Counseling for Results

Principles and Practices of Helping

Counseling for Results

Principles and Practices of Helping

Edward H. Scissons
University of Saskatchewan

Brooks/Cole Publishing Company
Pacific Grove, California

THIS BOOK IS PRINTED ON ACID-FREE RECYCLED PAPER

A CLAIREMONT BOOK

Brooks/Cole Publishing Company
A Division of Wadsworth, Inc.

Printed in the United States of America
10 9 8 7 6 5 4 3 2 1

Library of Congress Cataloging-in-Publication Data
Scissons, Edward H.
Counseling for results : principles and practices of helping / Edward H. Scissons.
p. cm.
Includes bibliographical references and index.
ISBN 0-534-19476-1
1. Counseling. 2. Helping behavior. I. Title.
BF637.C6S35 1992
158'.3—dc20 92-13414
CIP

Sponsoring Editor: *Claire Verduin*
Editorial Associate: *Gay C. Bond*
Production Editor: *Penelope Sky*
Manuscript Editor: *Betty G. Seaver*
Interior and Cover Design: *Laurie Albrecht*
Art Coordinator: *Lisa Torri*
Interior Illustration: *Roger Knox*
Typesetting: *Kachina Typesetting*
Printing and Binding: *R. R. Donnelley & Sons Company, Crawfordsville*

To the memory of Allon W. Fraser
Mentor, Colleague, Friend

PREFACE

Many books present counseling techniques independently of helping principles or theory, thus failing to address the novice counseling student's concern, "Yes, but what do I *do*?" This false dichotomy between helping principles and practices inspired me to write *Counseling for Results.*

This book is most decidedly about helping techniques. It addresses what counselors say and do in their helping relationships with clients. It approaches techniques as options leading to results. Results, after all, are what counseling is all about.

Counseling techniques are the legitimate outcomes of a process that starts with both a perspective on the nature of humanness and a definable orientation toward helping, and concludes with action by a counselor. This book thus links helping principles and counseling practices, encouraging students to discover the mysteries of counseling and to grow professionally.

Counseling for Results is primarily for entry-level helping professionals, particularly students with modest backgrounds in counseling. It will also be helpful to students who are pursuing noncounseling careers but who require an overview of the principles and practices that constitute the discipline. A common theme throughout is that counselors must recognize and be proficient at available options. They must also understand where these options fit in the overall counseling process. Because I provide a paradigm for analyzing and understanding this process, the book is a useful secondary resource for more sophisticated students who seek to integrate their knowledge of helping theories, principles, and practices.

To the Student

Counseling Is Good Honest Work

A carpenter saws and hammers. A surgeon cuts and sews. A truck driver steers and brakes. A police officer arrests crooks. And a counselor sits and talks. But a carpenter must know when to saw and when to hammer. A surgeon must know how to cut and when to do so in the right places. A truck driver must know how to steer the rig down the right road and when to brake. A police officer must know when to make an arrest and how to protect constitutional rights at the same time. And a counselor must *listen* and talk in such a way that clients are helped.

Just as there are good carpenters, surgeons, truck drivers, and police officers, there are good counselors. And just as there are carpenters you wouldn't let near your house, doctors you wouldn't let near your body, truck drivers who menace you on the highways, and police officers who ticket you and me instead of arresting real crooks, counselors vary a great deal in their effectiveness.

In most professions or trades there are both skills and beliefs that prescribe how the skills should be used. A carpenter must be able to use a miter box, drive nails without bending them, operate a table saw, and read blueprints. But the carpenter also works within an orientation that dictates the sequence of stages in building, limits the choice of woods for outside surfaces, and requires certain tolerances for the construction of cabinets. A carpenter's skills describe his or her individial abilities. A carpenter's orientation dictates how these skills should be put together to construct a building. Carpenters with very similar skills may operate under very different construction beliefs, either by choice or by necessity. Like carpenters, counselors possess complex skills, but because they have varying orientations, they use their similar skills in different ways, in different sequences, to achieve different intentions.

The study of counseling is the study of orientations and skills. An orientation provides a framework for what you should be doing and why you should be doing it. Skills provide a repertoire of what to say or do in your dealings with clients. If you are competent only in orientation, you are a philosopher. If you are merely skillful, you are a technician. A counselor needs to have mastered both aspects of the profession.

Organization

Because counseling is based on communication with a client, this book addresses what you do and say as a counselor. And because counseling is results-oriented, the focus is on what you want to achieve as a counselor in your relationships with clients, and on alternative ways of achieving those goals.

- Part I addresses counseling orientations and outlines a method for studying and analyzing popular schools of thought about counseling. For a treatment of individual theories, you are referred to works that consider counseling theories in detail.

- Part II outlines verbal and nonverbal communication skills. Effective communication is necessary no matter which counseling orientation you use in working with clients. *Part II gives you a basic understanding of the communication skills that are essential to your success as a counselor, so you may want to read it before you read Parts I and III.*
- Part III deals with the problems and issues that confront ordinary counselors. It addresses how theoretical orientations and counseling skills help resolve the problems you encounter as a counselor.

A word of caution before you go on! I often take a humorous and sometimes irreverent look at counseling and counselors. I have included many examples of counseling situations, some based on real life, some on familiar fairy tales. This is to take the mystery out of counseling and to encourage you to see how counseling skills apply to everyday fairy-tale life. I find it hard to believe that someone as reprehensible as the Wolf in Little Red Riding Hood would not seek counseling. You will read verbatim transcripts of his therapeutic sessions and those of other familiar characters throughout the text.

Acknowledgments

I would like to thank the colleagues throughout the United States and Canada who reviewed part or all of the manuscript. The book is richer for the unselfish contributions of Frank Asbury, Valdosta State College; Joshua Gold, Fairfield University; Iris Heckman, Washburn University at Topeka; Janet C. Heddesheimer, George Washington University; Eugene W. Jacobs, Presbyterian College; David Kendall, State University of New York at Brockport; Beverly Palmer, California State University, Domingues Hills; and Richard Percy, Vanderbilt University.

A special word of thanks is due my undergraduate and graduate students at the University of Saskatchewan, who have long served as a testing ground for many of the instructional techniques I describe throughout the book.

Finally, a word of appreciation to my family, Karen, Patrick, and Michael, who abided my early-morning hunt-and-peck typing, and for the dedicated professionalism of Claire Verduin, Gay Bond, Penelope Sky, and the entire Brooks/Cole production team.

Edward H. Scissons

CONTENTS

PART I

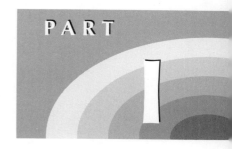

Counseling Principles and Theory

Learning Objectives

The chapters in Part I introduce you to a method for studying counseling theories or philosophical orientations to counseling. They provide the framework for counseling styles and skills you will study in subsequent chapters.

I do not analyze in detail the numerous approaches to counseling that are currently in vogue. Such a project requires a separate text, and there are many good ones from which to choose (check the references at the end of each chapter). After you complete Part I, you should be able to:

- outline a method you can use to compare and contrast approaches to counseling;
- articulate differing concepts of validity as they pertain to various approaches to counseling;
- demonstrate a results-oriented process for handling typical counseling situations;
- explain and critique your own orientation toward counseling;
- demonstrate your ability to put counseling orientations into practice; and
- explain the relationship among the goals of counseling, processes used to realize the goals, and techniques of counseling and counselor communication active within the processes.

CHAPTER 1

Assessing Counseling Orientations

The Theory of Theory

Let's face it. To some people, theory is very much akin to a scourge of locusts. If you mention theory, some look down their noses and say in a very deprecating way, "Well, that's just theory." For them, there is practice; practice is helpful. And there is theory; theory is useless. If only life and theory were so black and white!

The interesting thing about theory, at least counseling theory, is that everybody talks about it but very few can tell you what it is. In the physical sciences, theory refers to a connection postulated about relationships between a series of observations. The statement of a theory is used to explain observed phenomena and to predict other phenomena.

In counseling and many of the other social sciences, what are referred to as theories are really hypotheses about observations together with statements of values or beliefs. Although they seldom do so expressly, different counseling theories put different weights on the observation side and philosophical sides.

As a counselor, you must choose from many different orientations or approaches to counseling. Your choice is more than whether you will operate under the umbrella of a particular orientation. If you are like most counselors, you will eventually develop an orientation that is a hybrid of several orientations. Even if you do not clearly understand or express your orientation, you will still be operating under the framework of some sort of hybrid orientation. Your choice, as Shoben and associates (1956) aptly put it, is between ideas of human conduct that are well defined and formalized and ones that are not.

As part of your training, you will probably complete at least one course in counseling theory. Some of the theories you will study may be highly structured, similar to the elements of a theory in the physical sciences. Some will be more correctly described as a set of operating principles based upon a philosophical position that describes the nature of "humanness." To avoid confusion between the strict way that theory is usually described in the physical sciences and the way it is sometimes used in counseling, I will use the term *counseling orientation* to identify differing perspectives.

Counseling Orientations

To understand a counseling orientation, you must understand three key concepts and the relationships among them.

1. The *philosophy and purposes* of counseling are important aspects of a counseling orientation. The philosophy reflects a particular value system and is based on stated or unstated beliefs of what it means to be human. The philosophy under which a counseling orientation operates leads directly to counseling purposes—what counseling attempts to accomplish.
2. A *counseling process* flows from the purposes of counseling. A process outlines procedures or steps that are used by the counselor in conjunction with the client to realize the purposes of counseling. Often, a counseling process includes precepts (dos) and injunctions (don'ts) that function as general rules for counselors who operate under the orientation.
3. *Counseling techniques* translate counseling processes into the actual counselor behaviors. Counseling techniques are easily recognizable because they are stated as actions rather than intents. They are behavioral options for the counselor. Part II deals with the communication-based counseling techniques.

For a simplistic example of how the three concepts relate to one another, imagine you hold the philosophical position that being human requires that clients be totally responsible for their own behaviors. In your mind, this belief or value would define part of the nature of being human. One major purpose of counseling that might flow from your philosophical position is that counseling should help clients to make their own decisions.

Flowing from your purpose would be a process of counseling. The process might comprise several steps that would help clients to:

- understand the concern(s) that brought them to counseling;
- identify options for dealing with the concerns;
- examine the options fully; and
- make and implement choices.

It is likely that the steps would be better facilitated if you had established positive working relationships with your clients. What you do to achieve the relationships would also form part of your prescribed counseling process.

In addition to the process of counseling outlined above, you might be governed by the following precepts and injunctions as you and your clients work through the process:

- you should do nothing to influence the decisions your clients make;
- you should assist clients to do what they want to do (within certain bounds!); and
- you should ensure that clients examine fully the choices they are considering.

In carrying on with our simplistic example, your techniques of counseling would flow from your purpose of counseling and the abbreviated counseling process that has been outlined. Techniques that you might use to help clients to understand the concerns that brought them to counseling include:

- Questioning followed by listening. You might ask, "What brings you to talk with me today?" You might use listening to follow up on their responses. You could use relational questions: "How is this concern different from the concerns we talked about last week? How is it similar?" You might follow up these questions with further listening.
- You might have clients imagine they are explaining their problems or issues to others who are involved in the problems or issues. For example, you might ask a husband who is having problems in his marital relationship to pretend that his wife is sitting across from him, and have him explain his concerns to the envisioned wife. You might use questions and further listening to deal with clients' musings.

You can probably think of other techniques that would be appropriate to help your clients understand the concerns that brought them to counseling. (Part II provides further help.) Of course, there are many techniques that you could use at each step of the counseling process. Some techniques would work better with one client. Some would work better with another.

Validity of Counseling Orientations

Validity is the construct that you use to evaluate the effectiveness of a counseling orientation. *Validity* is a term borrowed from the research literature and asks a deceptively simple question. Does the "thing" (in this case the counseling orientation) do what it is supposed to do? Validity has several components that pertain to a study of counseling orientations: consistency, efficacy, and relevance.

Consistency is the aspect of validity that refers to the soundness of the relationships *within* each of the elements of the counseling orientation: philosophy and purposes, processes and techniques. Each element of an orientation's philosophy and purposes should be more or less compatible with every other element of its philosophy and purposes. Likewise for processes and techniques. For example, if a particular counseling orientation states that counseling should help clients to make their own decisions, it should not also state that counseling should teach clients specific ways of behaving.

Consistency also means that there should be a logical and smooth flow from one category to another within the counseling orientation. Philosophy should be reflected in purposes. Purposes should be reflected in process. Process should be mirrored in techniques. Techniques should be true to philosophy. There should be nothing incompatible *within* each category nor *among* the three categories. For example, if a particular counseling orientation states that a purpose is that counseling should help clients make their own decisions, a technique that allows the counselor to teach the client what had worked in the past for other clients would be inappropriate from the perspective of consistency.

If a counseling orientation has a high level of consistency, there will be no statements of philosophy, purpose, process, or techniques of counseling left "orphaned." This means that the relationship among them will be clear. There will be nothing represented in any one of the three areas that is not enacted in the other two areas. Of course, no counseling orientation does this perfectly, but logical progression is an important objective in the drafting of any counseling orientation.

Keep in mind that just because a counseling orientation is consistent within categories and clear in expressing the relationships between purposes, process, and techniques it does not necessarily follow that the orientation is flawless. A clear and logical relationship among and within categories is an indicator of high *consistency*, but *efficacy* and *relevance* are also important dimensions of validity.

Efficacy asks, "If a competent counselor follows the counseling process and uses the counseling techniques mandated by the counseling orientation, are the purposes of counseling fulfilled?" If one purpose is that counseling should help clients to make their own decisions, to what extent do the orientation's process and techniques, as used by a knowledgeable counselor, achieve this?

Relevance is the dimension of validity that provides a check on consistency. Relevance asks, "Do the philosophy and purposes of counseling make sense?" *Make sense* means that the philosophy and purposes of the

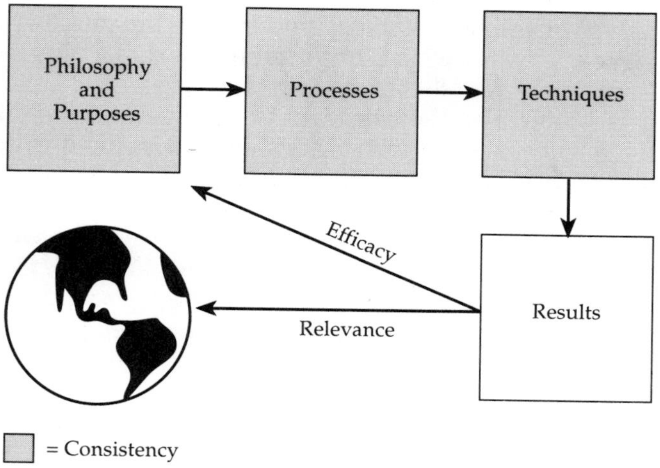

Counseling orientations and validity

counseling orientation must generally be compatible with the demands of the society within which the orientation must operate.

A demand for relevance poses thorny questions of any counseling orientation. Does use of the orientation by competent practitioners resolve individuals' problems? Does it help to reduce trauma for victims of crime? Does it help young pregnant women make informed decisions about their futures? Does it help those who are going through the breakup of a relationship? Presumably an orientation that did not help clients in these ways would be a poor one, no matter how eloquently presented or how solid the fit seemed among its philosophy and purposes, process, and techniques.

Consistency, taken on its own, might allow you to construct a counseling orientation in which the purpose of counseling is to help clients to love telephone poles. The process and the techniques that flow from the process would lead toward the sole purpose of fostering that emotion. Although consistency might allow you to put forward such a trivial approach, relevance would put into question your lucidity.

Keep in mind several things when you are using consistency, efficacy, and relevance to assess a counseling orientation:

1. The simpler the purposes of a counseling orientation, the higher its consistency. If you promise very little rather than much, it is easier to deliver what you promise.
2. The more complex and multidimensional the purposes of a counseling orientation, the lower its consistency. If you promise many things it

may be difficult to have process or techniques that can deliver what you promise. In fact, the means of realizing one purpose may be antithetical to realizing other purposes.

3. The simpler the purposes of a counseling orientation, the lower its relevance when relevance is defined in the broadest sense. If the sole purpose of an orientation is to foster a love of telephone poles and, even if the orientation can deliver on that purpose, nonlove of telephone poles is not a very significant problem in the world.
4. If you were actually to get a measure of relevance, the "relevance score" would always be lower than the "efficacy score" for the same counseling orientation. Efficacy determines how well the purposes of counseling have been realized. Relevance tells how important the purposes are to the world. By definition, relevance is always a lesser function of efficacy.

The above descriptions of the components of validity are imprecise definitions of things that are very complex. It is easy to discount a counseling orientation whose sole purpose is to foster an affinity to telephone poles. The validity of orientations based upon stereotypical differences between men and women, tenets of religions, distinctive cultures, the sanctity of marriage and the family, injunctions against homosexuality, or other nettlesome issues is less clear. Are such orientations, even if they are consistent, good counseling orientations? You can answer this question only if you are able to define operationally a good human being and correct human values.

Analyzing Counseling Orientations

For reasons of illustration, I have been clear in expressing the relationships between purposes, process, and techniques for an imagined counseling orientation whose sole philosophical position is that clients should be responsible for their own behavior. As you study actual counseling orientations, you will find that some are very clear in making associations between these three elements even if they do not use the same terminology I have used to do so. But some orientations do not express these relationships at all, and others express them haphazardly.

It is not uncommon for writings on counseling orientations to obscure the relationships between purposes, process, and techniques. A frequent deficiency is to define a technique as a goal instead of as a means to a goal. For example, some orientations might refer to listening as a fundamental counseling condition, whereas it is really a technique or behavior designed to evoke a fundamental condition. The fundamental condition is a certain type of positive relationship between counselor and client. Listening may not always be effective in promoting this condition, and other techniques might be more effective.

Let me take two counseling orientations that are in vogue today and examine them from the perspective of validity in the following way:

1. From a description of the orientation, choose statements that describe the philosophy (1a) upon which the orientation is based and the purposes (1b) intended by its use.
2. Outline the process (2a) that the orientation specifies should be used, as well as the associated precepts and injunctions (2b) that aid in operationalizing the philosophy and purposes.
3. Itemize counseling techniques that the orientation specifies are appropriate to set the process in motion.
4. Comment upon the consistency, efficacy, and relevance of the counseling orientation.

Rational-Emotive Therapy (RET)

The individual most closely associated with rational-emotive therapy (RET) is its genitor, Albert Ellis. With roots in classical psychoanalysis, Ellis experimented with a variety of therapies before first articulating his own brand of counseling in the late 1950s and early 1960s. Rational-emotive therapy is an example of an orientation to counseling whose tenets and practices are clearly presented—even though the framework and language for doing so is different from the methodology you have been studying. Perhaps because those who write about rational-emotive therapy are unequivocal in their descriptions, RET has a good measure of both popular support and opposition among counselors.

If you are not already familiar with rational-emotive therapy, it would be helpful for you to read Corey (1991) or one of the other resource books listed at the end of this chapter. To simplify the presentation of information regarding RET, it is keyed to the numbered points appearing in the list just above.

1a. Philosophy

The essence of the rational-emotive philosophy of humanness is the individual's responsibility, learned helplessness, transcendence of mind over emotion, and irrationality.

a. People are born with the potential for rational and irrational thinking.
b. People have many positive and negative predispositions.
c. People condition themselves to feel disturbed; they are not conditioned by external sources.

d. People have the biological and cultural tendency to think crookedly and to needlessly disturb themselves.
e. People invent disturbing beliefs and keep themselves disturbed about their disturbances.
f. People have the capacity to change cognitive, emotional, and behavioral processes to reduce their disturbances.
g. People mistake preferences for needs.
h. People have inborn tendencies toward growth and actualization; yet, they sabotage their movements toward achieving these because of crooked thinking and by learning self-defeating patterns.
i. Without intervention, people continue as they are even when they realize the way is self-defeating.
j. Emotions are the products of thinking; when we think something is bad we feel bad about that thing.
k. Anxiety results from blaming ourselves for our mistakes.
l. We have many irrational beliefs that cause us grief; many stem from societally expected ways of behaving and feeling.

1b. Purposes

The purposes of rational-emotive therapy center upon the necessity for indoctrination of the client to its theorems.

a. The essence of RET is showing clients that they can change the irrational beliefs that directly cause disturbing emotional consequences.
b. Counseling should help people to accept themselves as imperfect creatures who make mistakes.
c. Counseling should help people to learn to live more at peace with themselves.
d. Counseling should help clients to confront their value systems and reindoctrinate themselves with different values, beliefs, and ideas.
e. There are many goals that client and counselor pursue together, ranging from self-interest to scientific thinking and nonutopianism.

2a. Counseling Process

The process of RET counseling moves clients from understanding both what they are telling themselves and their belief systems about the particular circumstances that are impinging on them at the present. The process is then to teach them how to dispute the irrational beliefs that are causing them troubles. The process has four steps:

a. Show clients that they have incorporated many irrational beliefs into their belief systems.

b. Show clients that they continually reindoctrinate themselves with their irrational beliefs and are responsible for their own misery.
c. Help clients to modify their own thinking and abandon their irrational beliefs.
d. Challenge clients to adopt an RET philosophy of life so they will be free of problems in the future.

2b. Precepts and Injunctions

A number of rules for RET counselors form the net within which the counselor must operate:

a. Counseling should not dwell on past behavior, nor should it dwell on the recognition or expression of feelings.
b. The client and counselor should work together to transform an unrealistic, immature, and absolute form of thinking into a logical, mature, and empirical form of thinking.
c. The counselor should show full acceptance of clients yet relentlessly confront their irrational beliefs.

3. Techniques of Counseling

With rational-emotive therapy, as with most therapies, it is difficult, in outlining the overall orientation, to decide where process finishes and the techniques begin. It is particularly difficult to fathom from only reading about the orientation which technique among those listed below is appropriate for which stage in the process.

a. Pin clients down to irrational beliefs that motivate their disturbed behavior.
b. Challenge clients to validate their ideas.
c. Demonstrate to clients the illogical nature of their thinking and use a logical analysis to minimize their irrational beliefs.
d. Demonstrate to clients the fallacy of their beliefs; use absurdity and humor.
e. Convince clients that their irrational ideas can be replaced by more rational ones, and teach clients the new ideas.
f. Use open questions to identify problems to be dealt with.
g. Teach clients the basic tenets of the RET approach.
h. Assign cognitive and behavioral homework to clients.
i. Teach personal-responsibility language usage to clients; replace musts and shoulds with statements that mean "I have chosen. . . ."
j. Use imagined situations and role-playing to change clients' reactions to unpleasant situations.
k. Use behavioral techniques based on operant conditioning.

4. Validity

The simplest way to review a counseling orientation's consistency—the relationship between its philosophy and purposes, process, and techniques—is to take separate constituents of the philosophy and track their realization from philosophy through process to techniques. For example, one of the philosophical statements attributed to rational-emotive therapy is that people invent disturbing beliefs and keep themselves disturbed about their disturbances (Corey, 1991).

The philosophical position is compatible with assertions that the purposes of RET are to:

- change irrational beliefs of clients;
- help clients to accept themselves as imperfect;
- show clients they can change irrational beliefs; and
- help clients to confront their value systems.

The four-step process of rational-emotive therapy, as outlined by Corey (1991), has two main components: showing clients that they are operating on the basis of irrational beliefs; and helping them to operate within the RET paradigm. It is this process that is supposed to realize the purposes listed immediately above.

The techniques of counseling within a rational-emotive perspective, as described by Corey (1991), are described more in terms of what to do than in terms of where to do or how to do. For example, you are told to challenge clients to validate their ideas (Corey, 1991, p. 217). In what context is this to be done? What should you say? What do you do if clients disagree with you?

A second example of tracking a rational-emotive philosophical premise can be demonstrated from the belief that people have the capacity to change cognitive, emotional, and behavioral processes to reduce their disturbances. This philosophical position is compatible with assertions that the purposes of RET are to:

- help clients to understand their irrational beliefs in order to show them the relationships between the beliefs and their emotional states;
- help clients to pursue scientific thinking;
- help clients to be more accepting of themselves as imperfect creatures; and
- help clients to live more at peace with themselves.

Once again, the same four-step process cited in connection with the first example is used to effect these purposes. Techniques that might be used include assignment of cognitive and behavioral homework, use of imagined situations, role-playing, and teaching clients the basic tenets of RET.

Validity for RET or any other counseling orientation is not easily determined. Efficacy is perhaps the easiest to assess because it is the usual focus of research that addresses counseling outcomes. In general, the research has been reasonably supportive of RET's effectiveness (Corey, 1991) but not much more so than for other mainstream counseling perspectives. RET's relevance is evident in that RET techniques have been applied to a diversity of personal problems from alcoholism to vandalism.

Person-Centered Therapy

After being introduced in the early 1950s, nondirective counseling, later reborn as client-centered therapy, and most recently renamed person-centered therapy, the counseling orientation developed by Carl Rogers, remains one of the most popular therapies in use today. Its tenets have been taught to generations of counselors, psychologists, psychiatrists, and social workers. It is one of the few orientations celebrated enough to be instantly recognized by a single descriptor: Rogerian.

Although person-centered therapy has its roots in the writings and teachings of Rogers, he is by no means its only proponent. Other popular writers and practitioners, including Carkhuff (1969), Egan (1990), Ivey (1988), and Maslow (1971), are indebted to Rogers and he to them. Unlike rational-emotive therapy, person-centered therapy defies ready analysis according to the paradigm you have just learned. This is not because rational-emotive therapy is simple and person-centered therapy is complex. It is because person-centered therapy is older, is less definitely articulated, has continually evolved, and has been the subject of much more internal explanation and external analysis than RET. Rogers himself did not consider person-centered therapy to be fixed or completed. In his opinion it was more accurately described as a set of *tentative* principles (Rogers & Wood, 1984).

If you are not already familiar with person-centered therapy, it would be helpful for you to read Corey (1991) or one of the other resource books listed at the end of this chapter. To simplify my presentation of the orientation, I will present information in its regard keyed to the numbered points of the same list referred to earlier.

1a. Philosophy

a. People are essentially trustworthy.
b. People have a great potential to understand themselves and to resolve their own problems without intervention from a counselor; they are motivated to actualize themselves.

c. People are capable of self-directed growth. They will develop in a positive and constructive manner if they are involved in a therapeutic relationship or a climate of respect and trust.
d. Attitudes and personal characteristics of the counselor and the quality of the relationship between the counselor and client are prime determinants of the outcomes of the counseling relationship.
e. A counselor who is genuine, who is accepting and caring of the client, and who has the ability to become attuned to the subjective world of the client best facilitates the client's growth and development.
f. The primary responsibility for client change rests with the client.
g. The same principles of psychotherapy apply to all clients irrespective of degree of disturbance.
h. Human beings structure themselves according to their own perceptions of reality.

1b. Purposes

a. Counseling should help clients to discover new and more satisfying personal meanings about themselves and the world they inhabit.
b. Counseling should help clients in the growth process, not necessarily in the resolution of problems that bring them to counseling.
c. Counseling should help clients to be more accepting of conflicting and confusing feelings.
d. Counseling should help clients to become more open to their experiences and more accepting of others.
e. Counseling should help clients to appreciate themselves more and to show more creativity and flexibility.
f. Counseling should help clients to become less oriented toward meeting others' expectations and more true to themselves.

2a. Counseling Process

In person-centered therapy the process of counseling is not defined concretely. Loosely defined, it is phrased in terms of *statements of intent* for the counselor and client. Each part of the process is active throughout the time the client and counselor spend together; it is not undertaken and then dispensed with.

a. Clients must get behind the masks they wear, masks that were developed through socialization.
b. Counselors must create a climate of safety for their clients.
c. Counselors must create a therapeutic climate that helps clients to grow.
d. Counselors must create an atmosphere of freedom to allow clients to explore areas of their lives that are being denied or distorted.

e. The counselor must enter the world of the client.
f. Clients come to counselors experiencing discrepancy between their self-perceptions and their experiences of reality; counselors must help them to explore their feelings about the discrepancy.
g. Counselors should help clients to express their fears, anxiety, guilt, and other negative emotions.

2b. Precepts and Injunctions

a. The counselor should be concerned with the client's perception of self and the world.
b. The counselor should not choose specific goals for the client.
c. The counselor must demonstrate genuine caring, respect, acceptance, and understanding of the client.
d. The counselor does not need any specialized knowledge, nor is any accurate diagnosis of the client necessary.
e. The counselor should freely express and accept negative feelings.
f. The counselor should take actions to cause the client to believe that the counselor has an empathic understanding of and unconditional positive regard for the client.
g. The counselor should serve as a model for the client struggling toward greater realness.

3. Techniques of Counseling

What are usually identified as techniques of counseling in person-centered therapy fall on a continuum, with suggested behaviors for the counselor on one end (listen to the client) and very general admonitions for the counselor on the other end (be genuine). The behavior end of the continuum is easily and commonly understood. The admonitions end of the continuum does not represent behaviors; it represents *desirable inferences in the mind of the client.*

As a counselor, you cannot *be* genuine. You can talk or act in certain ways and hope that you bring about the inference by the client that you are genuine. Attribution of genuineness is made by the client, not by you. Although you can say and do things to influence the attribution, different clients would probably have to hear or see you do slightly different things before they would attribute to you the characteristic *genuineness.*

To make them compatible with the usual meaning of the word *technique,* I have operationalized the admonitions, translating them into *actual behaviors of the counselor.* Where this was not possible without doing violation to the intent of the counseling orientation, I have included the admonition under the categories that deal with the purposes of counseling or counseling process.

The behaviors to be exhibited by the counselor are

a. listen attentively to the client and voice an interpretation of what the client has attempted to communicate;
b. use nonverbal actions, such as eye contact, to show an interest in what the client is saying;
c. assert an acceptance of the client's rights to have feelings without necessarily accepting all behavior on the part of the client;
d. voice meanings or possible interpretations of the client's experiences of which the client may be only dimly aware; and
e. encourage clients to get closer to themselves, to get more in tune with how they are really feeling.

4. Validity

As with rational-emotive therapy, the consistency of person-centered therapy is partially determined by the quality of the relationship among philosophy and purposes, process, and techniques. In the case of person-centered therapy, the quality of the relationship is less easy to define than it is with rational-emotive therapy. This does not mean that the orientation necessarily has any less consistency than rational-emotive therapy. It does mean that the nature or degree of consistency of person-centered therapy is less easy to determine.

One element that bears tracking from philosophy through to counseling techniques is the assertion that primary responsibility for client change rests with the client. With a clear declaration such as this, the definition of *primary* is important because an extreme definition could cause you to say that none of the purposes I have previously cited flow from it. However, with a more middling definition, many of the purposes I have identified for person-centered therapy are compatible because they all contain the operant word *help. Help* implies everything from direct assistance to support. For person-centered therapy to be internally consistent, the definition of *help* must be skewed toward support.

As already noted, the process of counseling within a person-centered format is less clearly defined than is the case for some other orientations. This is a natural by-product of having purposes that are less definite and more subject to interpretation by individual clients or counselors. In fact, the process identified for person-centered therapy could not be said to lead to the purposes as already cited. The process neither prevents realization of the purposes nor leads directly to them.

In terms of the consistency paradigm that I have been using, the relationship between purposes and process is a possible threat to the consistency of a person-centered counseling orientation. The relationship between the two is not ill fitting but it is ill defined.

One aspect of the process that may be a threat to the consistency of the counseling orientation is the conundrum that develops when the client wants direction from the counselor, and the counselor, quite properly according to the tenets of the orientation, refuses to provide it. In doing so, the counselor is directing the client away from a path the client has opted for. Does this move the client away from self-determination or toward greater self-responsibility?

The precepts and injunctions associated with person-centered therapy are pretty much in accord with our philosophical assertion of client responsibility. They enjoin the counselor not to do things that take responsibility away from the client (choosing specific goals) but to do things that will facilitate the client's self-determination (modeling the expression of emotions).

The counseling techniques associated with person-centered therapy could be summarized to include reflection, listening, and modeling of appropriate behaviors by the counselor—these are in accord with the spirit of client self-determination. The only caveat is that because the techniques are not narrow in scope, the way the counselor uses them will determine how closely they parallel the philosophical stance of client self-determination. For example, not everything a client says is reflected upon. Decisions are made by the counselor in this regard. These decisions can move the client further away from or closer to self-determination and the counseling orientation further away from or closer to an acceptable level of consistency.

The validity of person-centered therapy has been the target of a good measure of research over the years. Efficacy studies have shown mixed results, with many of the studies having been plagued by hit-and-miss research design controls (Prochaska, 1984). Watson (1984), in a review of person-centered therapy, could find no basis for drawing definitive conclusions about the efficacy of the approach. Nonetheless, person-centered therapy has been used in many different venues and to address a variety of societal issues. Some researchers have indicated, however, that the approach is more appropriate for mainstream middle-class clients than for subgroup-member clients who are atypical in culture, education, or values.

It is impossible to find a counseling orientation that has the kind of textbook validity that I have been demanding of the two orientations introduced in this chapter. In practice, it is rare to find an orientation in which everything is as explicit in practice as I have optimized it in principle.

To summarize, in studying the relationships between the elements of a counseling orientation, there are several questions you should ask yourself:

1. Are the philosophy and purposes, process, and techniques of the counseling orientation consistent within and among one another? For example, are all of the purposes compatible with one another, or is there anything in the techniques of counseling that are not in accordance with the philosophy and purposes or the precepts and injunctions?
2. Are all purposes translated effectively into a counseling process? Is process translated effectively into techniques of counseling? Are any elements orphaned?
3. If competent counselors undertake the counseling process and use the techniques as enunciated for the counseling orientation, would the purposes of counseling be realized?
4. Do the articulated purposes of counseling make sense? Are they in accord with the needs of the client group? Do the purposes violate ethical or legal standards?

Putting Techniques into Perspective

If you are a typical counselor-in-training you are "technique hungry." You know that you will be faced with unfamiliar and stressful situations as a novice counselor and you want to know what to do. In counseling situations, your first question may be "What do I do or say?" It should be "What do I want to accomplish?" Asking the latter ensures that whatever you do is done for some purpose and prevents you from selecting techniques that are interesting but ineffective. The answering will aid you in selecting alternative techniques when your first selected technique is not effective.

Points to Consider

1. Why is there a different orientation toward the definition of a theory in the natural sciences than in the social sciences in general or counseling in particular?
2. How does a counseling orientation "grow" or expand to include new knowledge? For example, do new techniques have their origins in the purposes or process of counseling or are they formulated by other means?
3. What is the counseling orientation of a counselor you know? What is yours? How valid are the orientations?
4. The development of orientations to counseling are summarized in books such as Corey (1991). Which part of the orientations do you think came first: philosophy and purposes, process, or techniques? Do you think this differed for the different counseling perspectives? Why?

Suggested Readings

COREY, G. (1991). *Theory and practice of counseling and psychotherapy.* Pacific Grove, CA: Brooks/Cole. Chapter 7 deals with person-centered therapy; chapter 11 with rational-emotive therapy, as well as other cognitive behavioral approaches. Other chapters profile a variety of the counseling orientations currently in vogue.

GLADDING, S. T. (1988). *Counseling: A comprehensive profession.* Columbus, OH: Merrill. Chapters 3–6 provide a good overview of mainstream counseling orientations.

SCHULTZ, D. (1990). *Theories of personality.* Pacific Grove, CA: Brooks/Cole. Although not written specifically from the perspective of counseling, this book provides a solid overview of the basic orientations to personality on which counseling orientations are based.

CHAPTER 2

Counseling Orientations and Professional Practice

The Eclectic Counselor

It is probably safe to assume that the professional practices of most counselors are imperfect representations of any single counseling orientation. Most counselors do not profess beliefs and values that can be linked directly to any single style. Nor do most counselors operate on the basis of precepts or injunctions, or use counseling techniques that are representative of one orientation. Even though they may not clearly articulate their orientations, most counselors have orientations and methodologies drawn from many styles. Their styles are eclectic.

Eclectic means, quite literally, "drawn from many sources." *Eclectic* does not mean the absence of an orientation. Nor does an eclectic orientation permit an ill-defined, inconsistent, or random collection of philosophy, purposes, and techniques. An eclectic orientation is a very definite orientation but not an orientation with a "national-brand" label. Like shampoo in a nondescript bottle or tea in a plain white box, an eclectic orientation to counseling connotes a definite but not a "name" product.

Counselors who have an eclectic orientation do not operate solely from mainline perspectives. They draw their philosophical position and counseling purposes, as well as process and techniques, from several perspectives. They have a very definite perspective, but one that has many parents.

The criteria appropriate for evaluating mainstream counseling orientations are appropriate for evaluating an eclectic orientation. This means that an eclectic orientation should manifest a good measure of consistency within each of the three categories (philosophy and purposes, process, and techniques of counseling) as well as among them. In addition to a demand for consistency, an eclectic orientation is governed by the same demands for efficacy and relevance that were suitable for the orientations you studied in the previous chapter.

Very often what separates an eclectic orientation from one of the more mainstream orientations is the degree to which it is distinct from them. Within an eclectic orientation there may be very little that has not been borrowed from other orientations. This does not mean that there is anything wrong with eclectic orientations. It simply means that counselors who use them will have to work within perspectives that are not distinguished by name.

One thing to remember is that it is in the interest of someone who writes about his or her counseling perspective to emphasize its unique characteristics and to play down what has been borrowed from other perspectives. It's much like advertising, beer advertising, for instance. Schlitz wants to convince you that its product is different from and better than the brew Coors turns out—and vice versa. If you are a wise consumer—of beer or counseling orientations—you must become informed and thereby enable yourself to separate real from illusory differences.

It is not uncommon to hear counselors who have no articulated orientation whatever describe themselves as practicing within an eclectic orientation. More correctly, they should call themselves "weathervane" counselors because their orientations change with the winds in the field. Developing your own approach to counseling requires you to pick and choose, but to do so in a knowledgeable and defensible way. Developing your own approach also requires that you actively pursue perceptive criticism of your approach and seek to make it better.

Approximately half the counselors who report themselves operating under the aegis of one counseling orientation or another identify the orientation as eclectic (Corey, 1991). However, the word *eclectic* has many different connotations for counselors, ranging from the strict definition of a systematized approach that I have been advancing in this chapter to a loose operation that defies understanding. The proportion of counselors who operate under a clearly articulated eclectic orientation is significant, but probably less than the figure quoted by Corey.

Directive versus Nondirective Counseling

When I was first introduced to counseling, it was common to hear certain counseling orientations labeled as directive and others as nondirective. It still is not unusual to find counselors who believe themselves to be nondirective pejoratively referring to other counselors as "directive." I wondered then and wonder now what *nondirective* really means.

Part of the confusion about directive and nondirective counseling stems from a confusion between process and outcomes. The internal processes of all counseling orientations are directive. In each the counselor has a job to do, although the job differs from orientation to orientation. Within each perspective, the counselor is encouraged to do or say certain things and is discouraged from saying and doing other things. This is what gives each orientation its unique flavor.

Within each counseling orientation, the client is encouraged to behave in certain ways. The counselor might verify what the client has said, might support, or ask questions, or pursue some other course of action. Each behavior on the part of the counselor facilitates certain behaviors on the part of the client. The client is directed to express feeling, explain a feeling, investigate relationships, try new behaviors, and so on. This is what is meant by a directive process. Every counseling orientation except one that is random-chaotic has a recognizably directive process.

Within a counseling orientation that is directive in terms of outcome, the counselor determines or tries to determine the results of counseling for the client. The counselor might try to exert an influence on which decisions are considered by the client, as well as which way the client's decision should go. For example, in considering options, the pregnant teenager client might become convinced that abortion is the only real alternative available to her. Within an orientation that is directive in outcome, the decision of the counselor could have a considerable impact on the decision of the client. The orientation is based on the premise that someone other than the client knows what is best for the client.

If all counseling orientations are directive at the process level, very few are explicitly directive in terms of expected results. Most do not tell clients what to decide, although some are very clear in telling clients what types of decisions they must make. However, even within orientations that purport to be nondirective in terms of outcome, some counselors are very subtly directive and may influence clients in ways that were never intended by the counseling orientation.

There are probably instances where every counselor is directive in influencing client decisions. Sometimes this is conscious on the part of counselors and possibly justified in the long-term interests of clients. At other times, counselors may be unaware that they are subtly influencing the decisions made by clients. In all likelihood most counselors underestimate the amount of influence that they exercise.

Efficacy

Counseling orientations are important. They are particularly important for the counselor-in-training because they can provide a framework that allows learning. The practice of counseling within a more or less well-defined orientation raises counseling above a hodgepodge of unrelated techniques and beliefs. Counseling orientations can help you to understand where you are going with your counseling and help to identify what you ought to do to get there.

Perhaps the best reason for learning different counseling orientations and practicing the profession within an articulated framework is that doing so keeps you honest! If you practice within a framework wherein something is supposed to happen and where you are to use certain techniques to achieve that something, you have a benchmark against which to gauge your effectiveness.

A shopworn quip about doctors goes something like "The operation was a success but the patient died." For auto mechanics, it would go something like "I fixed your car but it still doesn't work." For investment brokers, "I invested your money wisely but now you are penniless."

One of the maxims of counseling, competent use of counseling techniques is necessary but not sufficient, carries the same general thought. This is so because success in counseling is not measured at the transaction-by-transaction level. It is measured in terms of outcomes. It is quite possible for a counselor to be thoroughly proficient in all of the requisite skills of counseling, to be operating within an orientation that is reasonable and coherent, and still to be ineffective. This is because counseling is Gestalt-like: its whole is more than the sum of its parts.

Effective counseling requires you to put together varying patterns of skills within a process that fosters the purposes you and your clients are trying to achieve. It is not enough to utter perfectly constructed statements. You must also choose what to say or do, where to say or do it, and where and how to use alternatives when your first choices are not as effective as you want them to be.

In operational terms, *efficacy* means "Does all that high-priced stuff really work?" Without a clear counseling orientation it is very difficult for you to answer that question because you don't have a good handle on what "really work" means. It is your counseling orientation, eclectic or otherwise, that tells you what you are striving to do. Efficacy is assessed in terms of whether or not you are able to do this.

For example, your counseling orientation might tell you that clients should be able to learn how to make decisions for themselves and indicates that your job is to help them do this, irrespective of the results of their decisions. You judge your effectiveness as a counselor in terms of how well your clients learn decision-making methodologies and in terms of whether your clients actually make and implement decisions.

Or, your counseling orientation might tell you that your job is to help clients to enhance their self-esteem, to feel good about themselves. Your techniques are directed toward effecting this development. In this instance efficacy is judged in terms of increases in self-esteem that result from the counseling experience.

Of course, a counseling orientation seldom has just one goal or value. More typically, there are multiple goals and multiple means. In such circumstances, efficacy is assessed by changes across several dimensions simultaneously.

When efficacy is high, when all of the important purposes of counseling are realized without significant negative side effects, little time is usually spent by the practicing counselor in studying why this is so. When efficacy is low or mixed, a study of the elements within a defined counseling orientation can help you to identify several reasons that success is eluding you. Ask yourself:

- Were the precepts and injunctions followed?
- Were the techniques applied with sufficient skill?

If the answers to both questions are no, you are faced with a technical problem: "How do you get better at what you already know you should be doing?" This is a difficult but not an insurmountable problem. If the answers to the questions are yes, your problem is not technical. Your problem is that your orientation does not provide a perfect translation from purposes to process to techniques. Put simply, your orientation expects more at the front end than the back end can provide!

Counseling orientations "grow" in techniques because counselors or researchers pursue better ways to do whatever their counseling orientations purport to do. The growth is a natural part of the development of an orientation and is one reason that, at the technique level, there is sometimes very little difference among orientations.

Counseling is doing. It involves interaction—what is said and done—between counselor and client. Counseling orientations must impact upon practice. To be distinct, an orientation must be different from other orientations in philosophy and purposes, but it must also be different in practice. If an observer of the counseling practices of two counselors who purport to practice under different styles cannot detect any differences between the counseling under the two styles, the distinctions between the two orientations may be more fiction than fact.

You may notice that others label you as a certain type of counselor because you have chosen to use a particular technique. You may find yourself labeled an "RET counselor" because you have challenged a client's beliefs. Another time you may be labeled a "Rogerian" because you have chosen to verify a client's feelings. Such attributions of your style occur because many people mistakenly characterize what type of counselor you are by one or two of your specific techniques.

Attribution of counseling style from one or two examples is a chancy business because at the discrete technique level, there is often very little to distinguish one orientation from another. This is particularly true for orientations whose basic philosophy and purposes may not differ in substantial ways from others. For example, you may find very little difference at the technique level between rational-emotive therapy and the other cognitive and behavioral therapies (Corey, 1991).

A counseling orientation is more correctly identified by its purposes than by its techniques. This is so because the same techniques are often used by different counselors to achieve different purposes. It is purposes and the philosophy upon which they are based that may require different sequencing of techniques or the use of alternative techniques to control for side effects that are considered negative within one orientation but not within another. This being the case, a single technique used by a counselor or a small sample of techniques do not provide sufficient evidence of an orientation.

When I Blow My Nose, My Head Aches

Unknown to my son, he once illuminated a key point about the practice of counseling within any counseling orientation. He was suffering from a bad cold and, like many seven year olds, his nose dripped continually. I encouraged him to blow his nose. Finally, tired of my badgering, he countered with, "Dad, when I blow my nose, my head aches." Eureka! The science of counseling moves forward one small step.

What my son illuminated in allegorical terms is that it is highly unlikely that any single counseling technique applied in a single instance will support all of the purposes of counseling. You cannot simultaneously blow your nose and soothe your head. In fact, certain techniques that support one purpose may be mildly antithetical to another purpose. This is a natural result of the multiple purposes of counseling.

Although the reality is that a single counseling technique used in a specific instance cannot support simultaneously all of the purposes of counseling, it does not mean that some purposes must be ignored or subverted. It does mean that when actions that support one purpose are concluded, other actions must be taken to support the purposes that either had been neglected or violated by what you did earlier. For example, you may hold that two of the purposes of counseling are to raise self-esteem and to increase rational thinking. Although these purposes are not antithetic, neither are they the same. Within a RET perspective, a counseling technique that may be appropriate for increasing rational thinking is a direct challenge by the counselor of a client's irrational beliefs. This may be an effective technique for the stated purpose but it may have the negative side effect of reducing the client's self-esteem. The wise counselor will not discard the direct challenge technique out of hand but may well use it coupled with other techniques that are more closely geared to increasing self-esteem. Both purposes of counseling can thereby be accommodated, albeit imperfectly.

Notions of main effects and side effects are common to all professions. Medication prescribed by a physician may have no purpose other than to control the unwanted side effects of another medication administered to save a patient's life. Engineers frequently need to add beams whose only purpose is to support weight-bearing main beams. Major league baseball players sometimes bunt, and risk being tagged out, in order to advance the positions of teammates. In your counseling *every single action* you pursue will not advance *every single purpose* of counseling even though, *taken as a whole,* your actions should be effective.

Personal Accountability and Counseling

Probably the most common and dangerous things that novice counselors do is to judge their effectiveness by what they do. The effectiveness of counseling is not judged in terms of competent adherence to a process. It is judged by what results from the process.

When counselors judge efficacy by adherence to a process, they put the responsibility for counseling outcomes solely in the hands of their clients. Of course, clients are responsible for their own behavior, but they are not responsible for all of the outcomes of counseling. It is the job of the counselor to facilitate positive change, although the precise definition and direction of that change vary from counseling orientation to counseling orientation. Adherence to a process, or adherence to a stock set of techniques, may aid in that process, but it is not effective counseling.

Let me reinforce this point with an analogy. As a teacher, I have seen individual students fail to complete successfully a course of mine. Unfortunate as this is (for the student!) and although I am unhappy about the situation, I know that it occurs from time to time. It results from some combination of my inadequacy as an instructor and the student's inadequacy as a learner. Still I sleep at night.

Perhaps I have been lucky because only a small number of students have done poorly in a course of mine. Yet I have seen this happen to other instructors on occasion. In such circumstances, the instructor can take little solace from retreating into a self-justified, "Well, I did the same for them as I did for everybody else. They must be stupid." The responsibility of instructors is not to follow a set of procedures, even well-defined procedures; it is to do whatever has to be done to ensure that most of their students learn. That responsibility can stand the violation of the occasional failure by a student. It does not hold up well in the face of large-scale failure.

To explain this analogy in terms of counseling, there will always be instances when you fail as a counselor. Failure is the nonrealization of the goals of counseling, and will occur once in a while no matter what you do. Failure on a large scale is another matter. It can be explained only by the incompetency of the counselor and/or the inadequacy of the counseling orientation within which the counseling was undertaken.

Efficacy and Choice

Put yourself in the position of trying to demonstrate a degree of empathy to your client. There are a variety of ways to attempt this. You might use a listening style of communication by feeding back to the client the concrete verification that you are "with" him or her. Or you might ask personal questions, or share personal information, or make supportive statements or statements that imply your positive reaction. Each alternative has the potential to demonstrate empathy. Perhaps one would work better than another. There is no "right" method, or at least if there is, its "rightness" must be judged in terms of how well the method accomplishes your goal of demonstrating empathy without at the same time giving rise to unpleasant side effects, such as diminished self-esteem on the part of the client.

In undertaking counseling, you must discipline yourself to operate on several "tracks" simultaneously. You must be aware of what you want to accomplish—your purposes in counseling. You must be aware of the particular counseling technique you have chosen to try to accomplish one or more of these purposes. You must collect information from the client to see if what you are doing is working. And you must be aware of alternative techniques you could use if your data collection from the client tells you that your original choices of techniques are not working out the way you want them to. It doesn't sound simple and it isn't.

For the effective counselor, counseling is a series of decisions about what to say and do. This is a far cry from an orientation to counseling that says "Follow these steps and things will be all right"—and then judges efficacy in terms of whether or not the steps were followed.

Decisions imply choice. Decisions imply the possibility of choosing wrong. But without the possibility of choosing wrong the counselor precludes the possibility of choosing right. This is the professional aspect of counseling, the aspect that raises counseling above a technical discipline. A technician can become very competent in applying a series of techniques but usually falls down in generalizing these techniques to new situations or in selecting and applying alternative techniques when the prescribed method does not work. To do this requires a touch of artistry together with skill—the mark of a professional.

No matter which counseling orientation finds favor with you, there are three questions that you must answer over and over throughout your counseling relationships:

- What can I do to achieve the goals of counseling?
- Am I being effective?
- What alternatives are available if I am not effective?

These questions are important at the micro level, where your purpose might be to get the client to talk about feelings. They are also important at the macro level, where your purpose might be to help the client to learn to make well-considered decisions. At either point, or at all points in between, the efficacy of the techniques must be judged in terms of the degree of success you are realizing at what you want to accomplish. Efficacy is much the same for counselors as for any other professionals. A well-sutured incision in a patient who dies on the operating table is not a cause for celebration. Neither should we glorify a perfectly constructed verifying statement spoken to a client who is no better off for having been exposed to counseling.

A results-oriented perspective such as you have been studying in this chapter is possible only if you think in turn of alternatives. It is alternatives that allow you to use another technique or to modify the suggested sequence of counseling when it seems that such a modification will be more effective in accomplishing what you want.

Being the Real You

One often hears beginning counselors or counselors-in-training make statements like "I could never do that," "It's just not natural for me or something I feel comfortable in doing," or "That's not the real me. I can't do that."

I thank fortune every time that I hear such statements that they did not represent the basic philosophy or the orientation toward training of the surgeon who repaired my injured eye or the anesthesiologist who delivered the mixture of gases that let the surgeon get on with her work. I doubt that cutting into eyeballs or putting tubes down throats was something that either of them would have called "natural" when learning these procedures. The activities became "natural" only after much work and practice.

The time to decide whether or not a particular counseling technique will be effective for you is not while you are learning it. Once you have learned to do something, you are in a much more objective position to evaluate whether you should do it. It's a lot like learning to dance. Last year, my fifteen-year-old son thought dancing was stupid; this year it's fun. The only thing I can identify that changed in the year was that he learned to dance. Now, if he were to advance arguments in favor of a danceless society, I would be much more inclined to believe that his opinions are based on objectivity rather than personal inadequacy!

If learning to counsel feels natural and easy when you first attempt it, you are probably not learning. Learning how to do something new is always uncomfortable. It should be! To be an effective counselor is to take risks, not ill-considered reckless gambles but risks that will help develop a repertoire of counseling techniques and procedures. Once you have developed your own repertoire, you will be in a good position to choose what you do. Your choices will probably be better because they will be based on something other than a rationalization that defends your limited skills.

Points to Consider

1. How do different professions handle the efficacy issue? Ask your local doctor, dentist, minister, undertaker, or pharmacist. Listen very carefully to what he or she tells you. How much of what that person calls efficacy is focused on adherence to a process? How much is results oriented?
2. What techniques have you identified to realize your purposes of counseling? What alternatives have you identified? What are the effects of these alternatives on the purposes of counseling you identified for your own orientation?

Suggested Readings

BURKE, J. F. (1989). *Contemporary approaches to psychotherapy and counseling.* Pacific Grove, CA: Brooks/Cole. Chapter 2 discusses the therapeutic process, culture, and impact of contemporary approaches to psychotherapy and counseling on counselors.

D'AUGELLI, A. R., D'AUGELLI, J. F., & DANISH, S. J. (1981). *Helping others.* Pacific Grove, CA: Brooks/Cole. Chapter 2 provides an understanding of the helper, particularly in terms of motivation, needs, and other personal factors.

EGAN, G. (1990). *The skilled helper.* Pacific Grove, CA: Brooks/Cole. Chapter 17 presents the author's notions about implementing the ideals of counseling in actual counseling situations.

GLADDING, S. T. (1988). *Counseling: A comprehensive profession.* Columbus, OH: Merrill. Chapter 2 offers an understanding of counselors, who they are and what they do.

KENNEDY, E., & CHARLES, S. C. (1990). *On becoming a counselor.* New York: Continuum. Chapter 6 deals with the counselor, asking the important question, "What is it like to be real?"

PHARES, E. J. (1992). *Clinical psychology.* Pacific Grove, CA: Brooks/Cole. Chapter 15 presents a research perspective on psychotherapy or counseling, providing a good treatment of the professional practice of a helping professional.

CHAPTER 3

Clinical Judgment

A Close Relative of Efficacy

If all of this talk about efficacy has turned you into an insomniac, you'll want to meet a close relative of efficacy: clinical judgment. Clinical judgment has been a hot issue in psychology since the turn of the century. The words may be different in different professions but clinical judgment has engendered passionate debate in fields ranging from stock brokering to medicine, in addition to counseling.

Judgment refers to the accuracy (read: validity) of decisions made by someone about some matter or another. Within counseling, *clinical judgment* refers to the accuracy or validity of judgments made by the counselor. Typically, the judgments are made about clients or about courses of action intended by a counselor. Judgments that counselors might make that would fall under the umbrella of clinical judgment would be deciding if a client was disturbed enough to require a referral, identifying the "real problem" of a client, or deciding how to deal with issues presented by the client.

Clinical judgment, as it pertains to counseling, deals with such matters as what information is used to make a decision and how the information is weighted or combined to make decisions. The rationale for studying the decisions of counselors is based on the belief that by understanding how decisions are made, a counselor can better understand the decision-making process and improve upon it.

Many impediments hamper understanding of the human decision-making process. Perhaps the biggest is that the processes we use for most of our decisions are not perceptible. If I were to ask you why you chose to do something, you could probably give me some idea, particularly in hindsight. But I would be surprised if you could identify all of the factors that went into making up your mind, and even more surprised if you were able to assign weights to them in terms of how important each was in helping you to make up your mind.

Counselor Errors

Counselor error can occur when the client is being assessed, when the client is being treated, or when effectiveness of counseling is being evaluated (Gambrill, 1990). Counselors may overlook important data or attend to irrelevant data, may select inappropriate or ineffective intervention strategies, or may evaluate counseling in terms of process rather than outcomes.

Put simply, the clinical judgment research shows mixed results in the quality of the decisions that counselors or clinicians make about clients. Some of the errors are the same kinds of errors we all make in deciding upon everything from which car to buy to where to eat dinner.

- The same type of information is weighted differently in different circumstances. For example, on one occasion the counselor might think it was very significant that the client had been abused as a child. On another occasion the information might be glossed over.
- In arriving at the same decision on two separate occasions or with two different clients, different information is used. For example, you might look at previous grades on one occasion in making an assessment of the educational potential of a prospective student. On another occasion you might look at motivational factors.
- Counselors sometimes make decisions based on very idiosyncratic factors and then look for reasons to justify the decisions.

The above broad categories of errors give rise to a number of specific mistakes that counselors make in dealing with clients (Foa & Emmelkamp, 1983; Gambrill, 1990; Kessler, 1978; May & Franks, 1985). Examples include failing to offer help that clients need or forcing them to accept help they do not need, using counseling procedures that hinder rather than help the client, using procedures that are inadequate to deal with the issues at hand, and predicting future client behavior inaccurately.

Gambrill (1990) outlines a number of strategies or rules of thumb that a counselor can use to improve the quality of decision making (see immediately below). Based on what you have studied in Part I, you could call these strategies precepts and injunctions.

1. Look for evidence that does not support your point of view. If you think a single issue might form the focus of a client's problem, look again. What are you missing? What evidence does not agree with your presumption?
2. Seek to understand contrary viewpoints. Ensure that you have taken the time to demonstrate that understanding. This is most easily accomplished through listening.
3. Pay attention to situational variables as a cause of behavior. It is almost always wrong to infer particular client attributes on the basis of behavior in a specific set of circumstances. Most behavior is context dependent.
4. Ensure that the meanings you ascribe to words are consistent and shared. It is particularly important for you and the client to use a vocabulary of shared meanings.
5. In collecting information from the client, find out what did not happen as well as what did happen. It is too easy to overemphasize the importance of a particularly intense example.
6. Identify where your personal values and beliefs impinge upon your ability to consider evidence objectively. What are your feelings about such subjects as abortion or homosexuality or religion? Do your opinions have an unrealized impact on what you hear or on the decisions you make in listening to clients?
7. Become knowledgeable. Get your facts straight. There is usually a body of academic knowledge concerning every issue you deal with. As a professional counselor, you should become increasingly familiar with the literature.
8. Do not rely on external resources to make decisions for you. Tests do not do so; they provide you with information. The utility of the information depends upon the validity of the tests you use and how you use them. You make and are responsible for your decisions.
9. Put problems into perspective. A focus solely on the present overestimates the apparent effectiveness of intervention and the severity of client problems.
10. When using questions, ask questions that fill in voids in your data. Once you identify what is missing in the information you require, you are in a better position to pose questions whose answers yield the information you require.
11. Resist the urge to accept simple understanding. Not all problems or solutions are simple or easily understood. If the issues you face are easily dealt with or if you find persistent themes from client to client, perhaps you do not understand the issues you face as well as you think.
12. Be aware of lies that look like truths. Very often concepts are presented

as dichotomous rather than continuous variables—reason and passion, for instance. Sometimes, because absolute truth cannot be found, we accept that everything is totally subjective.

Improving your clinical judgment can improve your effectiveness as a counselor. Efficacy focuses on outcomes. Clinical judgment focuses on the processes that precede outcomes. When efficacy is high, a concern with clinical judgment is superfluous, except from an academic perspective. You know that whatever you are doing is effective. When efficacy is low, a concern with clinical judgment is vital because only by improving the decision-making process you are using do you improve the outcomes you engender.

You study clinical judgment to increase the practical intelligence you will be able to call upon in your job as a counselor. For example, as a counselor you will be called upon to manage emotions, respond to setbacks, deal with procrastination or resistance, and respond to requests for advice. Your skills will be required to decide when such issues are present and also to decide how you will deal with them in an effective way. Let us suppose you are meeting with a female client for the first time. She is very reticent, cannot look you in the eye, talks in a monotone, is close to tears several times, and sighs profoundly whenever she mentions the future. Is she depressed? suicidal? angry? How will you decide? What will you do differently depending upon what you decide? These are the kinds of questions that test clinical judgment.

The question about *how* you will decide cuts to the heart of the human inferential process. How do you decide when you are in love? How do you decide when a salesperson is trying to trick you? How do you decide if you should accept an offer of employment? How do you decide if you will pursue a course of study?

In counseling, the decisions you make about the issues that bring your clients to counseling generally have an impact on your future actions with your clients. Quite likely, you do something different in dealing with a client who you infer is suicidal than with a client who you infer is bored. If you do not do something different, there is little point in putting yourself through the agony of deciding which inference is the more accurate.

This last point bears repeating because it has an implication for counseling that flows directly from the research on clinical judgment. In assessing issues that may have brought a client to counseling, you need not be more specific in your assessment than in your treatment. To take a ridiculous example, if you would do the same thing to deal with a suicidal client and a bored client, it would make little sense for you to expend much effort in deciding if a client were bored or suicidal. As long as you ascertained that the client was one or the other, your assessment would be specific enough to lead you to a course of action.

Of course, a concern for efficacy might cause you to reexamine your assumption that the same course of treatment would be appropriate for a suicidal client and for a bored client. Perhaps there is compelling evidence to suggest that this is not the case. If bored or suicidal clients merit different actions on your part, the decision you make about which condition is the more likely is important because the decision will lead your treatment in one direction or another. The information you look at and how you use it to make your decision are important determinants of how accurate you are in making a decision about your client.

Practical Suggestions to Improve Clinical Judgment

The clinical judgments of many counselors do not improve in quality because the counselors do not have a helpful system in that regard. They often make decisions at the automatic level, use information to make decisions that is vaguely defined and highly variable, differentially weigh the information they collect according to circumstances, and do not collect feedback about decision quality. Small wonder that researchers from Meehl (1954) to Dawes, Faust, and Meehl (1989) have identified many types of decision-making situations where actuarial or mathematical modeling techniques have equaled or bettered the decisions made by clinicians using personalized inferential processes.

Many of the decisions on which clinical judgment research is based are outcome oriented. An example would be a determination, on the basis of a set amount of information, about whether a client would be successful in pursuing further training. However, many of the clinical judgments that you will make as a counselor will be process oriented. You will make decisions about such issues as whether a client feels comfortable with you, the negative and positive impacts that your questions have on clients, choosing when and how to confront a client, and the willingness of a client to change. These are not decisions whose results can be assessed in terms of your overall effectiveness as a counselor because mistakes in one area can be confounded by successes in another. But they illuminate areas where you can improve the quality of your decision making and where your successes will contribute to your overall effectiveness as a counselor.

Gambrill's (1990) twelve strategies are important precepts and injunctions to consider when you are involved in a counseling relationship with a client. Like all precepts and injunctions, the strategies acquire their operational meaning at the *techniques* level. Let's look at how these strategies translate into actual counselor behavior in terms of the communications styles you studied in earlier chapters.

1. The ability to look for evidence that does not support your own point of view is an acquired art, certainly not one that untrained counselors are likely to practice. One of the ways to test inferences you make about a client is to listen for alternative meanings in what the client is saying, and then to check out the meanings through listening-based communication skills (Chapter 6).

2. Listening statements are a very useful way to understand contrary points of view and to communicate the understanding to the client. Be wary of communicating a judgment under the guise of a listening statement. Often only the inflection of your voice serves to distinguish the two. Remember that if the client argues with you, agrees with you, or questions why you have said what you have, he or she is hearing your opinion rather than a summary of what was said to you.

3. Examining situational variables almost always requires that you examine the past. This is most easily done by using questions to open an area, followed by listening statements to deal with the responses of the client to your questions. Examining situational variables also requires that you ask about other situations the client experienced that were similar to the situation that brought the client to counseling. This will help you and your client to understand better the context in which the behavior at issue occurred.

4. Paying attention to clients' verbal and nonverbal reactions is the best way to ensure that they assign the same meanings you do to the words you use. Do they look puzzled when you ask them a question? Do they answer a question in a way that indicates they have missed the meaning of a key word? Very often clients will not tell you directly that they do not understand what you have said. They will make an inference of meaning based upon what they did understand and proceed on the basis of the inference.

One other way to ensure shared meaning is to unobtrusively define unusual words when you use them. For example, you might ask, "Did you feel possessive when he told you about the other woman—that he was yours and yours alone?" This is similar to the technique of using synonyms to ensure that one of them conveys the meaning you want to be inferred. For example, you might say, "You were feeling angry—mad or enraged—by what he did to you?" Of course, you must be aware that synonyms always convey something slightly different from the word they are standing in for.

You might ask a question to ascertain exactly what the client understands by what you have said. For example, "What does it mean to you to be piqued?"—*piqued* being the word you want to be sure that you and the client interpret similarly.

5. During counseling, clients often cite peak or unusual experiences—notable positive or negative experiences in terms of ordinary life events.

They are most likely to tell what they did or what happened rather than what they did not do. Questions are often helpful to obtain a broader perspective, particularly if they are followed by listening. Coaching your client on the process of what you are doing is often helpful at this point. For example, you might say, "Amelio, you have told me how you reacted when she threw the sand in your face. Put that in the context of how she usually reacted to you, when you were angry and when you were not."

6. There is no such thing as a value-free counselor any more than there is a value-free bricklayer, doctor, lawyer, or professor. This being the case, it is important to identify the values you hold, how these values affect your relationships with clients, and how to manage the impact of your values on your counseling relationships. Start by focusing on and identifying your values. Then identify how you deal with communication from clients who agree or disagree with your values. If one of your values dictates an antiabortion stance, how do you deal with a statement from a client such as "There's just no other choice. I can't have a baby, not now"? How do you deal with a statement such as "I know I'll have to carry the baby. There's really no other choice"? If you are successful in managing the impact of your values on your counseling, you will not demonstrate a pattern wherein you react positively to one type of statement and negatively to another.

7. A concern for clinical judgment requires that you remain familiar with the ever-expanding body of counseling knowledge. You should know what the research tells us about the efficacy of one kind of treatment over another and the conditions under which one form or another of treatment is indicated. You should understand the alternatives to the resolution strategies you are using and other information that is based upon an objective analysis of what other counselors are doing. Each client you confront is unique, but each is likely to have something in common with others you have dealt with. The clinical judgment literature supports informed decision making.

8. Gambrill (1990) is quite correct. Tests do not make decisions for you. Counselors make decisions. Make certain you grasp the limitations of the instruments you are using, and that you examine alternatives to the hypotheses you develop from interpreting tests. Ensure that you use the test information the same way in differing circumstances.

9. This is very similar to strategy 3.

10. Before you ask questions of clients, identify what you want them to deal with in their responses. Too many questions, particularly closed questions, are asked simply to fill in time. For example, you may have decided that it is helpful for you to understand the sexual history of a client. What do you mean by sexual history? Once you have a clear idea of what you are looking for, you will be in a much better position to frame appropriate questions. You will also be in a better position to know when

you have the information you need and when there are gaps that remain to be filled.

11. As a counselor, you are constantly making inferences about your clients on the basis of what they have told you. Be certain that when you make an inference, you remain open to alternatives. Very often, once counselors make up their minds about something, they discount countervailing new information. Simple information often sounds more reasonable than it really is.

12. Think of most variables as continuous. Your clients are typically not happy or sad. Most often, most of them are some place between these two extremes. When you find yourself thinking that a client is something or other, ask yourself to what degree this is untrue as well as true.

Put simply, Gambrill's (1990) suggestions for the counselor share one thing: they focus on the counselor as *informed decision maker*. They seek to identify and improve upon the quality of the decisions the counselor arrives at. This is as true of decisions that affect process as it is of decisions that directly affect results. To rephrase an old Irish proverb, "An unexamined decision is not worth making."

Points to Consider

1. Recall the decisions you have made today. How did you make them? What information did you use and how did you weigh it? What evidence will you look at to see how effective your decisions have been? What do you expect to learn about decision making from examining the decisions you made today?
2. Ask several practicing counselors to tell you how they make decisions about clients. Identify consistencies and inconsistencies in what they tell you.
3. If you are involved in practicum or internship experiences as a counselor-in-training, keep a log of the decisions you make, the evidence you considered, and the accuracy of your decisions. Pay particular attention to decisions you make about clients.

Suggested Readings

GAMBRILL, E. (1990). *Critical thinking in critical practice.* San Francisco: Jossey-Bass. Summarizes much of the historical and recent literature that deals with clinical decision making as it affects the counselor. Highly recommended.

MEEHL, P. E. (1954). *Clinical versus statistical prediction: A theoretical analysis and review of the evidence.* Minneapolis: University of Minnesota Press. Probably the most quoted classic in the field of clinical judgment; written by a giant in the field.

SELIGMAN, L. (1990). *Selecting effective treatments.* San Francisco: Jossey-Bass. Based on the DSM-III method of categorizing mental disorders, this book is particularly helpful in identifying alternative courses of action to be recommended by a counselor or therapist.

CHAPTER 4

Applying Counseling Orientations

Where the Rubber Meets the Road

In previous chapters you looked at a method to study and critique counseling orientations. You also studied other factors, such as clinical judgment, that have an impact on what you do as a counselor. As a counselor, you need to understand the orientation toward counseling under which you operate. You also need to understand the mechanism by which you put your counseling orientation into practice.

The mechanism of applying counseling orientations is what allows you to make the transition from the stated philosophy and purposes, process, and techniques of your counseling orientation to the actual behavior you display in your relationship with your clients. The mechanism must be generic enough to apply to the multiplicity of counseling orientations that abound today, particularly the variety of eclectic orientations that typify much of modern counseling practice.

I outline ten steps below that seem to be sensible in making the transition from counseling orientations to counseling practice. Think of them as a flowchart for counseling.

1. Based upon the philosophy and stated purposes of the counseling orientation within which you are operating, identify the *goals or purposes* of counseling that are particularly appropriate to the case at hand. You should do this at the macro level, the end point at which you and your client part company, and at the micro level, the point at which you and your client part company at the close of a particular session.
2. Paying attention to the precepts and injunctions that apply to your counseling orientation, outline a *counseling plan* incorporating the process or steps that you will use to achieve the goals you have identified.

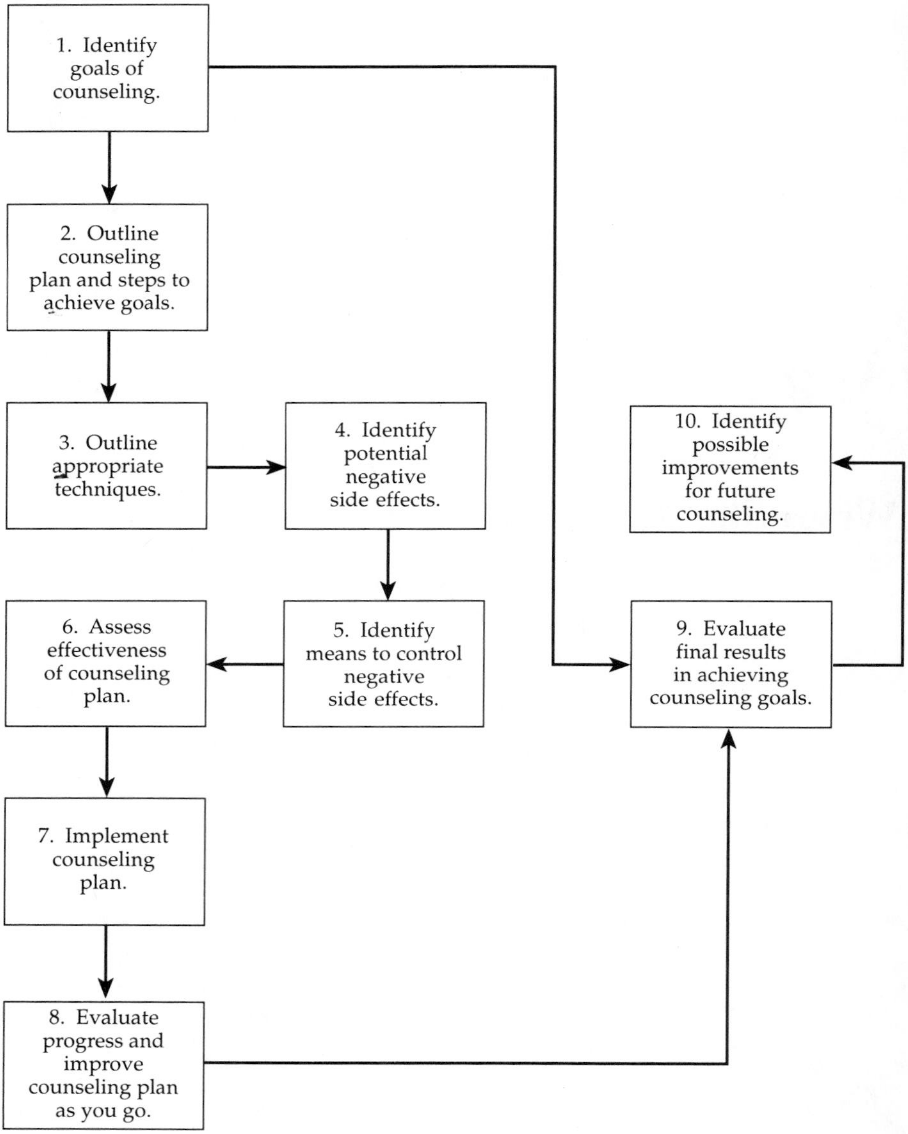

Flowchart of counseling process

3. Outline a variety of appropriate *techniques* that you can use to implement the counseling plan.
4. Describe possible *negative side effects* that might result from using the techniques you have chosen.
5. Outline how you will *control* or *accommodate* for the negative side effects you have identified.

6. Assess how well your plan will *achieve the goals* of counseling, and adjust your plan accordingly.
7. *Implement* your plan.
8. *Evaluate* the effectiveness of your plan as you are implementing it. Pay particular attention to alternative techniques you can use when your first choice does not have the desired result.
9. When you complete each session with the client and when you complete all sessions with your client, *evaluate* the extent to which the micro or macro goals of counseling have been realized—its *efficacy*.
10. Based on what you learned from your experience, *identify* what you would do differently if confronted with a similar situation in the future.

The first six steps in the flowchart represent planning. They are executed in advance of serious work with the client. The remaining four steps represent implementation and assessment of your plan. Using the two examples of counseling orientations that you studied earlier, person-centered therapy and rational-emotive therapy, I shall demonstrate how the first six steps of the flowchart might function with a case study similar to one you could confront in your work as a counselor.

Client Profile

Arnold is a forty-three-year-old unemployed professional. He is seeking assistance from a counselor employed by a local community college. Trained as an engineering technologist while in his early twenties, Arnold has held numerous jobs since, each for less than three years' duration. He now believes that in order to be successful with his life, he must find a new career, something he can be good at.

Arnold has been married twice. A seventeen-year-old child from his first marriage lives with him in his second marriage, and he has two children aged ten and three from his second marriage. Arnold's second marriage is not going well. His wife works as a secretary, although she would prefer to be at home with their preschool child, and she resents Arnold's "immature work attitude" that has seen him hold a string of mediocre jobs. Arnold has recently started drinking during the day, something he has not done since he swore off alcohol ten years ago. This has not helped his relationship with his wife, but he has met a number of cronies in a bar and feels that they understand him. He has become particularly close to a female divorced high school dropout ten years his junior whom he met in the bar, and she is willing to listen to his woes with an uncritical ear.

Arnold is a very discouraged individual. He has never been successful at a job, at anything. This condition he attributes to a poor career choice and bad luck. He is very prone to blame external circumstances for problems he encounters.

1. Goals

Rational-Emotive Therapy
Arnold's irrational belief that he cannot be successful at anything must be changed.

Arnold should learn to accept himself as imperfect, but not incapacitated by his imperfections.

Arnold should confront his inactivity, his failing relationship with his wife, his relationships with his friends, and his drinking.

Arnold should put in place a plan for the future.

Person-Centered Therapy
Arnold should be helped to see himself as he is and to accept himself.

Arnold should be helped to understand the often conflicting feelings that he has.

Arnold should be helped to understand that what he is experiencing is his life at present.

Arnold should be helped to pursue creative and flexible means to deal with life in a way that is true to how and what he really is.

2. Counseling Plan

Rational-Emotive Therapy
Help Arnold to investigate the irrational beliefs he holds.

Show Arnold how his irrational beliefs impact on his behavior.

Encourage Arnold to abandon the irrational beliefs he holds and to accept more rational beliefs.

Encourage Arnold to apply his revised beliefs to his future behavior.

Person-Centered Therapy
Encourage Arnold to talk about whatever is important to him.

Be accepting of anything that Arnold might say.

Help Arnold to explore discrepancies between his self-perceptions and his experiences of reality.

Encourage Arnold to express his feelings and negative emotions that might impact upon his life.

Be accepting and nonjudgmental.

Facilitate a feeling in Arnold that you are empathic—that you are "with" him.

3. Techniques

Rational-Emotive Therapy

Inform Arnold about the irrational beliefs that have guided his behavior and feelings.

Tell Arnold that only through changing his beliefs and acting on these changes will he ever be happy.

Teach Arnold about the principles of RET.

Ask Arnold to analyze his own behavior and beliefs and the impact of these on his current situation.

Assign Arnold homework to assess the rationality of proposed courses of action.

Person-Centered Therapy

Listen to what Arnold has to say, and reflect back to him your understanding of what he means.

Support Arnold's attempts at self-understanding through positive judgments.

Tentatively pose possible interpretations of Arnold's experiences to him to encourage him to reflect.

Support Arnold's decisions through positive judgments.

Assert your beliefs of Arnold's importance as an individual and your acceptance of him and his decisions.

4. Potential Negative Side Effects

Rational-Emotive Therapy

Arnold may rebel against accepting interpretations that you provide him.

Arnold may resist changing his beliefs.

Arnold may feel that you do not really understand him, that you are not interested in him as a person.

Arnold may not be capable of analyzing his own behavior.

Arnold may not do the homework you assign to him.

Person-Centered Therapy

Arnold may "talk around" issues that confront him.

Arnold may misinterpret your acceptance of him for acceptance of his behavior.

Arnold may not make decisions and may expect you to do so.

Arnold may feel that you are not prepared to help, that you are there to "just listen."

5. Controlling Potential Negative Side Effects

Rational-Emotive Therapy
Ask Arnold to identify alternative explanations to the ones he disagrees with.

Inform Arnold that he will never improve unless he changes the beliefs that guide his behavior.

Replace coaching with listening to help Arnold to understand that you are interested in him as a person.

If Arnold cannot analyze his own behavior, coach him on possible analyses and encourage him to consider these.

Do not set a definite time for the next appointment. Ask Arnold to call you to arrange for an appointment after he has completed the homework.

Person-Centered Therapy
Ensure that you do not inadvertently reinforce rambling by your facial and other nonverbal gestures.

Tell Arnold that you value him as a person, even though you may not always agree with what he has done.

Inform Arnold that you cannot make decisions for him but that you will help him to think about decisions he is considering.

Inform Arnold about the tenets of the counseling process you are using—that there is no place for you to make decisions for him.

6. Evaluate Your Proposed Counseling Plan

Rational-Emotive Therapy
There may still be weaknesses in the plan if the relationship between Arnold and you is not developed sufficiently well that he is open to your advice and counsel.

There are few alternatives available in the plan if Arnold is unwilling to accept the interpretations that you offer.

Person-Centered Therapy
A great deal of time may be required before Arnold is comfortable and willing to discuss important issues.

Arnold may use counseling as an excuse for real action in his life.

The six steps presented above are oversimplified for purposes of illustrating the counseling process I have outlined. Even though the two counseling orientations that are used as examples are dissimilar, both point out the *results dimension* common to all counseling orientations. Even though different orientations address different changes and do so in different ways, every successful orientation must make the transition from principles to practice.

Points to Consider

1. Follow the same six steps that I used to illustrate the counseling mechanisms for rational-emotive therapy and person-centered therapy to illustrate how you would handle this case using your own counseling orientation.
2. Study a real case with which you may be familiar. Use the two orientations used in this chapter's example as well as your own orientation.

Suggested Readings

KENNEDY, E., and CHARLES, S. C. (1990). *On becoming a counselor.* New York: Continuum. Part 2 of this book is particularly helpful in demonstrating the transition from principles to practice.

SELIGMAN, L. (1990). *Selecting effective treatments.* San Francisco: Jossey-Bass. This book is based upon the DSM-III method of categorizing mental disorders, and is particularly helpful in identifying alternatives to recommended courses of action by a counselor or therapist.

PART I

Summary of Key Points

1. The definition of a theory in counseling includes hypotheses about observations and statements of beliefs and values.
2. A counseling orientation comprises philosophy and purposes, process, and techniques.
3. The validity of counseling orientations is determined by their consistency, efficacy, and relevance.
4. Consistency of a counseling orientation lies in the soundness of the relationships among its philosophy and purposes, process, and techniques.
5. Efficacy of a counseling orientation refers to the effectiveness of the process and techniques in realizing the purposes of counseling.
6. Relevance of a counseling orientation refers to the utility of the orientation in addressing the demands of society related to counseling.
7. There is a linear relationship among the consistency, efficacy, and relevance of a counseling orientation.
8. Eclectic counseling orientations are drawn from many sources.
9. Eclectic counseling orientations can be analyzed and critiqued in the same manner as "name-brand" counseling orientations.
10. Most counselors operate under an eclectic umbrella.
11. Counseling orientations can be directive in process and/or intended outcomes.
12. All counseling orientations are directive in process to some degree.
13. The efficacy of counseling is judged by what happens to the client, not in terms of adherence to a process.
14. Counseling is multidimensional in purpose.
15. It is highly unlikely that any single counseling technique applied in a single instance will support all of the purposes of counseling.

16. There are usually many possible ways to accomplish a counseling goal.
17. Counselors must make decisions and be responsible for their decisions.
18. It is important to identify more than one means to deal with an issue in the event that your first choice is ineffective.
19. Learning new counseling techniques is difficult and usually feels unnatural at the start.
20. There are many impediments to making sound clinical judgments in counseling.
21. It is important to remain critical and analytical of counseling decisions you make.
22. You are responsible for your own decisions. Not deciding is a decision.
23. As a counselor, you operate on inferences. Inferences are opinions derived from your consideration of data.
24. Whenever possible, try to verify inferences drawn relative to clients.
25. There is no need for you to be more specific in your understanding of the issues that bring clients to counseling than you are in pursuing alternatives to deal with those issues.
26. Situational variables and the relationships between typical and atypical events are important considerations in understanding clients.
27. In practice, your orientation to counseling is defined by what you do rather than by what you say you do.
28. Many counseling techniques have negative as well as positive effects.

References and Additional Resources

BEUTLER, L. E. (1983). *Eclectic psychotherapy: A systematic approach.* New York: Pergamon Press.

BEUTLER, L. E. (1986). Systematic eclectic psychotherapy. In J. C. Norcross (Ed.), *Handbook of eclectic psychotherapy* (pp. 94–131). New York: Brunner/Mazel.

BISHOP, J. B., & RICHARDS, T. F. (1984). Counselor theoretical orientation as related to intake judgments. *Journal of Counseling Psychology, 31,* 398–401.

BLALOCK, H. M., JR. (1984). *Basic dilemmas in the social sciences.* Beverly Hills, CA: Sage.

BLAU, T. H. (1988). *Psychotherapy tradeoff: The technique and style of doing therapy.* New York: Brunner/Mazel.

BRABECK, M. M., & WELFEL, E. R. (1985). Counseling theory: Understanding the trend toward eclecticism from a development perspective. *Journal of Counseling and Development, 63,* 343–348.

BRAMMER, L., SHOSTROM, E., & ABREGO, P. J. (1989). *Therapeutic psychology: Fundamentals of counseling and psychotherapy* (5th ed.). Englewood Cliffs, NJ: Prentice-Hall.

BUDMAN, S. H. (Ed.). (1981). *Forms of brief therapy.* New York: Guilford Press.

BUDMAN, S. H., & GURMAN, A. S. (1988). *Theory and practice of brief therapy.* New York: Guilford Press.

BUGENTAL, J. F. T. (1987). *The art of the psychotherapist.* New York: Norton.

BURKE, J. F. (1989). *Contemporary approaches to psychotherapy and counseling.* Pacific Grove, CA: Brooks/Cole.

CAIN, D. J. (1987a). Carl R. Rogers: The man, his vision, his impact. *Person-Centered Review, 2,* 283–288.

CAIN, D. J. (1987b). Carl Rogers' life in review. *Person-Centered Review, 2,* 476–506.

CARKHUFF, R. R. (1969). *Helping and human relations: Vol. 1. Selection and human relations.* New York: Holt, Rinehart & Winston.

COMBS, A. W. (1988). Some current issues for person-centered therapy. *Person-Centered Review, 3,* 263–276.

COMBS, A. W. (1989). *A therapy of therapy: Guidelines for counseling practice.* Newbury Park, CA: Sage.

COREY, G. (1991). *Theory and practice of counseling and psychotherapy.* Pacific Grove, CA: Brooks/Cole.

COWEN, E. L. (1982). Help is where you find it. *American Psychologist, 37,* 385–395.

DAWES, R. M., FAUST, D., & MEEHL, P. E. (1989). Clinical versus actuarial judgement. *Science, 243,* 1669–1674.

DERLEGA, V. J., & BERG, J. H. (1987). *Self-disclosure: Theory, research, and therapy.* New York: Plenum.

DE RUBEIS, R. J., & BECK, A. T. (1988). Cognitive therapy. In K. S. Dobson (Ed.), *Handbook of cognitive-behavioral therapies* (pp. 273–306). New York: Guilford Press.

DIGIUSEPPE, R. A., MILLER, N. J., & TREXLER, L. D. (1979). A review of rational-emotive psychotherapy outcome studies. In A. Ellis & J. M. Whiteley (Eds.), *Theoretical and empirical foundations of rational-emotive therapy* (pp. 218-235). Pacific Grove, CA: Brooks/Cole.

DIMOND, R. E., HAVENS, R. A., & JONES, A. C. (1978). A conceptual framework for the practice of prescriptive eclecticism in psychotherapy. *American Psychologist, 33,* 239–248.

DRISCOLL, R. (1984). *Pragmatic psychotherapy.* New York: Van Nostrand Reinhold.

D'ZURILLA, T. J., & NEZU, A. (1980). A study of the generation-of-alternatives process in social problem solving. *Cognitive Therapy and Research, 4,* 67–72.

EGAN, G. (1990). *The skilled helper.* Pacific Grove, CA: Brooks/Cole.

ELLIS, A. (1973). *Humanistic psychotherapy: The rational-emotive approach.* New York: Julian Press.

ELLIS, A., & YEAGER, R. J. (1989). *Why some therapies don't work.* Buffalo: Prometheus Books.

ELSTEIN, A. S. (1988). Cognitive processes in clinical inference and decision making. In D. C. Turk and P. Salovery (Eds.), *Reasoning, inference, and judgement in clinical psychology.* New York: Free Press.

EYSENCK, H. J. (1966). *The effects of psychotherapy.* New York: International Science Press.

FOA, E. B., & EMMELKAMP, P. M. G. (Eds.). (1983). *Failures in behavioral therapy.* New York: Penguin.

GAMBRILL, E. (1990). *Critical thinking in clinical practice.* San Francisco: Jossey-Bass.

GARFIELD, S. L., & KURZ, R. A. (1977). A study of eclectic views. *Journal of Consulting and Clinical Psychology, 45,* 78–83.

GELATT, H. B. (1989). Positive uncertainty: A new decision-making framework for counseling. *Journal of Counseling Psychology, 36,* 252–256.

GLADDING, S. T. (1988). *Counseling: A comprehensive profession.* Columbus, OH: Merrill.

GUTSCH, K. U. (1988). *Psychotherapeutic approaches to specific DSM-III-R categories.* Springfield, IL: Thomas.

HAAGA, D. A., & DAVISON, G. C. (1989). Outcome studies of rational-emotive therapy. In M. E. Bernard & R. A. DiGiuseppe (Eds.), *Inside rational-emotive therapy.* San Diego: Academic Press.

HACKNEY, H. (1978). The evolution of empathy. *Personnel and Guidance Journal, 57,* 35–38.

HART, J. T. (1983). *Modern eclectic therapy: A functional orientation to counseling and psychotherapy.* New York: Plenum.

HEPPNER, P. P., & KRAUSKOPF, C. J. (1987). An information-processing approach to personal problem solving. *Counseling Psychologist, 15,* 371–447.

HOROWITZ, M., MARMAR, C., KRUPNICK, J., WILNER, N., KALTREIDER, N., & WALLERSTEIN, R. (1984). *Personality styles and brief psychotherapy.* New York: Basic Books.

IVEY, A. (1988). *Intentional interviewing and counseling.* Pacific Grove, CA: Brooks/Cole.

KATZ, J. H. (1985). The sociopolitical nature of counseling. *Counseling Psychologist, 13,* 615–624.

KENNEDY, E., & CHARLES, S. C. (1990). *On becoming a counselor.* New York: Continuum.

KESSLER, J. W. (1978). Potential errors in clinical practice. In J. S. Mearig (Ed.), *Working for children.* San Francisco: Jossey-Bass.

LAZARUS, A. A. (1986). Multimodal therapy. In J. C. Norcross (Ed.), *Handbook of eclectic psychotherapy* (pp. 65–93). New York: Brunner/Mazel.

LAZARUS, A. A. (1989). *The practice of multimodal therapy.* Baltimore, MD: Johns Hopkins University Press.

LEWIS, J. A., & LEWIS, M. D. (1986). *Counseling programs for employees in the workplace.* Pacific Grove, CA: Brooks/Cole.

MASLOW, A. (1971). *The farther reaches of human nature.* New York: Viking Press.

MAY, D. T., & FRANKS, C. M. (Eds.). (1985). *Negative outcome in psychotherapy and what to do about it.* New York: Springer.

MEEHL, P. E. (1954). *Clinical versus statistical prediction: A theoretical analysis and review of the evidence.* Minneapolis: University of Minnesota Press.

MEHRABIAN, A. (1981). *Silent messages: Implicit communication of emotions and attitudes.* Belmont, CA: Wadsworth.

MILLER, W. R., & MARTIN, J. E. (1988). *Behavior therapy and religion: Integrating spiritual and behavioral approaches to change.* Newbury Park, CA: Sage.

MURRAY, E. J. (1986). Possibilities and promises of eclecticism. In J. C. Norcross (Ed.), *Handbook of eclectic psychotherapy* (pp. 398–415). New York: Brunner/Mazel.

NORCROSS, J. C. (Ed.). (1986). *Handbook of eclectic psychotherapy.* New York: Brunner/Mazel.

NORCROSS, J. C. (Ed.). (1987). *Casebook of eclectic psychotherapy.* New York: Brunner/Mazel.

NORCROSS, J. C., & PROCHASKA, J. O. (1988). A study of eclectic (and integrative) views revisited. *Professional Psychology: Research and Practice, 19,* 170–174.

PATTERSON, C. H. (1985). *The therapeutic relationship: Foundations for an eclectic psychotherapy.* Pacific Grove, CA: Brooks/Cole.

PORTER, E. H. (1950). *An introduction to therapeutic counseling.* Boston: Houghton Mifflin.

PROCHASKA, J. O. (1984). *Systems of psychotherapy.* Chicago: Dorsey Press.

PROCHASKA, J. O., & DICLEMENTE, C. C. (1986). The transtheoretical approach. In J. C. Norcross (Ed.), *Handbook of eclectic psychotherapy* (pp. 163–200). New York: Brunner/Mazel.

ROGERS, C. R. (1942). *Counseling and psychotherapy.* Boston: Houghton Mifflin.

ROGERS, C. R. (1951). *Client-centered therapy.* Boston: Houghton Mifflin.

ROGERS, C. R. (1957). The necessary and sufficient conditions of therapeutic personality change. *Journal of Consulting Psychology, 21,* 95–103.

ROGERS, C. R. (1986). Reflections of feeling. *Person-Centered Review, 1,* 375–377.

ROGERS, C. R., & WOOD, J. (1984). Client-centered therapy: Carl Rogers. In A. Burton (Ed.), *Operational Theories of Personality.* New York: Brunner/Mazel.

SACHS, J. S. (1983). Negative factors in brief psychotherapy: An empirical assessment. *Journal of Consulting and Clinical Psychology, 51,* 557–564.

SCHULTZ, D. (1990). *Theories of personality.* Pacific Grove, CA: Brooks/Cole.

SCISSONS, E. H. (1985). *CareerScan: How to advance your career.* New York: Dembner Books.

SCISSONS, E. H. (1987). *Happily ever after: Making the most of your retirement.* New York: Dembner Books.

SELIGMAN, L. (1990). *Selecting effective treatments.* San Francisco: Jossey-Bass.

SHAPIRO, D. A., & SHAPIRO, D. (1982). Meta-analysis of comparative therapy outcome research: A critical appraisal. *Behavioral Psychotherapy, 10,* 4–25.

SHOBEN, E. J., JR., (1956). Behavioral theories and a counseling case: A symposium. *Journal of Counseling Psychology, 3,* 107–124.

STILES, W. B., SHAPIRO, D. A., & ELLIOTT, R. (1986). "Are all psychotherapies equivalent?" *American Psychologist, 41,* 165–180.

TROWER, P., CASEY, A., & DRYDEN, W. (1988). *Cognitive-behavioral counseling in action.* Newbury Park, CA: Sage.

WALEN, S., DIGIUSEPPE, R. A., & WESSLER, R. L. (1980). *A practitioner's guide to rational-emotive therapy.* New York: Oxford University Press.

WATSON, N. (1984). The empirical status of Rogers' hypotheses of the necessary and sufficient conditions for effective psychotherapy. In R. F. Levant & J. M. Shlien (Eds.), *Client-centered therapy and the person-centered approach: New directions in theory, research and practice* (pp. 17–40). New York: Praeger.

WEINRACH, S. G. (1980). Unconventional therapist: Albert Ellis. *Personnel and Guidance Journal, 59,* 152–160.

WESSLER, R. A., & WESSLER, R. L. (1980). *The principles and practice of rational-emotive therapy.* San Francisco: Jossey-Bass.

PART II

Communication and the Counselor

Learning Objectives

Part II introduces you to a method for assessing your communication with clients. It also helps you understand the implications of communicating in different ways with clients and provides skills-building practice. After you complete Part II you should be able to:

- describe a framework that explains types of communication with clients;
- outline the counseling implications of communicating with clients in different ways;
- articulate alternative statements that a counselor can use to help realize counseling goals;
- demonstrate an ability to respond in several ways to typical statements from clients;
- demonstrate an ability to use communication skills to advance the counseling process within one or more counseling orientations; and
- analyze communication styles at the typical speed of conversation in counseling.

CHAPTER 5

Effective Communication

Communication between you and your client is purposeful. Although the purposes of counseling vary from counselor to counselor and client to client, all counseling is designed to accomplish something. Just as you can drive without a road map, you can counsel with no specified purpose or destination. But trained counselors, like trained carpenters, truck drivers, surgeons, and police officers, want to get somewhere or achieve something. In fact, what differentiates the communication that a counselor has with a client from the conversation between two friends is the purpose of each conversation. Two friends might talk just to pass time. As a counselor, you speak with clients to accomplish something. Your effectiveness is judged on the basis of whether you are successful at it. By talking with your clients, you have the potential to effect a real difference in their lives (Evans, Hearn, Uhlemann, & Ivey, 1989).

The way you converse with a client is unique. Nobody else does it quite the way that you do. How you do it depends on many factors: your training, your counseling and noncounseling experiences, your counseling orientation, and your perceptions of the client you are dealing with, as well as such less defined factors as your level of nervousness.

In counseling interviews, you are confronted with choices. Because words are the tools of your trade, your most important choices deal with what you say and how you say it. What you say during counseling is a major factor in determining whether or not you achieve what you want to achieve. As a practicing counselor, you make many minute-to-minute operational choices that reflect a simple question: "What do I say now?"

What separates you from a less effective counselor are the goals you are trying to accomplish and your repertoire of actions to realize the goals. Without a well-developed repertoire, you try in vain to make counseling situations fit your limited abilities (Corey, 1986). To be a good counselor, you must respond flexibly and assuredly in many different situations. Making decisions is inescapable, and you must competently put your decisions into place in your conversations with clients.

An Example

As a counselor in a large community service agency, you deal with most clients on a drop-in basis. A female, approximately 30 years of age, asks to see you. She flops down in the chair opposite, saying, "I suppose I have to talk about this, but I don't know where to start."

From the five responses below, select the one that is closest to what you would be most likely to say in reply. It is unlikely that any of these responses is exactly what you would say, but probably one among them is an approximation.

1. You are not really too sure about talking to me today.
2. What is on your mind?
3. We will talk about whatever you want to talk about.
4. There is not much to be gained from holding back if something is bothering you.
5. It is never easy to talk to someone you don't know.

For most untrained counselors, *select* is the wrong word to describe what they would do in a real-life situation such as this one. *Select* implies a conscious weighing of alternatives and singling out the best. If you were an untrained counselor in a real situation, such as the example above, you would probably be functioning on autopilot. You would settle for what seems right at the moment. There would be, at best, a gap of only seconds between the statement by the client and your response. During that brief interval, if you were like most fledgling counselors, you would begin uttering the first appropriate response that comes to mind. There would be no conscious weighing of alternatives and choosing. You would simply react as best you could.

In the example above, there is a single measure that is suitable for assessing the effectiveness of your response: results. What counseling goals do you think are appropriate for this brief exchange with the client? What type of reaction do you think each of the five responses would summon from the client? When the client's response and the type of response you want from the client converge, that's success!

An Example—Continued

If you had made one of the five responses from the above example, you might expect certain responses from the client:

Counselor	Client
1. You are not really too sure about talking to me today.	1. Well, no I'm not.
2. What is on your mind?	2. What do you mean?
3. We will talk about whatever you want to talk about.	3. It's not that I don't want to talk.
4. There is not much to be gained from holding back if something is bothering you.	4. That's easy for you to say.
5. It's never easy to talk to someone you don't know.	5. Yeah.

In this example, different counselors, with differing philosophical or theoretical orientations, might each want to achieve something different from their exchanges with the client. They might be operating with goals or intentions that would result in their saying something different than a counselor who did not share these goals would say.

In such a situation you might want to achieve one or more of the following as a result of how you respond to the client:

- encourage a perception by the client that you are empathic, that you have a sensitivity to the client's concerns;
- instill a feeling of trust, competence, or confidence in the client;
- gain a better appreciation for the background of the client or a knowledge of the issues that bring the client to counseling;
- gauge the motivation of the client to change;
- determine if the issues that concern the client are ones that you are capable of addressing as a counselor; or
- challenge the client to think about why she is there or what she wants to achieve.

To complicate the issue further, no matter what type of initial response you use with clients, it will probably elicit responses from them that depend partly on how you answered the first time. When they respond to you, you will make other responses. You will be faced with choosing what to say, whether or not you are aware of making choices. The to-and-fro continues until you and your clients part company.

The goals or intentions of counseling are active throughout the counseling interview. Each exchange provides a fresh opportunity to realize the goals, and helps, hinders, or is neutral in terms of affecting the final result of the interview.

Visualize conversation in counseling as a tennis game. The client serves the ball with an opening statement, making a certain kind of "shot" that limits but does not define the kind of "return" you make. Your "return" also limits but does not determine the kind of response the client makes. In interpersonal communication, as in tennis, it is not possible to predict or influence perfectly the kind of "return" that a participant elicits. You can influence to a degree the possibilities open to your clients by what you say to them. And because what clients say is closely related to how they think or feel, you can also influence these important variables by how you choose to respond.

Suppose that rather than using one of the five responses proffered in the example, you reply haughtily, "When you decide you want to talk, make an appointment with my secretary." This response would be counterproductive because of the negative response it is likely to evoke. It would not be conducive to achieving any of the goals you want to achieve—unless you wanted to drive the client away.

No matter what you say when you respond to the client's opening remark, you will have many chances to influence the direction of the conversation. If the kind of response you get initially is not what you want, you will be able to try again. (As in tennis, when you switch from a forehand to a backhand shot!) When your turn comes around, you can duplicate the form of your first attempt or try a different tack. It is entirely up to you. Well, maybe not quite up to you.

It is possible to try different kinds of statements and responses in dealing with clients only if you are able to recognize differences in the style or forms of communication you are using and then to modify what you are saying and how you are saying it "on the fly." The skill is not easily mastered, particularly because in counseling, everything must be done at the speed of conversation.

If, as in the example you have just considered, the client opens the conversation by saying, "I suppose I have to talk about this, but I don't know where to start," you must:

- recognize what you want to accomplish by responding;
- identify several things you can say to accomplish what you want to accomplish;
- select what you are going to say;
- listen to what the client says in responding to you;
- ascertain if what you wanted to accomplish is being accomplished; and
- modify or augment your approach in light of the results you are obtaining.

This is a tall order, if for no other reason than it must be done quickly and with a sense of ease and facility that belies its difficulty.

Helping you to recognize what you want to accomplish with the client is the proper venue of counseling orientations or theories, the subject of Part

I. Identifying the alternatives you have available to help you accomplish the desired ends and identify when you are successful are technical skills. Of course, both are important. As Woody, Hansen, and Rossberg (1989, p. 55) so aptly put it, "Theory is, in fact, integral with practice." These skills form the nucleus for Part II.

Recognizing Interpersonal Communication Styles

How you communicate with your clients is more recognizable by others than by you. That's natural. You are much too busy trying to be helpful to analyze the hows and whys of your helpfulness. But analyze them you must if you are going to be able to change or improve in this important skill.

There are a variety of ways to understand and improve communication during counseling. Each way is based on four steps.

1. Use a framework that helps you to catalogue the styles or patterns of communication.
2. Study the styles or patterns and the implications of their use to achieve the goals you have in communication.
3. Appraise the use of alternatives to your preferred style(s) in order to better realize your goals in communication.
4. Practice the alternatives until you achieve mastery.

Communication categorization schemes can help you classify the statements you make to clients. The schemes do it by assigning each statement you make during counseling to a category that contains similar statements. Similarity is based on such factors as intent of the statement, likely reactions from clients when you use the statement, or potentially negative effects of the statement. However, because all categorization schemes work with the same "pie"—that is, what counselors say—they differ mainly in how they divide the pie and how they label each slice.

A categorization scheme is intangible. It takes what is said and puts it into one compartment or another. For example, a statement by a counselor such as "You've been upset for ten years about what happened and only now are you starting to talk about it" may be called clarifying, verifying, paraphrasing, perception checking, reflecting, or a multitude of other terms, depending upon the categorizer. The statement is unique, yet it is *similar* enough to other statements that we can group them all under a common label.

Communication categorization schemes can be helpful in learning how to counsel. They provide a framework to help you understand the typical kinds of statements used with clients. If a particular category of communication works well with a client, your ability to recognize that fact and then use statements representative of the category will enhance your performance. Conversely, if statements representative of a different category do not have the desired effect, your ability to recognize that fact and avoid bringing them into play makes you a better counselor.

Throughout this textbook, I employ a very elementary framework to categorize the communication between counselor and client. An adaptation of a framework first outlined by Porter (1950) and Jones (1967), the framework is one that I have taught to many students of counseling and one that has been field-tested in many situations. Keep in mind, however, that there is nothing sacred about any one categorization framework.

Analyzing Communication Patterns

A certain predictability is the rule in dealing with physical matters. Given the same sets of circumstances, a car will take the same distance to stop whenever it does so; comparable bullets will drop the same amount over a given distance each time they are fired; the length of time it takes the voice of an angry client to reach your ears is the same in each instance. In regard to physical matters, even when you don't enjoy the outcomes, you can be more or less assured of what will happen and plan accordingly. It is different in the realm of interpersonal communication. It is sometimes hard to understand why certain reactions from others follow certain actions we take. Reactions simply are not consistent either across individuals or within the same individual across time.

There are probably two reasons for unpredictability in the world of communication. The first reason is your misreading of a situation. Although a situation may look similar to one that occurred before, this is seldom the case. Differences are usually hard to detect or to assess in importance. The second reason is the complex interactive nature of communication. A client's responses are dependent not just on what you say but on factors such as the history of your interactions with the client, what the client perceives as having been said, or even how the client is feeling when you begin to speak. In theory it may be possible to take into consideration all of the factors in all their variety but it seldom works out that way. In practice it is difficult to decide which factors should be measured and it would be impossible to measure all of the factors even if you could decide upon the most salient. The two reasons then, foreclose certitude but do not render communication wholly undecipherable or unpredictable. It's just that you must be satisfied with far less of that about which you can be absolutely sure.

Although understanding or predicting communication patterns within counseling situations are elusive matters, it is possible to understand or predict at a level that will enhance your effectiveness. You will never be perfect, but you can be better! To do so, you must grasp how you communicate with others, and the implications of your styles of communication.

Buying an Electric Drill

Consider the following noncounseling example. Pretend that you purchase a new electric drill at a local building supply store. After a few days of use the drill quits working. You take it back to the store but without a bill of sale. The sales clerk asks if you indeed bought the drill at that store. Your immediate reply: "Of course, I bought it here. Why is it that you people are so damned keen to sell something, but as soon as anything goes wrong with it you look for some way to wriggle out of making things right?"

What type of response would you expect from the clerk? If you have witnessed a similar situation, you will know that the two most likely responses by an inexperienced clerk would be sheepish compliance or animosity: "Oh, I'm sorry. I didn't mean anything, but we're supposed to have the bill to make adjustments," or "If you don't have the bill of sale, I can't do anything. Sorry!"

Quite likely, had I asked you before the scenario started what you wanted, you probably would have told me a "no-hassle" exchange. Again, if I had asked you what might result from an inflammatory statement such as the one in the example above, you would probably be able to predict possible outcomes accurately. Why, then, did you make such a statement in the first place?

Most times, individuals get into problems in their communication with others because they do not think through what they want to accomplish. They rely on their "natural" manner of behaving with others, a manner developed over the years by incidental learning. In some cases incidental learning is very effective—witness a seasoned police officer using persuasion instead of raw power to deal with a potential tavern brawl. In other cases, such as domestic situations where the officer's presence may make things worse, persuasion is inadequate. But in both cases what is done is usually not consciously thought through and understood so it can be improved upon in the future. What is done is done!

Luckily, it is possible to improve communication abilities. You do this by studying the dynamics of what takes place in situations where you say something to someone, examining how you can influence the dynamics, and practicing alternative ways of doing so. For the would-be counselor, these steps are best attempted within the safety of a learning environment.

Before you begin reading the remainder of Part II, complete the Counseling Communication Inventory *in the Appendix. After you have completed reading Part II, read the short section in the Appendix that will help you to interpret your results on the self-administered questionnaire.*

Styles of Communication

One way to understand better the kinds of statements that you make during counseling is to analyze the responses your statements evoke from clients. Not that any single response statement by you will definitely lead to a certain kind of response by the client, but certain kinds of statements are more likely to do so. (An old proverb suggests to the traveler that if you know where you are going, you are more likely to get there! The proverb is just as appropriate for the counselor.)

Most of what a counselor does requires communication with clients. Conducting an intake interview, exploring the dimensions of a problem, discussing attempts to resolve a problem and encouraging and supporting clients all share an attribute: face-to-face communication. There are many ways to undertake such communication, many different styles to use.

In the remaining chapters of Part II you examine a communication categorization scheme that will help you to analyze your communication with clients. As you study, keep in mind that the communication styles used in counseling are not fundamentally different from the communication styles used in everyday relationships. Thus, you will find much of what is described to be appropriate to your noncounseling life as well.

Points to Consider

1. Identify circumstances in which you communicate in different ways. For example, how do you communicate at weddings, funerals, graduations, and religious celebrations, and in encounters with the law? What is similar or different about your behavior on these occasions?
2. Identify unique aspects of how you communicate. How are such ways different from those of your parents, brothers and sisters, friends, or significant others?
3. Identify situations in which your communication skills were particularly effective or ineffective. What has made the difference? If you had the opportunity to relive situations in which you were ineffective, what would you now do differently?
4. Identify situations in which you wanted to accomplish something in an exchange with someone. What did you say or do to bring this about?

Suggested Readings

BENJAMIN, A. (1969). *The helping interview.* Boston: Houghton Mifflin. Chapter 6 offers a good general introduction to communication within the context of counseling.

D'AUGELLI, A. R., D'AUGELLI, J. F., & DANISH, S. J. (1981). *Helping others.* Pacific Grove, CA: Brooks/Cole. Chapters 4–6 offer a perspective on communication based upon what the counselor says and hears.

STONE, G. (1986). *Counseling psychology: Perspectives and functions.* Pacific Grove, CA: Brooks/Cole. Chapter 9 offers a good introduction to communication and communicating from counseling and noncounseling viewpoints.

CHAPTER 6

Listening

"You are not very happy about the shift you've been put on."
"You did what you thought you were supposed to in your marriage and now nothing is working out."
"It's not much fun having a partner who doesn't pull his weight."
"When nobody tells you what to do, it is hard to get it right."
"When the room is the wrong color, it is hard for you to concentrate on what you are doing."

Unlike a question, a listening statement sounds out of place unless you hear the preceding statement. It is easy to visualize that some statement from the other person in a transaction must have precipitated each of the example statements above. Let's look at one possible statement for each of the five listening statements at the start of this chapter. When you pair each of the counselor's statements with client's statements, you will see the common elements of a listening style.

Client	**Counselor**
Why is it that I always seem to get a shift that conflicts with the one my wife has?	You are not very happy about the shift you've been put on . . .
I just did what I thought I was supposed to.	You did what you thought you were supposed to in your marriage and now nothing is working out . . .
Why did I get lucky enough to pull working with Jones?	It's not much fun having a partner who doesn't pull his weight . . .
Nobody tells you what to do, and when you make up your own mind, you get jumped on.	When nobody tells you what to do, it is hard to get it right . . .

I can't study here. It just drives me nuts.	When the room is blue, it is hard for you to concentrate on what you are doing . . .

Definition

A listening statement is a simple declarative statement to a client followed by an implied question that asks "You said this or meant this . . . didn't you?" Listening confirms your understanding of what another person is trying to tell you, and ensures that what someone wants to communicate to you and what you understand from him or her are similar in meaning. This communication from the client can be verbal or nonverbal, clear or vague (Egan, 1990). (Nonverbal communication is addressed in Chapter 11.) Depending upon the writer and the particular aspect of listening that is emphasized, listening is sometimes referred to as paraphrasing, perception checking, verifying, reflecting, or attending.

As you can see from the examples above, the person who uses a listening style replies to the other person with an understanding of what has been communicated along with an implied question, "Is that right?" This sets the stage for the other person to agree or disagree with the listener's perception and prevents misunderstandings.

- Listening can help to develop trust between counselor and client because listening demonstrates to the client that the counselor appreciates where the client is "coming from." Client trust in the counselor is an essential component of a successful counseling relationship (Orlinsky & Howard, 1986).
- Listening convinces clients that you understand them. Such conviction is usually beneficial as a prelude to successful resolution of issues or problems (Ivey, 1990; Martin, 1983).
- Listening encourages clients to reprocess what they have said to the counselor. Sometimes clients say something that they have not considered very thoroughly. Responding to the implied question, "Is that right?" prompts clients to consider what they have said and what they meant (D'Augelli, D'Augelli, & Danish, 1981). Sometimes, such reflection is the sole necessity for successful counseling.
- Listening ensures that you are on the right track. It can prevent your building a case based upon faulty inferences.
- Listening is an effective technique to collect information from a client. It is a desirable supplement to direct questioning because it avoids some of the latter's potentially negative side effects (Martin, 1983).

Certain aspects of a listening style are sometimes overused or used very superficially by someone who has a smattering of training in communication skills. A caricature would be a person who after your every statement looks at you intently and prefaces his or her reply with "I get the feeling that you mean . . ." or "What you are saying is . . ." or "It sounds like you mean (feel) . . ." or, worse yet, simply repeats what you have said.

When I was in graduate school, fellow students used to drive one another crazy by overusing listening statements, sometimes deliberately with an air of devilment, sometimes inadvertently because they thought it was the way that counselors are supposed to speak. An older professor gave us some "down-home" advice: "If you'd feel foolish saying it to longtime friends, don't say it to your clients!" He knew that "talking like a shrink" sounds unnatural and marks the speaker as fresh from a communication skills course. If someone is offended by your use of communication skills or thinks that you are speaking in another language, you are not likely to achieve what you have in mind by your use of the technique. To be effective, listening statements must sound like ordinary day-to-day conversation.

Sentence headers such as "I get the feeling that you mean . . ." or "What you are saying is . . ." or "It sounds like you mean (feel) . . ." are often used by the beginning counselor to buy time to construct the listening statement that will follow. Although there is nothing wrong with an occasional header, used too frequently they are annoying in the same way that the all-too-common "You know what I mean" is when it tags along after a statement. It is usually better to practice listening statements without the headers. This prevents your using them as a crutch that is difficult to do without when you become a full-fledged counselor.

Uses of Listening

The purposes of using listening with clients can be summarized under three rubrics: data collection, relationship building, and facilitating positive change. In practice, the purposes are usually realized simultaneously. For example, as a counselor you might collect data from clients about their relationships with their fathers and use listening to ensure that you have accurate information. At the same time you might use listening to build trust between you and your clients, to demonstrate that you care about them or to encourage them to focus on their feelings. Listening is not the only way to do these things but it is a very viable one.

Data collection is a major element of counseling. It is often important to find out about the background of the client, to understand the dimensions of the issues that bring the client to counseling, and to gain knowledge of the client's goals. Listening, in conjunction with other skills that you will study later, can be very effective in doing these things.

Listening is important when you want to collect data because questioning alone does not do the job. Even in situations such as police interrogation, where questions seem to be the order of the day, successful practitioners do not rely on questions alone. Listening is effective because of the typical reactions you get when you make listening statements to clients. Here are several examples.

Client	**Counselor**
I don't know why I love him so much. I shouldn't.	It's not good for you to love him but you do anyway . . .
Yeah. I mean, he beats me. I say that I'm never going to have anything to do with him, but after a while I do anyway.	Even when he hurts you, it just interrupts how you feel for him. You still go back time and time again . . .
Uh huh. I've tried but I just can't make myself leave him.	
Why does it matter if I go to school or not? Half of the people I know didn't finish school.	Part of you wants to finish school, but the other part says, "Why bother . . ."
Yeah. I mean what difference does it make? You can't get a job if you finish school or not.	If finishing school meant that you could get a job, that would be one thing. But, when it doesn't, who cares . . .
Well, I don't know. Finishing school would be good. I just don't know if I can make it or not.	
I know what to do. I'm just too damned chicken to do it. That's all.	If you were a braver person it would be easier . . .
Yes . . . no . . . I mean that somebody has to get hurt no matter what I do.	Somebody has to get hurt, and you don't want to be the person to do it . . .
Right. You don't know how hard it is to live with that kind of thing. I've had to go through that before.	
You don't know what it's like not being brave. I feel like such a coward, Dorothy.	Lion, you think that not being brave is being a coward . . .
Yes, Dorothy. A lion should be stouthearted. I'm not stouthearted, Dorothy.	You are not fearless because you are sometimes afraid, Lion . . .
Maybe. Sometimes, I'm brave. But, sometimes, I'm an awful coward.	

These examples point up two common reactions of clients to a counselor's listening: validation and elaboration. Validation means that listening statements are self-correcting. Once you make a listening statement, the client usually responds with answers that tell you if you are right, partly right, or wrong in your inferences. Usually, if you are wrong or partly right, the client will correct you by supplying additional information to make certain you draw a more accurate inference.

Elaboration means that listening encourages clients to supply additional information in the same or a related area. This customarily happens when you are correct in the inference you are verifying and the client responds with a "Yes, and . . ." answer. In the examples above, most of the responses by the client illustrate this aspect.

Relationship building is a major use of listening. Some writers have postulated and some research has demonstrated that client belief that the counselor (1) is trustworthy and (2) feels unconditional positive regard and empathy for the client is essential for effective counseling (Orlinsky & Howard, 1986). Listening by the counselor can help to bring about the belief.

Most often, the desired client belief cannot be imposed or willed. It is a side effect when listening is used for other reasons. For instance, just the act of attending carefully (necessary if appropriate listening replies are to be made) can leave clients feeling that you are empathic, interested in them and their problems, and trustworthy. If you use listening to follow up on things they say about themselves or feelings they express, these perceptions are augmented. Here is an example of how this might be done.

Client	**Counselor**
The hardest time is at night. That's when I feel most alone.	You are afraid at night because you can't avoid the feelings of being alone . . .
Yes. I mean that during the day there are people all around. Even though I don't have much to do with them, it's somehow reassuring.	At night you can't fool yourself any more . . .
I suppose that's true. What can I do about it anyway?	You are hoping there is something I can tell you that will make the night seem easier . . .
I can't seem to do anything right. Here I am in the same trouble again.	It's frustrating to go round and round in the same circles . . .
That's for sure. I swore that when I dumped Larry, I wouldn't go for men who were that way again.	Men who were hard on you, who hurt you . . .

Yes. Here I am again.	Hurt and angry—at him and yourself . . .
I'm not going to pass this year. I might as well drop out now.	You've finished the exams and you are scared silly to see the results . . .
Well, not everything. I might pass biology.	But everything else is pretty much a write-off, and that's not easy to admit . . .
Yes. I don't know what to do.	You are not sure what to do or a bit afraid to think of what you have to do . . .
It's so frightening in the forest all alone. I never know what will jump out at me from behind a tree.	Afraid because you are alone, Red . . .
Well, yes. You know what I mean. It's not so much that I'm alone but that I might not be alone, if you know what I mean.	Wolves . . . wolves are pretty scary . . .
That's for sure.	Knowing that wolves could be there makes it hard for you to get through the forest . . .

As you can see from these examples, there are only minor differences between using listening to collect information and using it to build a relationship with clients. One difference is in the choice of what is attended to and then verified with the client. When relationship building is the goal, there is a greater tendency to attend to the feelings of the client than to basic factual information. As a means to demonstrate the counselor knows how the client is feeling, there is also a tendency for the counselor to state the feeling that the client is experiencing even when the client has not expressed the feeling verbally. Of course, this does not mean that the only times that feelings are important are when relationship building is the goal. As you will see later, there are other reasons that will compel you to deal with feelings in counseling.

Facilitating positive change is another major reason for using listening. Listening does this by encouraging the reprocessing of information by clients. Very often clients say something that is not well considered. Listening can be helpful in such circumstances because it allows you to reflect back to them your understanding of what they wanted to communicate with the implied question, "Is that right?" This prompts clients to reconsider what they have said or how they are feeling, and often reconsideration leads to positive changes for clients.

Client	**Counselor**
I don't know. I never seem to have the time to talk with José. I mean to do it, but I don't have the time.	José isn't on your mind as much as you think he should be and you feel guilty about it . . .
(Pauses) Maybe . . . maybe if it was really important to me I would find the time.	Part of you is feeling guilty and part of you says, "If I really felt bad, I'd do something about it . . ."
I guess that's where I'm coming from. Maybe I need to quit feeling guilty about doing something I don't really think is wrong.	You'd like to quit feeling guilty for something others say is important . . .
I'm not sure what to do. I've never divorced anybody before.	Not sure what to do . . . not sure if you'll be able to do what you know you have to do . . .
Maybe that's it. I guess what I have to do is pretty simple.	From where you are sitting now, you have to leave. But you are not sure if you have the guts to do it . . .
Yes. I'm not sure how to start.	You're scared but you're game to do it . . .
I just have to build up my lungs. That's all. Brick houses can't be all that tough to blow down.	If your lungs were stronger, that would be all there was to it . . .
I'm not sure. I've never had to blow down a brick house before.	Stronger lungs might be one thing, but there are other things you are thinking about . . .
I guess there are. I've thought of one other thing. But I've always been so afraid of being trapped in a chimney.	You think you've got a better idea, Wolfy, but you're afraid to put it to the test . . .

Listening seldom accomplishes only one thing at a time. Even when listening is used to help in facilitating change, at the same time it can help you to collect information or to build a positive relationship with your client. The utility of listening in counseling dictates that whatever your philosophical or theoretical orientation, you should use listening frequently.

Even counselors whose philosophical orientations dictate that listening should be used as a major counseling technique do not use listening exclusively. Real counselors don't talk that way! Having said that, here are several counselor-client exchanges in which listening is used exclusively.

Client	Counselor
Why didn't I get the promotion to senior technician? I'm just as qualified, maybe more qualified than those who did.	As far as you are concerned, you were shafted somewhere . . .
Well, yes. Doesn't it look that way to you?	This thing has really got to you . . .
You are darn right it has. I thought that this time things were going to be done fairly. I guess I was wrong.	If it weren't for some unfairness somewhere up the line you would have been promoted . . .
Well, I suppose that if I had completed the upgrading course the department sponsored, it would have helped.	It would have looked better on your record to have had the course . . .
Well, maybe. But, why does that matter? I'm still a damned good operator and I've put in my time.	You've waited a long time for this and you're ticked off at the department and yourself because you didn't get it this time . . .
Yeah . . .	

Notice that this exchange between the counselor and the client does not resolve the problem. But it does set the stage for problem resolution. It is appropriate at the end of this short exchange for the counselor to move from collecting information to helping the client look at what could be done next time. Doing so will have more impact when undertaken at this point in the transaction than if the counselor had led off the conversation with questions or suggestions.

As you become more skillful in listening, you will become more comfortable in making statements that are based more on what you think others really mean by what they are saying than on the strict content of what they have said. This is referred to as making listening statements that are somewhat out of phase. Listening statements that are out of phase can be effective, but you must be careful in using them. With some clients, such statements can have the effect of "putting words in their mouths."

A listening statement can vary between zero degrees out of phase, when you repeat exactly what an individual has said to you, to 180 degrees out of phase, when you repeat exactly the opposite of what an individual has said to you. In practice, your listening statements will fall somewhere between these two extremes. Here is an example of progressively out-of-phase listening statements based on the same stimulus statement.

Stimulus	Responses
I don't know why I have to be paired with Robin. He is so dumb that I have to paint pictures for him.	You don't know why you have to be paired with that dumb Robin . . .

It's hard to understand the logic that assigned you to work with Robin . . .

Working with Robin is so difficult you begin to feel stupid—like you can't get your points across . . .

When you work with Robin, it makes you feel pretty inadequate . . .

You really enjoy the challenge of working with Robin . . .

Now, it is pretty unlikely that you would use most of the above listening statements, particularly the last two, because they seem to be far-fetched. But don't discard possibilities such as these out of hand. Sometimes clients will give you messages that are very oblique, messages to which listening statements that seem quite out-of-phase will be appropriate.

Another use of out-of-phase listening statements, even ones that are close to the 180-degree extreme, is in situations where clients appear not to be thinking about what they are saying. In such cases, statements that are extreme can encourage clients to think about the messages they are communicating to others. Of course, overuse of this tactic in inappropriate circumstances can make clients think you are sarcastic, stupid, or inattentive, three pitfalls of out-of-phase listening statements.

Negative Effects of Listening

Listening works, but it is not without pitfalls. Problems with listening arise when a counselor forgets that listening is only as good as the results that are achieved by using it—results that mirror its purposes: data collection, relationship building and facilitating positive change. In such cases a counselor forges ahead with listening solely because of a vague belief that listening is good even when it is evident (to others) that the client feels offended, misunderstood, or "counselor-phobic." The result is a client who does not yield good information, does not develop a favorable relationship with the counselor, and is not receptive to positive change.

One potentially negative effect to look out for when using listening is that you may convince clients that they feel certain emotions or that certain things are important when neither is so. Your clients may agree with everything you say, no matter how uncertain you yourself may be. This could come about because clients are unduly influenced by you or your opinions, or because they are not reflective and agree to everything you put forward as a possibility through your listening statements.

One way to test the two hypotheses regarding counselor influence is to offer clients disparate listening statements based on similar information. For instance, you might make a listening statement like "You love your mother and don't want to hurt her . . ." and a few moments later make a statement like "You dislike your mother intensely . . ." If the client agrees wholeheartedly with both, you will want to discuss the matter further. You should also be wary when using further listening statements with such a client.

You become aware of the potentially negative effects of listening or any other communication style by monitoring the effects on the client of what you are saying and doing. Is the client becoming less fearful, more open, less self-condemning, or more self-examining? Does the client agree with seemingly contradictory postulations that you put forward? Does the client appear confused or uncertain when responding to listening statements?

The goals you want to achieve through counseling provide a solid basis for assessing the effectiveness of the techniques you are using. The goals should be manifest in the client's progress and situation. If not, things are going wrong.

Summarizing—Multiple Listening

A special form of listening is often used in counseling: summarizing. Summarizing is the same as listening except that you use it to refer to several items that have been discussed earlier with the client. A statement such as "Robin, you attack the king's men to get their money. You use that money to give to poor peasants, and the more money you take the better you feel . . ." summarizes what the client has told you. But like all listening statements, it too turns the conversation back to the client to answer the implied question, "Is that right?"

Summarizing statements are often used to structure or refocus a conversation (Meier, 1989) and to draw meaning from a series of heretofore unrelated events. They are also used at a transition point in a conversation. For instance, in the example above, after Robin agreed with and perhaps elaborated on the counselor's summarizing statement, the counselor would be in a good position to move the conversation in a new direction. The counselor might then respond to Robin by saying, "I think I understand that pretty well. How do you feel about living on an exclusively venison diet?" This follow-up would explore Robin's dietary regimen. Or the counselor might respond by saying something like "Those things are pretty clear for you now. But I sense that it means more to you to steal the money from the king than it does to give the money away to the needy . . ." Such a follow-up would help to lead the conversation toward examining Robin's motivation. It is easier to ask a question that orients a conversation in a different direction if you demonstrate an understanding of where the conversation has been. Summarizing allows you to do just that.

It is difficult to gain an appreciation for summarizing by studying one transaction at a time, as I have been doing with examples thus far. In the final chapters of this textbook, you will see summarizing demonstrated in the context where it is most easily understood: extended dialogue from real counseling situations.

Points to Consider

1. What is your reaction to the obvious and persistent use of paraphrasing or listening techniques by others? What does the other person say that alerts you to their use of such techniques?
2. What is the effect of using a listening style with a reticent individual? What is the effect with a highly verbal person?
3. Experiment with different degrees of out-of-phase listening statements in your ordinary conversations with others.
4. Experiment by following up your use of questions by listening. Try following up with another question and see what differences you notice.

Suggested Readings

BRAMMER, L. E., SHOSTROM, E. L., & ABREGO, P. J.(1989). *Therapeutic psychology.* Englewood Cliffs, NJ: Prentice-Hall. Chapter 4 is particularly helpful in describing the place of listening within the goal of relationship building.

CORMIER, W. H., & CORMIER, L. S. (1991). *Interviewing strategies for helpers.* Pacific Grove, CA: Brooks/Cole. Chapter 4 helps you to understand the relationship between nonverbal behavior and clients' feelings, an understanding that helps you to listen accurately. Chapter 5 outlines different kinds of listening responses and provides you with numerous examples that demonstrate how they can be used in counseling.

EGAN, G. (1990). *The skilled helper.* Pacific Grove, CA: Brooks/Cole. Based on an approach that analyzes the individual verbal and nonverbal behaviors of counselors. Chapters 5 and 6 outline listening and offer helpful suggestions of what to do in order to translate the intentions of the counselor into practice. Chapter 6 covers empathy particularly well.

EVANS, D. R., HEARN, M. T., UHLEMANN, M. R., & IVEY, A. E. (1989). *Essential interviewing.* Pacific Grove, CA: Brooks/Cole. Chapters 4 and 5 show you how to reflect feeling and content in your counseling sessions. The counselor-client dialogue helps you to understand the relationships between what you say and the potential effects on your clients.

MARTIN, D. G. (1983). *Counseling and therapy skills.* Pacific Grove, CA: Brooks/Cole. Chapter 1 is particularly good at showing the relationship between how clients view your empathic statements and what you say to your clients. Chapters 2 and 3 provide another perspective on listening and vocabulary enrichment to make the transition from principles to practice.

STEWART, C. J., & CASH, W. B. (1985). *Interviewing principles and practices.* Dubuque, IA: Wm. C. Brown. Although written from an employment rather than a counseling orientation, Chapter 2 (pp. 43ff.) provides a good overview of the importance of listening in an interview situation.

WALSH, A. (1988). *Understanding, assessing, and counseling the criminal justice client.* Pacific Grove, CA: Brooks/Cole. Chapter 4 aids understanding of the relationship between listening and questioning, and provides some excellent suggestions about the impact of physical arrangements on listening in a formal interview situation. Although the criminal justice client is the focus of this book, much of what is outlined is appropriate for mental health counselors with a more general client orientation.

CHAPTER 7

Questioning

"How old are you?"
"Do you like ducks?"
"What happened at the staff meeting yesterday?"
"Why do you think you feel that way?"
"Can you think of any better way to do it?"
"How do you feel about having a parent who is close to death?"

Although dealing with widely different topics, all of the above statements share a characteristic: each asks a question. For most counselors, asking questions is an essential component of their interactions with clients. Asking questions seems like the natural thing to do.

Definition

A questioning statement is a request for information from a client. The request may follow up on an area that has been under discussion, may open a new area of conversation, or may solicit opinions from a client. Questions may be specific or general in nature.

There are two types of questions: closed and open. A closed question demands a specific answer. "How old are you?" "Where were you on Friday at 8:00 P.M.?" "Were you on a coffee break when the incident took place?" Each of these questions is closed. If a closed question is to be answered honestly, only one answer will do.

An open question is less specific. It does not target the kind of response that is wanted and allows for interpretation of the question by the answerer. "Tell me about your father." "What is important to you?" "How could you have done things differently?" In answering an open question, the answerer focuses on the aspects of the question he or she feels are most important or wishes to answer.

Questions are particularly useful in counseling if employed correctly (Phares, 1992). Skillful counselors put a questioning style of communication to good use. They gain the advantages of the style without reaping some of the less desirable effects.

- Questioning allows the counselor to focus the conversation on the aspects of the client's history or current circumstances that are beneficial. The counselor can move from topic to topic or explore one topic in greater depth.
- Questioning can reinforce or weaken the importance associated with a topic of conversation. If you ask the client several questions on a topic, the client will often infer that you think the topic is important. The inference might strengthen or weaken the importance the client ascribes to the subject. Questioning can also encourage clients to consider something they may have forgotten or put out of their minds.
- Questioning can help demonstrate that you are interested in a client. This is accomplished in counseling because it mimics a phenomenon that occurs outside counseling: we often infer that others are interested in us if they ask us questions about us. Of course, too many questions can have the opposite effect.
- Questioning is a function useful to listening. Questions elicit information; listening deals constructively with the information.
- Questioning can help clients clarify their problems. By asking penetrating questions or questions that address issues a client may not recognize as important, the counselor initiates a reflective process in the client that can lead to change.
- Questioning is a comfortable way of interacting with a counselor for many clients because many conversations in situations other than counseling are based on questions and answers.

Some counselors or trainers of counselors have strong views about how questioning should be used in counseling. Others have strong views that it should not be used at all. Very often these opinions are not based on an analysis of the effects of questioning but on doctrinaire beliefs. Like any style of communication, questioning has its place (Evans et al., 1989). It is not a panacea and it can be a poison. As Winnie the Pooh was apt to say, "It's all in your point of view."

Uses of Questioning

Think of the various reactions you have when people ask questions of you. Their questioning might indicate that they are interested in you—"How is that knee that you hurt last week?" You might feel that they are prying into something that is none of their business—"How often do you usually have sex in a week?" Or you might think that they are asking to obtain information they can use against you—"Where were you last Friday night at 8:30?" Answers to questions depend on how the respondent perceives the questions.

As was the case with listening, questioning is only as effective as the results that are obtained by using it. We often think that the sole purpose of questioning is to collect information. Although that purpose is uppermost, it is not the only purpose of questioning relative to counseling.

When you question a client, your originating question is important but perhaps less so than the supplemental questions you might ask. After your first question, do you probe for more details? Do you change the focus by asking questions on another topic? Do you ignore the client's answer and ask much the same question again? Or do you abandon questioning altogether and move on to a different communication style? Each alternative will probably produce different results.

When you ask questions, what you say after you get an initial response can strengthen, weaken, or change the reaction you got to your first question. For example, when you phone your employer to tell her you will be absent from work because of an injured knee, and she asks you several questions about your knee, do you feel that she is interested in your well-being? Or do you begin to feel that she is prying, perhaps to ascertain whether your knee is really as injured as you let on? Depending on how you perceive her questions, your answers change. You might become informative or you might become hostile.

Unless you are very aware, questioning might convey something unintended to your client. This is most likely to happen if you do not attend closely to the client's reactions.

The purposes of questioning clients can be summarized under the same three broad categories used for listening: data collection, relationship building, and facilitating positive change. As in the case of listening, the purposes are usually realized simultaneously when questions are asked of clients. As anyone knows who has ever watched a skillful counselor conduct an interview, there are probably as many ways to use questions as there are questioners! There are the matters of what questions to ask, their phrasing and sequence, and the tone or delivery techniques of the questioner.

Data collection is a natural use for questioning, but helpful information should not be taken for granted. The effectiveness of questioning must be judged in terms of how the listener perceives the questions. Here are several examples of asking questions to collect information.

Counselor	**Client**
Margaret, what happens when you and Augusto fight? What does he do? What do you do?	I try to raise an issue with him and he just gets mad. He won't listen. He thinks I'm stupid.
Do you bring up something and find that he ignores you, ignores what you've said?	He doesn't really ignore what I've said. He just takes off half-cocked when I say certain things to him.
What things?	Like, I told him he was inconsiderate, a boor, because he drank too much at the party.
Raphael, tell me what you liked about her in the first place? What did you find attractive?	She was good-looking. She seemed interested in me and what I was doing. Everybody liked her.
Did everybody like her?	Yeah. She seemed like a real good fit for me.
What does that mean, "a good fit"?	I had always gone out with women who were kind of flaky. You know, real space cadets. She seemed solid. Everybody thought so.
Gracie, tell me how it felt when you found out you weren't going to get the job.	I was devastated. I deserved the job a hell of a lot more than he did anyway.
Were you pretty mad too?	Yeah, I guess so. There's no way this thing was fair. Nothing is going to make me think that it is.
Is this the first time you were passed over for promotion? Or, has this sort of thing happened to you before?	It happened once before. That's why I left Allied Creampuffs. I thought things would be fairer here. I guess I was wrong.
Did the same thing happen at Allied?	Yeah. I thought there was only one stupid company to work for. Now I see that there are two.
Wolfy, when you saw Little Red, what did you think?	I couldn't think. My stomach was rumbling too much.
How long had it been since you had eaten?	A long time. There aren't that many people anymore who carry goodies through the forest. It's getting pretty desperate.

Is it the goodies or the person who carries the goodies that interests you the most?	Usually, it's the goodies. But, sometimes I get carried away.

Effective data collection also involves targeting the responses you want from your client. Targeting does not specify the particular answer you want but allows you to specify the area or domain you want your client's answers to address. As in the following examples, a response by a client may address several issues simultaneously. Subsequent targeted questions allow you to focus on an area that you want to pursue with your client.

Counselor	**Client**
What was there about the dance that bothered you?	I felt so awkward. Dancing seems so stupid. I felt like everybody was watching me.
Do you know how to dance?	Not really. Not very well anyway. I tried to learn but my sister gave up on me.
Are there some kinds of dancing that you can do . . . waltzes or jive?	No. I can't do anything very well.
Tell me about your relationship with your brother.	There's really not very much to say. We got along just fine, I thought. And, then one day he just blew his brains out. No "Help me." No "Goodbye." No nothing.
Were you older than he?	No, he was the oldest. He always bossed me around when we were kids. Said that *oldest* meant he had the right.
Was your relationship with him any different from your relationship with your other brothers and sisters?	No. He was always the bright one, the one who was supposed to do so well.
What kept you from school yesterday afternoon?	Nothing, really. I just wasn't there.
What were you doing instead?	Not much. Just horsin' around.
Were you with other students?	A few, I guess.
Jack, why do you look so perplexed?	I've got a problem. I've got this cow. I know I can trade her for some beans. The beans are supposed to be magic. But, what if they don't work?

Counselor	Client
How are the beans supposed to be magic? What are they supposed to do?	They're supposed to grow like crazy. That's what the farmer said.
What are they supposed to grow?	I'm not sure. Fruit or trees or something.

Although targeted questions are used in the above four examples in an attempt to collect information from the clients, they are used differently in each. In the first example, the questions are used to clarify ambiguous responses by the client. In the second and fourth examples, they are used to pursue a specific point brought up by the client in conjunction with other subjects. In the third example, the questions are used to pursue an area that was not addressed by the client and one about which the client was reluctant to disclose much information. In all four examples, for purposes of illustration, only questioning was used by the counselor. In a real situation, it is reasonable to assume that counselors use questioning as well as other communication styles in the counseling process.

Regarding the example of the nondancing client, you might ask yourself why the counselor did not focus on the client's feelings. The answer is simple. She chose not to. It was her professional opinion that it was better to collect information about the client's ability to dance and to continue in that vein until she had the facts she sought. Did her single-mindedness help or hurt the client? That is not an easy question. You could infer from the client's answers that the counselor's actions neither helped nor hurt the client; they simply provided information that might have been helpful in the course of counseling.

Relationship building is an important reason for questioning. It is often overlooked by some counselors who focus exclusively on the negative effects of questioning: the suspicion and hostility sometimes engendered in the client. Such counselors ignore potential benefits like demonstrating empathy and caring. Questioning can be helpful, hurtful, or neutral. Which of these depends on the care with which a particular question is constructed, how it is presented, and where it fits in the sequence of what else is said in the counseling session (Egan, 1990).

Below are three examples of questioning primarily to establish a positive relationship with a client. As in regard to the previous examples, keep in mind that questioning is not the only way to do this. In some situations questioning may not even be the preferred means. Questioning alone is used in these examples only for purposes of illustration.

Counselor	**Client**
Mary, tell me about yourself. What do you think are some important things I should know about you?	I have never thought much about that. I'm not sure there are important things about me that I could tell anyone.

What are some things you value . . . things that are important to you?	Honesty is really important. I hate it when people lie to me.
Are there times when that has happened to you, when someone has hurt you by deceiving you?	Boy, that's for sure. More often than I care to remember.
Brent, I want to hear your side of it. What happened that night?	Things just went haywire. The fuses started to blow on the main panel. Then the big short occurred and all hell just broke loose. I ran faster than I ever thought possible.
You weren't hurt in any way were you?	Not unless you count scarin' the crap outta me.
Was it as bad for you as it looked when we finally got the rescue team inside?	I don't think I was ever that scared before. You know what I mean.
Rapunzel, what is troubling you?	It's my hair. It's so long that it's driving me crazy. What can you do with hair this long anyway?
Do you sometimes think about cutting it off?	I do sometimes. Yet I keep thinking that this hair must be good for something—even when I am locked up in this dumb old tower.
What do you think you could be missing? How would cutting your hair hurt you?	I don't know. I just keep having this silly dream about a prince. I know it's foolish but I can't get it out of my mind.

As is evident from the above examples, several requirements are usually met when questioning is used to establish positive relationships with a client:

- the questions usually focus on the client or the client's feelings rather than on external matters;
- the client's responses to the questions are treated with respect;
- the questions are asked in such a way that they are not misinterpreted as judgmental by the client; and
- the client interprets the questions as indicating a concern for the client's well-being, safety, health, or like matters.

Questioning by counselors can help to *facilitate positive change* for clients. It can prod clients to consider issues or alternatives that have not been considered and to examine relationships between seemingly related variables that have previously been treated as independent. Of course, questioning is not the only way to achieve these aims.

For questioning to be effective in facilitating positive change for clients, they must view it in a certain way. The questioning must have a flavor of teaching or coaching about it. By using questioning toward that end, the counselor is saying to the client, "I think that such-and-such is important to think about. What do you think about this possibility?" For a question to be viewed more as a real inquiry than as advice, the client must sense a greater emphasis on the question than on an unstated judgment that may have formed the basis of the question. Here are several examples.

Counselor	**Client**
Yugi, what did you feel like before you hit Lugi?	I was mad. Really mad.
Were you aware of what you were doing when you did it?	Yeah. I mean that I'm not sure. Who cares, now, anyway?
If you were mad but not mad enough to lose control of yourself, what does hitting him tell you?	I guess I wanted to hit him. I've been so mad at him for the past week that I picked a fight I guess.
What was your relationship like with your wife, before she found out you had been fooling around?	Pretty good I guess. I mean we didn't fight much.
Were you close?	Close . . . No, not really, I guess, but we didn't fight much.
When she found out about your relationship with Goyda, things turned from a cold war to an open battle. Why?	I guess we couldn't pretend any more. Things were out in the open. Maybe I wanted it that way.
Tell me again about what it was like for you when things were good between you and your dad.	I always looked up to him. He always seemed to do everything right. I wanted to be just like him.
But then did you find out that he wasn't as perfect as you thought he was?	Yeah. He was a fraud. Everybody found that out when he was charged with evading income tax.
Were you angry that he had cheated on his income tax or disappointed that he wasn't perfect any more?	(Pauses) If you can't count on your dad, who can you count on?
Tell me again where it's at for you, Snow White.	All the men in my life are so short. And each one has a different problem. Why can't I ever find a real man?

Where do you look?	You know. The woods.
If you keep looking in the woods and you keep finding short men, what does that tell you?	I know I have to look somewhere else. But, where should I start?

Once again, keep in mind that questioning is used exclusively in these examples only for illustrative purposes. In a real counseling situation, you would probably use questioning as well as other forms of communication. When skillfully employed, however, it could be effective alone.

Questioning and Listening

Questioning is very frequently used in combination with listening in counseling. Questions that are broad in scope and some that are narrow provide the "openings." Listening further defines the openings, and validates and supplements inferences you make in consequence of your clients' answers. Astute use of the two techniques in concert will help you to collect more accurate information, build better relationships with your clients, and facilitate change more effectively.

Below are the same examples that were used to demonstrate the use of questioning in data collection, but now modified to show how listening and questioning can be effectively used together.

Counselor	**Client**
Margaret, what happens when you and Augusto fight? What does he do? What do you do? (Q)	I try to raise an issue with him and he just gets mad. He won't listen. He thinks I'm stupid.
He won't listen to you because he thinks anything you have to say isn't worth bothering about . . . (L)	He doesn't really ignore what I've said. He just takes off half-cocked when I say certain things to him.
What things? (Q)	Like, I told him he was inconsiderate, a boor, because he drank too much at the party.
He keyed on those words and flew into a rage . . . (L)	Yeah. I didn't mean to get him so darned mad.
Raphael, tell me what you liked about her in the first place? What did you find attractive? (Q)	She was good-looking. She seemed interested in me and what I was doing. Everybody liked her.
Everybody liked her and that helped you to see that she would be a good catch . . . (L)	Yeah. She seemed like a real good fit for me.

What does that mean, "a good fit"? (Q)	I had always gone out with women who were kind of flaky. You know, real space cadets. She seemed solid. Everybody thought so.
In comparison to other women, she stood out, if for no other reason than everybody else thought so . . . (L)	Yeah. She was a bit older and smarter and better looking than anyone I had ever dated.
Gracie, tell me how it felt when you found out you weren't going to get the job. (Q)	I was devastated. I deserved the job a hell of a lot more than he did anyway.
Devastated and pretty mad too . . . (L)	Yeah, I guess so. There's no way this thing was fair. Nothing is going to make me think that it was.
Others have tried to explain what happened but it still doesn't make much sense to you . . . (L)	Yeah. It can't be fair.
Is this the first time you were passed over for promotion? Or, has this sort of thing happened to you before? (Q)	It happened once before. That's why I left Allied Creampuffs. I thought things would be fairer here. I guess I was wrong.
Everything is starting to look like the past all over again . . . (L)	Yeah. I thought there was only one stupid company to work for. Now I see that there are two.
Wolfy, when you saw Little Red, what did you think? (Q)	I couldn't think. My stomach was rumbling too much.
You were hungry and out of sorts . . . (L)	Yeah. There aren't that many people anymore who carry goodies through the forest. It's getting pretty desperate.
Hungry enough that it was easy to mistake the messenger for the meal . . . (L)	I guess so. That was pretty stupid I guess.
Is that the first time you were confused like that? (Q)	For sure. I mean, usually it's grab the picnic basket and run.

There are only subtle differences between these examples and those you read earlier. That is because listening and questioning are used for the same purpose: collecting information. The only difference is that using questioning and listening together often yields better information, and it forestalls some of the potentially negative effects of questioning alone. Using the two techniques in tandem also provides you with an option for situations where the use of either technique individually does not do the job.

Questioning and listening also work well together in situations where relationship building is the goal. Here are the examples you read earlier, in which questioning was used alone to build a relationship with a client. In these revised examples, listening supplements questioning, although the goal of building a relationship remains the same.

Counselor	**Client**
Mary, tell me about yourself. What do you think are some important things I should know about you? (Q)	I have never thought much about that. I'm not sure there are important things about me that I could tell anyone.
It's not very easy telling those sort of things to a stranger . . . (L)	That's right I guess. I've never been one to blow my own horn very much.
What are some things you value . . . things that are important to you? (Q)	Well, honesty is really important. I hate it when people lie to me.
There have been times when this has happened, when someone has hurt you by deceiving you . . . (L)	Boy, that's for sure. More often than I care to remember.
Brent, I want to hear your side of it. What happened that night? (Q)	Things just went haywire. The fuses started to blow on the main panel. Then the big short occurred and all hell just broke loose. I ran faster than I ever thought possible.
Everything happened at once and nobody had prepared you for that kind of problem . . . (L)	That's for sure. I was scared silly.
Was it as bad for you as it looked when we finally got the rescue team inside? (Q)	I don't think I was ever that scared before. You know what I mean.
It's really easy to hear about these things happening to someone else but scary as hell when it happens to you yourself . . . (L)	You bet.
Rapunzel, what is troubling you? (Q)	It's my hair. It's so long that it's driving me crazy. What can you do with hair this long anyway?

Your hair is driving you crazy. Nothing you can do with it makes you feel very good . . . (L)	I keep thinking that this hair must be good for something—even when I am locked up in this dumb old tower.
If you thought it would be good for something sometime, that would be one thing. But now you're not sure . . . (L)	I just feel like a prisoner sometimes. I just keep having this silly dream sometimes about a prince. I know it's foolish but I can't get it out of my mind.
What do you think about the prince? What do your dreams tell you? (Q)	I know he's out there someplace. You can see what I mean, can't you?

These examples, in which listening supplements questioning to build relationships, differ only modestly from the earlier examples where questioning alone was used for the same purpose. However, the two styles together in these examples do a better job than does questioning alone.

Teaming questioning and listening is perhaps most beneficial when the intent of the counselor is to facilitate change. In the revised examples of questioning's being used for that purpose, listening has a supplemental effect.

Counselor	**Client**
Yugi, what did you feel like before you hit Lugi? (Q)	I was mad. Really mad.
You were mad . . . he was there . . . and boom . . . (L)	Yeah. I mean that I'm not sure. Who cares now, anyway?
You'd like to forget it but nobody will let you . . . (L)	I guess I wanted to hit him. I've been so mad at him for the past week that I picked a fight I guess.
You know what happened and you'd like to forget it but it isn't that easy . . . (L)	I guess so. It was stupid. I felt better and worse after I did it.
What was your relationship like with your wife, before she found out you had been fooling around? (Q)	Pretty good, I guess. I mean, we didn't fight much.
There weren't many fights but there wasn't much closeness either . . . (L)	Close . . . No, not really I guess.
When she found out about your relationship with Goyda, things turned from a cold war to an open battle. Why? (Q)	I guess we couldn't pretend any more. Things were out in the open. Maybe I wanted it that way.

You made sure she found out because you didn't know of any other way to get things moving . . . (L)	Yeah. Kinda stupid, isn't it.
Tell me again about what it was like for you when things were good between you and your dad. (Q)	I always looked up to him. He always seemed to do everything right. I wanted to be just like him.
He was your idol but one day the bubble burst . . . (L)	Yeah. He was a fraud. Everybody found that out when he was charged with evading income tax.
You were disappointed that he wasn't perfect, and felt like a fool and embarrassed to have him for a father . . . (L)	(Pauses) If you can't count on your dad, who can you count on?
You are mad at him for what he has done to you . . . stolen your trust, your belief . . . (L)	Yeah, I guess it was stupid to look up to him that way. He's no more perfect than anybody else.
Tell me again where it's at for you, Snow White. (Q)	All the men in my life are so short. And each one has a different problem. Why can't I ever find a real man?
No matter where you look there are no real men . . . (L)	True. I've looked in the woods nearly everywhere.
Have you looked anywhere else but the woods? (Q)	No. What's wrong with the woods?
If you keep looking in the woods and you keep finding short men, what does that tell you? (Q)	I know I have to look somewhere else. But, where should I start?
You are not sure where else to look . . . (L)	I've never thought that men could be anywhere but in the forest.

Keep in mind that the counselor's intention in these four examples does not change because listening is now used in conjunction with questioning. As it was when questioning was used alone, the goal is to facilitate client change. Using questioning and listening together can often improve the odds that this will happen.

Negative Effects of Questioning

More so than with listening, questioning must be used judiciously if you are to avoid negative side effects (Ivey, 1988; Long, Paradise, & Long,

1981). To illustrate, the use of closed questions, particularly back-to-back closed questions, has the effect of making answerers feel a bit as though they are under siege. Their answers may become guarded and indefinite as they seek to prevent you from tripping them up as you persist.

It is difficult for someone to feel that a question from a boss, like "when did you get to work this morning?" is a simple request for a time. It is more likely to be seen as a request for information that can be used against the answerer. Such a view will probably adversely affect the answerer's response.

For most people, particularly streetwise people, questions asked of them can throw out warning signals, similar to the cues one gets in the game of chess when an opponent opens a game in a certain way. This means that the answers provided are not so much answers that you want but responses designed to throw you off the scent.

You might think that because closed questions have untoward side effects, open questions are the way to go. Not quite! Open questions are less likely than closed questions to arouse suspicion, but they are also less likely to produce the specific answers you want (Evans et al., 1989).

Skillful counselors know that a blend of open and closed questions often produces the best information from a client. An open question is used to open up an area, and a judicious mixture of open and closed questions is then used to flesh it out. Information collection can be enhanced even more by integrating a questioning style with other styles, particularly listening.

Although you cannot completely eliminate the negative effects of a questioning style, by being careful to balance open and closed questions, you can limit negative outcomes. Here is a sample of a predominantly questioning style by a workplace counselor interviewing a client to gather information about how a serious technical problem developed. Keep in mind that this example is not designed to resolve the issue. The example is provided solely to demonstrate a balance of open and closed questions in the information-collection process.

Counselor	**Client**
I want you to think through the whole situation. What happened? (Q)	Nothing. It was just an ordinary day. Then all hell broke loose and John started screaming for an emergency shutdown of the equipment.
Did you notice anything wrong at any time before that? (Q)	No, not really.
Not really? (Q)	Well, I mean that I had a kind of funny feeling ever since the shift started. I couldn't put my finger on anything, but it just didn't seem right.

Something was wrong, but you couldn't put your finger on anything . . . (L) What did you do about that? (Q)	Well, there was nothing I could put my finger on, so there was nothing I could do. I just chalked it up to nerves. I guess it wasn't.
Something was wrong, but you didn't know what it was, so you just chalked it up to nerves until John started screaming . . . (L)	That's right.
Is that it? Can you think of anything else I should know about the incident? (Q)	Nothing. I mean it seemed so ordinary that I can hardly remember it.

Notice how the conversation opens with an open question, moves to closed questions, then a listening response, closed questions, a listening response and concludes with an open question. The issue is not resolved as a result of this exchange nor should you expect that it would be. This is data collection not problem resolution.

One problem that some counselors have is asking questions in such a way that they either imply the answers they want or make a suggestion or express a judgment in the guise of a question. It is hard to see a question such as "Do you think that it was a very smart idea to ignore how you felt?" as a simple question. Nor is it likely to be interpreted as a simple question by the client. In a counseling session, the real definition of the styles used is made by the client.

In a case such as the workplace example above, it is likely that the listener will see the question as judgmental and react accordingly. Similarly, a question such as "Do you think that maybe next time you should check out your suspicions instead of ignoring them?" would be seen as coaching or inferring, styles that can also engender negative side effects. (These two styles are discussed next.)

To employ a questioning style skillfully, you must remain very aware of the reactions to your questions. Is the client becoming defensive or providing answers that are evasive or off the topic? Are the answers long-winded or sketchy? Does the client understand your questions? You must be aware of the reactions to questions, if you are to extract the maximum amount of information.

Points to Consider

1. Think back to situations in which you tried to carry on a conversation with a reticent person. What did you say? Most of us ask uncommunicative people far too many closed questions in the vain hope that this strategy will "open them up."

2. Listen to a good radio or television interviewer. To what extent does he or she use questioning? What other styles does the interviewer use in conjunction with questioning?
3. How do you react to badgering? When a person asks questions of you, what do you do when you feel uncomfortable about responding?
4. What alternatives are there to questioning in the solicitation of information from another person?

Suggested Readings

CORMIER, W. H., & CORMIER, L. S. (1991). *Interviewing strategies for helpers.* Pacific Grove, CA: Brooks/Cole. Chapter 6 describes what the authors call "action responses" and provides helpful guidelines for using questions in counseling.

D'AUGELLI, A. R., D'AUGELLI, J. F., & DANISH, S. J. (1981). *Helping others.* Pacific Grove, CA: Brooks/Cole. Chapter 4 (pp. 72ff.) provides a solid introduction to the questioning technique. Counselor-client dialogue is used to good advantage to demonstrate the impact of questions.

EGAN, G. (1990). *The skilled helper.* Pacific Grove, CA: Brooks/Cole. Chapter 6 (pp. 141ff.) outlines important suggestions that can govern the use of questions in counseling. The author includes dialogue to demonstrate key points.

EVANS, D. R., HEARN, M. T., UHLEMANN, M. R., & IVEY, A. E. (1989). *Essential interviewing.* Pacific Grove, CA: Brooks/Cole. Chapter 3 will help you to understand the potential outcomes of asking particular kinds of questions. It also highlights practical dos and don'ts in the use of open and closed questions, particularly for purposes of collecting information.

MARTIN, D. G. (1983). *Counseling and therapy skills.* Pacific Grove, CA: Brooks/Cole. Chapter 5 (pp. 79ff.) describes the use of differing types of questions in counseling from a particularly conservative perspective.

MEIER, S. T. (1989). *The elements of counseling.* Pacific Grove, CA: Brooks/Cole. Although his treatment of questions is brief, the author points out very clearly several situations where questions are inappropriate or poorly asked.

STEWART, C. J., & CASH, W. B. (1985). *Interviewing principles and practices.* Dubuque, IA: Wm. C. Brown. Although written from an employment rather than a counseling perspective, Chapter 4 provides a good overview of questioning techniques that are helpful in counseling as well as employment situations.

CHAPTER 8

Coaching

"The best way to deal with problems is to face them head-on."
"To make a clean break with your husband, you should do it while the opportunity is right."
"At a job interview, make certain that you are neatly groomed and don't act officiously."
"If you are going to use needles, make certain they have not been used before."

As was the case with listening statements, coaching statements sound out of place or very obtrusive unless you hear the preceding statements from the client and counselor. Here is an example of one statement from a client that could precede the coaching replies by a counselor that appear above.

Client	**Counselor**
I don't know what to do about my dad. He's just as old and cranky as can be.	The best way to deal with problems is to face them head-on.
I don't know how to leave him. It all seems so complicated.	To make a clean break with your husband, you should do it while the opportunity is right.
How should I act when I get the interview?	At a job interview, make certain that you are neatly groomed and don't act officiously.
I do up with a needle. It's faster that way.	If you are going to use needles, make certain they have not been used before.

Definition

Although on widely different topics, these replies by a counselor shown just above share a characteristic: they provide advice on behavior and feelings in particular circumstances. Advice or suggestion-giving is the essence of a coaching style of communication. Used judiciously, it can make the difference between a good and a not-so-good counselor (D'Augelli et al., 1981).

Coaching statements usually express or imply behavioral suggestions, and are presented in a manner that says, "Please consider this course of action," "Here is what I think about that," or "Have you thought about this or that?"

- Coaching statements can express an answer to a factual question posed by a client. In such cases, the role of the counselor becomes one of technical expert.
- Coaching can suggest that the client consider some sort of change in what he or she is doing or thinking. It can prompt a client to consider alternatives.
- Coaching can weaken or reinforce positions held by clients. There is sometimes a complementary relationship between a counselor's coaching statements and the resultant position of a client, and sometimes an antithetical relationship.
- Coaching implies a negative judgment on the behaviors or thoughts of the client that led to the coaching statement by the counselor. In athletics or counseling, a coach does not try to teach something to someone who has already done well in the coach's assessment.
- Coaching can help demonstrate that you are interested in a client.
- Coaching can help teach the client the process of counseling that you are using. It can help the client learn his or her role as a client in much the same way that an agenda outlines the role of a participant at a meeting.
- Listening is a useful adjunct to coaching. Listening helps you to deal with the actions by clients that ensue from coaching.
- For many clients, use of a coaching style by a counselor is a comfortable kind of interaction. But comfort is a two-edged sword because it can lead to increased dependency.
- Coaching can help clients to resolve their problems, but like all styles, coaching itself is not without problems.

As was the case with questioning, coaching elicits strong views from some counselors and trainers of counselors about how it should be used. Some counselors rely on it almost exclusively. Others avoid it to the same degree. Advocates of each position usually focus on either the possible advantages or disadvantages of coaching.

The debate about whether coaching is an appropriate counseling technique centers on how directive the counselor should be. Although the debate is a matter of values, beliefs, and philosophy, keep one thing in mind: coaching statements can be used for many reasons. As you will see in the next chapter, some of the reasons are very much in accord with even a very nondirective philosophy of counseling. Coaching, like any style, must be judged in terms of results, whether it fosters favorable counseling outcomes without precipitating unpleasant side effects.

Uses of Coaching

The purposes of using coaching with clients can be summarized in four broad categories: providing factual information; promoting the counseling process; building the counseling relationship; and fostering client change.

Providing factual information is important in counseling. This is particularly true when counseling is undertaken in an educational or employment setting where a key role of the counselor is that of information-giver. Questions by clients about topics ranging from academic entrance requirements to personal financial management demand answers. Very often the answers are based on a coaching style of communication.

In answering clients, you must be careful to ensure that unintended messages are not being communicated along with the facts. The messages might include "You are stupid because you didn't already know this," or "Listen to me because I'm always right," or "Make sure you check with me before you do anything." Such messages might bring about an emotional reaction from the client or uninformed compliance, even though you think you are simply providing information.

Here are several examples of using coaching to answer factual questions:

Client	**Counselor**
What credits do I need to get into first year?	You need seven credits, and two of them must be in English.
Why do I need seven?	Seven is the minimum number for admission. Most students have eight and some have nine.
How often do they do a performance appraisal here?	The first one is done after you have been here three months. After that, every year.
What happens if you don't do well on the first one?	The first one is called your probationary review. After it is done, the company has to make the decision about whether or not you will be taken on as a permanent employee.

I don't know how I am going to balance my budget. There is always too much month left at the end of the money.	We have to balance your budget with the amount that is there. The agency can't exceed the guidelines.
This is not going to be easy. How do they expect us to do everything on this little bit of money?	The agency sets the guidelines based on the average costs for a typical student.
How long will my nose get?	There is really no limit on that, Pinocchio. It all depends on you.
Do you mean it could get longer yet?	You have what we call a "fibber's nose," Pinocchio. The more you fib, the longer it will get.

With respect to each of these examples, keep in mind that coaching was used for illustrative purposes only. The counselor could have used any style but chose coaching. If these had been actual—not imagined—situations, I think I would have been tempted to substitute questioning or listening for coaching at several points. How about you?

Coaching for the purpose of providing factual information is more complex than it may first appear. Sometimes a client will pose a very significant issue in the guise of an uncomplicated question. "You can't get pregnant the first time, can you?" is probably not a hypothetical question when asked by a frightened adolescent. The counselor who does not recognize its intensely personal nature and responds, "You can get pregnant any time, first time or not," misses the point. A simple-sounding request for information is not always what it seems to be.

Although most counselors don't think very much about it, a key purpose of coaching is to *promote the counseling process.* During counseling, the counselor teaches the client what to do—that is, how to be a client—by providing cues to certain ways of behaving. Some of the cues are these:

- encourage the client to focus on certain aspects when background information is being compiled;
- instruct the client about the process that will be used; for example, tell the client that it is time to move from discussing a problem to considering possible solutions;
- encourage the client to deal with an issue more completely or prompt her or him to consider other issues;
- inform the client about reasonable expectations or outcomes of counseling; and
- prompt the client to shift from one part of the counseling process to another.

Here are some examples that illustrate how coaching can be used to facilitate the counseling process.

Client	**Counselor**
I just need somebody to tell me what to do, that's all.	Chico, you are the only one who can decide if you are confident enough to take a job on high steelwork.
And then there is the other issue: What am I going to do about Loras? I can't love him or leave him.	Before you tell me about Loras, there are a few more important things about Lorenzo we should talk about.
What should I do? I know I can't handle having a baby.	You are going to have to decide at some point in the near future, Barbie, but you don't need to decide this minute. You'll feel better about any decision you make if you make it very carefully.
It's just back to the same old thing again. They growl at me. I get hurt. I get angry. I walk out.	Goldilocks, you need to look at ways to deal with the hurt so that you don't always end up alone in that same big forest.

Coaching alone is not the best way to facilitate the counseling process, but it is a helpful component. In a real situation, you might initially use coaching statements in much the same way as illustrated by the foregoing examples, but you would probably also bring in listening and questioning to deal with the reactions your coaching statements evoke.

At first blush, it may be difficult to see how coaching can be used in *building the counseling relationship*. After all, one of the reasons that some counselors avoid making coaching statements is because they may hinder development of a positive relationship. Coaching statements can have this effect, but they can also help to promote a positive relationship. The difference between the extremes has to do with how coaching is used.

For coaching to be beneficial in building relationships, clients must infer that you are helpful and concerned. It is important that your coaching not be interpreted in the same light as a "clean-up-your-room" command directed at a rebellious adolescent. If your clients react negatively to your coaching, the counseling relationships suffer to one degree or another.

Some examples follow of coaching statements made by a counselor primarily to build a better relationship. Because it is impossible to make coaching statements whose only purpose is to build relationships, these statements have other intents as well. Irrespective of the other intents, is the counseling relationship likely to be improved by what is said?

Client	**Counselor**
There are so many things I should be doing with my life. I never seem able to get off my duff.	Many people have a hard time taking that first step. We need to talk about a plan that will help you to be successful—a plan that you'll feel good about.
It just seems that everything I do screws up. I feel like giving up. Nothing's going to work anyhow.	The thing that will work for you is something you believe in. Nobody can make you do anything.
I can't decide whether or not I should stay in school. I'm doing kinda okay, but it's just so damned depressing being here.	If you are depressed, you are not likely to do very well. I guess we need to take a look at how you are feeling no matter what you eventually decide to do.
When I'm with the prince everything seems fine. It's when I go to sleep that I worry I may never wake up.	Well, Snow White, you know you are going to have to sleep sometime. What you and I need to talk about is something you can do that will make you less anxious.

When you make coaching statements to foster counseling relationships, you usually focus on your clients' feelings. Even though suggestions are conveyed, they are directive in terms of counseling processes rather than client outcomes. The advice focuses on *how* you want them to decide what to do rather than *what* you want them to do.

To be effective, you must keep your "antenna" up to monitor client reaction. Look for subtle cues in what clients say, their tone of voice, facial expressions, and body posture. Clients for whom coaching is serving its relationship-building purpose are likely to look directly at you, smile, appear interested in what you are saying, and agree with your process-oriented suggestions.

The most obvious reason for using coaching in counseling is to *foster positive client change*. For some novice counselors and for most people who have not had direct experience with professional counseling, coaching is the essence of counseling. "You tell me what to do. I'll do it. And that's that!"

There is no reason to think that coaching will be more effective in fostering positive client change than any other style of communication. The difference between coaching and the other styles is that coaching appears proactive. It looks as though some sort of direct action is being taken that will result in change.

When coaching is used to foster positive client change, it usually takes the form of advice. The advice can range from a suggestion that the client consider some behavior or idea to a very strong exhortation to act in a certain way. Each extreme has advantages and disadvantages. You must keep in mind potential unintended outcomes of coaching.

- Coaching that is accepted can have the unwanted side effect of increasing client dependence. ("You helped me. I need you.")
- Coaching that is not accepted can have the unwanted side effect of increasing client commitment to an alternative course of action. ("Anything you say is wrong. I must be right.")
- Coaching can cause a client to reject responsibility for outcomes. ("I did it your way. It's not my fault if something goes wrong.")
- Coaching can have negative effects on the relationship between client and counselor. ("I hate people who tell me what to do.")
- Coaching can seduce counselors into thinking that they are being effective or into discounting their responsibility for counseling outcomes. ("I told him what to do. If he's too defiant to listen, there's nothing more I can do.")
- Coaching that is "right" and accepted may diminish client self-confidence. ("It seemed so easy for my counselor. I must be stupid not to have thought of that.")

The above caveats should not prevent you from using coaching to foster positive client change, but they should make you cautious. Here are several examples of using coaching primarily to foster positive client change.

Client	**Counselor**
I want to move ahead. But I keep getting stuck in the past.	At some point you will have to accept the past for what it is—over. You need to start focusing on your present, where you are now.
I've tried everything. I must be too stupid to pass algebra.	Everything you've tried hasn't worked. That doesn't mean that something different won't click for you. Have you considered using a private tutor?
It's my nose. I'll never be happy as long as I have a nose like this.	If that's the case, you'll probably always be unhappy. Your nose isn't going to go away, and you'll be unhappy as long as you let those feelings rule your life.

I'm just so darned unhappy. That third house just won't seem to blow over no matter what I do.

Wolfy, you've tried the same approach time and time again. Let's talk about something different. How about chimneys . . .

As you read through the examples of coaching in this chapter, it might be hard to deduce the specific intentions of the counselor. Is the counselor trying to establish a good relationship with the client, provide factual information, promote the counseling process, or foster positive client change? Identical coaching statements by different counselors could be made for any or all of these reasons.

A single coaching statement is seldom made in response to a single statement from a client. Counseling is give-and-take. What is said before a particular statement is as important as what is said after. In a real counseling situation, communication styles are combined.

Coaching, Questioning, and Listening

Even its most zealous advocate does not use coaching exclusively. Good coaching depends on a mix of styles. You have already studied questioning and listening. Let's look at how they work with coaching.

- Listening is a profitable way to deal with a client's negative reaction to your coaching because it can help you to deal constructively with that circumstance.
- Listening and questioning are often used before coaching to ensure that your coaching is on track and to encourage client receptiveness.
- Listening and questioning can soften the "edge" of coaching statements and lessen the likelihood of unpleasant side effects.

Here is an example of a situation where coaching alone was used by the counselor, followed by an example of the same situation but where the counselor combines coaching with listening and questioning.

Client

I don't know what it is about my husband. He seems to think that the world was meant to have him at its center.

Counselor

Sometimes husbands have to learn that things can't always be the way they want them to be. (C)

Client

That's for sure. But it's a lot easier said than done.

Counselor

What you need is a plan. Something you can use to organize yourself—something that will make certain you are successful. (C)

What do you mean?	If you want to change the circumstances that affect you, you need to think about how you are going to do it. You need a plan. (C)
I don't think anything is going to change him. He's been doing everything his way for far too long.	Why don't you try doing . . . (C)

Client	**Counselor**
I don't know what it is about my husband. He seems to think that the world was meant to have him at its center.	He thinks only of himself and you seem to come up short . . . (L)
Yes. That's for sure. Everything is me, me, me.	Sometimes husbands have to learn that things can't always be the way they want them to be. (C)
That's for sure. But it's a lot easier said than done.	It's a lot easier to decide what you want to do than to get on with doing it . . . (L)
I've always been a person who planned things out and then got on with doing them.	What you need then is a plan. Something you can use to organize yourself—something that will make certain you are successful. (C)
What do you mean?	If you want to change the circumstances that affect you, you need to think about how you are going to do it. You need a plan. (C)
I don't think anything is going to change him. He's been doing everything his way for far too long.	You've tried many things . . . (L)
I've tried talking to him, but that doesn't seem to work because he doesn't listen.	Do you try talking to him right at the time or do you wait until he has cooled down? (Q)
I guess that I let it all hang out as soon as it happens. I believe in being honest.	Why don't you try doing . . . (C)

Negative Effects of Coaching

If you've ever coached children in athletic activities, you know that it's not easy, even when you possess technical expertise from which they can benefit. Sometimes, no matter what you say, it is taken the wrong way. What does *wrong way* mean when it comes to coaching?

Recall that a coaching statement has two components: one explicit, one implicit. The explicit part says, "Do things this way." The implicit part says, "The way you were doing things was not right." When clients take your comments in the wrong way, they are focusing on your implicit rather than your explicit meaning. They think you are telling them that they were in error; you think you are telling them how to do things right. Both are important misapprehensions.

Some athletic coaches and counselors who use coaching statements are very proficient in the coaching style. Their implicit meanings do not come across as uppermost. The style apparently is natural to them. Their antennae pick up any incipient negative reactions, and they use this information to modify what they are saying in time to deflect adverse consequences. Here are several examples.

Client	**Counselor**
I'm not sure what I should be doing. Every time I decide to go in one direction, I get nervous.	That's a very natural way to feel. Making choices always means there are certain paths you decide not to walk down. (C)
That's easy for you to say. You don't know what it's like to feel stopped in your tracks.	As soon as you make a choice, you feel like a noose has been tightened around your neck . . . (L)
Yes. I keep thinking that I am locking myself into something that I won't really want to do.	Maybe you need to delay making a choice until you are more certain, until you are ready to live with the consequences. (C)
That's it! I don't have to decide.	What will you do if you don't decide? (Q)
I guess that I'll have to decide sooner or later or the decision will be made for me.	You can delay making a decision for a while—to give you time to collect more information, but you'll have to decide sooner or later . . . (L)
Yeah. I guess that's it.	So, let's decide when you have to make the decision and work backward from there to decide what you have to do. (C)
I know that if I get Horatio out of my life everything will be fine. Without him, all of my troubles will be over.	With Horatio gone, you'll still have other things to deal with—drugs and the kids . . . (L)
Oh, Allah! What's the use? Nothing's ever going to change.	It's hard to think that when you have dealt with one problem, there will be others waiting out there for you . . . (L)

For sure. Won't it ever end? First Lucretia. Now Horatio. What's next?	You've had problems with Lucretia, but you've pulled through. You've got problems with Horatio, but you've decided how you are going to handle them. You'll probably always have to deal with things you don't want to deal with. (C)
(Sighs) Yes. But I wish it didn't have to be this way.	It would be easier if you didn't have to handle so many things . . . (L)
(Brightens) Yes. But I guess that's just the way it is and I'll have to deal with it. I've done it before and I guess I can do it again.	Just one more problem that you can handle . . . (L)
But you'se got to see da briar patch is still withs me, no matters what I do.	Br'er Rabbit, the briar patch is never going to leave your mind completely. We need to talk more about how you can deal with your life in spite of your thinking about the briar patch. (C)
That's plumb easy fer you ta say. You'se never lived in da briar patch.	The experience is something that is going to follow you forever . . . (L)
Oh boy! I feels so lost sometimes wid'out that there patch to goes back to.	How do the others handle it? (Q)
Br'er Bear, he just too stupid to knows no different. Br'er Fox, he just say that's what is and that's that.	But you are not stupid and you can't ignore how you feel. (C)
No, siree. Dat's for sure.	So, what you and I need to talk about is how you can get on with your life, even though you feel as bad as you do. (C)

Avoiding a negative reaction when you use coaching is as much a matter of how you say as what you say. To maximize the chances that your clients will focus on the explicit meaning of your coaching, modulate the tone and volume of your voice, and keep your voice nonaccusatory and unemotional. Do not sound exasperated or defensive if you get unexpected reactions; you should not have a vested interest in your advice. Try to offer your coaching statements in a manner that prompts clients to consider them reasonably, and if they disagree with you, respond with equanimity. (Chapter 11 presents a more complete review of implicit communication.)

The other potential negative effect of coaching is compliance by the client and a dependence on you as the "fountain of knowledge." To deal with this possibility, monitor client reactions carefully. If a client agrees with you without suitable reflection, challenge him or her to assess the alternative carefully. Do not proceed simply because a client agrees with you. Here are the three examples that you have just considered, modified to show different negative client reactions to coaching. Notice how the counselor deals with them.

Client	**Counselor**
I'm not sure what I should be doing. Every time I decide to go in one direction, I get nervous.	That's a very natural way to feel. Making choices always means there are certain paths you decide not to walk down. (C)
So what should I do? I'm so hopeless at making those kinds of decisions on my own.	Are you afraid to make those kinds of decisions or do you find that you are not happy with what you decide? (Q)
I keep thinking that I am locking myself into something that I won't really want to do.	Maybe you need to delay making a choice until you are more certain, until you are ready to live with the consequences. (C)
That's it! I don't have to decide.	You'll have to decide sometime. But, maybe you won't have to decide this very minute. (C)
Even that would be of some help.	You can delay making a decision for a while—to give you time to collect more information, but you'll have to decide sooner or later. (C)
When will I have to decide?	Let's explore that and then work backward from there to decide what you have to do to get to that point. (C)
I know that if I get Horatio out of my life everything will be fine. Without him, all of my troubles will be over.	With Horatio gone, you'll still have other things to deal with—drugs and the kids. (C)
That can be so hard. What do you think I should do?	You are hoping that I can give you some direction on those things . . . (L)
I'm so tired of having to make decisions. I just want somebody to tell me what to do.	You've had problems with Lucretia but you've pulled through. You've got problems with Horatio, but you've decided how you are going to handle them. You'll probably always have to deal with things you don't want to deal with. (C)
(Sighs) Yes. But I wish it didn't have to be this way.	It would be easier if you didn't have to handle so many things . . . (L)

(Brightens) Yes. But I guess that's just the way it is and I'll have to deal with it. I've done it before and I guess I can do it again.

Just one more problem that you can handle . . . (L)

But you'se got to see da briar patch is still withs me, no matters what I do.

Br'er Rabbit, the briar patch is never going to leave your mind completely. We need to talk more about how you can deal with your life in spite of thinking about the briar patch. (C)

That's just so true.

You want to talk about something other than the briar patch? (Q)

Nevers hurts to talk, I guesses.

How do the others handle it? (Q)

Br'er Bear, he just too stupid to knows no different. Br'er Fox, he just say that's what is and that's that.

But you are not stupid and you can't ignore how you feel. (C)

No, siree. Dat's for sure.

So, what you and I need to talk about is how you can get on with your life, even feeling as bad as you do. (C)

If you compare the responses by clients and counselors from this set of examples with the previous set of examples, you will note many similarities. In both sets, the counselor uses listening or questioning to follow up on responses the client makes to the counselor's prior coaching statements. This is done whether or not the client's responses were expressed as uncritical acceptance or as an emotionally charged disagreement.

A guitar is one of the easiest instruments to play. After learning a few chords, many people play passably well. But it is a difficult instrument to play beyond that level. Similarly, many people—perhaps almost everyone—try their hands at coaching. In casual conversation, for instance, coaching is very predominant. However, few people, in sports or counseling, are able to express coaching statements skillfully enough to reap only the advantages of the style.

Points to Consider

1. Think back to the reactions you experienced when others used a coaching style in dealing with you. What did they do or say that elicited particular reactions?
2. Compare an educator whom you consider to be good with one whom you consider to be poor. How do they differ in their use of coaching?

3. How does a counselor who is laissez-faire in style use coaching to orchestrate this style throughout counseling?
4. When you deal with children, what separates the occasions when your coaching statements are effective from those when your statements are not?
5. Observe athletic coaches whose players appear to be happy. How do they interact with the players? How do they teach?

Suggested Readings

CORMIER, W. H., & CORMIER, L. S. (1991). *Interviewing strategies for helpers.* Pacific Grove, CA: Brooks/Cole. Chapter 16 describes what the authors call "action responses" and provides helpful guidelines for using questions in counseling.

D'AUGELLI, A. R., D'AUGELLI, J. F., & DANISH, S. J. (1981). *Helping others.* Pacific Grove, CA: Brooks/Cole. Chapters 14–17 provide many examples of how coaching by the counselor is used to influence both counseling processes and outcomes.

EGAN, G. (1990). *The skilled helper.* Pacific Grove, CA: Brooks/Cole. Chapter 10 outlines important ways that counselors should coach clients, particularly when coaching is intended to help clients undertake a process of reflection, healing, and decision making.

LEWIS, J. A., & LEWIS, M. D. (1986). *Counseling programs for employees in the workplace.* Pacific Grove, CA: Brooks/Cole. Chapter 4 is particularly helpful in outlining the place of coaching in the facilitation of the counseling process.

OKUN, B. F. (1992). *Effective helping.* Pacific Grove, CA: Brooks/Cole. Sections of this book dealing with interpreting and informing could be particularly helpful in your study of coaching.

SACK, R. T. (1985). On giving advice. *AMHCA Journal, 7,* 127–132. An excellent article dealing with giving advice, particularly in crisis situations.

TEYBER, E. (1992). *Interpersonal process in psychotherapy.* Pacific Grove, CA: Brooks/Cole. Chapter 4 details the use of coaching responses, primarily to influence the process of counseling. The dialogue and examples cited will help you understand the implications of using coaching responses in your counseling.

THOMPSON, C. L., & RUDOLPH, L. B. (1992). *Counseling children.* Pacific Grove, CA: Brooks/Cole. Chapter 2 contains an interesting section about giving advice in the counseling of children.

CHAPTER 9

Inferring

"That was damned fine work you did in exploring the different options that are open to you."
"Anybody who thinks like that deserves anything she gets."
"That's a good idea. I like it."
"Don't look so glum."
"You've worked very hard to get where you are."

Statements such as these—inferring statements—form a cornerstone of human conversation. You hear them in taverns, classrooms, churches, counseling offices, and just about anywhere that people gather and converse. In everyday conversation they sound routine and are expected, even when you may not agree with them.

Definition

Inferring statements have a common element. Each one communicates an opinion to another person. The inferring statement may reflect the speaker's view of an external situation or the speaker's feelings about something that the listener has done or thought or proposes to do or think. In counseling, as in the rest of life, inferring statements may be positive or negative.

- An inferring statement can evoke a very powerful reaction from the listener, even in circumstances where the reaction is not shared with the speaker.

- Because of potentially adverse results, an inferring statement by a counselor must be expressed very carefully. This is particularly true when a negative inference is being communicated.
- Communicating your inferences to clients can prompt them to examine aspects of their lives or can strengthen their intransigence.
- Clients frequently interpret positive inferences as supportive.

Sometimes counselors needlessly confuse inferring statements with coaching. The two are easily distinguished. A negative inference is the implicit part of a coaching statement; the explicit part is a suggestion for action. An inferring statement stops with expression of opinion. A coaching statement starts with an implied expression of your opinion but carries on with suggestion for further action. For example, a statement such as "To make sure you are eligible for the scholarship, you need to complete the bottom part of the form" made to a prospective student who submits an incomplete scholarship application is a coaching statement. However, it is based upon an implicit judgment: the form handed in did not fulfill requirements. A negative inferring statement in the same circumstance might be "You did not complete the whole form." Either statement *might* elicit an adverse reaction from the student, but the negative inferring statement is more likely to do so.

Sometimes a counselor will confuse listening with inferring. A listening statement and an inferring statement may have the same declarative part, the part that says, "It's like this for you . . ." The difference is that listening follows up this declaration with an implied "isn't it?" thereby checking out a tentative hypothesis. Inferring begins and ends with expression of the counselor's opinion.

As a counselor, you find it hard to escape drawing inferences about your clients. This does not mean that you should share the inferences with them without regard for their reactions. On the contrary, your inferences must be communicated strategically in order to achieve one or more goals of counseling.

As anyone who has ever had a compliment paid to another person "taken the wrong way" can attest, communicating inferences is a tricky business. Sometimes the most damning negative inferences are received objectively. Sometimes inferences of a highly positive nature are rejected out of hand. The difference between the two extremes has to do with the unintended messages that piggyback on inferences. In a statement such as "You still have a way to go before you will be ready to commit to any job," it is easy for your client to "hear" "You are incompetent" or "You are lazy." Such interpretations of the unspoken but nonetheless communicated "You are . . ." statements can hinder the fostering of the goals of counseling.

The likelihood that unintended messages will be communicated depends more on what you say after your original inferring statements than the original inferring statements themselves. If you follow an inferring statement about a decision that needs reevaluation by another inferring statement like "It's taken you a long time to get to the point of thinking constructively about this," the chances of an unintended negative message are increased. On the other hand, if the follow-up statement is of a coaching nature, something like "Let's go through the decision-making steps again to see where you got off track," a more positive reaction by the client would probably result.

As a counselor, you will attach importance to being nonjudgmental in terms of clients as human beings. However, many good counselors use inferring statements at many points during a counseling interview to deal with client behavior or proposed behavior. They do so very skillfully and thereby minimize untoward side effects.

Uses of Inferring

The use of inferring in counseling has two purposes: to build the counseling relationship and to foster positive client change, including reinforcement of the counseling process. Either purpose entails more risk than do other communication styles. High risk is not *necessarily* bad. Positive results can sometimes be aided by great care in your use of inferring statements.

Building the counseling relationship is a use for inferring that is familiar to you. Other communication styles can do this as well, although each employs different means. Inferring statements can help in building the relationship because they often are put into service to initiate and structure relationships outside counseling. Hence, clients may be predisposed to their use.

Although positive inferring statements are generally more effective than their opposites in building the counseling relationship, do not totally dismiss negative statements. The latter can be part of the picture if they are expressed in ways that the client perceives as fair and beneficial. ("My counselor must think I'm important because she makes the effort to point out shortcomings in what I am doing.") Here are several examples.

Client	**Counselor**
So what should I do? I love my kids but I want a good education too. If I stay at home, I think I'll go nuts.	You've identified the two important things in your life pretty well, and you are right that you can't have them both perfectly.
It's just so depressing all the time. The more I try, the harder things seem to go for me.	Of course you feel depressed. You've been through hell. But you've done the right things. You've survived.

I shouldn't have hit him. I guess he deserved it, but I still should have tried something else.	No, you shouldn't have hit him. That didn't solve anything. But, it takes a lot of courage to admit something like that.
I think I'm on the right track now. I feel better about that new wall the king's horses and king's men and I are putting up.	Humpty, the important thing is how you feel about what you are doing.

Although these examples do not reveal responses by the clients to the counselor's inferring statements, their responses are critical. Responses tell you if your inferring statements have been effective. In the examples above, the clients' responses would tell you if the counseling relationships have been hampered or hindered by the counselor's inferring statements. If the latter, you would want to follow up with something that deals with that circumstance. Fortunately, there are few final sayings in counseling!

Keep several points in mind when you use inferring statements to build the counseling relationship.

- Positive inferences that are not deemed credible by clients may hamper the development of positive counseling relationships. ("You are a liar. I don't trust you.")
- Some clients may not agree with your inferences; disagreement need not mean that the counselor-client relationship will suffer. It is still possible for clients to feel that you are empathic, caring, and genuine. ("If you care enough to comment, you care.")
- Be sure that you don't get into trading inferring statements with clients. ("I'm right." "No, you are wrong." "No, you are wrong, I'm right.")
- All inferring statements, particularly negative inferring statements, should be expressed in terms of behaviors, not in terms of the behaving individual. ("Love you but hate your dance steps.")
- Don't try to soften up a client with positive inferring statements as a prelude for a negative inference or zinger. ("Your breath is clean, your teeth are white, *but* your head is empty.")
- Some clients will refute or be suspicious of all positive inferences either expressly or implicitly. Their experience may be that such statements usually precede the expression of negative inferences. ("Yes, but what do you really think?")
- Monitor the nonverbal support you lend to inferring statements. If you use nonverbal cues to reinforce negative inferring statements, you may maximize clients' negative reactions and jeopardize the counselor-client relationship. ("Don't frown at me. I couldn't be as bad as your expression implies.")

The above points should not deter you from using inferring statements as one means to foster positive relationships with your clients. However, your knowledge of these possibilities should make you cautious: carefully note the reactions of your clients.

Inferring is more frequently employed *to foster positive client change* than for any other reason. This is not to say that inferring is the best way to bring about change but it is a viable way. Inferring statements are sometimes confrontational, designed to focus clients' attention on some aspects of their lives or of the counseling relationship that they may have preferred to ignore.

To foster positive client change, inferring statements are usually directed toward clients' actual or proposed actions.

- Positive inferring statements are usually made in support of client movement toward a goal.
- Negative inferring statements are usually made to combat client inertia or to avert client action or proposed action that is deemed ill-considered, dangerous, or illegal by the counselor.
- Inferring statements are often used in a confrontational fashion to challenge clients who resist the counseling process or who ignore or discount important information about themselves.

Here are some examples.

Client	**Counselor**
So, I have finally decided to get on with my life. I can't keep worrying all the time about what might have been.	That's right. At some point you have to accept the past for what it is and move forward.
I think I might as well give up. Everything I try doesn't seem to work anyway.	That might seem like your only alternative, but it's not going to get you very far.
So, what does it matter if I take drugs or not? Who cares what happens to me?	Danny, it seems as though every time you get close to dealing with your dependency on drugs, you pull back. You lose hope and start to feel that nothing will work for you. I'm not sure that's going to get you very far.
I think that saying goodbye to Wendy was the hardest thing I've ever done.	It was hard but it was necessary, Peter. You knew she couldn't stay with you in Never Never Land forever.

As with coaching, the kinds of statements you use immediately following an inferring statement—positive or negative—are very important. Observe your clients carefully to ascertain whether they have become defensive, angry, distant, or offended by what you have said. If they have, listen or question to deal constructively with their reactions.

Exercise care in expressing negative inferences about clients' behaviors. Do so only when proposed actions may be self-destructive or illegal, or may entail irreversible consequences, and when more conservative counseling techniques have been unavailing.

- If you express a negative inference, do not bolster it with more negative inferences. Deal with reactions to what you have said before moving on to something new. Remember that client agreement with your negative inference is not necessarily constructive.
- You must leave a client free to accept or refute your inferences, particularly negative inferences. A negative inference can be an "arrester" that encourages reflection and reconsideration. So employed, it can prepare a client for coaching or questioning styles of communication that you might bring into play to encourage reflection and decision making. Your clients are unlikely to benefit much from your use of inferring statements unless you follow them up properly.
- A negative inference about how the counseling process is proceeding can be a means to get things back on track. In such cases you will be more successful if you phrase the statement so that if blame is to be attributed, it is attributed to you rather than your client. For example, statements like "I don't think we're making much headway in discussing your relationship with your wife" or "I don't think I was very clear in explaining what I wanted you to focus on in talking about your relationship with your wife" are preferable to "You haven't been very clear in describing your relationship with your wife."
- All inferring statements, particularly negative inferring statements, are more beneficial if made sparingly. Used too frequently, they quickly lose their edge and net more adverse side effects than positive main effects.
- A positive inference is often an "encourager to action"; the favorable message with respect to past behavior reinforces such behavior. It is important to integrate positive inferring statements with other communication styles to maximize their impact.

Inferring, Coaching, Questioning, and Listening

Inferring statements are never used on their own in counseling. It is in association with other styles that they gain their utility. Here are several examples of using positive inferring statements together with statements that are indicative of other styles:

Client	**Counselor**
I tried talking to him last night, but it just didn't work out.	He wouldn't listen to you . . . (L)

No, he listened, but he didn't seem to care about anything that I said.	It's good that you tried. At least you can feel good about having made an effort. (I)
I suppose. For all the good it does.	You had really put a lot of hope in things working out if you got up the courage to talk with him . . . (L)
Yeah. A lot of good that did me. Now he thinks that I'm mad at him.	Don't judge yourself too harshly. You tried. Maybe he is not very interested in changing things. (I)
He doesn't think there is anything the matter.	He thinks things are fine and you know that they aren't . . . (L)
Yeah. What am I going to do?	Yes . . . what?
I must be stupid. Everybody else in algebra did okay. Why do I have to be the one to fail?	Everybody else did all right, and you flunked . . . (L)
Yeah. How stupid can you get.	I don't think you are stupid, Arlenzo, just because you failed algebra. (I)
Yeah, well, tell that to my mom. She'll kill me.	Pretty much afraid to tell her . . . (L)
She's going to know anyway. I mean, they mail the grades home anyway. I must be dense not to have seen this coming.	Are you hoping that if your mother thinks you are dumb, she'll go easier on you? (Q)
(Smiles) What do you mean?	Sometimes people go easier on those they think can't do any better. (C)
(Sighs) I guess my mom knows I'm not dumb.	No, you are not dumb, Arlenzo. (I)
What can I tell her? She's going to kill me.	Okay. Let's talk about how you are going to explain this to her. Why don't you explain it to me first. (C)
I didn't study. I had three basketball games the week before the examination. I hate algebra.	You were heavy into basketball, and algebra is a pretty tough subject for you to get down to studying . . . (L)
It's the ticking that drives me crazy. I hear it at night in my bed. I hear it when I'm at the wheel. It's that Pan who did this to me.	Peter Pan makes you hear ticking . . .? (L)

He did this to my hand.	It's resourceful of you to seek me out to talk about this, Captain. (I)
That crocodile won't quit 'till he's got me. I can hear him now. You hear him, don't you?	You've handled it well this far, Captain. (I) We need to explore the ticking a little more—to separate when it's real from when you are imagining it. (C)
But, it always sounds the same. It's so loud sometimes that I can't hear Sneed tell me where we are.	It always sounds the same, but sometimes you know it's real and sometimes you know it's not . . . (L)
It's got to be real when I'm on the water. I can just feel it in my bones.	When you hear the ticking on the water, it sounds real. When you hear it at other times, Captain, it's just your imagination. (C)

In the examples above, notice how positive inferring statements are followed by listening or coaching statements. It is the blend of styles used that determines how successful an exchange will be.

Here is an example of negative inferring statements used in conjunction with other styles.

Client	**Counselor**
I was in the classroom when it happened, but I didn't really hit her.	You were there, but you didn't touch her . . . (L)
Not exactly.	You hit her but, you didn't mean to . . . (L)
Yeah. I guess so.	Grace, you know I can't condone hitting anyone in school, whether you meant to or not. (I)
Yeah, I guess.	You are thinking that it's unfair for me to come down on you . . . (L)
Well, it wasn't just my fault. There were others there too.	Can you tell me about that? (Q)
They kinda egged me on.	They were kind of pushing you to do it, and you didn't want them to think you were chicken . . . (L)
Maybe that was it. It all kind of happened so fast.	Grace, one good rule of thumb is that when a bunch of people are egging you on to do something, they're usually trying to get you to do something that's going to get you in trouble. (C)

Yeah. I was kinda dumb, I guess.	It's not dumb to let this kind of thing happen to you once—if you learn from it. (I)
Okay.	Okay. Now, how do you want to clear this thing up? (Q)
I guess I should tell Marge that I'm sorry.	Guess so . . . but I sense you'd rather not do that. (I)
Not really. What am I supposed to do? Just walk up to her in front of everybody and just beg her forgiveness?	It's going to be hard for you to do it if you have to do it in front of everybody . . . (L)

In the above example, the counselor is directive but still uses listening, coaching, and questioning to reinforce and follow up on inferences. Remember that the purpose of making an inferring statement in a situation like this is to improve future behavior. Nobody can change the past but sometimes an assessment of the past can help in planning for the future.

Sometimes, of course, it is more productive for the counselor to disregard the past and to focus entirely on the present or future, as the exchange below illustrates.

Client	**Counselor**
I think this has been the hardest six months of my life. Ever since I lost my husband in that accident, it's been like I'm living in a black hole.	Looking back on it, you are wondering how you lived through it . . . (L)
Yes. But I did and I suppose that's something.	It's more than something. It's a lot! (I)
But I still get so lonely. Sometimes I go into the bedroom at night and half expect to see him there reading a book.	That's a very natural feeling, Eleanor. Natural, but still very strong for you. (I)
It's not always like that. Sometimes, I'm just fine. Then, all it takes is some little thing and I feel like I just fell down the well again.	Mostly you are okay, but sometimes it feels like you are back at square one all over again . . . (L)
Yes. Last week I saw Jack's sister—the first time since the funeral. We looked at each other and then we both burst into tears. It's crazy. I can't go on my whole life riding a roller coaster like this.	I don't think you will Eleanor. (I) Are these spells getting more frequent or less frequent for you? (Q)

Oh, they happen less often but when they do . . . bam!	You are down a bit on yourself for continuing to grieve in this way. (I) Don't be, Eleanor. (I) The way you feel is natural and what you feel is natural. (C)
That doesn't help very much.	You'd feel better knowing how to stop feeling this way than knowing that others feel this way too . . . (L)
Yeah. I need to figure out how to stop feeling this way, or at least start doing better with it than I am right now.	I'm not sure you will be too successful in stopping the feelings. (I) They will taper off, but you may always feel them occasionally. (I) Let's talk about how you can better manage them as they arise. (C)

Notice how the counselor in the above example uses negative inferring statements but also includes positive inferring and other communication styles. Notice particularly which style the counselor calls upon after making an inferring statement. Here is another example:

Client	**Counselor**
So, I asked the gentleman to show me his pies. But he refused.	He didn't want to sell you his pies . . . (L)
I guess not. He kept mumbling about pennies.	Did he want pennies from you, Simon? (Q)
Well, maybe he did. But I just told him to show me first his wares. He said pennies. I said wares. He said pennies. I said wares. Indeed, he must be dense.	Might it be that he reacted badly because you refused to show him your pennies . . .? (I)
I couldn't show him my pennies. I didn't have any.	You made him think you did have pennies but were just being difficult . . . (L)
I suppose that was pretty simple.	Simon, you may meet the pieman going home. (C) How else might you handle him? (Q)

You no doubt have recognized by now that effective communication by a counselor requires a variety of styles. The utility of each is amplified in combination. In fact, you might say that a counselor's orientation requires several communication styles rather than a particular style in interpersonal exchange.

Negative Effects of Inferring

In one of my earlier lives, I trained police officers in techniques for handling interpersonal disputes, the kinds of disputes that take place in taverns and family kitchens. The communication techniques they studied were very similar to those you are studying, although the officers' goals were very different from your goals in counseling clients.

To keep the officer trainees alive beyond the end of their first week on the street, I spent a good deal of time helping them to understand the inflammatory side of inferring statements, particularly negative inferring statements. Such statements have the potential to arouse negatively persons to whom they are directed, especially those already in a state of excitement. When agitated suspects are on the receiving end, they may respond in kind but at a higher emotional level. What's more, untrained officers usually come back with an even more intense rejoinder. After two or three escalating exchanges, the only thing left for the parties is "fight or flight."

In counseling, of course, fisticuffs are frowned upon, so the wise counselor attends closely to client reaction to inferring statements. If a client becomes angry or more emotionally charged when you make an inferring statement, think twice before you make another. With some clients you will need to avoid inferring statements altogether because of adverse reactions such clients exhibit or express to even positive inferences.

Inferring statements entail other negative effects of which the counselor must be aware:

- Positive inferences can be addictive for clients. Your clients may become dependent on your approval. To forestall this possible eventuality, limit your use of inferring statements. Encourage clients to assess their own actions.
- Following up one inferring statement with another increases the chances of adverse side effects.
- Because of their previous life experiences, you must avoid altogether using inferring statements with some clients, who might include clients who have undergone verbally abusive relationships, clients who are very withdrawn, clients who are reluctant to manifest negative reactions even when they have such reactions, and clients who are very dependent upon others to make decisions for them.

Points to Consider

1. Have you ever responded negatively to a positive comment? What did you do? How did the other person react? What ensued?

2. Identify situations where you may have paired an inferring statement with a question or a coaching statement. How did the others respond? Why do you think they responded the way they did?
3. Recall reactions you received to negative inferring statements you made. What factors mediated a reaction of compliance or one of animosity?
4. Experiment following up an inferring statement with varying communication styles. Do you gain a different reaction from following up with a listening style than a coaching style?
5. Observe teachers or athletic coaches whom you respect. How does each use inferring?

Suggested Readings

COREY, G. (1990). *Theory and practice of group counseling.* Pacific Grove, CA: Brooks/Cole. The author provides a good treatment of how to use confrontation skills within a group-counseling perspective.

COREY, G. (1991). *Theory and practice of counseling and psychotherapy.* Pacific Grove, CA: Brooks/Cole. Chapter 6 provides a good overview of confrontation from a Gestalt perspective.

COREY, M. S., & COREY, G. (1989). *Becoming a helper.* Pacific Grove, CA: Brooks/Cole. Chapter 3 outlines, in a practical and easily understandable way, the place of confrontation in the helping process.

CORMIER, W. H., & CORMIER, L. S. (1991). *Interviewing strategies for helpers.* Pacific Grove, CA: Brooks/Cole. Chapters 14–19 provide numerous examples of how to use inferring to influence the outcomes of counseling.

EGAN, G. (1973). *Face to face.* Pacific Grove, CA: Brooks/Cole. Chapter 8 provides a good overview of confrontation within a small-group counseling framework.

EGAN, G. (1990). *The skilled helper.* Pacific Grove, CA: Brooks/Cole. Chapter 8 includes a discussion of challenging, a particular kind of inferring that may be more implicit than explicit.

EVANS, D. R., HEARN, M. T., UHLEMANN, M. R., & IVEY, A. E. (1989). *Essential interviewing.* Pacific Grove, CA: Brooks/Cole. Chapter 8 deals with confrontation, an essential counseling skill that is based upon inferences by the counselor.

GLADDING, S. T. (1988) *Counseling: A comprehensive profession.* Columbus, OH: Merrill. The author provides a number of practical suggestions for confronting clients within the context of a helping relationship.

IVEY, A. E. (1988). *Intentional interviewing and counseling.* Pacific Grove, CA: Brooks/Cole. Chapter 8 provides an overview of the author's confrontation techniques. Included is a self-assessment scale that measures the impact of confrontation.

MARTIN, D. G. (1983). *Counseling and therapy skills.* Pacific Grove, CA: Brooks/Cole. Chapter 4 outlines the author's perspective on confronting.

OKUN, B. F. (1992). *Effective helping.* Pacific Grove, CA: Brooks/Cole. At several points the author describes confrontation skills that blend coaching and inferring styles as outlined in this text.

CHAPTER 10

Supporting

"That's too bad about your father."
"I'm sure that things will improve soon . . ."
"Don't feel bad, I'm sure things will work out."
"I know things aren't too great for you right now."
"I know just how you are feeling."
"That's really nice for you."

As was so for each of the styles presented thus far, supporting has specific characteristics associated with it. Supporting statements are widespread, particularly in the world outside counseling.

Definition

Supporting statements communicate interest, commiseration, backing, encouragement, compassion, or sympathy. Assertions such as "I'm sorry," "That's too bad," "I wish you didn't feel so bad," and "I'm happy for you" are examples of supporting statements you might hear in conversations. In counseling and out, supporting statements are common.

A supporting statement often sounds like a platitude. This is not necessarily bad because platitudes are a part of social custom. That is the case, say, with "I'm sorry" expressed at a funeral to a grieving friend. The statement communicates compassion and acknowledges that you "feel" for your friend. In some ways, it also communicates "I wish you didn't feel this way because I don't know how to handle it and I feel uncomfortable. Please stop!"

The use of supporting statements is a social grace as well as a method of relating with others. In some ways supporting statements are like the "Good morning"–"Good morning" exchange with workmates when you meet first thing each day. If the exchange is completed, no importance is attached to it. If not, if someone neglects to answer your "Good morning" in the usual manner, you may become disconcerted.

- Supporting statements are prevalent outside counseling, and the client experiencing difficulties may assume that someone who is going to help him or her will make them.
- When you say something that is supportive, it is often the case that you must follow up with a statement that revives the conversation. Statements like "I'm sorry" spoken at funerals usually do not lead anywhere or prompt extended replies. A lagged conversation can almost always be brought back to life by questioning or listening.
- Supporting statements can communicate caring to a client, and can sometimes help in building the counseling relationship.
- Supporting statements can be made in response to a client's positive or negative assertions.

Occasionally, even though your heart is in the right place, your clients do not interpret your supporting statements as helpful. The statements may sound perfunctory to them, may sound as though you are paying only lip service to their problems. The caricature of this type of response is the television advertisement for a cold remedy in which a person is waiting at a bus stop, looking miserable. A passerby remarks, "I know how you feel." "No, you don't." "Oh, yes I do!" "Oh, no you don't!"

It is easy to poke fun at supporting statements, but they are a necessary form of conversation—mainly because they are expected and others may feel uncomfortable if you don't deliver. Still such statements are seldom effective on their own. Statements made immediately before a supporting statement are important but statements made immediately after are critical.

From what was said earlier about conversation stoppers, you know that any statement in the wake of a supporting statement must restart the conversation. For example, if a counselor is told by a client something like "It's hard to keep your mind on what you are doing when you've got a sick kid at home," and chooses then to offer a supporting statement like "I'm sorry to hear about your kid's being sick," the counselor will have to be prepared to rescue the lagging exchange, perhaps with a question, perhaps with a coaching or inferring statement.

Uses of Supporting

A major reason for using a supporting style is to build the counseling relationship. A secondary reason is to acknowledge issues that a client brings forward as preparation for dealing with the issues constructively.

As you have seen, *building the counseling relationship* is something that all communication styles can do, although each does so differently and any one style may or may not work to advantage with individual clients. Supporting statements may help to build the relationships between you and your clients because the style mimics the way that empathy, understanding, or compassion is often shown to them elsewhere. Thus, your clients may relate well to supporting statements or may even expect that you do.

Here is an example of how supporting statements are typically used in a noncounseling situation.

Person 1	**Person 2**
The harder I work for my sisters, the behinder I get.	Oh, I'm sorry to hear that.
Yeah. They're so mean. It's always "Cindy, this . . ." or "Cindy, that . . ." There's never a moment's rest.	Gosh, that's really tough for you.
Tough? You bet it is. They're always going dancing, but do you think I ever get the chance to go? No siree. Just work, work, work.	That's a crying shame.
At least it's nice to talk to somebody who understands these things.	It's not easy being a fairy godmother either.

Here are several examples of supporting statements used in a counseling context.

Client	**Counselor**
Since Gromethius left, everything has been miserable. I feel really bummed out.	That's too bad. I'm really sorry to hear that.
Finally, I've got everything going my way. I'm happier now than I ever thought possible.	Super! That's just great. Good for you!
When I'm with Gerry, everything is clear as can be. As soon as she leaves, my world falls apart.	That's a tough one for you.
Tell me what to do. I'm so damned confused I don't have a clue.	That's a pretty scary way to have things.

As you read these examples, keep in mind that no counselor would desert the conversation after only one supporting exchange with a client. Even in situations where counselors make supporting statements to clients as a means to build counseling relationships, they would not end there. Supporting statements would be followed by statements indicative of other styles that reinforce productive counseling relationships, resume the counseling process, or effect other goals.

A clear distinction must be made between a supporting style of communication and the client's feelings of being supported in the counseling relationship. The latter may be brought about by any communication style. The former is a particular communication technique used by the counselor to make the client feel supported or for a variety of other important reasons.

A distinction should also be made between a supporting and a listening statement. For example, a statement like "That's a pretty scary way to have things" could be interpreted as listening or supporting, depending upon how the counselor says it. The statement will be heard as listening if the inflection is lifted at the end of the sentence as though putting the implied question "Isn't it?" If the statement comes across as a simple declarative sentence, it will be supportive. A supporting statement asserts how the client feels: "You feel this way." A listening statement queries: "You feel this way . . .?" The difference between the two is subtle but important.

Supporting *prepares the client to deal constructively with issues* in the same way that it helps to build the counseling relationship. Some clients need to hear supporting statements to make them more disposed to take constructive action on issues that affect them. Perhaps this is because they have been exposed to supporting statements outside counseling. Using a supporting statement with such individuals can help you to move forward in the counseling process.

Client	**Counselor**
Everything always seems to happen to me. Today my stupid car wouldn't start. Yesterday it wouldn't shut off.	That's too bad, Pythagoras. (S)
For sure.	Pythagoras, run through what happened and what you did. Perhaps we can learn something from it. (C)
Okay. Well, I left the lights on and the stupid battery ran down.	You forgot to turn the lights off last night . . . (L)
Yeah. I was pretty hammered I guess.	It's easy to forget something like that when you've had a few too many. (I)
Oh, for sure. I don't know why it wouldn't shut off. Just kept a bangin' and a whirrin'.	Had you drunk anything yesterday afternoon? (Q)

Oh, yeah. Lots, for sure. For a while I kept trying to turn off the radio instead of the ignition.	I think we should probably talk a bit more about your drinking, Pythagoras. Sounds like it's something that has caused you a bit of grief of late. (C)
The way I feel today, nothing can bother me. Everything's just great.	I'm glad to hear that, Gorgo. (S)
Oh yeah. Even thinking about school can't bring me down.	School is something you'd rather put out of your mind . . . (L)
(Sighs) Yes.	But that's easier said than done . . . (L)
I'm not sure that today's so great after all.	I would guess that you would rather not talk about school, Gorgo. (I) Or is part of you thinking that you'd better deal with it? (Q)
I guess I have to get a few things straight. I suppose that I can't drift through this thing forever.	You'd rather not think about school when you are feeling good but you know you have to . . . (L)
(Sighs) Yes.	Okay, Gorgo. We need to talk about your attendance and your grades. (C) Where shall we start? (Q)
I don't think I'll ever find them. They're just gone that's all.	Don't feel so bad, Bo-Peep. I'm sure we'll be able to think of something. (S)
No. They're never going to show up. I can just feel it.	Nothing I say is going to change your mind, is it? (Q)
Well, what am I supposed to think? I'm usually so careful with my flock.	You are upset with yourself for letting them get lost . . . (L)
I guess I am. It's not as if they'll come home on their own.	Bo-Peep, let's take a run through your options. You can leave them alone and maybe they'll come home or you can put some kind of plan into place to find them. (C) How do you feel about those two options? (Q)

Supporting and Other Styles

As in the examples you have just read, supporting statements are seldom used exclusively. When you use them, you usually do so to deal with specific statements from clients to achieve specific ends. You probably follow up your supporting statements with other styles that are designed to bolster the ends you were pursuing through supporting statements or to help you pursue other aims.

The reason for the sequence is that other styles, such as listening, to an extent not possible with supporting statements, can help to build the counseling relationship and achieve other counseling goals at the same time. For instance, listening can build the counseling relationship and simultaneously encourage the client to reflect upon her lot in life or her feelings toward her sisters.

Below is the noncounseling example you read earlier, but now with the addition of supporting as well as other styles:

Person 1	**Person 2**
The harder I work for my sisters, the behinder I get.	Oh, I'm sorry to hear that. (S)
Yeah. They're so mean! It's always "Cindy, this . . ." or "Cindy, that . . ." There's never a moment's rest.	They always want things immediately and you have to do it . . . (L)
That's for sure. They're always going dancing, but do you think I ever get the chance to go? No siree. Just work, work, work.	That's a crying shame. (S) Is this something that's been bothering you for a long time? (Q)
Too long. There's nothing I can do about it until Mr. Right comes along. But at least it's nice to talk to somebody who understands these things.	Don't be so sure that there's nothing you can do about it, Cindy. (I) What you need is the right attitude—and a little help from this wand. (C)

Here are two examples of how to use a supporting style in conjunction with other styles in exchanges between counselors and clients.

Client	**Counselor**
It was so hard. I told him that he and I were history and he just looked at me blankly. It was like he didn't believe me—or didn't care.	You finally got up the nerve to tell him and it didn't work out the way you wanted it to . . . (L)
That's for sure. I'm not sure if things are over now or not. We just seem to pretend that I hadn't said anything.	It's not easy to do these things. It's harder when the problem still seems unresolved. (S)
That's for sure.	What's your next step? What do you want to do now? (Q)

I don't know. It's almost like I've lost the courage to do anything right now.	I'm sorry to hear you've taken it so badly. (S) I guess that since you've been unsuccessful once, it seems all too easy to think that you could be that way again . . . (L)
That's for sure. I don't know how I got up the guts to tell him in the first place.	But you did, and I'll bet you could do it again if you decided to. (C)
Don't count on it.	I don't mean exactly the same thing, but let's review what happened and see what it tells you about what you tried to do. (C)
I don't know what I'm going to do about my grades. If I don't smarten up, I'm going to flunk out.	I'm sorry to hear that, Pericles. (S) Have they been going down with your working or going down with your not working? (Q)
Not working, I guess. At least, not very hard.	And now you are afraid your chickens are going to come home to roost . . . (L)
Yeah. I don't know if I can pull out of this or not.	Pericles, you've already made an important first step. You've admitted to yourself that you need to do something about how things are going. That's not an easy thing to admit. (I)
I guess not.	Okay, let's talk a bit more about what kind of pickle you are in and what might help you to pull yourself out of it. (C)

Negative Effects of Supporting

A supporting style requires that you pay close attention to your client. Some clients will warm to your use of it; others may find you condescending.

The apt counselor is able to communicate support to the client yet at the same time not communicate a willingness to accept any and all kinds of behavior. He or she can demonstrate empathy, understanding, or sympathy and simultaneously indicate that there is a counseling job to perform that may conflict with expressions of support for and acceptance of everything the client does.

The fine line between support and unilateral acceptance of all kinds of client behavior is maintained by using supporting statements in conjunction with other kinds of statements. It is quite possible to show support and in the same exchange make inferences, coach, ask questions, and listen.

A supporting statement is most effective when it is preceded by a listening statement that demonstrates that you understand the situation you are providing support for. This prevents your making empty supporting statements that leave the conversation hanging. Rather than successive supporting statements, questioning, inferring, or coaching statements are often preferred immediately after a supporting statement to further the conversation.

Points to Consider

1. In television soap operas, what types of reactions are customarily made to supporting statements? What might account for such reactions?
2. Identify the styles used to rekindle a conversation in a funeral situation after a supporting statement such as "I was so sorry to hear that Bessy-Sue had passed away."
3. Propose several supporting statements you could make in response to a report of "bad news" from your spouse or good friend.
4. Compose supporting statements that do not stop conversations.

Suggested Readings

BURKE, J. F. (1989). *Contemporary approaches to psychotherapy and counseling.* Pacific Grove, CA: Brooks/Cole. Chapter 7 provides a good overview of Adlerian approaches to counseling and the Adlerian notion of encouragement.

COREY, G. (1990). *Theory and practice of group counseling.* Pacific Grove, CA: Brooks/Cole. Chapter 3 provides a useful treatment of a leader's supporting within the context of group counseling.

COREY, G. (1991). *Theory and practice of counseling and psychotherapy.* Pacific Grove, CA: Brooks/Cole. Chapter 12, particularly pp. 299ff., provides a good review of counseling techniques, including supportive styles. Chapter 3 provides an overview of Adlerian approaches, along with the place of encouragement in assisting clients.

EGAN, G. (1990). *The skilled helper.* Pacific Grove, CA: Brooks/Cole. Chapter 2 provides a context for supporting within a helping model. The chapter is particularly helpful in its discussion of the relationship between supporting and confronting.

IVEY, A. E. (1988). *Intentional interviewing and counseling.* Pacific Grove, CA: Brooks/Cole. Chapter 2 identifies a supporting style as part of attending behavior.

MUCHINSKY, P. (1990). *Psychology applied to work.* Pacific Grove, CA: Brooks/Cole. Chapter 11 provides interesting insights into theories of leadership, including supportive leadership, although the book is not about counseling.

CHAPTER 11

Implicit Communication

Until this point I have been writing as if communication were an entirely verbal process. Of course, it is not. Communication can be achieved through words but also through other, less direct means such as tone of voice and body language. As anyone who has tried to find a toilet in a foreign land can attest, implicit communication can be both creative and powerful.

Implicit communication is of two slightly different forms. Each can reinforce, weaken, or contradict the message conveyed by the other or by the explicit communication conveyed by words.

1. *Body language* is what most people think of when they think of implicit communication. Body language includes all aspects of facial and body positioning that convey a message to others. This can include such actions as grimacing or smiling, avoiding eye contact or staring, crossing one's legs, and leaning forward.
2. The *structure of language* also conveys a great deal of implicit meaning. For example, what do you infer differently from "I hate Gorgo" and "It would be easy to hate Gorgo." The structure of language is mitigated by *inflection* as another key component of implicit language. Meaning can be altered very significantly by emphasizing one syllable or another or by modulating the volume and intensity of your voice.

Much of implicit communication occurs without conscious notice, certainly without conscious remark. This is true for both sender and receiver. Because of this, implicit communication is more difficult than explicit language to control. Implicit language is also easier for listeners to misinterpret.

Implicit communication is not something about which you have a choice to use or not to use. Nor is it restricted to face-to-face encounters, telephones being the mainstay of communication for many people. Implicit communication is constantly in play whenever you are involved in interactions with others. In your professional work as a counselor, you must learn to *manage* implicit communication, to use it as you use explicit communication: to further what you want to accomplish as a counselor.

Body Language

An offensive beer commercial, common in my part of the world, goes something like this. The scene is a crowded youth-oriented bar, full of the merriment that—we are supposed to believe—can be generated only by the sponsor's product. At one end of the bar sprawl three "real men," laughing and gesturing at—you guessed it—three winsome "young things" at the other end of the bar. The camera pans to one of the men, who has managed to catch the eye of one of the women. She looks away. He laughs and momentarily gazes heavenward. She looks back. He is still looking at her. They both laugh. They move close together, spontaneously touching as they obviously enjoy the sponsor's product. It must be a low-budget commercial. Except for the laughing, there are no words.

Counseling involves verbal interaction between client and counselor, but it also involves interaction of a more physical nature, the same kind of communication the television sponsor hopes will induce you to buy its brand of beer. As in commercials, body language in counseling is language with a purpose—or it ought to be.

Body language is used by the counselor to reinforce a verbal message or to convey a message that cannot be transmitted easily with words. The client does likewise, although perhaps not always with the same degree of premeditation as does the counselor.

Understanding Client Body Language

As a counselor, you must pay attention to client body language. Clients can ask questions, give opinions, and describe feelings without uttering a sound. Body language can be explicit, as in giving someone "the finger," but most body language is more subtle than the spoken word. You must be vigilant to tune it in and to validate the inferences you form of its meaning.

One element to monitor is the apparent contradiction by body language of verbal communication. You might notice, say, that a client seems to be angry—clenched teeth and tensed neck muscles—but is vocally laying claim to being in a state of serenity. Or you might hear a client, while laughing, profess great unhappiness over a marital separation. Or a client might declare that there is no problem but be unable to look you in the eye.

Of course, the above illustrations do not *necessarily* indicate a conflict between the spoken word and body language, although they hint strongly at one. Your lack of certainty occurs because drawing inferences from body language is less easily done than drawing inferences from the spoken word. To clear up conflictive meanings, you must apply finely honed communication skills in a method similar to the method you would use for conflictive meanings in wholly verbal communication: sharing your perception of the conflict with the client through dialogue. For example, in the matter of the seemingly angry client who vocalizes serenity, you could respond in the following ways:

- "Part of you feels happy, but part of you is still angry over what has happened . . ."
- "You are very angry about what happened but it is difficult for you to talk about it . . ."
- "The part of you that wants everything to be all right is fighting with the part of you that is still very mad . . ."
- "When Wolfy attacks you, you understand why he does it but it still makes you angry . . ."

Note that each suggestion brings up the dichotomy of interpretation in a muted way, a way that allows the client to discuss the matter without feeling blamed. This is an important aspect in the process of resolving a dichotomy of meaning. The client must not get a sense of censure or judgment as a result of the mixed message conveyed. It is very easy for the client to interpret your side of the conversation as, "On the one hand I hear this. On the other hand, I hear that. What's the matter with you?"

Many counselor-trainees have trouble with the proper interpretation of client body-based communication. What do lowered eyes mean? How different is the manifestation of joy versus sadness? What do tight lips connote? In this regard, Cormier and Cormier (1991, p. 68) provide an excellent summary of nonverbal behaviors typically exhibited by clients and *possible* meanings you can ascribe to such behaviors.

Do not forget that body language is culturally and geographically bound. This is true at the macro level; many differences are evident among national and ethnic groups. It is also true at the micro level; many differences crop up in similar groups that are geographically separated. Until you become thoroughly familiar with the characteristics of the groups you deal with, you will make a goodly number of errors in interpreting body-based language.

Suggestions for Dealing with Client Body-Based Communication

1. It is not unusual for a client to display some incongruity between verbal communication and body communication. Very often one moderates or accentuates the other, and in such cases it may be of little importance for you to inquire into the differences.
2. When there is a considerable difference between a client's two kinds of communication, try pursuing *each* in turn. It is not always necessary or desirable to confront a client about differences in a transmitted message. In fact, doing so sometimes causes him or her to be more circumspect in body communication, thus depriving you of a valuable source of counseling information.
3. Monitor the relationship between your physical communication and that of your clients. Perhaps your unintentional body transmissions are having unintended effects on the behavior of your clients.
4. Try introducing comments about a client's body behavior as part of a listening-based summarizing statement rather than as a singular event. For example, you could say, "The hardest thing you have to handle right now is the loneliness, the fact that there is nobody at home you can count on and *you are pretty damned mad about being left out in the cold . . .*" (The italicized words are an inference drawn from body communication.)
5. An occasional temptation is to ask clients the meaning of their body-based communication. Remember that it is usually easier to get clients to agree with your inferences as to possible meanings than it is to elicit their explanations of meanings. Unfortunately, it also happens that clients sometimes agree with your incorrect inferences.

Understanding Your Own Body Communication

Body communication is not the sole domain of clients. As you do in your everyday life, in your role as a counselor you continually telegraph body-based messages to your clients. Although you might be cavalier about the messages you transmit in your everyday life, you cannot be quite so indifferent during counseling.

To varying degrees, your body message can reinforce or obscure the message you convey to clients through words. There is nothing wrong with either message provided that both are conveyed intentionally for therapeutic effect. Operating without your deliberate control, your body behavior ceases to be an ally and may prevent your accomplishing your counseling goal.

Perhaps the most common body communication that you must remain aware of as a counselor are mannerisms that may have become almost automatic to you and hence unnoticed but that *may* annoy clients. Examples are playing with your hair or a pen, scratching your ear or buttocks, staring out the window, smiling perpetually, or doodling on a note pad. In many cases personal quirks will be as neutral in the counseling setting as in the everyday world. In other cases, however, they may be detrimental.

Probably one of the best ways to ascertain your mannerisms is to videotape yourself during mock or real counseling sessions (the latter requires client permission). View the tape yourself, and if possible with a colleague or friend, as a check for habits that have become such a part of you that you are no longer aware of them. I think it was through this exercise that I first found that my obsessive polishing of my glasses was annoying to some people. It took some time to learn to counsel with smudged eye-panes!

Eye contact and physical proximity are also key physical means of communication with clients. Very often counselors are more comfortable than their clients about direct eye contact and being seated closely together. Although neither is likely to spark a client revolt, neither is likely to help the counseling relationship if it makes the client restive. Whether we like it or not, clients set the standards for what makes them comfortable in nonverbal exchange with counselors.

Cormier and Cormier (1991, p. 82) outline a number of counselor nonverbal or body-based behaviors, together with their *possible effects* on clients. Although the listing is far from exhaustive, it is a good place to start in analyzing their relevance for your professional development. Of course, the most important thing is not the reactions clients *might* have; it is the reactions they *do* have.

By keeping constantly alert to the reactions of clients, you will be able to ascertain the effects of your body communication. Do clients look away when you fix your gaze on them? Do clients lose their train of thought when you, once again, scratch your buttocks? Do they move back in their chairs as you lean forward in yours? Do they seem more animated and chipper when your demeanor is upbeat?

Deciphering client reaction to body communication is not easy. At issue is a point that has undoubtedly been brought home to you in your classes on research design: inferring causation from correlation. Because a client appears to demonstrate a certain reaction in one or more instances to an action of yours, it does not *necessarily* mean that your action caused the reaction, although the likelihood of this may be high. To know for certain, you must *vary* your action to see if the reaction of the client also varies. As in research, if systematic variation of what you do occasions systematic variations in the client's reaction, you have a pretty good idea that the former causes the latter.

In operational terms, this means that you need to *experiment* with your body messages to clients. Use a particular behavior. Stop using it. Try substituting another. Pay close attention to client reactions. This is perhaps the best way to sensitize yourself to the effects your body communication have on others.

Suggestions for Managing Your Body Communication

1. Do not rely on how you react to the body behavior of others to predict how your clients might respond to the same behavior on your part. Each person has as unique a reaction to body communication as to verbal communication. What might be titillating to one might be off-putting to another. Rely on collecting your own information about actual reactions rather than on supposed reactions as your touchstone.
2. Remember that elements of body communication include attire and personal demeanor. What might be free-spirited to you might be slovenly and unprofessional to your clients. Possible effects are readily investigated through systematic change on your part. Perhaps a beloved fluorescent tie or a décolleté frock would be better reserved for dimly lit settings.
3. The office or other location where you meet clients may also convey messages that help or hinder your counseling efforts. Generally, subdued decor allows a room to fade into the background of client awareness and thereby removes a possible impediment to the purpose at hand.
4. Experiment with matching closely your verbal and body-based communication. If you are talking about happy events, look the part. If you are discussing a serious matter, a sober mien is appropriate.
5. Experiment with taking notes and not taking notes throughout counseling sessions. When you take notes, assess the effects of writing and not writing after a client has discussed a certain point that may or may not be important.

The Structure of Language

Oral language has a dimension that goes beyond the words spoken. The paralinguistic dimension includes the actions we take to highlight or to gloss over certain aspects of what is being said. It also includes language structure, such as use of the active or passive voice and double-edged communication like sarcasm. As is the case with body communication, the varying of expressed-language structure is used by both clients and counselors to convey meaning.

Suppose a client is talking with you about her husband's possible infidelity. In describing an event between him and another woman, she says one of the following:

1. Gretta was making love to him.
2. He was making love to Gretta.
3. The two of them were making love.

What differences in interpretation would you make among the assertions? Which one shows a greater acceptance of what the client's husband did? Which one places more or less blame for what happened on Gretta or the husband?

Suppose a student is talking to you about feeling depressed near the end of the school term. In describing his feelings, he says one of the following:

1. I feel just awful. I don't know what to do.
2. It's just awful. It's hard to know what to do.
3. Everybody's feeling awful. They're just trying to find out what to do.

What differences in interpretation would you make among the expressions of feeling? Do you detect differences in the willingness of the client to take personal responsibility? Does the client feel different in each statement?

Mehrabian (1981), in his excellent primer on implicit communication, describes a number of stylistic differences used to express varying degrees of attraction or preference, terming them indicative of an approach-avoidance concept that is important in understanding the meaning attributed to language. The differences evident to you in the examples below are representative of this approach-avoidance dimension.

Approach Statement	**Avoidance Statement**
Here is Adelaide.	There is Adelaide.
These things really bother me.	Those things really bother me.
I can't understand what you mean by this.	I can't understand what you mean by that.
I am really depressed.	I have been really depressed.

In the four paired statements the differences are telegraphed by using different demonstrative pronouns, adjectives, or verb tenses. One or more of the three instruments are often used to add subtle shades of meaning to language, in counseling and in everyday circumstances.

In counseling, an awareness of language styles that signify approach or avoidance can help you to understand better messages that your clients try to convey to you. Attuning yourself to the subtle aspects of language will enable you to frame more intuitive listening statements for validation by your clients. It will also help you to avoid hearing and responding to only part of what the clients tell you.

It is primarily through listening and questioning that you will be able to validate the inferences that you make as a result of focusing on language structure. Remember, there is nothing fundamentally different in the substance of what is communicated through the nonverbal medium. Once you form the inference, it can be validated in the same way it would be if the communication had come to you through verbal means.

In addition to client use of the structure of language as a means to communicate to you, you too can use it to advantage in your communication with clients. It can help you to frame listening or questioning statements that, although true, are more likely to be accepted by clients than if they feel you have approached too close too quickly. Consider the following examples of client statements followed by counselor listening responses that are slightly different based upon language structure:

Client	**Counselor**
I don't see how I can love a person like that.	You love him but don't know if you should . . .
	It's not easy to love someone who cheats on others . . .
	You loved him but that wasn't easy for you . . .
I've always been afraid of trying too hard.	When you try hard, you are afraid of how you might feel if things don't work out . . .
	It's not easy to try hard in case things don't work out the way a person wants . . .
	You haven't tried too hard because you would be afraid of failing . . .
I've always been a happy person. And now . . .	You are afraid of what your future will look like . . .
	It's hard to move from happiness to sadness . . .
	You were happy and then you were sad . . .

Notice how the counselor in the above examples uses different pronouns and verb tenses to make the listening statement more or less personal for the client. The statements by the counselor can use the person pronoun *you,* and the present tense to frame a listening statement that is personal and immediate. Or the impersonal pronoun *it,* and the past or future tense to depersonalize or distance the counselor's inference from the client.

Using language structure subtly can help you to "ease in" to the feelings and deeply personal meanings expressed by your clients. Rather than initially responding to a client with a listening statement that is intensely personal, you can allow the client to warm to you as you progressively move from a language structure that is *impersonal and past* to *personal and present.* This sometimes helps to ensure that clients are not frightened into silence.

The interpretation of implicit communication is also dependent on factors such as volume, tone, and enunciation. For example, how are the meanings of the following sentences changed for you if the underlined words are emphasized by inflection? How are they changed if, in addition to emphasis by inflection, volume is increased when speaking the underlined words?

I saw her.	*You* can't make me.
I *saw* her.	You can't make *me.*
I saw *her.*	You can't *make* me.

Of course, expressing and interpreting are something that both you and your clients do quite naturally. In the case of clients not versed in communication skills, expressing is most often subliminal and interpreting private, not subject to verification through active means. In your case, although you will probably express and interpret subliminally in many instances, you have the capacity to do so with deliberate control.

In communication with clients, you must ensure that the messages you convey through volume, tone, and enunciation are the messages you want to convey. Otherwise, client reaction may not be what you want. More important, the reaction to your unintended communication may not be telegraphed to you, and you may never have the chance to clear up the misinterpretation. In deciding what you are going to say to clients, think through possible meanings that could be attributed to it, depending upon how you say it. Focus carefully on client reaction to see if what you wanted to communicate was communicated.

A final aspect of implicit language is double-edged communication, usually expressed as sarcasm. Sarcasm is most often spoken by clients in response to real or imagined negative inferences directed at them. For example, you might make an observation about something a client has done. The client might respond by saying, "Well, I *suppose* you must be right. After all, you *did* go to college." In effect, the client has responded to a perceived inferring statement with another inferring statement, this one expressed within the relative safety of sarcasm.

Sarcasm allows the speaker to deny the implied meaning, usually by saying something like "Oh, but I didn't mean that," and then repeating the original statement but with decidedly different emphasis on key words. For this reason, it is elusive and hence troublesome to deal with.

There is really no reason for you to use sarcasm as a counselor, although you might be confronted by it if your clients use it. Should that occur, you can usually deal with it in the same way that you respond to inferring statements expressed orally: listening statements. As indicated in earlier chapters, listening statements are probably your best response in most situations.

Suggestions for Managing Language Structure in Counseling

1. In framing listening statements, make it a practice to start from a point at which you mirror the pronouns, verb tense, and adjectives used by your client. This will make you more aware of circumstances where you consciously decide to deviate from this standard.
2. In listening to clients, look for deviation from their usual patterns of implicit communication. This could include changes in language structure, body communication, or volume, tone, and enunciation. Altered patterns usually indicate something.
3. Simply because you are aware of possible messages being conveyed to you by the client does not *necessarily* mean that you must immediately respond to the messages or immediately resolve differences between explicit and implicit messages. Sometimes it is better to ignore a message or to "store" it in your memory bank for use at a later, more fruitful point.
4. Playback of video or audio recordings of your interviews with clients can sometimes help you identify your own implicit language patterns, as well as those of your clients. It can also be helpful to have clients view or listen to their own tapes; sometimes language patterns that do no harm in counseling can cause problems in everyday life. Watching themselves, with interpretation assistance from you, can sometimes increase their self-awareness.
5. Focus on client body communication to help you interpret language structures, such as sarcasm, whose meanings are not immediately clear to you. Very often there is a congruity between the two.

Points to Consider

1. Watch situation comedies and soap operas on television to see how implicit language is handled in popular culture. Remember that such programs also exert a subtle teaching influence on viewers, as well as express how the writers see the world of implicit communication.
2. Encourage your clients to talk about and monitor their use of implicit language. Very often their communication difficulties with others in their environments are only partly related to their explicit language.
3. Attend a mime event to sensitize yourself to the subtlety and power of implicit language.
4. With a friend practice transmitting and receiving implicit messages that

are congruent or incongruent with explicit messages you are trying to express.

Suggested Readings

COREY, M. S., & COREY, G. (1989). *Becoming a helper.* Pacific Grove, CA: Brooks/Cole. Chapter 4 contains a useful section dealing with nonverbal communication in the transmittal of human values.

CORMIER, W. H., & CORMIER, L. S. (1991). *Interviewing strategies for helpers.* Pacific Grove, CA: Brooks/Cole. Chapter 4 includes an excellent treatment of all forms of nonverbal behavior.

D'AUGELLI, A. R., D'AUGELLI, J. F., & DANISH, S. J. (1981). *Helping others.* Pacific Grove, CA: Brooks/Cole. Chapter 3 provides a good overview of nonverbal behavior, including such matters as the importance of dress and physical setting on counseling.

EGAN, G. (1990). *The skilled helper.* Pacific Grove, CA: Brooks/Cole. Chapter 5 offers an overview of nonverbal behavior within the general framework of attending skills as used by the counselor.

MEHRABIAN, A. (1981). *Silent messages: Implicit communication of emotions and attitudes.* Belmont, CA: Wadsworth. This book is an invaluable resource for the student of implicit language. Although not written from a counseling perspective, it presents much information appropriate for counselors or counselors-in-training.

OKUN, B. F. (1992). *Effective helping: interviewing and counseling techniques.* Pacific Grove, CA: Brooks/Cole. Chapter 3 includes a useful section on nonverbal communications, and Appendix A includes a valuable guide for observers of nonverbal processes.

SHERTZER, B., & STONE, S. C. (1980). *Fundamentals of counseling.* Boston: Houghton Mifflin. Section 2 provides a good integration of verbal and nonverbal communication techniques and principles.

PART II

Summary of Key Points

1. Counseling encompasses beliefs or theoretical orientations as well as skills. An understanding of both is vitally important.
2. In counseling, communication is purposeful, directed toward achieving *something.*
3. The communication between client and counselor is interdependent. How each communicates with the other depends in part on how the other communicates in turn.
4. Different orientations to counseling dictate differing goals for the communication between client and counselor.
5. To alter the pattern of your communication with others, you must learn and practice alternative ways of responding.
6. A listening statement is a simple declarative assertion followed by an *implied question,* "You said this or meant this . . . didn't you?"
7. Listening is used to collect data, build the counseling relationship, and facilitate change by clients.
8. Listening statements vary in how closely they parallel the words spoken by a client.
9. Multiple listening or summarizing is often used to structure or refocus a conversation.
10. Questioning is a request for information from the client.
11. A closed question seeks a specific answer. An open question allows for an interpretation of the question by the answerer.
12. Questioning is used to collect data, build relationships, and facilitate positive change.
13. Listening is frequently used in conjunction with questioning to collect information.

14. Coaching provides advice to others about how they should behave or feel in particular sets of circumstances.
15. Coaching provides factual information, helps to build the counseling relationship, and fosters positive change by the client.
16. Coaching statements contain implied negative inferences that form the basis for the advice given.
17. Inferring communicates an opinion about what another has done or thought or intends to do or thinks.
18. Inferring is used to build the counseling relationship and to foster positive change by the client.
19. It is usually effective to use listening to follow up on the responses that others voice to your coaching and inferring statements.
20. Supporting statements assert interest, commiseration, backing, compassion, or sympathy to others.
21. Supporting statements can help to build the counseling relationship and prepare the client to deal constructively with issues that he or she confronts.
22. Implicit communication comprises body language and meanings conveyed by the structure of verbal language and inflection.
23. The interpretation of implicit language is culturally and geographically bound.
24. You communicate the composite of your verbal and implicit communication to others.

References and Additional Resources

ANDERSEN, B., & ANDERSON, W. (1985). Client perceptions of counselors using positive and negative self-involving statements. *Journal of Counseling Psychology, 32,* 462–465.

BARKER, L. L. (1971). *Listening behavior.* Englewood Cliffs, NJ: Prentice-Hall.

BARTH, R. P., & GAMBRILL, E. (1984). Learning to interview: The quality of training opportunities. *Clinical Supervisor, 2,* 3–14.

BATSON, C. D., O'QUIN, K., & PYCH, V. (1982). An attribution theory analysis of trained helpers' inferences about clients' needs. In T. A. Wills (Ed.), *Basic processes in helping relationships.* Orlando, FL: Academic Press.

BEIER, E. G., & YOUNG, D. M. (1984). *The silent language of psychotherapy: Social reinforcement of unconscious processes* (2nd ed.). New York: Aldine.

BENJAMIN, A. (1969). *The helping interview.* Boston: Houghton Mifflin.

BERNSTEIN, L., BERNSTEIN, R., & DANA, R. A. (1974). *Interviewing: A guide for health professionals.* New York: Appleton-Century-Crofts.

BINGHAM, W. V. D., MOORE, B. V., & GUSTAD, J. W. (1959). *How to interview.* New York: Harper & Row.

BITTNER, J. R. (1983). *Each other: An introduction to interpersonal communication.* Englewood Cliffs, NJ: Prentice-Hall.

BOOK, H. E. (1988). Empathy: Misconceptions and misuses in psychotherapy. *American Journal of Psychiatry, 145,* 420–424.

BRAATEN, L. J. (1986). Thirty years with Rogers' necessary and sufficient conditions of therapeutic personality change: A personal evaluation. *Person-Centered Review, 1,* 37–50.

BRAMMER, L. E., SHOSTROM, E. L., & ABREGO, P. J. (1989). *Therapeutic psychology: Fundamentals of counseling and psychotherapy* (5th ed.). Englewood Cliffs, NJ: Prentice-Hall.

BROWN, J. E., & SLEE, P. T. (1986). Paradoxical strategies: The ethics of intervention. *Professional Psychology: Research and Practice, 17,* 487–491.

BURKE, J. F. (1989). *Contemporary approaches to psychotherapy and counseling.* Pacific Grove, CA: Brooks/Cole.

CANTRIL, H. (1940). Experiments in the wording of questions. *Public Opinion Quarterly, 4,* 330.

CLAIBORN, C. D., WARD, S. R., & STRONG, S. R. (1981). Effects of congruence between counselor interpretations and client beliefs. *Journal of Counseling Psychology, 28,* 101–109.

COREY, G. (1986). *Theory and practice of counseling and psychotherapy.* Pacific Grove, CA: Brooks/Cole.

COREY, G. (1990). *Theory and practice of group counseling.* Pacific Grove, CA: Brooks/Cole.

COREY, M. S., & COREY, G. (1989). *Becoming a helper.* Pacific Grove, CA: Brooks/Cole.

CORMIER, W. H., & CORMIER, L. S. (1991). *Interviewing strategies for helpers.* Pacific Grove, CA: Brooks/Cole.

CRABLE, R. E. (1980). *One to another: A guidebook for interpersonal communication.* New York: Harper & Row.

D'AUGELLI, A. R., D'AUGELLI, J. F., & DANISH, S. J. (1981). *Helping others.* Pacific Grove, CA: Brooks/Cole.

DEVITO, J. A. (1983). *The interpersonal communication book.* New York: Harper & Row.

DOHRENWEND, B. S. (1965). Some effects of open and closed questions on respondent's answers. *Human Organization, 24,* 175–184.

EGAN, G. (1973). *Face to face.* Pacific Grove, CA: Brooks/Cole.

EGAN, G. (1990). *The skilled helper.* Pacific Grove, CA: Brooks/Cole.

EMMERT, P., & EMMERT, V. (1983). *Interpersonal communication.* Dubuque, IA: Wm. C. Brown.

EVANS, D. R., HEARN, M. T., UHLEMANN, M. R., & IVEY, A. E. (1989). *Essential interviewing.* Pacific Grove, CA: Brooks/Cole.

FLEURIDAS, C., NELSON, T. S., & ROSENTHAL, D. M. (1986). The evolution of circular questions: Training family therapists. *Journal of Marital and Family Therapy, 12,* 113–128.

FRETZ, B. R., CORN, R., TUEMMLER, J. M., & BELLET, W. (1979). Counselor nonverbal behaviors and client evaluations. *Journal of Counseling Psychology, 26,* 304–311.

GELSO, C. J., & CARTER, J. A. (1985). The relationship in counseling and psychotherapy: Components, consequences, and theoretical antecedents. *Counseling Psychologist, 13,* 155–243.

GERRARD, B. A., BONIFACE, W. J., & LOVE, B. H. (1980). *Interpersonal skills for health professionals.* Reston, VA: Reston.

GLADDING, S. T. (1988). *Counseling: A comprehensive profession.* Columbus, OH: Merrill.

GLADSTEIN, G. (1983). Understanding empathy: Integrating counseling, developmental, and social psychology perspectives. *Journal of Counseling Psychology, 30,* 467–482.

GOLDHABER, G. M. (1983). *Organizational communication.* Dubuque, IA: Wm. C. Brown.

GORDEN, R. L. (1980). *Interviewing: Strategy, techniques, and tactics.* Pacific Grove, CA: Brooks/Cole.

HAMILTON, C., PARKER, C., & SMITH, D. D. (1982). *Communication for results.* Belmont, CA: Wadsworth.

HARPER, R. G., WIENS, A. N., & MATARAZZO, J. D. (1978). *Nonverbal communication: The state of the art.* New York: Wiley.

HAYNES, S. N., & JENSEN, B. J. (1979). The interview as a behavioral assessment instrument. *Behavioral Assessment, 1,* 97–106.

HELLER, K., DAVIS, J. D., & MYERS, R. A. (1966). The effects of interviewer style in a standardized interview. *Journal of Counseling Psychology, 30,* 501–508.

HERSEN, M., & TURNER, S. M. (Eds.). (1985). *Diagnostic interviewing.* New York: Plenum Press.

HILL, C. E., & GORMALLY, J. (1977). Effects of reflection, restatement, probe, and nonverbal behaviors on client affect. *Journal of Counseling Psychology, 24,* 92–97.

HILL, C. E., SIEGELMAN, L., GRONSKY, B. R., STURNIOLO, F., & FRETZ, B. R. (1981). Nonverbal communication and counseling outcome. *Journal of Counseling Psychology, 28,* 203–212.

IVEY, A. E. (1988). *Intentional interviewing and counseling.* Pacific Grove, CA: Brooks/Cole.

JONES, J. E. (1967). Helping relationship response tendencies and occupational affiliation. *Personnel and Guidance Journal,* 671–675.

KAHN, R. L., & CANNELL, C. F. (1982). *The dynamics of interviewing.* New York: Wiley.

KNAPP, M. L. (1978). *Nonverbal communication in human interaction.* New York: Holt, Rinehart & Winston.

KRIVONOS, P. D., & KNAPP, M. L. (1975). Initiating communication: What do you say when you say hello? *Central States Speech Journal, 26,* 115–125.

LAGEMANN, J. K. (1965). The delicate art of asking questions. *Reader's Digest, 86* (June), 87–91.

LEWIS, J. A., & LEWIS, M. D. (1986). *Counseling programs for employees in the workplace.* Pacific Grove, CA: Brooks/Cole.

LONG, L., PARADISE, L. V., & LONG, T. J. (1981). *Questioning: Skills for the helping process.* Pacific Grove, CA: Brooks/Cole.

MARTIN, D. G. (1983). *Counseling and therapy skills.* Pacific Grove, CA: Brooks/Cole.

MEHRABIAN, A. (1981). *Silent messages: Implicit communication of emotions and attitudes.* Belmont, CA: Wadsworth.

MEIER, S. T. (1989). *The elements of counseling.* Pacific Grove, CA: Brooks/Cole.

MUCHINSKY, P. (1990). *Psychology applied to work.* Pacific Grove, CA: Brooks/Cole.

NISBETT, R., & ROSS, L. (Eds.). (1980). *Human inference: Strategies and shortcomings of social judgement*. Englewood Cliffs, NJ: Prentice-Hall.

OKUN, B. F. (1992). *Effective helping: Interviewing and counseling techniques*. Pacific Grove, CA: Brooks/Cole.

ORLINSKY, D. E., & HOWARD, K. I. (1986). Process and outcome in psychotherapy. In S. L. Garfield & A. E. Bergin (Eds.), *Handbook of psychotherapy and behavior change* (3rd ed., pp. 311–381). New York: Wiley.

PAYNE, S. L. (1951). *The art of asking questions*. Princeton, NJ: Princeton University Press.

PEARSON, J. C. (1983). *Interpersonal communication*. Glenview, IL: Scott, Foresman.

PENN, P. (1982). Circular questioning. *Family Process, 21*, 267–280.

PHARES, E. J. (1992). *Clinical psychology* (4th ed.). Pacific Grove, CA: Brooks/Cole.

PHILLIPS, G. M., & WOOD, J. T. (1983). *Communication and human relationships: The study of interpersonal communication*. New York: Macmillan.

PORTER, E. H. (1950). *An introduction to therapeutic counseling*. Boston: Houghton Mifflin.

ROLOFF, M. C. (1981). *Interpersonal communication: The social exchange*. London: Sage.

RUFFNER, M., & BURGOON, M. (1981). *Interpersonal communication*. New York: Holt, Rinehart & Winston.

SACK, R. T. (1985). On giving advice. *AMHCA Journal, 7*, 127–132.

SEAY, T. A., & ALTEKRUSE, M. K. (1979). Verbal and nonverbal behavior in judgements of facilitative conditions. *Journal of Counseling Psychology, 26*, 108–119.

SELBY, J. W., & CALHOUN, L. G. (1980). Psychodidactics: An undervalued and underdeveloped treatment tool of psychological intervention. *Professional Psychology, 11*, 236–241.

SELTZER, J., & HOWE, L. W. (1987). Poor listening habits: Identifying and improving them. In *The 1987 annual: Developing human resources*. San Diego: University Associates.

SHERER, M., & ROGERS, R. (1980). Effects of therapist's nonverbal communication on rated skill and effectiveness. *Journal of Clinical Psychology, 26*, 696–700.

SHERTZER, B., & STONE, S. C. (1980). *Fundamentals of counseling*. Boston: Houghton Mifflin.

STEWART, C. J., & CASH, W. B. (1985). *Interviewing principles and practices*. Dubuque, IA: Wm. C. Brown.

STEWART, J. (1982). *Bridges not walls: A book about interpersonal communication*. Boston: Addison-Wesley.

STONE, G. (1986). *Counseling psychology: Perspectives and functions*. Pacific Grove, CA: Brooks/Cole.

TEYBER, E. (1992). *Interpersonal process in psychotherapy*. Pacific Grove, CA: Brooks/Cole.

THOMPSON, C. L., & RUDOLPH, L. B. (1992). *Counseling children*. Pacific Grove, CA: Brooks/Cole.

TOMM, K. (1987). Interventive interviewing: Part I. Strategizing as a fourth guideline for the therapist. *Family Process, 26*, 3–13.

TOMM, K. (1987). Interventive interviewing: Part II. Reflexive questioning as a means to enable self healing. *Family Process, 26*, 167–183.

WACHTEL, P. L. (1980). What should we say to our patients? On the wording of therapists' comments. *Psychotherapy: Theory, Research, and Practice, 17,* 183–188.
WALSH, A. (1988). *Understanding, assessing, and counseling the criminal justice client.* Pacific Grove, CA: Brooks/Cole.
WATZLAWICK, P. (1978). *The language of change: Elements of therapeutic communication.* New York: Basic Books.
WOLVIN, A. D., & COAKLEY, C. G. (1982). *Listening.* Dubuque, IA: Wm. C. Brown.
WOODY, R. H., HANSEN, J. C., & ROSSBERG, R. H. (1989). *Counseling psychology: Strategies and services.* Pacific Grove, CA: Brooks/Cole.
YOUNG, D. W. (1980). Meanings of counselor nonverbal gestures: Fixed or interpretive? *Journal of Counseling Psychology, 27,* 447–452.
ZUNIN, L., & ZUNIN, N. (1975). *Contact: The first four minutes.* Los Angeles: Nash.

PART III

Practical Counseling

Learning Objectives

Part III deals with the kinds of everyday issues and concerns you will confront in your role as a counselor, and pays particular attention to those that are most common early in your career. For many of you, these experiences occur during your training, in practically oriented courses, or in on-the-job supervised practicums. After you complete this part of the text, you should be able to

- identify practical alternatives in commencing a counseling relationship;
- identify the types of issues that you will confront in your first meetings with clients and viable means to address the issues;
- integrate your knowledge of communication skills and counseling orientations in thinking about how you will work through the counseling process with clients;
- recognize the types of blocks or impediments you will confront in counseling and the means that you can use to overcome them;
- identify the means that you can use to move your counseling from initial meeting to conclusion;
- recognize the types of problems that clients are likely to bring forward in counseling, together with suitable means that you will use to deal with these matters.

CHAPTER 12

The Initial Interview

The initial interview is a time of uncertainty and anxiety for both client and counselor, particularly the novice counselor. For the client, counseling may be a new experience, may involve an admission of personal defeat, and may be partially or wholly involuntary. For the novice counselor, even though counseling usually occurs on home turf, it is a time of apprehensiveness over what to do and how to do it. You want to appear credible, establish a workable relationship, and deal effectively with whatever the client brings forward. For you and the client, the first counseling session is a time of exploring and learning.

During the first session you and your client get acquainted, and you establish the "ground rules." The interview is of great value because first contacts are likely to leave lasting impressions on both parties.

In counseling interviews, as in other types of interviews, setting is important. Privacy is vital, as are physical arrangements, such as chair or desk placement, which bear on the development of a good relationship. At the very least, arrangements should not adversely impinge on the process or outcome.

Physical arrangements conducive to good counseling do not necessarily mean that if you were the client, the setting would ease your mind. For instance, you the counselor might be most comfortable in an environment that some of your clients would find threatening or unsuitable. The client may expect a setting akin to that of other professionals they have dealt with in the past—doctors, lawyers, and the like: a setting that is neither stiffly formal nor so informal that the unwritten rules of interpersonal encounter are blurred.

Of course, it is impossible to create a space and an ambience that all clients will fancy. Typically, furniture placement is conducive to counseling but not noticeably so. This allows the main environmental variable—*you*—to change and react according to the demands of the situation, not to the room.

Some good starting points for physical arrangements and your initial behavior are listed below. Keep in mind that these are only starting points and that you must be alert to the client's reactions to everything you do as a counselor.

- Greet your clients by name and introduce yourself in a friendly manner. Use a simple greeting such as "Master Splinter, I'm Rock Steady. Come on in."
- Most clients probably expect to shake hands when you first greet them. Your grip should be solid, not crushing or limp.
- Arrange your office so clients can choose seating from among two or three alternatives. This allows them to establish their preferred distances. Leave a daily calendar or a personal item on your chair as a "reservation."
- Smile. Show that you are looking forward to being of help.

How you change and react during the initial interview depends upon your perceptions of how the interview is affecting the client, and upon how you think the goals you and the client want to accomplish through counseling are being framed. As your perceptions of what is happening form, your behavior modifies accordingly.

Goals

There are two types of goals to focus on during the initial interview. The first type has to do with your client; the second, with you. Goals that affect your client refer to reasonable expectations of change on his or her part after the session is concluded. Although different counseling orientations will impose expectations beyond those listed below, your client ought to depart with *at least* the following:

1. an understanding of what counseling is all about, including a reasonable expectation of its outcomes;
2. the beginnings of feelings of trust and safety in discussing matters with you;
3. a belief in your interest in him or her and expressed concerns;
4. a belief in your competence as a facilitator of development; and
5. a positive orientation toward counseling that promotes an enthusiastic approach to it.

You should also pursue several goals in your own behalf throughout the session:

6. an understanding of the issues that bring your client to counseling;
7. an understanding of the expectations that your client has for counseling and for you as a counselor;
8. an assessment of your ability or inability to deal with the counseling issues that confront you;
9. an assessment of the commitment of your client to change; and
10. an understanding of counseling processes and techniques you could use in subsequent sessions.

The first-session goals are ambitious, and important to keep in mind as you and your client get to know each other. They will seldom be pursued directly. For example, you might not have explicitly discussed your orientation toward counseling, but then do so if your client declares firmly that it is up to you to solve the problems brought to you. You might not have expressly asked your client about a willingness to change, but by the end of the session you should be able to declare your opinion on the likelihood of changing as a result of counseling.

Opening the Interview

The first counseling interview with a new client is like the first interview in other contexts that you and your client have experienced—employment interviews, police interrogation, survey interviews, and the like. Because the tone established at the beginning of an interview often persists throughout, the first few moments are critical. As in a footrace, a good start does not guarantee a good finish, but a poor start may preclude one.

In any new interpersonal situation you make many inferences based upon the minute-by-minute information you collect. At first meeting you may observe an unusual facial expression, a tepid handshake, and a nervous laugh, and hence infer that the person is fearful, perhaps stupid, or deceitful. Your inferences are your own and may be very different from the inferences of others meeting the same person.

In unfamiliar situations your inference-generating tendencies are exaggerated. You "read things into" your observations much more than you may do in situations where you are at ease. In accustomed situations you remain alert to the unusual, but the inferences you drew earlier are still serving you in good stead.

Counseling is but one example of an interpersonal situation that is ripe for generating inferences. As in any new interpersonal situation, during the first few minutes of a counseling session your client forms many inferences. Accordingly, what you do then dramatically influences client opinion of you and of counseling. To recite the overworked sales maxim, "You never get a second chance to make a first impression!"

A distinction must be made between *collecting* and *using* information. Regarding the goals you have for your client, you want to know to what extent they have been realized. Regarding the goals you have for yourself, you want to collect data that will allow you to have an informed opinion. In both cases, you will not *necessarily* take immediate action based upon this knowledge. For example, you might collect information throughout the first session that would lead you to infer that it is unlikely your client will change. You do not have to confront the client with the inference nor need you abandon counseling him or her altogether. It does mean that you can use the information in an appropriate way, in a way that would be impossible if you hadn't collected it in the first place.

A ten-step generic flowchart for counseling was outlined in Chapter 4. The first step requires that you state the macro, or overall, purposes of counseling, as well as the micro purposes that are appropriate for the particular session you are handling. The ten generic goals listed above are specific examples of the micro purposes for an initial counseling session, and therefore are handled in accord with the flowchart.

The ten generic goals, or micro purposes, for the initial counseling session must be kept in mind when you initiate contact with any of your clients. Even though you may not always pursue the goals directly, you must do *something* to facilitate the inferences you want your clients to form. To help you better understand the options available toward that end, some appropriate techniques that you can use are presented below. The techniques conform to step three in the flowchart in Chapter 4.

Client-Based Goals

1. Understanding Your Approach to Counseling

Clients have many different ideas about counseling and counselors, all of which depend to one degree or another upon such factors as prior experience with counselors, beliefs in the opinions of others, and contact with soap operas and other manifestations of pop psychology. Some equate counseling with teaching, and hope thereby to find answers to their troubles. Some see counseling as a chance to "pour out their hearts" and do not expect much more than that relief. Others regard counseling as an opportunity to validate past actions or future intentions. It is rare to find clients without preformed notions about counseling no matter how willing or unwilling they are to be open with you.

You can help your clients to understand your approach to counseling by a variety of means. Sometimes you will do so overtly, as a coach reveals a football play to the players. Sometimes you will do so subtly, in much the same way that chess strategy becomes evident to an observer during the course of a game.

- One excellent way to communicate your counseling orientation to clients is to be congruent: *live your orientation.* It is confusing if you espouse the necessity for clients to make their own decisions and then turn around and tell them what to do.
- Use situational responses by clients as points from which to inform or reinforce what counseling is all about. For example, if a client says, "I just can't make a decision. Which pizza should I order?" you might initially respond with a listening style: "Michaelangelo, you're so confused about which pizza to order that you've given up on finding a solution yourself . . ." Following a response to your listening statement, you might make a coaching statement such as "I can't really make a decision for you Michaelangelo. I can help you to examine your choices and maybe that will help you to see your way more clearly." In most instances, the message needs to be reinforced throughout the initial session.
- It may be helpful to include a *brief* statement of how you counsel as part of your introductory remarks. You might say, "Michaelangelo, my clients often find it helpful when I explain to them what it is I do, how I might be able to help them. As a counselor, I try to help you to understand yourself better. I want you to understand the alternatives available to you as well as their implications." However, do not think that such remarks ensure an understanding of what counseling is about. Clients are often very distraught and self-concerned during the initial interview and may not hear what you say, no matter how well put.
- Support actions by your clients that are in accord with what you believe counseling to be about. For example, if your client moves closer to making an informed decision, a positive inferring statement from you might be appropriate. You might say, "Michaelangelo, you've worked hard to decide which pizza to order. I think you'll find that you're more satisfied with your decision than if you had just ordered the first one that came to your mind."
- With clients, reinforce the principle that counseling is action oriented. Although actions vary from perspective to perspective, your clients should have the impression that *something* will change as a result of counseling.

2. Developing Feelings of Trust and Safety

Counseling often involves discussing feelings and matters that are otherwise private, an unusual dropping of reserve with someone newly met. Although clients may be motivated to enter counseling as a means to ameliorate pain, it does not necessarily follow that they will be *initially receptive* to the openness deemed appropriate.

Clients' feelings of trust and safety do not just happen. They grow, usually slowly, and they are influenced by what you do as a counselor.

You cannot impose trust, but you can create an atmosphere in which clients will be more disposed to risk self-disclosure. This advice parallels social rules of encounter governing other situations, such as within a family or a love or friend relationship.

A goodly number of techniques and practices promote an atmosphere of trust and safety for your clients, the following among them:

- *Do not violate the trust or confidence of clients.* Nothing worries a client more than hearing a counselor relate some piece of information to which the counselor has been made privy. Be wary of telling "battle stories" to enhance your credibility or build up your image, even if they do not include names or other identifying details.
- *Handle the initial client disclosures with care.* It is usual for clients to take tentative risks or to test you with mildly personal information before they go into more intimate matters. Be cautious about communicating inferences, even positive ones, during the first few minutes of encounters with clients.
- *Listen to your clients.* Even within counseling orientations that do not favor listening, active listening can be a worthwhile tool during the early stages of the initial interview. A frequent inference we make about persons who listen to us is that they are interested in us, that it is safe for us to speak freely. Although listening may be antithetical to your desire to appear as an "expert," as someone who can help clients in the direct way that many of them expect, the risk of a negative perception's developing on the part of clients is minimal.
- *Make plain your policy and that of your agency on confidentiality.* Do not guarantee more than you can legitimately offer. It is better to stop someone from saying something before he or she says it than to explain after the fact why you cannot hold confidential something already said.

3. Telegraphing a Concern for Your Clients

The relationship that should develop between counselor and client is facilitated by the belief of the client that the counselor cares about him or her. The belief is sometimes referred to as *unconditional positive regard* by person-centered counselors (Egan, 1990). Of course, the belief is a client inference, but a counselor can do much to foster such a helpful inference.

Showing concern for your clients is very much akin to instilling feelings of trust and safety in them, the subject of the previous section. What you do not do is as important as what you do.

- Not all clients will infer concern from the same behavior on your part. What one client may see as concern, another client may see as aloofness, and another as excessive chumminess. This means that you must see telegraphing concern as a *result you want to achieve* not as one or more things you actually do. You must keep your perceptive "antenna" up to collect the information that will tell you if what you are doing to show concern is actually working.

- Different ethnic and social groups show concern for others in different ways. You will be more successful in telegraphing concern to your clients who are members of a particular group if you use behaviors that group interprets as showing concern than if you use behaviors that would demonstrate concern to you if you were the client. For example, in counseling delinquent inner-city teenaged boys, some success has been achieved by a "tough-love" stance on the part of the counselor. The rationale seems to be that the counselor cares enough to be firm, something that many adults in the boys' lives in the past have not been. The same actions by the counselor might be interpreted quite differently by members of other groups.
- In counseling and many other areas concern is often shown by listening. It is almost always difficult, however, to listen without giving evidence of disagreeing with statements that conflict with your own values. In fact, some clients will "test" you with such statements just to see how they affect you. A good point to keep uppermost in your mind is that clients should find it impossible to tell from your listening responses whether you agree with their opinions.
- Some counselors mistake displaying sympathy for the telegraphing of concern. You will recall that one of the potentially negative side effects of a supporting communication style is that clients may feel you are responding stereotypically, feigning interest in them. To show concern, it is usually safer to listen than to commiserate openly.

4. Demonstrating Your Competence

In self-initiated counseling, clients come to see you because they think doing so will help them. They believe that what you do will be beneficial. This is the same type of believing that steers you to a particular physician, hair stylist, or carpenter.

As a counselor, you are always walking the fine line between the role of the expert, a godlike figure who usurps the responsibility of clients to deal constructively with their own problems, and the role of an amateur for whom positive outcomes are random events. You want your clients to believe that you are competent to assist them, but you do not want them to be overly dependent on you for what they do and how they do it.

In the initial counseling session, work at generating the inference in the mind of your client that you are proficient at what you do, that the process you are embarking on together will ultimately be helpful. When you accomplish this, the client may invest enough of himself or herself to be helped.

- *Believe in yourself.* You are a trained professional. You have proprietary skills and understandings. If your approach is uncertain, your clients may infer that you are incompetent. Exhibit purpose and confidence in your stock of knowledge and abilities.
- *Do not manifest shock or astonishment at what you hear from clients.* Maintain a professional perspective that allows you to listen in a clinical—but not detached—manner. Your own feelings should not interfere with the course of therapy.
- *Dress and conduct yourself in ways that connote professionalism.* Although standards in dress and demeanor vary from agency to agency, be aware that your appearance conveys a message. If the impression you make on the client is not on the plus side, everything else you do throughout the initial session will need to be especially effective to make up for a poor start.
- *Master the body of factual matters that pertain to your counseling practice.* Whether you deal with battered spouses, financially insolvent clients, teenagers with career concerns, or some other problem area, you should know the resources in your community and farther afield that can be brought to bear.

5. Telegraphing a Positive Orientation

Does having your teeth drilled by a dour dentist add to the pain? Does having your hair cut by a sullen stylist lessen the pleasure of a salon visit? Does buying provisions from a glum grocer add another dimension of cost? Yes, yes, and yes. In the same vein, clients want to be served by an upbeat counselor and to have a positive experience. Improvement is more likely if they approach counseling as a potentially beneficial step rather than as an ordeal. Counseling can often be hard work for counselor and client alike, but, it need not be a time of grim endurance.

- Enthusiasm about what you are doing can be contagious and infect your clients. Be the part. Smile! Bless the world with your good grace and cheer. If you cannot be genuinely happy in counseling, perhaps you have made an incorrect career choice.
- Encourage your clients to look at the positive aspects in their lives' environments, rather than solely at the downside. This does not signify that you discount the problems that bring your clients to your door but that the clients ought not to dwell unduly on them. Encouragement is often accomplished by summarizing statements wherein you focus on what

has gone right as well as what has gone wrong. For example, "Michaelangelo, you were very confused about which pizza to order. These feelings sometimes overwhelmed you to the point that you could think of nothing but pizza. However, the more you dwelt on the decision, the more you knew you needed to do something constructive. And that's what brought you in to see me . . ."

- Wear bright, cheerful attire. Sunny colors in office furnishings and decor help to minimize gloom. It is no accident that professionals from obstetricians to undertakers present themselves and surroundings in ways that reinforce the images they want to convey to their clientele.

Counselor-Based Goals

6. Understanding Precipitating Issues

Almost all orientations to counseling require the counselor to understand the issues that bring clients to counseling. Although such understanding unfolds over the entire counseling process, it begins during the initial session.

During the opening moments of the initial session, some clients lay out the issues that brought them to you with remarkable clarity and candor. Other clients will be equally frank but about issues that subsequently prove to be related only indirectly to the real issues that are troubling them. Still others will be oblique, obtuse, or deceptive; such behavior is usually more pronounced in involuntary clients.

A cliché in counseling has it that the issues first presented by clients are seldom the impelling issues. There is a kernel of truth in the cliché, but only a kernel. As a counselor, you must *validate* your inferences about the issues presented. Validation is important whether the issues are clothed in clear and apparently unambiguous language or in confused and perhaps misleading language.

- Do not act upon your inferences without first verifying them, at least in some fashion. A good first step is to state your inferences to the client, inviting reaction. For example, you might say, "Michaelangelo, you're concerned that Master Splinter isn't quite the mentor he used to be, that his ideas were fine for the sewer but that they can't quite cut it in the real world . . ." As with all listening statements, it requires your client to reprocess what has been said and seeks for a confirming reply.
- Verify important inferences through multiple means. For example, in dealing with the potential for spousal abuse, you might initially verify your inferences through listening. You might say, "You feel unhappy because your husband sometimes hits you, pushes you around . . ." Subject to a positive response, you might validate your initial inference

by questioning and further listening. This will help you to understand the extent and intensity of the problem your client faces. You might say, "Think back through the past three weeks. How many times did he hit you or push you? What did he do?"

- Do not forget client feelings in your eagerness to collect factual information. Beginning counselors sometimes treat the initial interview simply as a fact-finding exercise. It is at least equally important for you to gain a perspective on feelings relative to the issues at stake. If you do not do so, you may be communicating the unspoken message that only factual matters are important and your client may resist sharing feelings with you.
- Verify problems or issues even when they are expressed point blank. Occasionally, clients make statements that are untrue or far less definite or significant than they indicate. For example, the outburst "I hate him! How could anybody love somebody who treated 'em like that?" sounds absolute. But it may not be. It could be verified by an out-of-phase listening statement: "You love him, even though he hurt you badly . . ." Or by a question: "Are you telling me that you hate him or that you love him?" In any event, it is prudent to verify any initial inference you make before going on.
- In verifying the inferences you make about client issues remember to look for *relationships between variables* or *relationships between circumstances* that ought or ought not to be associated. Say you hypothesize that a client is depressed in the clinical sense of the term based upon a self-report; look for information that is often associated with depression. For example, withdrawal from social contact, weight gain or loss, or repeated periods of tearfulness. Individuals seldom manifest all of the characteristics typically associated with a particular counseling concern, but it is common to manifest more than one.
- As in the data-collection processes of all other professions, *changes from the ordinary* are important. For example, a person who is depressed today and who has a history of depression probably manifests a different kind of concern than a person new to depression.
- Remember that attempting to understand the concerns of your clients is meant to *lead somewhere*. As stated earlier, there is no point in being more specific in the attempt than you will be in your reactions to what you have learned. (If you would do the same thing for a headache and an earache, there is little to be gained by ascertaining if the condition is one or the other.)

7. Understand Your Clients' Expectations

An earlier point asserted the necessity for you to educate clients about counseling. It is equally important for you to understand the expectations that your clients have for you as a counselor and for the counseling relationship. This does not mean that you change who you are and what you do to comport with client expectations, but you are probably better off knowing the expectations so you can deal constructively with differences between them and reality as you know it.

- The simplest but not necessarily the best way to find out about your clients' expectations is to ask them. "Michaelangelo, what do you expect will change for you by coming to see me?" "Donatello, how do you think that meeting with me will help you to deal with your problems with Splinter?" Keep in mind that some clients will be affronted by a direct approach. They may reason that you are telling them their expectations are wrong.
- Clients are more likely to communicate their expectations to you indirectly than directly. They may ask, "What should I do?" and thereby indicate that they think your role is that of sage. They may respond freely only when asked a direct question, thereby relegating you to the role of interrogator. Or they may continually evade any hint of a sense of responsibility for their lives, thereby treating you as an acquiescent sponge.
- Be consistent or, at least, be inconsistent on a predictable basis in your dealings with clients. If you are willing to guide clients on some occasions, it is difficult to do otherwise on other occasions.

8. Counselor, Know Thyself!

Cabinetmakers do not customarily frame houses. Heart surgeons do not deliver babies. Family lawyers do not handle corporate accounts. And only foolish counselors think that they can handle clients with any and all kinds of personal problems.

Once you have a reasonable perspective on the concerns that motivate your clients to seek counseling, you must make professional decisions about your ability to address the concerns. At one end of the continuum, most counselors employed by counseling agencies would feel inadequate to deal with severely schizophrenic clients. At the other end of the continuum, most such counselors would probably feel competent to deal with clients undergoing the breakdown of a personal relationship. Most clients you will encounter in your day-to-day work as a counselor will range between these two extremes.

Professional ethics and legal liability mandate that you not deal with professional matters beyond the scope of your ability. But the limits to competency are ill-defined. You cannot handle all the problems presented by your clients, but at the start of your career you may feel that you cannot handle any of them. Both extremes are inaccurate.

- Do not be afraid to ask others for help. There is nothing wrong with using the initial meeting with a client purely as an introductory session. There is no requirement that you immediately begin to deal with the problems the client brings forward. Seeking assistance in interpretation or approach is integral to your growth as a counselor.
- Be prepared to stretch your capability. There is a first time for everything you do, and all beginning professionals must be prepared to take a degree of tempered risk.
- Acquaint yourself with reputable referral possibilities. The more familiar you are with community resources relative to a wide variety of concerns, the more prepared you are to deal with a broad range of counseling situations.
- Be aware of your own values and their influence on your counseling. Abortion, incest, battering, theft, adultery, and child molestation are situations you may confront as a counselor. Undoubtedly, your values have led to convictions with respect to them, convictions that may be very different from those of your clients. Remember that during counseling, your role is to *understand and assist* your clients, not to be confrontational. If you cannot set aside your personal opinions when dealing with clients professing or living disparate values, you will find counseling to be very trying.

9. Assessing Client Motivation to Change

Counseling is *change oriented.* Change involves thoughts, feelings, and behavior. At best, change is difficult and stressful for clients. At worst, acutely painful. Still, without change, counseling is little more than a trifling exercise for client and counselor alike.

During the initial counseling session, it is important that you ascertain the extent to which your client is willing or motivated to change his or her beliefs, feelings, and behaviors. Although the level of readiness does not remain stationary as counseling progresses, knowing its base point will help you to *pace* yourself in the counseling process. For example, if a client is unwilling to change, the intractability must first be addressed, not the nature or extent of any particular change.

- Although a history of *demonstrated willingness* to change is not a perfect predictor of future willingness, it is a good indicator. Find out how your clients have weathered other situations calling for flexibility. Have they been willing to take risks? Do they have a history of changing more than whining? Use questioning and listening styles to investigate.
- Listen carefully to your clients' analyses of their concerns. To what extent do they take personal responsibility? To what extent do they expect or want others to accommodate to them?

- When your clients talk about troublesome issues in their lives, do they freely discuss possible improvements to be wrought by themselves or do they skirt topics that might entail some rearranging of the status quo? If you introduce the potential for change, is it embraced?

10. Understanding Your Options

One reason that you collect information during initial interviews is to help you to refine and delineate your actions. Counseling orientations provide *options* in regard to processes you employ and in techniques. Information allows you to make a considered match between problem and remedy. Which in turn requires an intimate knowledge of the counseling orientation within which you operate. Vacillation in deciding what to do does not augur well for a beneficial outcome.

- Be wary of *interpreting* client concerns only in terms of what *you* can do to help your clients deal with those concerns. Some counselors speak of interesting techniques they have "up their sleeves," and do so in such a manner that it is evident the techniques are "one size fits all." The *concerns of the client* should be uppermost, dictating the counseling processes and techniques that are put into service.
- Train yourself to think in terms of *options* as you collect information about clients. Options pertain to alternative hypotheses about the concerns of your clients as well as alternatives about what you might do to address the concerns.
- Keep current with the research literature on problem areas within your purview. Much of such literature centers on *efficacy*.

Points to Consider

1. As you watch live or videotaped initial counseling interviews, pay particular attention to the *process* used by the counselor. Even though the process is seldom articulated in advance, every initial interview follows one.
2. Using a counseling case study of your own choosing, outline how you would pursue the ten goals discussed in this chapter.
3. What other goals for an initial counseling interview are dictated by your counseling orientation?

Suggested Readings

BENJAMIN, A. (1969). *The helping interview.* Boston: Houghton Mifflin. Chapters 1–4 provide a good overview of the author's orientation in connection with the initial interview.

EGAN, G. (1990). *The skilled helper.* Pacific Grove, CA: Brooks/Cole.

GLADDING, S. T. (1988). *Counseling: A comprehensive profession.* Columbus, OH: Merrill. Chapter 7 is a good introduction to important factors in establishing a counseling relationship.

KENNEDY, E., & CHARLES, S. C. (1990). *On becoming a counselor.* New York: Continuum. Part 2 explains, for the novice counselor, the practicalities of the intake interview.

MARTIN, D. G. (1983). *Counseling and therapy skills.* Pacific Grove, CA: Brooks/Cole. Part 2 provides a practical orientation to the issues confronting the counselor in the initial interview.

OKUN, B. F. (1987). *Effective helping.* Pacific Grove, CA: Brooks/Cole. Chapter 2 addresses building a helping relationship between client and counselor.

PASCAL, G. R. (1983). *The practical art of diagnostic interviewing.* Homewood, IL: Dow Jones-Irwin. This book offers a good overview of the interviewing process, albeit from a somewhat clinical or medical perspective.

SCHULMAN, L. (1984). *The skills of helping.* Itasca, IL: Peacock. Chapter 3 explains the author's unique orientation to the initial counseling interview.

TEYBER, E. (1992). *Interpersonal process in psychotherapy* (2nd ed.). Pacific Grove, CA: Brooks/Cole. Provides a sound description of one perspective on structuring initial interviews.

WALSH, A. (1988). *Understanding, assessing, and counseling the criminal justice client.* Pacific Grove, CA: Brooks/Cole. Chapter 4 presents an insight into initial interviews within the context of a selected (criminal justice) client base.

CHAPTER 13

Facilitating Change

I am struck by how akin counseling is to gardening. A gardener cannot germinate a seed. A seed sprouts when the time and conditions are right for the seed. A gardener cannot bloom a flower. A flower blooms according to an ancient timetable all its own. A gardener tends a plant and is *sometimes* rewarded by the genesis of great beauty. Yet the beauty is the flower's alone.

As a counselor, your job is to *facilitate* client change. *Facilitate* is a multifaceted term encompassing subtly different dimensions, such as aiding, expediting, hastening, encouraging, easing, and simplifying. Sometimes *to facilitate* means little more than to observe and to be still. At other times it is passionate labor, with an intensity and a directedness that belies counseling's subtle nature.

Although not everything that you do as a counselor results in demonstrable change for each and every client, client change is the measure by which the overall efficacy of your counseling must be judged. Depending upon your particular orientation toward counseling and the counseling situations you confront, changes that you must bring about through counseling take many forms:

- changes in clients' feelings about their past, present, or future circumstances;
- changes in clients' behavior in future circumstances;
- changes in clients' understanding of themselves or of events they have confronted or might confront;
- changes in clients' knowledge or proficiency;
- changes in clients' beliefs or attitudes about themselves or others;
- changes in clients' understanding of their seemingly discordant drives, beliefs, values, or needs.

If you think back to points in your life when you encountered change, you will probably agree that contemplating or experiencing change can be stressful. This is true even when change is positive, such as embarking upon a close relationship. It is the process of change that begets anxiety.

Change is threatening because it involves risk-taking, moving from the accustomed to the unaccustomed. Even if a client's present circumstances are hurtful and unpleasant, they are familiar and have been coped with, however badly. The unknown holds who knows what, and anticipation enlarges upon the worries. The uncertainty and anxiety are magnified if the client has a mixed track record in handling previous life changes.

It may be difficult for you to appreciate the mixed feelings that your clients bring to changes they believe are a result of counseling. From your perspective, the changes under consideration would require only modest enterprise on their parts, particularly in light of present circumstances. Perception of risk, however, is a very personal thing.

Think of the dilemma facing a 35-year-old female client who is considering ending an unhappy fifteen-year marriage. On the one hand, she may be driven by a desire to escape a relationship she perceives as abusive, sexually unfulfilling, remote, and stifling. Powerful motivators indeed, and if they were the only elements in the change equation, there would probably be little doubt about her course of action.

But other elements have bearing as well on what she will eventually decide. She brings knowledge of some of these elements to counseling; others she will probably comprehend as a result of counseling. The countervailing elements may include:

- a lack of confidence in her ability to survive emotionally on her own;
- concerns about the effects of a divorce on her children or extended family members;
- values or religious conflicts about the permanence or sanctity of marriage;
- financial worries;
- concerns about her ability to initiate intimate interpersonal bonds in the future;
- thoughts of loneliness now or in later years;
- feelings of failure as a person and anxiety about the reactions of others; and
- loss of pride because she is giving up, a belief that there is something wrong with her.

At the time your clients first approach you for voluntarily initiated counseling, they are usually more motivated by current pain than by worry about what future changes may bring. Otherwise, they would probably not arrange to meet with you. But the balance of present pain versus future uncertainty is a tenuous one and may change several times during the counseling sessions.

You facilitate change for clients by managing the counseling process, which is not a naturally occurring phenomenon. It is mandated by the counselor's orientation and is imposed on the counselor-client relationship by the counselor. To facilitate change, you must deal constructively in the counseling relationship with threats to the carrying out of the counseling process.

Handling Barriers to Change

As dictated by particular counseling orientations, the counseling process consists of *stages*, each of which has goals. The goals vary among counseling orientations and range from building an effective relationship with your client to the formulation of specific action plans by your client. Change requires the removal of impediments to the successful realization of these goals.

Two concerns arise in your role of facilitator. The first pertains to barriers that frustrate your working your way through a particular stage of counseling. The second concern pertains to barriers that thwart your attempts to move on to new stages.

By way of illustration, an early stage common to many counseling orientations includes a goal that can be stated as "Establish the issues that bring the client to counseling." The barriers you might experience in working through this stage are similar to the barriers you might find in other stages of your counseling process. They are put in place by your clients to handle their discomfort in dealing with personal matters under your encouragement. Often the barriers are not expressed overtly, and many times, clients are unaware of what they are doing.

Because the barriers to change in this stage of the counseling process are like those in later stages, they merit our giving thought to countermeasures. At one level, the initial exchange seems simple. It is often initiated with a straightforward question such as "Bo Peep, what brings you to talk with me today?" However, the client's answer may not be simple. It may be colored by many factors, including:

- a lack of faith in you as a confidant or confidante;
- an aversion to disclosing potentially embarrassing personal matters;
- a reluctance to admit past failures;
- an uncertainty about what you mean by your question;
- a recognition that talking about problems might lead to change;
- a fear that you might negatively judge what you hear;
- a desire to present a picture that represents what the client wishes were true; or
- a dread of failure.

In most cases, no matter which of these factors are germane, the client will usually reply in some fashion. It is from the answer and the ensuing dialogue that you will deduce if your client is communicating other than surface meanings. For example, from "Oh . . . nothing really, I guess" you might infer that "nothing" is inaccurate. Quite probably, the true answer is "something" that your client is shying away from sharing. The oblique answer is a barrier to change.

In handling a barrier to change presented by a client, you should keep several factors in mind. It is important to discover the nature of the barrier as well as to identify potential means you can use to overcome it.

1. Ascertain if the barrier relates to a misunderstanding or communication obstacle between you and your client. In hearing "Bo Peep, what brings you to talk with me today?" the client may think you want to know the form of transportation used, and the reply might imply having arrived by means of walking.
2. Find out if your client is reacting poorly to you *as an individual*. Does the client feel comfortable, ill at ease, or trusting? What is being considered may not be the barrier; it could be you and the prospective relationship.
3. Determine if the barrier stems from a lack of knowledge or meager insight on the part of the client.
4. Establish if the barrier is a reaction to the technique you are using.

Barriers to successful counseling are worthy of reflection from two perspectives. In the first, if you think that one or more of the grounds may be important, you will want to *validate* your sense of what is going on. In the second, if you are correct, you will want to know how to *resolve* the matter.

Miscommunication as a Barrier

Miscommunication happens within the counseling relationship and out, but the former may be the more prone to errors than the latter. This is because communication within the counseling relationship is likely to be different in format or style and to deal with very different topics than everyday conversation. Very seldom are you invited to share your deepest and darkest secrets in a sidewalk encounter.

Because conversation within the counseling relationship is probably a new experience for many of your clients, you must be aware of possible misapprehension of what you say and what you hear. Your clients are learning to understand what you really mean, and undoubtedly make mistakes as they do so. And vice versa.

Validation

- Use active listening. For example, to the Bo Peep reply "Oh, nothing really, I guess," you could counter with "You're not certain about what I'm looking for . . ."
- Rephrase your question. In the example of Bo Peep, you could respond with "What kinds of concerns have been bothering you?" If this produces a more direct answer than did your colloquial "icebreaker," it is evident that your first question was misunderstood.

Resolution It is relatively easy to resolve miscommunication once you are certain that it is the issue.

- Use a statement that reflects upon what you tried to do followed by a question. For example, you might say, "I think I may have misled you, Bo Peep. What I meant was, What kinds of things are on your mind that you want to talk about with me?"
- Minimize your use of proprietary language. The more you deviate from language patterns and vocabulary that are easily understood by your clients, the more apt they are to misunderstand you. Remember that vernacular articulated with afflatus deportment is recurrently fathomed with complication.

Dealing with Personal Reactions

Just because clients understand what you say does not mean that they will necessarily walk arm in arm with you down the counseling path. Perhaps they do not like you, do not feel comfortable with you, nor trust you. These possibilities can lead to the same type of oblique responses from your clients that occurred in the Bo Peep miscommunication cited above.

It is unlikely that your clients will let you know directly that trust and comfort are problematical. Rare indeed are clients who, when you ask them why they have come to see you, look you in the eye and say, "I am reluctant to answer that question directly because I neither feel comfortable with you nor trust you!" Yet you may speculate that this is the problem. If, upon validation, your hunch proves correct, you must deal constructively with the barrier before moving on.

Validation

- Listen carefully for half-responses or hesitant responses from your clients. If a client starts to say something and then recants or veers off into an oblique response, it may be indicative of fear or mistrust.
- Take note of client evasiveness in answering personal questions, or use listening responses that deal with their private feelings.

- Pay attention to nonverbal behavior. Do clients avoid your glance, squirm when you look at them, or move away from you?

Resolution

- Try using a supporting statement after an evasive response from your client. Then follow up with listening responses before posing another question. For example, "Bo Peep, I think most people find it difficult at the start to talk about what is on their minds. It's hard to talk about things that bother you when you scarcely know the person you're talking to . . ."
- Avoid confronting your clients directly through inferring and coaching statements such as "You're uncomfortable talking with me. Relax." This may make your clients even more uneasy.
- Use a supporting statement, followed by a rephrasing of your question. You could say, "Bo Peep, many times people are hesitant when they first come to talk with me. What I wanted to know was the kinds of things that have been of concern to you. Perhaps that would be a good place to start."
- Pull back to less personal issues before reintroducing the topic later in your conversation.
- Avoid staring at your clients. Let them establish eye contact with you before you respond in kind. Respect clients' personal space.

Lack of Knowledge or Insight

Your insights are not your clients' insights. Your knowledge is not theirs. Clients will sometimes be unwilling to move forward in the counseling process because they lack sufficient insight or understanding. They may not grasp what has already been dealt with or they may not be convinced that the process will help them. If you attempt to proceed under such conditions, your clients may put barriers in the way of what you are trying to accomplish.

Validation

- A summary statement followed by a question is one way to see if your client has integrated or internalized what has gone on. For example, you could say, "Bo Peep, you have told me about your fear of the wolf, your poor relationship with your father, and your love of your grandma, the only person you've ever really trusted. From where you are sitting, do you see any relationship between these three things?" If Bo Peep sees none, it is premature for you to encourage her to come to grips with the possible connection you see.
- Use a listening statement to check out your inference of your client's lack of insight or understanding. For example, you might say, "Bo Peep, you

have many things on your mind and find it difficult to tie them all together . . ."

- Be alert to circuitous speech from your clients. Skipping from one idea to another is one sign that insight is blurry or infirm.
- Try to discern the extent to which your clients take responsibility for their own actions. Clients who blame others for their woes and who reject accountability are not ready to move to phases of the counseling process that address change on their part.

Resolution

- A coaching statement can be used in conjunction with questioning to focus client understanding or to foster insight. For example, you could say, "Bo Peep, when you talk to me about the wolf, your father, and your relationship with your grandma, I sense that you assess everything in your future in terms of what has happened to you in the past. How does that work for you? Do you sometimes feel that you can have no future because your past has been frightful?"
- Use questioning followed by listening statements to focus your clients on the matters they have brought forward. For example, you could say, "Bo Peep, you have told me a bit about your relationship with your grandma. Tell me how that relationship was different from the one you had with your father." Then, follow Bo Peep's answer with a listening response.
- Use delicate inferring statements followed by coaching statements to keep your clients' attention on the tasks at hand. For example, you might say, "Bo Peep, we seem to be moving from topic to topic very quickly, and I can't quite understand everything. Let's try to deal with one area before we move on to another."
- Use listening responses to concentrate on selected aspects of your clients' conversations. For example, if Bo Peep has talked about the wolf, her father, and her grandma in a single sentence, you could say, "Bo Peep, your relationship with the wolf seems to be important to you . . ."

Techniques as Barriers

Although I am a counselor rather than a client at this point in my life, I have not always been so enlightened! I was once the one sitting in the big soft chair, exhilarated by a counselor's hanging on my every word! Yet, even as she dangled, all was not well. I put up barriers, not to my counselor but to what she was doing.

The procedure to which I erected barriers I later recognized as the *empty-chair technique,* a common means of encouraging insight as practiced by the Gestalt school of counseling, among others. I was asked to speak to the imagined figure of my estranged spouse in the empty chair, to speak in a manner that I might not have dared had she actually been there. The poltroon in me took over. I didn't so much refuse as tell my skeptical counselor that I had nothing to say. The kind of behavior requested was foreign to me and would have been embarrassing. The only people within my limited range of experience who talked to themselves were a good deal more psychologically indisposed than I imagined myself to be. Of course, I couldn't actually voice these convictions to a counselor who seemed genuinely interested in helping me, so I remained "unenlightened."

In my observations of counseling since my awkward experiences of years ago, I have noticed that I am not the only client to react poorly to a technique. Different clients react in different ways to different techniques. A technique that facilitates the opening up of one client can promote the closing down of another.

As a counselor, you use techniques in order to achieve something, not as ends in themselves. When a client does not react well to a technique, it is the technique that is wrong, not the client!

Validation

- When a client becomes resistant to engaging fully in the counseling process *after* your introduction of a new technique, suspect that the technique may be unsuitable in that instance.
- Look to changes in client reactions as you use different counseling techniques. It is usual to observe mild discomfort or uncertainty as you vary techniques. Be alert for instances where these become pronounced or act as impediments.
- If a client asks why you are doing something or why you are asking him or her to do something, do not take this as a simple request for factual information. It is likely that the client feels uncomfortable with what is taking place.
- If, after explaining to a client a new tack you will take in a subsequent counseling session, the client misses that session, look for possible reasons that go beyond those that are stated.

Resolution

- If a client is apprehensive or resistant to a technique you are using, do not ignore these cues and push ahead. Discuss and resolve the concerns before proceeding. For example, you might say, "Bo Peep, you seem to be uncomfortable with what we are trying to do now. Tell me about that . . ." Then, use listening and supportive statements to handle Bo Peep's reply.
- Try using a different technique to accomplish what you want to accomplish.

- If you are unsuccessfully using a technique for which there is no viable alternative, initially pull back and work on bettering your relationship with your client. Reintroduce the technique at a later time.

Confronting Clients Successfully

Facilitating change on the part of your clients very often means that you must confront them. Confrontation within counseling does not have negative connotations, but it may be uncomfortable or embarrassing for you or your clients.

Confronting a client requires that you bring into the open a feeling or idea or issue that, up to that time, has been left unexpressed. These feelings, ideas, or issues may include:

- observations about the client's behavior during counseling;
- comments on the quality of the relationship between you and the client; and
- assertions about the responsibility of the client for his or her own problems and solutions.

Confronting a client during counseling is not completely dissimilar to the confronting you may have done in your personal or business relationships. In these instances, as in counseling, confronting is a means to change something. Often what you seek to change is the process by which you and someone else are relating to each other. Confronting does not solve a problem. It sets the stage for solving a problem.

Perhaps the hardest aspect of confronting is getting started. If you think back to a time you may have confronted a friend or lover about an aspect of your relationship, you will know that mustering the courage to bring up an unpleasant matter is not easy. Dealing with the matter once it is "on the table" is often effortless by comparison.

Introducing Confrontation with Clients

Confrontation with a client usually begins with a direct or implied inferring statement. The counselor says, in effect, "I think thus-and-so about this-and-that." Successful confrontation involves two distinct steps: (1) formulating the confrontational initiative, and (2) dealing constructively with the reaction from the client.

Consider the situation outlined earlier in this chapter of the 35-year-old female client who is considering ending an unhappy marriage of fifteen years. The client, let's call her Jalyn, has already shared with you much of the pain and frustration she feels and has long felt. You have listened attentively, summarized appropriately, and have tried several times to focus Jalyn on considering the alternatives that face her. Each time you encourage her to reflect upon what she might do with her life, she introduces new problems that confront her.

Counselor	Client
Jalyn, you have shared many things during the times we have met. You have talked about the fear you have of being alone, the effects of your relationship on your children, and the anxiety over holding yourself up as a failure for the world to see. Each time I see you taking a tentative step toward thinking about what you will do with your life, you seem to pull back, back to looking at more of the issues that might prevent you from taking action. (I)	Yeah . . . I don't know. It just seems so hopeless. Sometimes I know that I should get on with my life, but then when I even think seriously about it, it feels like the bottom of my stomach will fall out. Maybe I am just wasting my time—and yours.
The more you think about what you might like to do, the more scared you become . . . (L)	How can I get over that? I mean, I know I want to do something with my life. I'm just so damned scared. I mean, what if things don't work out? I could be worse off than I am now.

Notice how the counselor references the confrontational observation in terms that support but that do not communicate "You've failed" to the client. The confrontational statement "breaks the ice" and positions the counselor to help the client to deal with an impediment to progress. Here are two examples of another way to effect the same thing, this time using questioning as an initial step.

Counselor	Client
Jalyn, what is troubling you? What is preventing you from looking at what you might do to help yourself through this troubling time in your life? (Q)	I'm just afraid to start, that's all. I can't think about doing anything, really. I mean, what if I can't really do anything about my life?
You're afraid to talk about how you could handle your situation because you're fearful that I might push you to do something before you're ready . . . (L)	Maybe I'm not sure if I will ever be ready.

Counselor	Client
Wolf, something appears to be bothering you. (I) What is causing you to look so down in the mouth? (Q)	I've just reached the end of my rope. I used to think that I'd never meet a house I couldn't blow down. Now, that's all behind me.
You used to think you were invincible, that any house you wanted to blow down was yours. That didn't work, so you've been afraid to try again . . . (L)	Maybe I've had life as good as it gets. It would be awful to think that I had to start all over with just plain old straw houses.

Notice how, in both examples, the counselor uses listening to deal with the reactions of the client to the original confrontational statement. In both cases the confrontational statement has identified an issue that merits attention. This allows the issue to be brought forward and dealt with. Using this strategy is much more constructive than pushing ahead as if no impediments existed.

Dealing with Clients' Reactions to Confrontation

Although initiating confrontation is often difficult, it is not the only important part of the confrontation process. No matter what you say to begin the process, the client will likely respond to you in some fashion. To be effective as a counselor, you must work with the response to accomplish your desired ends. Of course, it is daunting if a client reacts adversely. Such reaction may take one of several forms:

- withdrawal into silence;
- verbal attacks on you and the legitimacy of your observations; or
- denial of the validity of what you said.

An adverse reaction can occur when your confrontational statements, no matter how well or poorly put, are accurate as well as when your statements are inaccurate. For example, in the situation with Jalyn described above, she could have responded to the first statement by the counselor with "There's nothing troubling me. I'm not afraid to look at anything about me." Would the response have been based on the counselor's inaccurate inferences that led to the confrontation statement? Or, would it indicate that the counselor was accurate but that Jalyn was defensive because she was being asked to deal with issues that were upsetting? Simply on the basis of Jalyn's response, it is difficult to know which possibility is closer to the mark.

It is important to understand the reasons for clients' adverse reactions to your confrontational assertions. You would probably want to respond differentially to reactions stemming from disagreement with your inferences, misunderstanding of what you said, or a desire to avoid dealing with the issues you raised.

Listening statements are probably the most appropriate means of ascertaining the why of an adverse reaction to a counselor's confrontational statement. Here are two more examples, based upon earlier situations.

Counselor	**Client**
Jalyn, what is troubling you? What is preventing you from looking at what you might do to help yourself through this troubling time in your life? (Q)	There's nothing troubling me. I'm not afraid to look at anything about me.
There is nothing that is troubling you just now . . . (L)	Well, maybe a few things, but I can still look at them. I'm not afraid of doing that.
Some things are troubling you but you're willing to look at them head-on . . . (L)	Yeah.
Perhaps we should talk more about some of those things if we're going to get anywhere. (C)	Okay, sure.

Counselor	**Client**
Wolf, something appears to be bothering you. (I) What is causing you to look so down in the mouth? (Q)	What do you mean? There's nothing wrong with me. I'm still twice the wolf that most wolves are.
It's upsetting to think that someone might think you were sliding backward a bit . . . (L)	It's not easy being a wolf, you know. There are responsibilities, books, royalties, pressure all the time.
When you think about all of the pressure, you sometimes worry that maybe you're not up to it any more . . . (L)	Maybe. But I'm still pretty ferocious. These false teeth are every bit as good as the real things.
You're worried, but still have pretty good control of what you do . . . (L)	That's r-r-roar right.

Notice how the counselor uses listening statements to ascertain what the client may mean by what has been said. Once this is established, a coaching statement is used to refocus the conversation. Here is another example, based upon a different type of adverse response by a client.

Counselor	Client
Jalyn, you have shared many things during the times we have met. You have talked about the fear you have of being alone, the effects of your relationship on your children, and the anxiety over holding yourself up as a failure for the world to see. Each time I see you taking a tentative step toward thinking about what you will do with your life, you seem to pull back, back to looking at more of the issues that might prevent you from taking action. (I)	I'm doing the best that I can. Those things aren't easy to deal with you know. All you have to do is listen to me or talk about them. I have to live my life after I leave here.
It's upsetting you that I don't seem to think that your problems are as difficult as you know they are . . . (L)	It's not easy living my life just now. Sometimes a person wants to do something about it and can't.
You want to do something about your life but there are things that are stopping you from doing that . . . (L)	That's right. My old man might not be all he is supposed to be, but I don't have many options.
Every time you think about doing something, the old fear thing sets in . . . (L)	For sure.
Maybe we need to deal with the fear thing if you're going to be able to handle your concerns. (C)	The fear thing. Yeah, the damned fear thing.

Once again, the counselor uses listening techniques to move the client to talk about her reaction to the confrontational statement. The counselor does not react defensively to the challenge by the client. The situation ends with the client more disposed to deal with the matters that were raised by way of confrontation.

A Final Word on Facilitating Change

Facilitating change by clients is the primary job of the counselor, irrespective of counseling orientation. Helping clients to change is not something at which you will ever become wholly proficient. As you grow in professional experience, so too will grow your realization that there is much more that you need to learn. Like all professionals, counselors are never afforded the luxury of thinking that they have "arrived."

Points to Consider

1. As you begin your career as a counselor or an apprentice counselor, keep track of stumbling blocks you encounter. When you have the time to do so, work through alternative means to deal with these situations in preparation for similar stumbling blocks in the future.
2. In observing the work of counselors, pay attention to their techniques vis-à-vis interruptions or blockages in the counseling process. Because many counselors are not totally aware of the process and techniques they use, you may gain more insight through observation than by asking them to identify their techniques and to tell you the uses to which they are put.
3. Ask other students to observe you in mock or real counseling situations. Encourage them to focus on what you do and how you do it. You might also find it helpful to videotape your counseling encounters and then analyze your own performance.

Suggested Readings

BRAMMER, L. E., SHOSTROM, E. L., & ABREGO, P. J. (1989). *Therapeutic psychology: Fundamentals of counseling and psychotherapy* (5th ed.). Englewood Cliffs, NJ: Prentice-Hall. Chapter 6 deals with the actions of the counselor in facilitating change by clients.

COREY, G. (1991). *Theory and practice of counseling and psychotherapy.* Pacific Grove, CA: Brooks/Cole. Chapter 13 provides a good overview of how different counseling orientations can be applied to common counseling issues.

CORMIER, W. H., & CORMIER, L. S. (1991). *Interviewing strategies for helpers.* Pacific Grove, CA: Brooks/Cole. Provides practical suggestions on dealing with resistance to change by clients.

EGAN, G. (1990). *The skilled helper.* Pacific Grove, CA: Brooks/Cole. Chapters 4, 8, 10, 13, and 17 are particularly helpful in understanding the role of the counselor in facilitating change.

GAMBRILL, E. (1990). *Critical thinking in clinical practice.* San Francisco: Jossey-Bass. Chapter 12 covers issues pertaining to the counselor's decision making.

IVEY, A. E. (1988). *Intentional interviewing and counseling.* Pacific Grove, CA: Brooks/Cole. Chapter 11 includes an excellent presentation on influencing strategies for counselors.

MEIER, S. T. (1989). *The elements of counseling.* Pacific Grove, CA: Brooks/Cole. Chapter 2 details a much simplified analysis of strategies that counselors can use to help clients to change.

TEYBER, E. (1992). *Interpersonal process in psychotherapy* (2nd ed.). Pacific Grove, CA: Brooks/Cole. Describes means to move the counseling process toward a successful conclusion.

CHAPTER 14

Concluding Counseling

In the previous chapter, I likened counseling to gardening, with the counselor as gardener and the client as flower. Permit me to continue with my poetic license! In gardening there comes a time when the toil of the gardener is no longer needed. Whatever assistance the gardener can give to the growth and development of the flower has been given. The flower is as it should be. It does not need further water, nourishment, or sunlight. It is ready for harvesting, propagating its seed, or decorating a fragrant bouquet. The flower may not be perfect but the gardener has done whatever has been possible to make it so.

Of course, clients are not flowers nor are counselors gardeners. Yet there comes to counseling, as to gardening, a time for moving on, beyond the bounds of the helping relationship. Individual counseling sessions must be concluded and the counseling relationship itself must be discontinued at some point. Proficiency in doing both is the mark of a competent counselor.

Concluding Counseling Sessions

In some instances there will be only one counseling session with a client. This may be so when the client wants information that can be readily provided or when it is evident that the issues the client brings forward are either exceptionally simple or beyond the mandate or skill of the counselor. In many cases, however, the client will meet with the counselor more than once, sometimes frequently, before the counseling relationship itself is terminated.

There are several goals that the counselor should keep in mind in concluding a counseling session with a client. These goals cut across many different counseling orientations.

- When possible, it is better to end a counseling session on a positive note than on a negative one.
- A counseling session should be ended in such a way that the client is motivated to attend the next session.
- Clients should not feel that they are being "kicked out" before they are ready to leave.
- Orderly operation of the counseling practice should be maintained. Clients should not be required to wait for unreasonable lengths of time to begin their sessions because other clients have overstayed their sessions:

Your clients know that their interviews have a prescribed duration. They understand that you must see other clients and that you cannot allow sessions to run over. Still, in the heat of intense or worthwhile sessions, rational understanding may not always be uppermost in their thinking.

Several practices are helpful in successfully concluding counseling sessions:

1. It is easier to conclude a session if the conclusion is not a surprise. Start the session by stating its length. For example, you might say, "Cornelius, we will have one hour together this morning. Let's start by . . ." Or you could say, "Jackie, each of our sessions together will last an hour or a little bit less. The first thing . . ."
2. Do not violate the stated length of a session without a good reason. A counselor will sometimes extend a session without alerting the client that this is due to some special circumstance. As a result, the client may infer that the counselor's time constraints are very elastic. If you extend a counseling session, inform your client of the reason. For example, you might say, "Julio, we will be able to spend an extra half hour together today because my next booking was canceled. Perhaps that will give us the opportunity to . . ."
3. As much as possible, refrain from opening up new areas, particularly ticklish ones, near the scheduled end of a counseling session. If the client does so, be prepared to listen but address your comments to how you will deal with the matter in the next session. For example, if a client brings up a particularly difficult relationship in the last minutes, you might use an inferring response to deal with the client's initial statement and follow with a coaching statement such as, "Maxine, I sense that the matter of your relationship with your father is an important one. I doubt that we will be able to deal with it adequately today because we have only about five minutes left. Perhaps next week we should devote as much time as we need to talk about your relationship with your father.

In the meantime, why don't you think more about what you will want to talk about next week . . ."

4. Be prepared to compromise your usual interview time constraints in the event of a *genuine emergency*. Emergencies do not occur as a rule, and if they start to become the rule rather than the exception, you will need to assess your counseling strategies.
5. Near the end of a counseling session, move its focus to the future rather than the past or present. The easiest way to do this is to summarize what you have just done as a way to direct your upcoming activities. For example, you might say, "Zorb, we have accomplished quite a lot today. You were able to talk through your relationship with your wife even though I sense that was difficult for you. You were also able to speak more positively about your future than has been the case before. I hope we can continue with these developments next week. Perhaps at that time we can . . ."
6. If your counseling orientation allows for "homework" by your clients, the discussion of such activity is a natural bridge between the current session and subsequent sessions. For example, you could say, "Jardine, there are several things you can do during the week we are apart that will help us in our time together next week. Perhaps the most helpful thing would be . . ."
7. As the scheduled end for the session approaches, use nonverbal cues to reinforce what you are communicating to the client about the conclusion of your session. Your tone of voice should become *slightly* more upbeat and neutral rather than communicating intense interest in what the client is saying. You might look at your watch or a clock on the wall. In some cases, when the client does not decipher your more subtle cues, you might need to stand up while saying something like "Robin, it looks like our time today has pretty much passed. Remember those last few points we talked about. They will be a good place to start next time." Then move toward the door, perhaps reaching out to touch the client on the shoulder as a means to prompt the client to action.

Concluding the Counseling Relationship

Counseling relationships, like most human relationships, are finite. Perhaps the main difference between them is that the counseling relationship is often concluded in a calculated manner, a manner through which both parties know that it has come to an end. Of course, this is not always so, and in those cases there is no definite end point. Counselor and client simply drift apart with no formal marking circumstance. In fact, it has been stated that the single most frequent way that a counseling relationship is concluded is by the client's not appearing for a scheduled session—or thereafter.

It is a tacit if not a stated purpose of most counseling orientations to prepare clients to deal with their worlds without ongoing professional assistance. Counseling is intended to be a brief interlude in what are otherwise self-guided lives. Even when this goal is not realistic for an individual, most counseling orientations are directed toward aiding him or her to function without perpetual assistance from the counselor. In this respect, counseling's purpose is often to help clients surmount certain barriers in their lives so they then can manage without counseling by the better use of resources already available to them, such as friends, relatives, support and interest groups or other potential helping affiliations.

As in noncounseling relationships that both you and your client have experienced, concluding a counseling relationship varies from client to client. Those that I have concluded ranged from partings where a client and I separated amicably but were each probably glad to be rid of the other to partings that led to tears on both sides. Of course, the conclusion to most counseling relationships falls somewhere between these two extremes.

Keep several points in mind in concluding a counseling relationship. Although generic, each will obviously apply more to some counseling orientations than to others.

- A counseling relationship is more easily concluded if its conclusion is not a surprise to the client.
- All other things being equal, the longer the duration and the greater the intensity of a counseling relationship, the more extended and intricate the process of concluding.
- It is easier to conclude a counseling relationship when both partners believe it appropriate to do so.
- Some clients resist concluding the counseling relationship, as do some counselors.

Although all of your clients probably understand that their relationships with you must eventually end, they may not approach the end with enthusiasm. It is usually necessary for you to do something—to put some process into place—to conclude the relationships. Depending upon your orientation to counseling, the process may involve several elements.

1. It is usually more difficult to conclude counseling relationships that are indeterminate in length. If the relationship has been carried on with no indication of when it might end, your client may infer that you are concluding for extraneous reasons; for example, that you have given up hope! With this in mind, it is usually preferable to conduct your counseling *in stages,* consciously advancing from stage to stage. For example, you might say, "Janine, it is difficult to know how much energy and time we will need to devote to addressing the issues you have shared

with me. Let's see how things go for the next three weeks and assess at the end of that time if we need to continue meeting."

2. Provide options to your clients. If you feel that the time is appropriate to end a counseling relationship, rather than doing so immediately and unilaterally, you might say, "Jorgen, I sense that you are getting a pretty good handle on the issues that first brought you to see me. Are you feeling the same way or would you feel more comfortable meeting one or two more times before we see how you handle things without further help?"
3. Soften the perceived permanence of concluding the counseling relationship by leaving open a "door" to a future relationship if such becomes necessary. For example, you might say, "Copernicus, I sense that you are still feeling a bit uncertain about not coming to see me any more. Why don't you try things on your own for the next three weeks, see how things are going, and then call me if you still feel uncertain?"
4. If you work at an agency that limits the amount of assistance that can be provided to any one client, inform clients of this reality sooner rather than later. For example, you might say, "Katrine, in order for us to work with a client for more than four sessions, we must present the situation to a committee of counselors for approval. Let's work on the basis that we will be successful over the next four weeks and talk about this requirement after we have met three times."
5. Review the progress clients have made and discuss with them how they will handle the period immediately following the conclusion of counseling. For example, you might say, "Thales, it seems that over the past two months you have made good progress in overcoming your obsession with water. You now think of water only occasionally and are much less certain that it is the prime element of the universe. Sooner or later, you are going to meet other philosophers who remember how things used to be for you. How are you going to handle the situation?" Then use your comments and those of your client to build a bridge to concluding the counseling relationship.
6. Try to conclude the counseling relationship on a positive note. Very often this can be accomplished by reviewing client progress. A review also serves as a natural bridge from helping to departing. For example, you might say, "Charmin, when I first met you three months ago, you said that you had to start making decisions about your life. You've done just that. You have decided to go back to school and will begin in the fall. You've decided to offer your baby for adoption immediately after birth. And you've decided to put on the hold the relationship you had with the baby's father. Each decision was difficult, but still you made them. I sense that you're really getting a new hold on your life."
7. Do not be afraid to voice your own feelings about ending the counseling relationship. This can often serve as an impetus for your client to share similar feelings. For example, you might say, "I'm both happy and sad

that our time together is drawing to a close, Pythagoras. I'm happy that you'vebeen able to work out the fear that you've always had about arithmetic, but I will really miss our talks about those theorems. You have such a command of the area."

8. In the final period before concluding the counseling relationship tread particularly carefully the fine line between creating undue dependence upon you as a counselor and conveying uncaring detachment. Neither close off the possibility that you will see your client again nor communicate the necessity of doing so. For example, you might say, "Galileo, I am glad that you are feeling better about handling whatever life might throw at you over the next while. Of course, I'll still be available to assist you if you run into something you're uncomfortable about handling. But, I think you're pretty well equipped to deal with most of what you're likely to confront."

Points to Consider

1. Observe how relationships with other professionals are concluded. From doctors to lawyers to undertakers, each group conducts itself in somewhat different ways. Of course, there is considerable variability within each group as well as among professional groups.
2. Observe counseling relationships as presented in the mass media through soap operas and the like. How real are they? Remember that for first-time clients, these examples may be the only ones in their experience.
3. Identify several opening statements you could make to introduce the concluding stages of counseling to clients.

Suggested Readings

BRAMMER, L. E., SHOSTROM, E. L., & ABREGO, P. J. (1989). *Therapeutic psychology: Fundamentals of counseling and psychotherapy* (5th ed.). Englewood Cliffs, NJ: Prentice-Hall. Chapter 5 deals with concluding counseling relationships and individual interviews.

EGAN, G. (1990). *The skilled helper.* Pacific Grove, CA: Brooks/Cole. Chapter 18 provides a good overview of the time dimension in counseling, as well as strategies to conclude the counseling relationship.

GLADDING, S. T. (1988). *Counseling: A comprehensive profession.* Columbus, OH: Merrill. Chapter 9 offers a fine understanding of the termination process and issues pertaining to it.

SCHULMAN, L. (1984). *The skills of helping.* Itasca, IL: Peacock. Chapters 5 and 15 give an overview of the termination process from the perspectives of individual and group counseling.

TEYBER, E. (1992). *Interpersonal process in psychotherapy* (2nd ed.). Pacific Grove, CA: Brooks/Cole. Includes an overview of the termination process.

CHAPTER 15

Professional Ethics and Counseling

Ethics permeate everything we do. Personal ethics are the freely chosen basic moral principles that govern our day-to-day actions and our relationships with others. Professional ethics are a combination of freely chosen personal standards and the guidelines or rules mandated by a profession, in the present instance, counseling.

Within the constraints of the legal system, you have a good deal of latitude in formulating your personal ethics. You have the right to love others or to hate them, to behave in a kindly manner or to be mean spirited, to tell lies or to be truthful, to engage in monogamous or polygamous sexual relationships. People with ethics different from yours may not like what you do, may avoid you, or confront you strenuously, but you are free to do what you like and still call yourself an ethical human being.

Professional ethics are more constricting. They do not define what is good or bad about everything you do as a counselor, but they do set guidelines or firm rules that cover much of your behavior as a counselor. For example, it has always been considered unethical for a counselor to divulge private matters shared by a client in confidence, unless required to do so by law. It has not always been so clearly considered unethical for a counselor to engage in consenting sexual activity with clients, although that is a much more clearly proscribed edict today.

Professional codes of ethics have been developed to ensure consistent standards of practice in potentially contentious areas, to prevent legal problems or embarrassing incidents that bring disfavor on the profession, and to provide a framework for counselors to assess the professionalism of their practices. Professional ethics range from firm rules, the breaking of which can cause you to be ejected from professional organizations or counseling agencies, to suggestions from fellow professionals, which probably represent a loose pooling of the shared personal ethics of a number of other counselors. Individual counseling agencies typically practice under ethical guidelines that are a combination of generally mandated rules that cover all counselors and specific guidelines that are germane only to a particular agency.

As a counselor, you will probably practice under the aegis of one or more professional national or local associations. A professional group is likely to have its own code of ethics, although you will find much that is common among associations. For example, you may be a member of a national association of counselors, such as the National Board for Certified Counselors, and of a state or provincial association of school counselors. Because each deals with clients and counseling situations that are partly unique, each has developed its own code of conduct to govern the conduct of its members.

There are many shared elements in the professional ethics of the many associations representing counselors. In the main, the standards inherent in the ethics center upon what you do with your clients. The following areas are often covered by ethical standards:

- competency as a counselor
- relationships with clients
- confidentiality
- due process in counseling

Counselor Competency

It may come as a shock to you, but even after you have completed your period of training and seasoned yourself "on the line" as a counselor, you will still not be perfect! You will still not be qualified to handle each and every counseling situation with which you are confronted.

Ensuring that you are competent to handle the life situations presented by your clients is an important ethical consideration in counseling. It is also an increasingly important legal consideration. In counseling, as in orthopaedic surgery, automotive repair, or accounting, holding yourself out to the public as a provider of a service brings with it the legal responsibility to be a competent provider. If you are not, you may be chastised by your colleagues, disciplined by your professional association, or successfully sued by your clients.

The competency of counselors is not an either/or thing. Probably few counselors are ever *totally competent* to handle all of the types of issues with which they are confronted. Competency is governed by *reasonableness* more than by any absolute measure. Reasonableness asks, "Is it reasonable for this counselor to assist this individual with this problem?" Reasonableness dictates prudence in selecting what you do and how you do it. Reasonableness does not dictate that you deal with exactly the same counseling concerns in exactly the same way. Reasonableness would, however, preclude your use of tap dancing as a means to resolve marital disputes!

Selecting the types of cases you handle as a counselor means walking the fine line between professional growth on one hand and malpractice on the other. As with any professional, your skills are generalizable. To agree to help a new client you need not have previously dealt with *exactly* the same type of client with *exactly* the same types of concerns. However, you are required, by ethics and law, to exercise *good judgment* in providing professional services. Unaided, you should not deal with concerns nor should you use counseling interventions in which you are not versed.

Several guidelines are worth following to ensure that you do not run afoul of ethical guidelines respecting competency in counseling.

1. Although it may seem too obvious to mention, make sure that you read the ethical standards for the professional groups that regulate or guide your practice. It is surprising how many counselors equate personal ethics with professional ethics, even though the two are often quite different.
2. The more serious the issues posed by your clients, the more conservative you should be in deciding to provide counseling services on your own. For example, when counseling clients who are potentially suicidal or clients who may take other actions that are irrevocable, it is not a time to experiment with untried methodologies.
3. Do not be afraid to admit that you are not capable of providing assistance in specific instances. Refer the individual to counselors whose expertise is more appropriate than your own. Referring clients does not mean that you must turn your back on them, and the referring should not be communicated to clients in that manner. Preface your remarks in such a way that clients feel you are acting in their best interests, not foisting them off on someone else. For example, you could say, "Martha, your concerns about the financial area are very troubling to you. They are also concerns a little out of my league. What I would like to do is to arrange for you to see another counselor who is far more proficient than I am in the financial area. Of course, I will still be available to see you, but I think at this point you will be better served by someone who knows more than I do about some of the matters we have discussed."
4. Do not be afraid to ask for advice from other counselors or other helping professionals. In some instances you may want to involve an ally as a cocounselor (with your client's permission). This will aid you in dealing

with the immediate situation, and also will ensure that you gain more competence to deal with such matters in the future.

5. Read and continue your professional study. There are always new things "under the sun" and you have the ethical responsibility to be as informed as you can be about dealing with clients. Although counseling principles and techniques have a much longer shelf life than developments in solid state electronics, knowledge about counseling is an ever-growing field and requires your ongoing attention to keep abreast of change and improvement.
6. When you deal with situations that are out of the ordinary, keep records of what you did and why you did it. Pay particular attention to what you said and the reactions you obtained.

Relationships with Clients

Relationships with clients should be professional. Counseling relationships involve a degree of professional formality and distance that distinguishes them from personal relationships, which are not bound by convention. A professional relationship does not mean you are aloof from the client, but it does set limits on the nature and degree of the relationship.

Probably the most touted impropriety in counselor-client relationships is when a relationship includes a sexual dimension. Because of the potential for exploitation, the ethical standards of most professional counseling groups prohibit counselor-client sexual relationships of any kind, irrespective of the apparent willingness of the client. The operating practices of most counseling agencies reinforce this ethic through stiff censure or termination of employment for a single incident, irrespective of the apparent willingness of the client. Depending upon the circumstances, legal sanctions and lawsuits are also likely consequences. Put simply, the most constructive advice for a counselor to follow with respect to client-counselor sexual relationships is "Don't!"

Sexual relationships aside, it is always difficult to determine where a professional relationship leaves off and the personal relationship begins in your dealings with clients. For most counseling orientations, part of the counseling relationship is the requisite that you establish a trusting, caring, and helping liaison with the client. These characteristics are also intrinsic to relationships between friends, yet counseling is not solely a friend-to-friend relationship.

One thing that differentiates the client-counselor relationship from the friend-to-friend relationship is the *mutuality of needs satisfaction* in the latter: each partner has expectations that a personal need or needs will be satisfied therein. If this does not prove to be true, if the relationship is one-sided in terms of needs satisfaction, the relationship often falters. Contrariwise, the client-counselor relationship focuses on meeting the needs of the client, sometimes to the exclusion of the needs of the counselor. In this respect, counseling is a service-oriented profession.

Of course, it is impossible to separate completely your needs from those of your clients. You are not an automaton. However, you must remain aware of the possibility that meeting your needs through the counseling process might interfere with your ability to help your clients meet theirs. If you have a high need to control, you might further undermine a dependent client. If you are still plagued by the memory of a poor relationship with your parents, you might not be the right choice to help others handle their relationships with their parents. To paraphrase the edicts of several professional associations, you ought not to let your personal problems interfere with your ability to provide quality care. You ought not to seek through client relationships the satisfaction of your needs; they are more properly met through relationships with friends, colleagues, or therapists.

Several worthwhile guidelines can help to ensure that you do not go awry in respect to your relationships with clients:

1. Do not socialize with your clients. The more contact you have with a client outside the counseling context, the more blurred the counseling relationship becomes.
2. Be wary of touching a client in any manner that could be misinterpreted as sexual. Of course, all counselors have given a pat on the back, touched an arm, or held a hand on occasions when the situation dictated that such actions were appropriate. However, physical contact should be infrequent; should be used with clients of both sexes and should be of short duration and different in form and intent from sexual contact. A bit of wisdom offered me while I was still a graduate-trainee was to pretend that all counseling sessions were being conducted behind a one-way pane of glass, and on the viewing side was the chairperson of the departmental ethics committee—that's not the sort of image to breed overly familiar relationships with clients!
3. Monitor your actions to ensure that you are not addressing your own personal issues through your counseling. If many of your counseling sessions seem to take a similar direction, try to ascertain whether it results from your subtle steering. It is sometimes helpful to have a colleague who knows you well observe your counseling sessions. He or she may pinpoint behavior that self-analysis did not uncover.
4. If in doubt about whether it is appropriate to expand a client relationship to include an activity that may not be considered appropriate by some, be conservative. Seldom will you lose by consulting with peers before pursuing potentially perilous actions.

5. If you experience problems in maintaining professional rather than personal relationships with clients, consider counseling for yourself. There are too many possibilities for productive personal relationships with nonclients for you to think of clients in that respect. If it does not seem so to you, perhaps you need assistance.
6. If you receive any hint that a client has a concern with your sexual behavior or if you are confronted with formal complaints, seek legal assistance.
7. If you are working with a client for whom you have a strong physical attraction, end the relationship promptly through referral to another counselor. If it becomes obvious that your client has a strong physical attraction for you, do likewise.
8. Discuss the limits of the counselor-client relationship with your clients when it is appropriate to do so. Do not be afraid to let them know that because the relationship is professional, it can be *only* professional.

Confidentiality

The confidential relationship between client and counselor is a relative rather than an absolute matter. This is true from a legal as well as from an ethical perspective. This means not that you are free to discuss the private affairs of your clients with whomever you choose but that there are some circumstances when you are compelled legally and ethically to do so. However, breaches of the privacy of the counseling relationship are *exceptions.*

Probably no ethics issue other than that of a sexual relationship between counselor and client is as important as confidentiality. Confidentiality is an issue with which you will be confronted on a daily basis as a result of the nature of counseling and the organizational circumstances surrounding your practice. Although violations of the confidentiality injunction are seldom as well publicized or penalized as are violations of the sexual prohibition, opportunities for violation of the former are obviously more pervasive than of the latter.

The simplest way to express the requirements of the confidentiality ethic in counseling is that, except in defined circumstances, your freedom to disclose details about your clients is limited to what your clients have *agreed in advance* is to be made accessible to others. This would include matters ranging from releasing information about whether an individual was a client of yours to the release of intimate details about the counseling itself.

The confidentiality ethic is not dependent upon whether the private information is released with good intentions on the part of the counselor. It is the *act of releasing* that is at the crux of violations of confidentiality. Thus, it would be wrong from the perspective of professional ethics for you to release information about a client to an individual who ultimately helped the client, even if the client were later to thank you for doing so.

In my experience most breaches of the confidentiality ethic by counselors are inadvertent rather than malicious; they occur in the informal give-and-take between one counselor and another or between a counselor and another professional. For example, it is not uncommon when one counselor mentions to an associate the name of an individual, for the associate to disclose that he or she has worked in the past with that client, perhaps even elaborating on the revelation in some way. The associate's remark is offhand, unplanned, and violative—albeit perhaps in a minor way—of the confidentiality ethic.

The most effective way for a counselor to deal with the confidentiality issue is through *prior advice and consent*. This means that you must advise the client of the confidential nature of the counselor-client relationship *before* any disclosure of information and gain consent before proceeding. In many counseling situations, this caution from the counselor is verbal and informal. In other situations, it may be done formally, perhaps even in writing.

It is imperative to practice the prior-advice-and-consent edict in circumstances where it is not solely up to you whether to reveal confidential client information. This can include such legal matters as knowledge about the commission of certain crimes, awareness of planned criminal activity, or possession of information regarding the transmission of dangerous communicable diseases. Vis-à-vis the legal system, counselors cannot always offer the same guarantees of confidentiality as can other professionals, such as lawyers.

It is also important to practice prior advice and consent when your organizational affiliation imposes an obligation to reveal certain information. For example, you may be required by the private social agency that employs you as a counselor to reveal the names of clients, the nature of their problems, and the amount of time devoted to each client.

You will usually avoid successful lawsuits and satisfy the ethics of your profession regarding confidentiality by making certain that clients know *in advance* the kind of information you may or must reveal to others. Clients are then free to decide whether they will make you privy to compromising information. In my own practice I *always* warn clients verbally, early in the counseling relationship, about the limits to confidentiality. In some circumstances I follow the verbal warning with a written warning; in rare circumstances I solicit written acceptance of the terms that have been described and agreed upon. The habit of invariably delivering a caveat in regard to the limits of confidentiality can help to protect you against instances of forgetfulness or oversight.

In addition to the general suggestions just offered about confidentiality, several guidelines, if followed, will ensure that you do not run afoul of ethical practices in that regard.

1. When in doubt, say nothing. If you are not certain about the propriety of revealing information about a client, do not do so. Remember, there is no way to undo a breach of confidentiality.
2. Consider giving informational leaflets to all new clients. In addition to outlining your policy on confidentiality, the leaflets can address payment policy, hours of service, emergency procedures, and the like.
3. Formal clarification of the limits of confidentiality are particularly important when you are dealing with clients who may not be seeking your services on a purely voluntary basis. Examples might include criminal justice clients or students.
4. When a client appears ready to reveal a specific matter that was addressed by your earlier general admonition regarding confidentiality, interrupt to reaffirm your earlier warning. For example, you might say, "Helgar, it seems as though you are about to tell me something that may have to do with criminal activity. I would be happy to talk with you about it, but I must caution you that I may not be able to hold these matters as secret as you might want me to. There are legal requirements for me to reveal certain information related to criminal matters. I want to remind you of that before you go on."
5. Make certain that you understand the legal requirements of every government level, as well as the ethics of your professional association(s) that impinge upon the limits to your confidentiality with clients. Some issues that abridge confidentiality, such as suspicion of child abuse, are almost universal. Others, such as potential transmission of communicable diseases, come into play less frequently.
6. In dealing with minors, master the legal and ethical requirements with respect to divulging certain kinds of information to parents or guardians, which vary from location to location. Also be aware that parental permission may be antecedent to the release of confidential information about a minor, even when the minor has agreed to the release.
7. If an unwarned client inadvertently blurts out something that might impinge upon a matter about which you cannot offer confidentiality, interrupt as soon as possible. Offer a partial and imprecise interpretation of what you have heard (erring on the side of understatement) followed by your admonition. For example, you might say, "Charlee, you are starting to talk about a case of potential child abuse. You have not told me anything definite yet but before you go on . . ."
8. When a client has given you permission to release confidential information to someone, remember that it is a *specific permission.* It does not extend to others, even if they are associated with the individual for whom permission had been secured.

Due Process in Counseling

Due process in counseling is obviously related to your competency as a counselor. However, the concept goes further than competency. Due process involves *what you do* as a counselor, irrespective of your preparation and experience. Thus, it is possible for a counselor who is professionally qualified to handle a case to do so in an incompetent and unethical manner.

Because counseling is imprecisely defined relative to other professions, such as law or medicine, there is a smaller body of standard practice to use as a benchmark to help you determine if you have deviated from accepted norms. Although it is easy to see that recommending chicken soup as a treatment for family problems is imprudent and reckless, other actions that you might take as a counselor are less clearly definable as right or wrong—ethically or legally.

Due process in counseling means that you must take *reasonable actions* to deal with the counseling issues with which you are confronted. To be safe, you must pursue courses of action that are comparable (but not necessarily the same) as those that other professionals could conceivably pursue in similar circumstances. Due process might also address the consistency with which you take similar actions with different clients to deal with similar counseling concerns. For example, do you sometimes use standardized instruments to assess stability in cases of a potentially suicidal client and sometimes not?

Concerns with due process can focus on inadvertent mistakes as well as conscious choices to pursue a course of action that the client or others judge as ineffective or harmful. The former is analogous to the sponge left in the patient's body by a surgeon. The latter is analogous to a psychiatrist's use of a frontal lobotomy to deal with depression instead of conventional drug therapy.

Concerns with due process are usually defined in *hindsight*. This means that if you make a mistake or consciously select an inappropriate course of action that subsequently proves to be effective, you may be thought of as a creative innovator, even though knowledgeable others would not have condoned what you did. (Even counselors can get lucky!) If you take the same actions and things do not work out, complaints may be lodged against you and you may be judged to be incompetent. (You can't beat the odds for long!)

A concern with due process is limiting but ought not to curtail your creativity as a counselor. There is no requirement to follow exactly the same process with every client you deal with or to treat all clients in the same way as your colleagues might do. However, all actions you take as a counselor must be defensible in terms of being the reasonable actions of a competent professional.

Due process is a concept that many counselors ignore. This is because errors in due process do not usually come to light unless a complaint is lodged by a client, usually through a professional association or by means of civil litigation. However, it is folly to ignore due process and to act as if you are in your own world once you close the office door. What you do within your office walls must stand the scrutiny of others, even when that scrutiny is infrequent. Remember that in a case where due process is called into question, it is not how you behaved on *average* but how you behaved in a specific incident that matters.

Several guidelines, if followed, ensure that you do not run afoul of professional ethics respecting due process.

1. Approach your counseling in an orderly and systematized manner. Be aware of what you are doing and why you are doing it. If you elect to take or not take a particular course of action with a client, make sure the decision is a conscious one and cannot be interpreted by others as whimsy, neglect, or an overly laissez-faire attitude.
2. Pay particular attention to the consistency and acceptability of your actions in high-risk cases. Although all cases at times can be categorized as high-risk, situations involving potential suicide, criminal activity, and child abuse are more likely to be so.
3. When in doubt, involve other professionals in your counseling process. Because you need not furnish identifying information, this does not violate the confidentiality of the client.
4. Do not take refuge in *not doing something* as a means to deal with potential risk. The requirement of due process covers what you do not do every bit as much as it covers what you do.
5. Manage the support or administrative aspects of your practice in an orderly and professional manner. This includes such matters as the scheduling of appointments, fees and fee collection practices, and the soundproofing of premises.
6. Do not promise anything. Because you are only one character in a multifaceted play, you cannot guarantee results. Be particularly careful in your use of supporting statements ("Everything will be just fine . . ."); they are readily misunderstood as guarantees of outcome.
7. Keep notes of what you do. Nothing is as unreliable as memory, particularly in instances where you must testify in very specific terms about what you did or did not do.
8. If you have any doubt that a client understands or accepts what you will do or how you will do it, provide a written summary to the client.
9. Consider the use of therapeutic contracts. Such contracts detail what you will do and what is expected of the client. Although quasi-legal documents at best, they are decidedly better than nothing.
10. Due process is important, but do not become obsessed by it.

Points to Consider

1. Talk to several counselors about ethical problems they encounter in their day-to-day practices. How do the problems differ by type of practice?
2. Interview several clients to find out what they understood by the confidential relationship. How aware were they of its limitations?
3. Read the codes of ethics of several professional counseling associations. How are they similar? How do they differ? How do they differ from your personal ethics?
4. Create several scenarios that pose ethical dilemmas for counselors. Discuss them with your friends and with fellow counselors-in-training.

Suggested Readings

BRAMMER, L. E., SHOSTROM, E. L., & ABREGO, P. J. (1989). *Therapeutic psychology: Fundamentals of counseling and psychotherapy* (5th ed.). Englewood Cliffs, NJ: Prentice-Hall. Chapter 12 describes the relationship between personal and professional values.

COREY, G. (1991). *Theory and practice of counseling and psychotherapy*. Pacific Grove, CA: Brooks/Cole. Chapter 3 provides an excellent overview of ethics in counseling.

GLADDING, S. T. (1988). *Counseling: A comprehensive profession*. Columbus, OH: Merrill. Chapter 10 furnishes a good overview of morals, the law, and counselor ethics.

SHERTZER, B., & STONE, S. C. (1980). *Fundamentals of counseling*. Boston: Houghton Mifflin. Chapter 16 of this volume remains a fine overview of ethical and moral perspectives on the practice of counseling.

WOODY, R. H., HANSEN, J. C., & ROSSBERG, R. H. (1989). *Counseling psychology: Strategies and services*. Pacific Grove, CA: Brooks/Cole. Chapter 12 constitutes a good perspective on ethics, with particular attention to legal matters.

CHAPTER 16

Common Questions and Concerns

Starting out as a counselor can be intimidating. There is so much to remember and there are endless opportunities to embarrass yourself publicly. There is the constant worry that you will do something wrong, harm your clients in some way or get in "over your head."

It has been my experience that counseling students of all theoretical persuasions begin (and sometimes conclude) their professional training with similar questions and worries. Most center on how to deal with clients under specified conditions. Often the concerns are expressed as "How do I . . ." or "What should I do if . . ." As with most questions asked by neophytes, they sometimes seem very simple but are often deceptively complex.

In this final chapter I profile the actual questions that, in my experience, are repeatedly asked by students of counseling or by counselors just beginning their careers. Where such questions are uncomplicated, I try to offer uncomplicated answers. Where they are not, and that is in the majority of cases, I point out *considerations that are important in addressing the matter*. Many of the questions raised here have also inspired the examples in other chapters.

Please keep in mind that this chapter is not a cookbook. The answers to most of the questions asked by students of counseling are highly dependent upon the analytical framework of the answers. There is seldom any such thing as a neutral answer or one that everyone will agree with. In fact, within even a single analytical framework, answers to apparently simple questions are often far from obvious or clear.

In succeeding editions I hope to include more questions about counseling as raised by counselors in training. Please use the removable page inside the back cover of this book to write down your questions as you progress through training as a counselor. I would appreciate very much if you would send a copy of your questions to me at the address listed on the reverse side of the removable page.

Questions and Responses

1. How Do I Deal with a Client Who Is Compelled to See Me?

As sunny as your disposition is, there may be many instances where you must offer assistance to someone who, at least initially, would rather be anywhere else but with you. Your work assignments as a counselor employed by an institution, such as a school, prison, or social service agency, may dictate that most of your clients initially see you because they are compelled to do so.

Because a client is compelled to see you does not, of itself, mean much. Sometimes what clients are compelled to do and what they might do under no compulsion are not dissimilar. At other times clients who are compelled to see you may not be especially reluctant about doing so. In short, the element of compulsion does not *necessarily* lead to problems.

- Do not let your worry about seeing a client who is seeing you under duress cloud your initial presentation of yourself. Approach the situation as you would any other client situation, with an air of optimism and hope. The concern with compulsion is sometimes stronger on your part than on your client's.
- Remain alert for signs that clients do not want to be with you; these could range from withdrawal or disinterest to open hostility. Deal with the aversion in the same way that you would if it arose from other reasons.
- Listening and reflecting feeling are very helpful in confronting clients who are signaling that they would rather not be in counseling. For example, you might say, "Claudine, I sense that coming to see me was not something you would have done if you had had a choice . . ." or "Gerald, you would rather that we did not have to meet today . . ." Then wait for a response and deal with it as you would any other.
- Coaching and mild inferring statements can sometimes be helpful in dealing with a client who is made to see you. For example, you could say, "Julio, I know that you were told that you had to come to meet with me. That's probably not the best way for the two of us to meet. However, I hope we will be able to work together. I would certainly like to give it a shot."
- Resist the urge to comment negatively on the client's minor manifestations of a negative attitude. It is usually best to ignore small irritants, such as a surly tone of voice, to demonstrate that you will not be "hooked" into responding in judgmental ways. Be positive.

- Use inferring followed by coaching followed by questioning to confront your clients directly. For example, you might say, "Caroline, we seem to be at a bit of a stalemate here. I want to work with you but I sense that you're not quite ready for me to do that yet. Is there something I could do differently that would get us working together?" Deal with the response, even a very negative response like "Nope" through listening.
- Do not give up hope. Many clients who have been compelled to see you are accustomed to others' halfhearted attempts to help. Showing that you have staying power, that you will not be discouraged easily, is quite often enough to break through a client's resistance.

2. What Should I Do When Clients Themselves Resist Change and Yet Want Everyone Else to Change?

This is an issue that is seldom presented clearly to you, at least in the beginning. Very rarely does a client say, "I don't want to change anything about myself. I want everyone to change to accommodate me." But clients occasionally telegraph messages that cause you to infer that that is how they feel.

How you choose to handle client resistance to change depends to a large measure on your orientation toward counseling. Some orientations, such as person-centered therapy, are more likely to go with the client's flow, gently feeding back to the client the counselor's observations about a lack of movement. Other orientations, such as RET, dictate a more direct approach: confronting the client with the issue as a means to break through. In simple terms, whatever you do to handle client resistance to change should be true to your orientation to counseling.

- It is important that you separate a general or absolute resistance to change on the part of your clients from a resistance to change *on your terms* or on your timetable. Many times, clients are not resistant to change in absolute terms but, like flowers in a garden, have their own maturation schedules. Greater patience on your part may now and then be necessary. Counseling, after all, is not a footrace.
- As a counselor, you *facilitate,* not mandate, change by clients. You can help clients to recognize their reluctance and help them to understand the implications of their decisions to stand pat. You cannot impose change except by extremely coercive measures that are not normally a part of counseling. You can lead a horse to water, but . . .
- It is helpful on occasion to validate your hypotheses about a client's unwillingness to change. There are two hypotheses to test. The first is your observation that your client is resistant to change. The second is your inference that your client accommodates this resistance by wanting others to change. Listening techniques can be very effective in validation.

For example, you could validate the first hypothesis by saying something like "Lone Ranger, the idea of living your life without your mask is hard for you to accept right now. It makes others uncomfortable when you wear it all the time, but it may at times seem to be the only friend you have . . ." You could validate the second hypothesis by saying something like "Rather than taking off your mask, it may seem easier to hope that everybody else will become more accepting of you the way you are . . ." Deal with the client's responses through further listening and questioning.

- Use inferences followed by questions to give clients choices about the directions they want to pursue. For example, you might say, "Mr. Pan, part of you wants to come back into the real world but part of you wants everyone else to come to Never Never Land. Would you rather spend our time together talking about how to bring you back from Never Never Land or about how to get others to Never Never Land?" Use listening to deal with the response.
- Summarizing followed by coaching sets the stage for you to focus the client on the next step in the counseling process. For example, you could say, "Bo Peep, we've talked about your problem with your lost sheep. You shared with me your anger toward the other shepherds who haven't helped you find them. You have said you want to get the sheep back and you've identified a number of places where you think they could be hiding. Still, it's hard for you actually to start looking for them. The next step would probably be for us to talk about what's stopping you from moving forward, from finding those sheep and bringing them home."
- Your counseling orientation may allow you to become very directive in dealing with a client who is disinclined to change. For example, you might make strong coaching and inferring statements, probably following up the client's responses by listening. For example, you might say, "Mario, I sense that, no matter what you do, you won't be able to get the others to tell you where the princess is hidden. You can either live with this reality or we can look for ways for you to find her without their help. The choice is really yours to make."
- If you have shared the counseling process you follow with your client at the commencement of your time together, reviewing where you are in terms of the process and where you have yet to go can be very helpful. For example, you could say, "When you and I first got together, I talked about the process we could use to help you deal with your fear of kryptonite, Superman. I think we have come to the point where you have some decisions to make. Do you want to move on to consider what you're going to do with the situation you face or do you need to spend more time where you are right now?"
- Initiate an interruption in the counseling process to give your client time to think. A one- or two-week hiatus in meetings, with the firmly ex-

pressed expectation that the client must decide upon a course of action once counseling recommences, can yield rewards.

3. Can I Be a Friend to My Clients? A Counselor to My Friends?

It would be easy to answer questions relative to friendship as a component of the client-counselor relationship with a very glib no. But although that response is sound, it is not complete nor is it very satisfying for the questioner.

Can I be a friend to my clients? a counselor to my friends? are two distinct questions, but they share one element: both address the nature of the professional counselor's relationship to the world. One approaches the relationship from a professional-to-personal angle; the other, from a personal-to-professional angle.

The issue embodied in the first question, friend to clients, is dealt with in Chapter 15. The counselor-client relationship has some of the attributes of a relationship between friends, but differs in being results oriented and in focusing on meeting the needs of the client. And the process of the relationship is managed by one of the partners, the counselor.

The issue embodied in the second question, counselor to friends, is less easy to deal with in a precise way. It is probable that even before you began your training to be a counselor, you have been approached by friends to discuss their concerns. Such instances were probably informal and unplanned, but they may become more frequent as others recognize that you are on your way to becoming an "expert."

In counseling friends the issue is where to draw the line. On the one hand, as all friends do, you probably become involved as an informal helper in friends' personal concerns. But crossing the line that separates friendly counsel from professional counseling assistance is usually not a good idea. The roles of counselor and friend are different in nature and purpose, and it may be impossible for you and your friends to work through the built-in conflicts that result from trying to operate within mixed role definitions.

As a friend, you have a vested interest in the specific outcomes of your relationships with others. As a counselor, you have a professional but not vested interest in the outcomes of your relationships with others. You may be the exceptional individual who is able to juggle both types of relationships successfully, but be aware that if you try to be both friend and counselor, you may end up being neither.

How can you handle the requests that friends may make for assistance, particularly for "friendly advice"? Probably the best way is to use your listening and questioning skills to understand the problem. Resist the urge to offer advice because now that you are an "expert," you run the risk that

8:30-5 8½
5
35
2
37½
Cruz & Candy
Graham –

your adv … plain to them that you cann … quire professional assistanc … source. Do not try to becor …

- It is m … es to friends than it is to r …
- Think … persons who have intim … nclude your friends' close … nship could hamper your … ionships with your frier …

4. V … I … ty to Help … heir Lives?

Most counselors have not led textbook p … . They may have been lied to, cheated on, or abused in ways that are similar to their clients' ways. Counselors may come from dysfunctional families or have unresolved and long-standing problems with parents, spouses, or lovers. Counselors, like their clients, may once in a while question what they are doing or where they are going. Counselors get depressed, suicidal, angry, hurt, and yet are sometimes asked to help others resolve these very problems.

If perfection in one's own life were a prerequisite to helping others with theirs, few of us would qualify as counselors. Besides, those who do would be pretty boring people! Counseling sometimes entails helping others to deal with issues that may be partially or wholly unresolved in your own life. Good counseling also means knowing when circumstances in your own life are preventing your clients from receiving quality counseling.

Having endured a divorce does not mean you are incapable of helping others to do so. Having an abusive spouse or parent does not mean that you are disqualified from assisting others in similar circumstances. In both instances, the issue is the same: To what extent do your experiences *interfere* with your ability to help others? Ideally, experiences of yours that mirror those of your clients should enhance that ability or at least, not interfere with it.

Perhaps the most important thing with respect to your own experiences is to be *aware* of the impact they have had upon your life. It is one thing to deal with a client who is enduring the breakup of a relationship when you *understand* the impact on you of your own relationship problems. It is quite another thing when you lack such understanding.

I recall the experiences of a male colleague who was counseling a male client who was undergoing a very messy divorce. Knowing that my colleague had been through the same thing less than a year previously, I was curious about the influence that that might have upon his treatment of the client. My colleague recounted how, with his help, the client had been able to sidestep the actions of a greedy wife. It seemed evident to me that my colleague, whose normal orientation to counseling was exceptionally laissez-faire, had been very directive in providing advice. I pointed this out and was met first with stunned silence. Then, sheepishly, "Sounds like I might have been giving him the advice I wished someone had given me, doesn't it?"

- If you have gone through a major disruption in your life, be alert for its potential effects on your counseling. Rather than deny to yourself that your experiences have influenced you, be vigilant in seeking to understand the effects.
- Be particularly aware of using a coaching style in counseling situations that mirror your own experiences. Very often, there is an unspoken notion that what worked or did not work for you will do the same for your clients.
- Be alert to the necessity of referring your clients to others when their problems are "too close to home."
- Be vigilant for outcomes that are similar across clients when you deal with clients whose problems parallel your own. Perhaps you are doing or not doing something of which you are unaware that nets similar results.
- Take advantage of opportunities for professional retreats or values-exploration sessions. Such activities can help you to understand yourself better and indirectly help your clients.

5. What Do I Do If I Make a Mistake In My Dealings with a Client?

Perhaps one of the biggest fears of counselors-in-training is making grievous errors, ones that not only embarrass them but harm their clients in some way. It is easy to say that you learn only by making mistakes. It is more difficult to face a mistake and rectify it.

The best way to deal with mistakes is not to make them! That is why other professionals, from the pilot who uses a checkoff list before launching an aircraft to the surgeon who makes certain that somebody counts the sponges used in surgery, *systematize* what they do. Of course, planning cannot prevent mistakes; it only helps to eliminate predictable mistakes.

Adherence to a consistent counseling process can help you to eliminate predictable mistakes. This includes the mistakes of collecting insufficient information, offering widely varying assistance to clients with similar problems, or using a counseling technique you are unqualified to use. If you consciously decide what you are going to do before you take action, you are far less likely to make an impulsive mistake.

Counselors are perhaps more fortunate than other professionals in that the human personality is quite robust. By *robust* I mean that there is a reasonably broad range of allowable actions by the counselor that constitutes effective performance. The range of what constitutes effective performance by a counselor is far broader than that allowed the brain surgeon, if one were to make a comparison between counseling and neurosurgery. Failure to make a perfect listening statement at the appropriate time is not nearly so life threatening nor as irreversible as failure to fashion a perfect suture!

No matter how many predictable mistakes you prevent, you will never eliminate mistakes altogether. You will occasionally say the wrong thing at the wrong time, select inappropriate techniques, or make erroneous inferences. It is to be hoped that you will recognize when you make an error and rectify it.

Perhaps the most difficult and important thing you will do as a counselor is to monitor your own actions on an ongoing basis. This is so because most of the errors you make in counseling are recoverable. For example, if you realize that you ought to have made a listening statement at some point in a conversation but instead asked a question that caused your client to change topics, all is not lost. You can return to an earlier point in the conversation simply by referring to that point again. For example, you could say, "Rapunzel, a moment ago you were speaking about your hair, about how much it meant to you. Tell me more about that." Or you could say, "Simple Simon, when you were speaking about the pieman a few moments ago, you sounded angry, as though he was the last person you wanted to meet . . ." Although there may be a best time to do something in a counseling session, missed opportunities can be retrieved.

- Debrief yourself after you complete a counseling session. If you find that you have neglected to do something or have done something that is inappropriate, alert yourself to pick up on that matter in a subsequent meeting.
- Do not be afraid to admit to a client that you have made a mistake as a prelude to getting yourself back on track. For example, you might say, "Little Miss Muffet, a few minutes ago when you mentioned eating curds and whey, I guess I overreacted. They've never been my favorite foods, but that doesn't mean they're not good for you. Tell me a bit more about why you think curds and whey attract spiders to you . . ."
- In deciding what you will do in your time with a client, try to keep alternatives in mind. Having a "Plan B" can help you to be more adaptable when it becomes obvious that what you are doing is ineffective. It can also help to prevent you from proceeding down an unrewarding path simply because you don't know what else to do.

- Do not forget that mistakes include errors of omission as well as commission, although the latter are certainly easier to identify. Counselors-in-training sometimes take an unduly cautious approach, reasoning that even if they do not help the client, they will not make things worse.
- Remember that the most insidious kinds of errors are the ones you do not notice. Therefore, do not be too hard on yourself when you catch a mistake; it is to your credit that you do so. You will usually be able to deal constructively with almost any error.

6. How Do I Deal With Clients Who Want Me to Tell Them What to Do?

The tenets of most counseling orientations do not encourage a tutorial relationship between counselor and client. This does not mean that you won't be confronted by clients who want you to tell them what they should do. Their expectations are expressed both subtly and directly.

Chapter 12 deals with the necessity of ensuring that your clients understand the framework within which your counseling takes place. Doing so is a good *preventive practice* that helps deal with expectations of your clients for direct tutelage but may not be sufficient to deal with the more misguided of those expectations.

It is probably easiest to recognize and deal with an outright request for advice. For example, a client might say, "I just don't know. Should I break up my marriage or not?" Use listening as your initial response: "You're finding it pretty difficult to decide what to do, and you are hoping that I might be able to make the decision for you . . ." You might follow up an affirmative reply with "I don't think that's a question that I can answer for you, or anybody can answer for you. I'll help you work it through but I can't make up your mind for you." It is important that whatever you say, you not sound as though you have judged the client negatively because of the request for advice.

Some clients are more subtle in asking for advice. They are very adept at putting off decisions or acting on their own in the hope that you will edge them toward a decision out of frustration with the pace. Clients who more artfully ask for advice can be recognized by moves such as:

- suggesting actions they *might* take and then backing away in the hope that you will intervene;
- asking how others have dealt with similar problems;
- telling you that decisions they have made have not worked out;
- speaking openly about a fear of deciding anything;
- acting in a resistant fashion at any point in the counseling process that comes close to decision making; and
- adopting a fatalistic stance, "It doesn't matter what I decide to do, what will happen will happen."

Aside from recognizing when clients are subtly requesting you to make decisions for them, other means at your disposal to deal with this situation are not markedly different from what is available to you to deal with direct requests for information. In both cases, you need to reaffirm the position stated in earlier remarks to clients, but in a manner that is gentle and encouraging to them.

Several other points bear on handling requests from clients that you make decisions for them.

- It is more likely that clients will expect you to make decisions for them if you are prone to use a good deal of coaching in your counseling. After all, if you give advice in one set of circumstances, why not in another?
- The matter of clients expecting you to make decisions for them cannot be resolved once and then forgotten. It is probable that clients will return to the expectation at different points throughout the counseling process.
- Be aware of the possibility that clients may want you to make decisions for them because they may not want to make decisions that disappoint you. You may need to reaffirm your support for clients irrespective of the decisions they make.
- In helping clients to assess or evaluate decisions they are considering, be wary of using inferring statements. It is very easy to convey the impression that you prefer one solution over another whether or not you actually do.
- Help your clients to recognize the compromise nature of all decisions. Sometimes clients want you to make decisions for them because they can see no *perfect solutions* on their own.
- Be supportive of your clients' fledgling attempts at decision making. It is appropriate to support the process, even when you must help your clients to evaluate (perhaps even negatively) the decisions that result from the process.

7. What Do I Do When I Suspect That a Client Has Fallen in Love with Me or with the Counseling Process?

For some of your clients, you may be the sole significant person in their lives. You may be the only one with whom they can share secrets, admit weaknesses, or dream dreams. And the counseling process itself can also be very powerful for clients. Counseling may be the only productive life process they have engaged in for some time, the only one they can see as leading somewhere. Small wonder that some clients become devotees, both of the process they are engaged in and the animator of that process—you.

The issue with respect to clients falling in love with you or with the counseling process is not one of misplaced affection. The issue is one of feelings that clients have that may interfere with the counseling process. For example, clients who have fallen in love with counseling may be reluctant to take steps that, although helpful for them, might serve to end the counseling relationship. Clients who are falling in love with you may not be in the best position to deal constructively with the matters that brought them to counseling in the first place. Counseling and the counselor can become part of clients' problems rather than an avenue to deal constructively with the problems.

Recognizing the excessively positive feelings of clients for counseling or for you is the first step in facing that phenomenon. Although it happens, seldom do clients look you squarely in the eye and tell you that they love you! However, they usually provide you clues that may cause you to suspect that it is so.

- Clients who are excessively flattering in their comments about you, your appearance, or the help you are providing may be losing perspective. You're good but you're not perfect!
- Clients who continue to return for help with new problems or with rekindled old problems may be growing dependent on counseling as a process or on you as an individual.
- Be alert for clients who seek to expand the counseling relationship into something quite other. Requests to meet you for coffee, invitations to their homes, or other personal invitations are indicative of intentions in that regard.
- Clients who buy you presents or who express a great deal of interest in your personal affairs may be more interested in you than in resolving the matters that brought them to counseling.
- Be alert for clients who repeatedly tell you that you are the only person they can talk to. You want to be helpful, but you do not want to create a strong dependency on you or on the counseling process.
- Clients who try to initiate physical contact with you may be attempting to meet needs other than those that are usually met through counseling. Of course, you must be aware of cultural and ethnic differences when interpreting these actions by clients.

The infatuation of a client with you or with the counseling process is a delicate matter. On the one hand, you do not want the infatuation to interfere with the effectiveness of the counseling. On the other hand, you do not want the way you deal with the infatuation to drive the client away. If you have had to deal with the unwanted attention of another person in your personal life, you will recognize the dilemma. It is easy to say no. It is more difficult to say so in a manner that does not damage your previous relationship with the individual.

Probably the most effective way to deal with the infatuation of a client is to take *preventive measures.* Although some clients probably do not require much encouragement from you to develop feelings of infatuation, others may be inadvertently encouraged by actions of yours that convey over-familiarity. The counselor-client relationship is *professional.* To the extent that you allow the line between professional and personal to become blurred, you contribute to the distorted expectations of clients. Refer to Chapter 15 for a more complete discussion of the relationship between client and counselor.

Expressions of infatuation by clients can be dealt with by actions on your part that range from ignoring to confronting. The ignoring end of the continuum is probably most appropriate for the mild expressions of infatuation that probably characterize many counselor-client relationships. Ignoring, combined with a heightened awareness by you of the necessity to maintain a professional presence throughout the remainder of counseling may be all that is required. Ignoring may not be sufficient in some circumstances, and there could be other reasons, such as a desire to help clients better understand their emotions, that dictate a more proactive approach.

In confronting a client about a possible infatuation with you or the counseling process, it is important to do so in a way that encourages further dialogue and that does not sound judgmental. As in a situation when you are trying to fend off unwanted attention in your personal life, in counseling it is easy to give feedback to clients in such a way that they take offense. The message they hear in such circumstances is "You are doing something that indicates to me that there is something wrong with you."

A listening statement or a diplomatic inferring statement, one that leaves open the possibility that you are wrong, is often an appropriate way to initiate a confrontation with an infatuated client. These styles are suitable because your client may be unaware of the infatuation that you have deduced to be an issue. The matter will need to be raised in a very diplomatic, perhaps even circuitous, manner. For example, you might say, "I am beginning to get somewhat worried because I am not sure that I will be able to meet the needs you hope will be met by coming to see me as a counselor . . ." In most cases, the client will respond with a "What do you mean?" statement. You can then reply with something like "I guess it feels to me that you would like our relationship to be more personal than counselor to client, and that is difficult for me." The client will probably respond with a denial, in which case you can respond with listening to clarify the denial. You can then follow up your listening statement with an apology for your own erroneous inference. For example, you could say, "Sometimes I pick up on signals that are unclear. I usually try to check them out as I did with you just now. I hope you can understand my concern." Then move on with the counseling process, ensuring that you maintain a professional distance in subsequent conversation.

If the client agrees with your initial inferring statement and verbalizes an attraction to you or infatuation, you are faced with a different issue. The softest message that can be communicated to the infatuated client is that the counseling process and ethics of the counseling profession do not allow for the development of close personal relations between clients and counselors. It is usually not necessary—even if true—to add that you would not be interested in such relations. For example, you might say, "It sounds as if what you are feeling right now is fairly strong for you . . ." Follow up the client's reply with a listening statement. Then, you might say something like "I am not sure how to handle what you have just told me. I know that personal relations between counselor and client are not something that is allowable, during or after counseling takes place. I hope we will still be able to work together, but I will understand if you would rather that someone else worked with you." Then you might discuss the matter with the client in greater detail.

Once you have "broken the ice" with the client and discussed the infatuation in a clinical manner, it may be that you will be able to reestablish a somewhat more formal client-counselor relationship. If this is not possible, you have little alternative but to terminate the counseling relationship and to refer the client to someone else.

- Deal professionally with initial requests by a client for personal contact. When a client invites you out for coffee or to attend a social event, it may be easier for you to plead unavailability than to deal with the matter directly. Nonetheless, the latter course is preferable to tacitly encouraging unrealistic expectations.
- If you experience more difficulties with infatuated clients than your peers, examine your own actions carefully. Perhaps you unknowingly telegraph encouraging messages.
- Protect your professional credibility. If you have doubts about your ability to handle the solicitations of an infatuated client, reassess your offer to continue counseling to the individual.
- If you actually express any reciprocation of your client's infatuated feelings, or feel strongly compelled to do so, terminate the counseling relationship. Do so professionally, while ensuring the counseling interests of your clients are properly handled.
- When you encounter clients in social situations, be pleasant but maintain an appropriate professional distance.

8. How Do I Decide Which Issues to Deal with First?

If life were uncomplicated, clients would arrive with single problems on their minds. You would help each to deal constructively with the problem and life would go on. Of course, life and counseling are seldom that simple. In reality, you will probably encounter many clients who have a number of unresolved concerns in their lives, concerns that may or may not be related to one another. Even clients who present unidimensional matters at the start of counseling may tender more multidimensional concerns as you become more familiar with them. For many novice counselors, the question they must constantly deal with is, What do I do first?

Most counseling orientations are silent on the matter of how to organize your counseling when a client confronts you with multiple items. Several factors are important to consider in helping you to decide.

- The *relative severity* of the issues presented is important. Quite obviously, concerns that may lead to suicide are more important than concerns about long-term career choice.
- The *timeliness* of concerns expressed by the client is important. Concerns that will have an immediate impact may need to be dealt with before concerns that have long-term effects.
- The *relatedness* of issues brought forward by the client is important; you may choose to deal with related issues simultaneously.
- The *wishes of the client* will probably be a major deciding factor in organizing the help you provide. Clients who are motivated to deal with a specific issue are usually better prospects to resolve that issue than they would be if they were pressured into dealing with other matters.

The more you are aware of the full range of concerns brought forward by your clients, the more information you have to help you to deal effectively with them. This does not mean that you should interrogate clients to gain a full appreciation for the range of their concerns. It does mean that you must be sensitive throughout counseling to matters that may not have already been brought forward.

In most instances, it is appropriate to allow the client a major voice in deciding which issues will be dealt with. A useful way to focus the client on such a decision is a summarizing statement. For example, you could say, "Mr. Pan, you've told me about your problems with Mr. Hook. You've talked about your mixed feelings for Wendy. And you have shared with me your deep concern for the Lost Boys. These are all issues that have been on your mind for some time. Which one would you be most interested in working through, so that you are better able to understand your feelings and options?"

Sometimes clients do not recognize that some of the issues that they have brought forward as separate may be linked to other issues they have or have not brought forward. For example, a client who is undergoing a marital breakdown, partly as a result of abusing his wife, may have disclosed that he was abused as a child. Yet he may see these as two separate issues. Indeed, they *may* be. However, you might want to broach the possible relationship between these two matters with your client as a prelude to discussing either one individually. You might use summarizing followed by a question to do so. For example, you might say, "Sean, you have talked about your feelings before and after you hit your wife. Earlier you talked about how it felt to be on the other end of things, when you were younger and had a father who hurt you. Are those two things related in any way for you?"

In dealing with a matter of timeliness, you are concerned both with the feelings of your client and the external demands of the world. For example, you may have a client who, among other things, is considering a return to school. You know that unless the application for admission is submitted by a certain date, there will be no decision to make. You would probably want to make certain that your client first understands the external deadline and then see if he or she wants to deal with the matter. If the client does not, the matter may already be resolved by default. You might say, "Delphia, you have brought up a number of subjects this afternoon. You've talked about the lack of relationships in your life just now, your weight problem, and your feelings about your mother, who may be close to death. You've also talked about the possibility of returning to school in September. I'm wondering how serious the school question is for you. If it is serious, we should probably talk more about it very soon because the deadline for admission is in two weeks . . ." Of course, you must remember to return to the other issues identified by your client, whether or not you deal constructively with school admission.

Don't forget that the decision to pursue one issue or another in counseling is seldom irrevocable. You usually have many opportunities to refocus the discussion on matters raised earlier but then set aside. In fact, you may need to refocus your counseling sessions at many points as matters wax and wane in their salience for the client and for counseling's success. Counseling is seldom a linear process.

- If a very important issue is brought up during the course of counseling, be prepared to redirect your efforts toward it. It is not uncommon for clients to introduce a major issue part way into the discussion of a minor issue or issues.
- Occasionally, a client may want to move fairly superficially from issue to issue. In that event you may be dealing with a client who is resistant to change, not one who has problems in determining priorities. (See question 2, this chapter, for information in that respect.)
- In some instances, perhaps many, the sequence in which you consider issues may not really matter. If you are concerned about the ordering of issues, ask yourself if it really makes a difference which comes first.

9. How Do I Know When I Have Done All That I Can for a Client?

Every professional has limitations. Your limitations as a counselor are a combination of several factors; training, experience, personal characteristics, and the nature of the "chemistry" that develops between you and the client. With some clients you are very effective. With others you are ineffective. With still others, perhaps the majority, you are *partially effective.* It is essential that you realize when you have been as effective as you are likely to be, when further effort by you will net only modest returns for the client.

Like all professionals, you are pressured to be efficient. Pressure comes from the agency that employs you, the demands of a heavy caseload, your professional pride, or your own bank account if you are a freelancer. Efficiency means that time spent with clients must be worthwhile. It must contribute to meeting the goals of counseling. It is important for you to recognize when you have done as much as you reasonably can for a client. This frees you to pursue other activities through which you may be more productive. It also frees the client to pursue other resources, if need be, or to get on with his or her life without further counseling assistance, if that is appropriate.

The effectiveness of the counselor-client relationship is not necessarily linear. There are undoubtedly times when your counseling is very helpful. Other times you may reach a plateau, where nothing that you do seems to be particularly fruitful. Counseling should not be stopped simply because you and your client are going through a period where the gains are modest. It should be concluded at the point where it seems that further gains are unlikely or unnecessary, or where other resources are likely to be more productive.

It is always easier to ascertain that you have helped the client as much as you can if you and the client together initially identified the counseling's goals. Goals help you to know when you have reached the natural end of the relationship. In the interim they also help guide toward accomplishment of the desired ends and give you and your clients a framework for decisions on the course of counseling and postcounseling matters.

It is probably never absolutely certain when you have done all that you reasonably can to help a client. However, several points might help you to arrive at the termination decision.

- There is probably a minority of clients with whom you are not a good fit. This is the "chemistry" element in all human relationships. Simply because the chemistry does not feel right with a certain client is not, in itself, sufficient grounds to decide that your counseling will be unsuccessful with that client. The client may not share your feelings. The feelings may lessen with further contact. It may not be necessary for there to be good chemistry for the client to be helped significantly. However, the absence of good chemistry *might* be an indicator that counseling will not be as promising as you and your client may be hoping.
- Changes in the *pace* of forward movement is an indicator of when the

effectiveness of counseling may be winding down. Although variability of pace is expected throughout counseling, prolonged sluggishness may indicate the approach of a natural conclusion. (Of course, it may also indicate that you are proceeding through difficult but important matters.)

- The wishes of the client are an important consideration in deciding when you have done all that you can. If a client is still satisfied with the progress being made and help that is being provided, this *may* be an indication that all is not complete. Of course, common sense must come into play here; the client could have become highly dependent on the counseling relationship and want to maintain it for its own sake.
- The overall demands of your workload is another consideration in your decision that you have done as much as you can with a client. You must balance giving continuing service to a client against giving service to other clients, some of whom may have been waiting a long time.
- In some situations it is helpful to *suspend* counseling for a defined period when it appears that there is a lull in productive activity. This gives the client opportunity to reflect on the desirability of continuing, and may motivate resumption with renewed vigor.
- Referral to another counselor but *not terminating* your relationship with the client can sometimes be helpful. This allows the client to explore other options in a safe atmosphere.
- It may be necessary for you to continue counseling for a short while beyond the point when your professional judgment indicates that you are not being effective. The client may need time to feel comfortable ending the relationship, or changed circumstances may render the relationship more productive.

10. How Do I Help My Clients to Survive Outside the Counseling Relationship?

The purpose of a job interview is to predict the performance of the candidate *on the job,* not to judge performance during the interview. The purpose of counseling is to help the client to cope outside the counseling relationship, not within it. In that sense, the counseling relationship, like the job interview, is *directed toward external criteria.* The true test of counseling is how it helps clients to handle the problems and concerns that led them to pursue assistance in the first place.

How do I help my clients to survive outside the counseling relationship? is a seemingly simple question but it cuts right to the heart of counseling. It is, after all, what counseling is all about. Therefore, everything you do as a counselor should be directed toward client survival in the world beyond counseling.

Different counseling orientations answer the question in different ways. Some orientations rely upon the self-awareness gained by the client during counseling to carry the day outside counseling. Other orientations teach the client how to handle specific life events outside counseling. Most orientations are between these two extremes.

Generalizability to the outside world of what is absorbed during counseling sessions by the client ought to be a dominant theme in all counseling, even though counselors of varying orientations will implement the theme in varying ways. In addition to the means mandated by the counseling orientation within which you practice, the following general principles are worthy of your consideration in helping you prepare your clients for life on the "outside."

- If your orientation to counseling provides for a skills-development component, use examples drawn from clients' own experiences to illustrate key points. Encourage clients to use their own experiences in role-playing or in simulation situations.
- Devote a portion of counseling sessions to activities that help clients focus on what they could do in the intervals until their next counseling sessions. If you are able to help clients anticipate problems, they will be better positioned to explore ways to deal with problems when they come up.
- Encourage self-development reading or other structured activities by clients in the intervals between counseling sessions. This can help to dissuade them of the notion that counseling is a "fifty-minute encounter" divorced from the rest of life.
- Where appropriate, encourage clients to participate in reputable self-help groups in the intervals between counseling sessions.
- When circumstances allow, encourage clients to identify resources in their everyday worlds that will help them meet some or all of their needs addressed by counseling.
- Combine group and individual counseling to provide clients with varying perspectives on the matters that concern them. If suitable, encourage "buddying."
- Encourage each client to keep a journal of important events, reactions and feelings that occur in the intervals between counseling sessions.

Points to Consider

1. Keep a journal of common issues and problems that confront you in counseling. Discuss these matters with colleagues, fellow students, or in your counseling classes.
2. In contemplating a question dealing with counseling, think of how it could be addressed from differing counseling orientations. If an orientation is silent on a particular point, try to intuit how the orientation might deal with the point by how it addresses similar matters.

3. If you are taking counseling courses taught by several instructors, find out how each one would address particular questions pertaining to counseling. Try to correlate differences with the counseling orientation as well as with the personal perspective of each instructor.
4. On the removable page inside the back cover of this book write down your unanswered questions as you progress through your training as a counselor. Send the page to the address listed on the reverse side.
5. Ascertain if a directory that lists local self-help groups and other sources of out-of-counseling assistance for your clients is available. If not, compiling such a directory would be a desirable and praiseworthy undertaking.

Suggested Readings

KANFER, F. H., & GOLDSTEIN, A. P. (Eds.). (1986). *Helping people change.* Elmsford, NY: Pergamon Press. This collection is a compendium of methods and procedures of counseling that will be helpful in answering the questions of beginning counselors. Although comprising a variety of counseling perspectives, it provides a good balance between principles and practices.

KENNEDY, E., & CHARLES, S. C. (1990). *On becoming a counselor.* New York: Continuum. Written from the perspective of the nonprofessional counselor, this book provides practical suggestions on diverse matters ranging from using the telephone to handling AIDS patients.

SELIGMAN, L. (1990). *Selecting effective treatments.* San Francisco: Jossey-Bass. Using a case study format, this book offers suggestions for handling the types of cases likely to be encountered by counselors. It also provides excellent access to current treatment research.

PART III

Summary of Key Points

1. The initial counseling interview is a time of exploring and learning for counselor and client alike.
2. Physical arrangements of the counseling office and your personal demeanor are important considerations in creating a positive first impression.
3. During the early stages of the initial interview the client is drawing many inferences about you and the counseling process.
4. It is important to develop the goals of counseling in concert with the client and to ensure that he or she understands your approach.
5. Counseling is more effective if you are able to help the client to trust you and to feel safe in the counseling relationship.
6. It is important that the client feels your concern and sees you as a competent helper.
7. An understanding of the issues that bring the client to counseling and his or her expectations of the counseling relationship is important.
8. Undergoing change is difficult; the clients usually experiences feelings and concerns that may support or hinder change.
9. It is important to recognize and deal with barriers to change that the client may initiate.
10. In dealing with possible barriers to change, validate your inferences that there are barriers and then put in place processes to deal with them.
11. Confronting the client must be done in such a way that a strong negative inferring component is not telegraphed.
12. It is important to recognize when the counseling relationship should be concluded and to take positive steps to do so.

13. Personal ethics differ from professional ethics in counseling as in other professional activities. Professional ethics are mandated or generally accepted rules of conduct.
14. It is essential that you be competent to deal with the counseling concerns brought forward by the client.
15. The relationship with the client is professional and must not become personal or intimate.
16. Confidentiality is a relative rather than absolute concept. It is imperative to inform the client of the limits of confidentiality before compromising information is divulged.
17. A concern for due process means that you must take reasonable actions to deal with the concerns of your client.
18. The client who is compelled to see you should be approached positively, and the forced attendance should be dealt with matter-of-factly.
19. When the client exhibits resistance to change, it is important to recognize when the resistance is only to change on your terms.
20. It is potentially compromising to be a friend to your clients and to be a counselor to your friends.
21. It is highly desirable to be aware of unresolved issues in your own life because they may affect your ability to help clients.
22. There are few unrecoverable mistakes in counseling. The first step in correcting a mistake is to recognize that you have made one.
23. Remain alert for clients who want to expand their relationships with you to include a personal dimension.
24. The relative severity, timeliness, and relatedness of issues are important considerations in deciding which issue to tackle first. So too are the wishes of the client.
25. You have limitations as a counselor. It is essential that you recognize them.
26. Counseling should be focused on helping clients to handle the world outside counseling better.

References and Additional Resources

ABRAMOWITZ, S. I., BERGER, A., & WEARY, G. (1982). Similarity between clinician and client: Its influence on the helping relationship. In T. A. Wills (Ed.), *Basic processes in helping relationships.* Orlando, FL: Academic Press.

ADLER, J. E. (1987). On resistance to critical thinking. In D. N. Perkins, J. Lochhead, & Bishop (Eds.), *Thinking: The second international conference.* Hillsdale, NJ: Erlbaum.

AGUILERA, D. C. (1986). *Crisis intervention: Theory and methodology.* St. Louis: Mosby.

AHIA, C. E. (1984). Cross-cultural counseling concerns. *Personnel and Guidance Journal, 62,* 339–341.

AKAMATSU, T. J. (1988). Intimate relationships with former clients: National survey of attitudes and behavior among practitioners. *Professional Psychology: Research and Practice, 19,* 454–458.

AMERICAN ASSOCIATION FOR COUNSELING AND DEVELOPMENT. (1988). *Ethical standards* (rev. ed.). Alexandria, VA: Author.

AMERICAN ASSOCIATION FOR COUNSELING AND DEVELOPMENT. (1989, January). Knowledge of cultural values helpful to counselors. *Guidepost,* p. 14.

AMERICAN ASSOCIATION OF MARRIAGE AND FAMILY THERAPY. (1988). *Code of ethical principles for marriage and family therapists* (rev. ed.). Washington, DC: Author.

AMERICAN MENTAL HEALTH COUNSELORS ASSOCIATION. (1980). *Code of ethics for certified clinical mental health counselors.* Falls Church, VA: Author.

AMERICAN PSYCHIATRIC ASSOCIATION. (1986). *Principles of medical ethics, with annotations especially applicable to psychiatry.* Washington, DC: Author.

AMERICAN PSYCHOANALYTICAL ASSOCIATION. (1983). *Principles of ethics for psychoanalysts and provisions for implementation of the principles of ethics for psychoanalysts.* New York: Author.

AMERICAN PSYCHOLOGICAL ASSOCIATION. (1981). *Ethical principles of psychologists* (rev. ed.). Washington, DC: Author.

AMERICAN PSYCHOLOGICAL ASSOCIATION, DIVISION OF COUNSELING PSYCHOLOGY. (1979). Principles concerning the counseling and therapy of women. *Counseling Psychologist, 8,* 21.

ANDERSON, C. M., & STEWART, S. (1983). *Mastering resistance: A practical guide to family therapy.* New York: Guilford Press.

ANSCOMBE, R. (1986). Treating the patient who "can't" versus the patient who "won't." *American Journal of Psychotherapy, 40,* 26–35.

APONTE, H. J., & WINTER, J. E. (1987). The person and practice of the therapist: Treatment and training. In M. Baldwin & V. Satir (Eds.), *The use of self in therapy* (pp. 85–112). New York: Haworth Press.

ARKES, H. (1981). Impediments to accurate clinical judgement and possible ways to minimize their impact. *Journal of Consulting and Clinical Psychology, 49,* 323–330.

ATKINSON, D. R., MORTEN, G., & SUE, D. W. (Eds.). (1989). *Counseling American minorities: A cross-cultural perspective* (3rd ed.). Dubuque, IA: Wm. C. Brown.

ATWOOD, J. D., & CHESTER, R. (1987). *Treatment techniques for common mental disorders.* New York: Jason Aronson.

AUBREY, R. F. (1983). The odyssey of counseling and images of the future. *Personnel and Guidance Journal, 61,* 78–82.

AXELSON, J. A. (1985). *Counseling and development in a multicultural society.* Pacific Grove, CA: Brooks/Cole.

BAIRD, K. A., & RUPERT, P. A. (1987). Clinical management of confidentiality: A survey of psychologists in seven states. *Professional Psychology: Research and Practice, 18,* 347–352.

BALDWIN, B. A. (1980). Styles of crisis intervention: Toward a convergent model. *Journal of Professional Psychology, 11,* 113–120.

BARAK, A., PATKIN, J., & DELL, D. M. (1982). Effects of certain counselor behaviors in perceived expertness and attractiveness. *Journal of Counseling Psychology, 29,* 261–267.

BARCLAY, J. R. (1984). Primary prevention and assessment. *Personnel and Guidance Journal,* 475–479.

BATES, C. M., & BRODSKY, A. M. (1989). *Sex in the therapy hour.* New York: Guilford Press.

BECK, N. C., LAMBERTI, J., GAMACHE, M., & LAKE, E. A. (1987). Situational factors and behavioral self-predictions in the identification of clients at high risk to drop out of psychotherapy. *Journal of Clinical Psychology, 53,* 511–520.

BEERS, T., & FOREMAN, M. (1976). Intervention patterns in crisis interviews. *Journal of Counseling Psychology, 23,* 87–91.

BERENSEN, B. G., & MITCHELL, K. M. (1974). *Confrontation: For better or worse.* Amherst, MA: Human Resource Development Press.

BERGIN, A. E. (1971). The evaluation of therapeutic outcomes. In A. E. Bergin & S. L. Garfield (Eds.), *Handbook of psychotherapy and behavior change: An empirical analysis.* New York: Wiley.

BERMAN, J. S., & NORTON, N. C. (1985). Does professional training make a therapist more effective? *Psychological Bulletin,* 98, 401–407.

BETHUNE, H. (1985). *Off the hook: Coping with addiction.* London: Methuen.

BLOCK, P. (1981). *Flawless consulting: A guide to getting your expertise used.* Austin, TX: Learning Concepts.

BLOOM, M., & FISCHER, J. (1982). *Evaluating practice: Guidelines for the accountable professional.* Englewood Cliffs, NJ: Prentice-Hall.

BORCK, L. E., & FAWCETT, S. B. (1982). *Learning counseling and problem-solving skills.* New York: Haworth Press.

BRUCKNER-GORDON, F., GANGI, B. K., & WALLMAN, G. U. (1988). *Making therapy work.* New York: Harper & Row.

BUGENTAL, J. F. T., & BUGENTAL, E. K. (1986). A fate worse than death: The fear of changing. *Psychotherapy, 21,* 543–549.

BUTCHER, J. N. (Ed.). (1987). *Computerized psychological assessment.* Hillsdale, NJ: Erlbaum.

CAMPIONE, J. C. (1989). Assisted assessment: A taxonomy of approaches and an outline of strengths and weaknesses. *Journal of Learning Disabilities, 22,* 151–165.

CARROLL, M. A., SCHNEIDER, H. G., & WESLEY, G. R. (1985). *Ethics in the practice of psychology.* Englewood Cliffs, NJ: Prentice-Hall.

CELOTTA, B., & TELASI-GOLUBSCOW, H. (1982). A problem taxonomy for classifying clients' problems. *Personnel and Guidance Journal, 61,* 73–76.

CHAMBERLAIN, P., PATTERSON, G., REID, J., KAVANAGH, K., & FORGATCH. M. (1984). Observation of client resistance. *Behavior Therapy, 15,* 144–155.

CIMINERO, A. R., CALHOUN, K. S., & ADAMS, H. E. (1986). *Handbook of behavioral assessment* (2nd ed.). New York: Wiley.

CLAIBORN, C. D. (1982). Interpretation and change in counseling. *Journal of Counseling Psychology, 29,* 439–453.

COMBS, A. W. (1986). What makes a good helper? A person-centered approach. *Person-Centered Review, 1,* 51–61.

CORCORAN, K., & FISCHER, J. (1987). *Measures for clinical practice: A sourcebook.* New York: Free Press.

DEUTSCH, C. J. (1985). A survey of therapists' personal problems and treatment. *Professional Psychology: Research and Practice, 16,* 305–315.

DYER, W. W., & VRIEND, J. (1975). *Counseling techniques that work: Applications to individual and group counseling.* Washington, DC: APGA Press.

EBERLEIN, L. (1987). Introducing ethics to beginning psychologists: A problem-solving approach. *Professional Psychology: Research and Practice, 18,* 353–359.

EGAN, G. (1985). *Change agent skills in helping and human-service settings.* Pacific Grove, CA: Brooks/Cole.

EGAN, G. (1990). *The skilled helper.* Pacific Grove, CA: Brooks/Cole.

ELLIOTT, R. (1985). Helpful and nonhelpful events in brief counseling interviews: An empirical taxonomy. *Journal of Counseling Psychology, 32,* 307–322.

ELLIS, A. (1971). *Growth through reason.* Hollywood, CA: Wilshire Books.

ELLIS, A. (1984). Must most psychotherapists remain as incompetent as they are now? In J. Hariman (Ed.), *Does psychotherapy really help people?* Springfield, IL: Charles C Thomas.

EYSENCK, H. J. (1984). The battle over psychotherapeutic effectiveness. In J. Hariman (Ed.), *Does psychotherapy really help people?* Springfield, IL: Charles C Thomas.

FISCH, R., WEAKLAND, J., & SEGAL, L. (1982). *The tactics of change: Doing therapy briefly.* San Francisco: Jossey-Bass.

FOREST, J. J. (1988). Self-help books. *American Psychologist, 43,* 599.

FOWLER, R. A. (1985). Landmarks in computer-assisted psychological assessment. *Journal of Consulting and Clinical Psychology, 53,* 748–759.

FRETZ, B. R. (1981). Evaluating the effectiveness of career interventions. *Journal of Counseling Psychology, 28,* 77–90.

FULERO, S. M., & WILBERT, J. R. (1988). Record-keeping practices of clinical and counseling psychologists: A survey of practitioners. *Professional Psychology: Research and Practice, 19,* 658–660.

GAMBRILL, E. (1988). The state of the art in practice evaluation. In N. Gottlieb (Ed.), *Perspectives in direct practice evaluation.* Seattle: Center for Social Welfare Research, School of Social Work, University of Washington.

GARFIELD, S. L., & BERGIN, A. E. (Eds.). (1986). *Handbook of psychotherapy and behavior change* (3rd ed.). New York: Wiley.

GLADSTEIN, G. (1977). Empathy and counseling outcome: An empirical and conceptual review. *Counseling Psychologist, 6,* 70–77.

GOLDBERG, D. C. (Ed.). (1985). *Contemporary marriage: Special issues in couples therapy.* Pacific Grove, CA: Brooks/Cole.

GOLDBERG, R. L. (1970). Man vs. model of man: A rationale, plus some evidence, for a method of improving on clinical inference. *Psychological Bulletin, 73,* 422–432.

GOODYEAR, R. K., & BRADLEY, F. O. (1980). The helping process as contractual. *Personnel and Guidance Journal, 58,* 512–515.

GOTLIB, I. H., & COLBY, C. A. (1987). *Treatment of depression.* Elmsford, NY: Pergamon Press.

GREENBERG, L. S. (1986). Change process research. *Journal of Consulting and Clinical Psychology, 54,* 4–9.

GUY, J. D. (1987). *The personal life of the psychotherapist.* New York: Wiley.

HARIMAN, J. (Ed.). (1984). *Does psychotherapy really help people?* Springfield, IL: Charles C Thomas.
HARVILL, R., JACOBS, E., & MASSON, R. (1984). Using "props" to enhance your counseling. *Personnel and Guidance Journal, 62,* 273–275.
HAYNES, S. N. (1978). *Principles of behavioral assessment.* New York: Gardner Press.
HERR, E. L., & NILES, S. (1988). The values of counseling: Three domains. *Counseling and Values, 33,* 4–17.
HILLERBRAND, E., & STONE, G. L. (1986). Ethics and clients: A challenging mixture for counselors. *Journal of Counseling and Development, 64,* 240–245.
HINES, M. H. (1988). How to fail in private practice: Thirteen easy steps. *Journal of Counseling and Development, 67,* 253–254.
HOGARTH, R. M. (1987). *Judgement and choice: The psychology of decision* (2nd ed.). New York: Wiley.
HOPKINS, B. R., & ANDERSON, B. S. (1985). *The counselor and the law* (2nd ed.). Alexandria, VA: AACD Press.
HOUTS, A. C. (1984). Effects of clinician theoretical orientation and patient explanatory bias on initial clinical judgements. *Professional Psychology: Research and Practice, 15,* 284–293.
HUXLEY, A. (1963). *The doors of perception.* New York: Harper & Row.
KANFER, F. H., & GOLDSTEIN, A. P. (Eds.). (1986). *Helping people change.* Elmsford, NY: Pergamon Press.
KARLINS, M., & ABELSON, H. I. (1970). *Persuasion: How opinions and attitudes are changed.* New York: Springer.
KENNEDY, E., & CHARLES, S. C. (1990). *On becoming a counselor.* New York: Continuum.
KITCHENER, K. S. (1988). Dual role relationships: What makes them so problematic? *Journal of Counseling and Development, 67,* 217–221.
KOTTLER, J. A. (1986). *On being a therapist.* San Francisco: Jossey-Bass.
KOTTLER, J. A., & BLAU, D. (1989). *The imperfect therapist: Learning from failure in therapeutic practice.* San Francisco: Jossey-Bass.
KRAMMER, S. A. (1986). The termination process in open-ended psychotherapy: Guidelines for clinical practice. *Psychotherapy, 23,* 526–531.
KUPERS, T. (1988). *Ending therapy: The meaning of termination.* New York: New York University Press.
LAMBERT, M. J. (1982). *The effects of psychotherapy.* New York: Human Sciences Press.
LARKE, J. (1985). Compulsory treatment: Some methods of treating the mandated client. *Psychotherapy, 22,* 262–268.
LEAMAN, D. R. (1978). Confrontation in counseling. *Personnel and Guidance Journal, 56,* 630–633.
LEVENSON, J. L. (1986). When a colleague practices unethically: Guidelines for intervention. *Journal of Counseling and Development, 64,* 315–317.
LIDZ, C. W., MEISEL, A., ZERBAVEL, G. E., CARTER, M., SESTAK, & ROTH, L. (1984). *Informed consent: A study of decision-making in psychiatry.* New York: Guilford Press.
LLEWELYN, S. P. (1988). Psychological therapy as viewed by clients and therapists. *British Journal of Clinical Psychology, 27,* 223–237.

LONDON, M. (1982). How do you say good-bye after you've said hello? *Personnel and Guidance Journal, 60,* 412–414.

MANTHEI, R. J. (1983). Client choice of therapist or therapy. *Personnel and Guidance Journal, 61,* 334–340.

MAYS, D. T., & FRANKS, C. M. (Eds.). (1985). *Negative outcome in psychotherapy and what to do about it.* New York: Springer.

METZGER, L. (1987). *From denial to recovery: Counseling problem drinkers, alcoholics, and their families.* San Francisco: Jossey-Bass.

MEUHLEMAN, T., PICKENS, B. K., & ROBINSON, R. (1985). Informing clients about the limits to confidentiality, risks, and their rights: Is self-disclosure inhibited? *Professional Psychology: Research and Practice, 16,* 385–397.

NACE, E. P. (1987). *The treatment of alcoholism.* New York: Brunner/Mazel.

NELSON, R. O. (1983). Behavioral assessment: Past, present, and future. *Behavioral Assessment, 5,* 195–206.

PAAR, D. W. (1988). Helping can hurt. *Journal of Counseling and Development, 67,* 107.

PAPP, (1984). *The process of change.* New York: Guilford Press.

PARLOFF, M. B. (1986). Psychotherapy outcome research. In A. M. Cooper, A. J. Frances, & M. H. Sacks (Eds.), *The personality disorders and neuroses.* Philadelphia: Lippincott.

PASCAL, G. R. (1983). *The practical art of diagnostic interviewing.* Homewood, IL: Dow Jones-Irwin.

PATTERSON, C. H. (1984). Empathy, warmth, and genuineness in psychotherapy: A review of reviews. *Psychotherapy, 21,* 431–438.

PEDERSEN, P. (1988). *A handbook for developing multicultural awareness.* Alexandria, VA: American Association for Counseling and Development.

PEELE, S. (Ed.). (1988). *Visions of addiction: Major contemporary perspectives on addiction and alcoholism.* Lexington, MA: Lexington Books.

POPE, K. S., TABACHNICK, B. G., & KEITH-SPIEGEL, P. (1987). Ethics of practice: The beliefs and behaviors of psychologists as therapists. *American Psychologist, 42,* 993–1006.

POPE, K. S., TABACHNICK, B. G., & KEITH-SPIEGEL, P. (1988). Good and poor practices in psychotherapy: National survey of beliefs of psychologists. *Professional Psychology: Research and Practice, 19,* 547–552.

REMLEY, T. P., JR. (1985). The law and ethical practices in elementary and middle schools. *Elementary School Guidance and Counseling, 19,* 181–189.

RIDLEY, N. L., & ASBURY, F. R. (1988, March). Does counselor body position make a difference? *School Counselor,* pp. 253–258.

RIORDAN, R. J., MATHENY, K. B., & HARRIS, C. W. (1978). Helping counselors minimize reluctance. *Counselor Education and Supervision, 18,* 6–13.

RITCHIE, M. H. (1986). Counseling the involuntary client. *Journal of Counseling and Development, 64,* 516–518.

ROBERTSON, M. H. (1986). Training eclectic psychotherapists. In J. C. Norcross (Ed.), *Handbook of eclectic psychotherapy* (pp. 416–435). New York: Brunner/Mazel.

ROBINSON, S. E., & GROSS, D. R. (1986). Counseling research: Ethics and issues. *Journal of Counseling and Development, 64,* 331–333.

SAPER, B. (1987). Humor in psychotherapy: Is it good or bad for the client? *Professional Psychology: Research and Practice, 18,* 360–367.

SCHULMAN, L. (1984). *The skills of helping.* Itasca, IL: Peacock.

SELIGMAN, L. (1984). Temporary termination. *Journal of Counseling and Development, 63,* 43–44.

SELIGMAN, L. (1990). *Selecting effective treatments.* San Francisco: Jossey-Bass.

SENOUR, M. (1982). How counselors influence clients. *Personnel and Guidance Journal, 60,* 345–350.

SHEELEY, V. L., & HERLIHY, B. (1986). The ethics of confidentiality and privileged communication. *Journal of Counseling and Human Service Professions, 1,* 141–148.

SIMONS, H. W. (1976). *Persuasion: Understanding, practice, and analysis.* Reading, MA: Addison-Wesley.

SIMPSON, M. A. (1987). *Dying, death, and grief: A critical bibliography.* Pittsburgh: University of Pittsburgh Press.

SMITH, M. A. (1982). *Persuasion and human action.* Belmont, CA: Wadsworth.

STEARNS, A. K. (1984). *Living through personal crisis.* New York: Ballantine.

STENSRUD, R., & STENSRUD, K. (1981). Counseling may be hazardous to your health: How we teach people to feel powerless. *Personnel and Guidance Journal, 59,* 300–304.

STRUPP, H. H. (1986). Psychotherapy: Research, practice, and public policy (How to avoid dead ends). *American Psychologist, 41,* 120–130.

STRUPP, H. H., & HADLEY, S. W. (1985). *Negative effects and their determinants.* In D. T. Mays & C. M. Franks (Eds.), *Negative outcome in psychotherapy and what to do about it.* New York: Springer.

SUE, D. W. (1981). *Counseling the culturally different: Theory and practice.* New York: Wiley.

SUE, S. (1988). Psychotherapeutic services for ethnic minorities: Two decades of research findings. *American Psychologist, 43,* 301–308.

TAMMINEN, A. W., & SMABY, M. H. (1981). Helping counselors learn to confront. *Personnel and Guidance Journal, 60,* 41–45.

TURK, D. C., & SALOVEY, P. (1986). Clinical information processing: Bias inoculation. In R. Ingram (Ed.), *Information processing approaches to psychopathology and clinical psychology.* Orlando, FL: Academic Press.

TUROCK, A. (1978). Effective challenging through additive empathy. *Personnel and Guidance Journal, 57,* 144–149.

TUROCK, A. (1980). Immediacy in counseling: Recognizing clients' unspoken messages. *Personnel and Guidance Journal, 59,* 168–172.

VANDECREEK, L., & ANGSTADT, L. (1985). Client preferences and anticipations about counselor self-disclosure. *Journal of Counseling Psychology, 32,* 206–214.

VANDENBOS, G. R. (1986). Psychotherapy research: A special issue. *American Psychologist, 41,* 111–112.

VARGAS, A. M., & BORKOWSKI, J. G. (1982). Physical attractiveness and counseling skills. *Journal of Counseling Psychology, 29,* 246–255.

WARD, D. E. (1984). Termination of individual counseling: Concepts and strategies. *Journal of Counseling and Development,* 63, 21–25.

WATKINS, C. E., JR. (1983). Transference phenomena in the counseling situation. *Personnel and Guidance Journal,* 62, 206–210.

WATKINS, C. E., JR. (1985). Countertransference: Its impact on the counseling situation. *Journal of Counseling and Development, 63,* 356–359.

WIDIGER, T. A., & RORER, L. G. (1984). The responsible psychotherapist. *American Psychologist, 39,* 503–515.
WIGGINS, J. (1984). Clinical and statistical prediction: Where are we and where do we go from here? *Clinical Psychology Review, 1,* 3–18.
WIGGINS, J., & WESLANDER, D. (1979). Personality characteristics of counselors rated as effective or ineffective. *Journal of Vocational Behavior, 15,* 175–185.
WOOLFOLK, R. L., & LEHRER, P. M. (Eds.). (1984). *Principles and practice of stress management.* New York: Guilford Press.

APPENDIX

Counseling Communication Inventory

Here are twenty entry-level adult counseling situations. In each situation the client makes an initial statement that requires a response from the counselor. Five possible responses are given. On the Answer Sheet on page 230, rank in order the five possible answers from your first to your fifth choice, according to how you think you would respond in the cited situation.

Duplicate the answer and scoring sheets that follow these questions, and use the copies to record your answers and to score and profile your results.

1. A woman in her 30s wants assistance with her elderly mother, who lives with her. With a touch of annoyance in her voice, the woman says, "My mother is lonely and has nothing to do during the day."
   a. Your mother takes up a lot of your time because she has no outside interests?
   b. How long has your mother lived with you?
   c. You need to come up with some ideas to get your mother active again.
   d. Having an elderly person underfoot can drive a person nuts.
   e. Don't let this get you down. Things will work out.

2. Your client, a 30-year-old male, presents an array of complaints about his wife. He begins, "My wife needs glasses that I can't afford, and even if I could, that wouldn't make any difference. I think she needs a psychiatrist."
   a. Then why are you here?
   b. Your wife is unhappy and so are you?
   c. You will have to look at issues one at a time if you are to sort out your problems.

d. From what you are saying, I think you both need someone to talk with.
e. It is not easy to have personal problems.

3. Your client, a female aged 24, talks with slurred speech and smells of liquor. She starts out, "Life isn't worth living. Nobody cares what happens to me."
   a. There is always someone who cares.
   b. How long have you been drinking heavily?
   c. You feel all alone right now?
   d. I want you to start at the beginning and tell me what is going on in your life.
   e. You are depressed and the booze is not helping you.

4. A 50-year-old woman is very upset because her unemployed son has moved back home. She begins, "When my son left home four years ago, I thought that I was finished raising my family. We fight every day. I want him out of my home."
   a. Boy, life sure has its trying moments.
   b. Why did you let him move in if you didn't want that?
   c. Life would be easier without your son at home?
   d. I guess you are going to have to ask him to leave.
   e. Obviously, this is not a happy situation for you or your son.

5. Your client is worried about her husband, who drinks excessively and is belligerent. She begins, "Recently he said that he would beat me up if I didn't watch what I was doing. I'm not doing anything."
   a. You love him but are afraid of what he might do?
   b. Do you believe him?
   c. Don't worry. I am sure that we can work everything out.
   d. Tell me what you think he would do if he were provoked.
   e. It's not right for one person to cause so much pain and worry for another person.

6. Your client is very upset. He feels that his marriage is falling apart and wants to save it. On occasion his wife has threatened to file for divorce and to take the children with her. Your client is frightened by the threat and says, "I don't know what I will do if she leaves."
   a. What a worry . . .
   b. You love your children very much and don't want to lose them?
   c. You need to focus on what is in the best interests of the children as well as the family as a whole.
   d. Do you want to try to save your marriage or just try to gain custody of your children?
   e. Kids are not enough to hold a poor marriage together.

7. A male client has been suffering from a fear of open spaces for some time. His fear is becoming so intense that he frequently misses work.

He states, "I'll lose my job if this keeps up and I can't afford to have that happen again."

a. How many jobs have you lost because of this fear?
b. You have lost jobs before because of this condition and you don't want to lose another job?
c. It is very normal to want to hold your job.
d. Tell me about the events that occurred in past jobs that resulted in your losing your job.
e. Boy, life can be really tough.

8. Your client is a widower with two young children. He feels that he cannot manage to earn a living and raise the children at the same time. He begins by saying, "I think that I am going to crack with all of this stress. I can't handle kids and my job at the same time."
   a. Don't feel bad. I'm sure it's not that bad.
   b. You have reached your limit and the demands at home and work are not going to change?
   c. How long have you been feeling this way?
   d. Perhaps you need to evaluate alternatives to the ways you currently do things at home and at work to reduce your stress.
   e. Don't let this situation beat you. I am sure you have been through worse times and survived.

9. Your client is about to retire next year. He is worried about the financial and personal aspects of retirement. He starts out, "What am I going to do with all of my time? I have always worked and loved it. And the money! I'll have to reduce my standard of living."
   a. Don't worry. It takes a while to get used to change.
   b. Exactly what are your worries about retirement?
   c. Retirement has been on your mind for quite a while and you are scared?
   d. I am glad that you came to talk with me about your retirement concerns.
   e. I want to hear more about the different worries you have when you think of retirement.

10. Your client, a female about 40, feels tired. She cannot sleep and has lost her appetite. She begins by saying, "I don't understand what is going on. I feel jumpy and my chest is tight all the time."
    a. That really must be a downer for you.
    b. Are there recent events that have changed in your life?
    c. You feel anxious but you don't know why?
    d. The more you worry, the more pains you will get in your chest.
    e. Try to think of recent events that may be related to your anxiety.

11. Your client, a young female, has problems with her live-in boyfriend. She says that she loves him very much but that he is very demanding

of her time. "He is driving me crazy. He wants me to stay home with him all of the time and to ignore my friends. I can't do that."

a. You want some time to spend with your friends?
b. Why don't you go out anyway?
c. Your boyfriend is too possessive. You seem like a responsible person.
d. Give me an idea of the kinds of things you would rather be doing.
e. Lots of men are like that.

12. Your client's husband hit her and pushed her down the stairs the night before you met her. She took their children and slept at a friend's house. She says to you, "I am afraid to go back home and I can't drag my neighbors into my personal affairs."
   a. Let's see if we can find you a safe place until we sort out this thing.
   b. Do you have another place to go where he can't find you?
   c. You don't know what your husband will do if he finds you?
   d. If you were at risk, you did the right thing.
   e. I know this is scary for you.

13. Your client, a young male, is very sad. His girlfriend has just left him and he has no outside activities to occupy his leisure time. He begins, "I lost my girl. Got nothin' to do. And the job ain't too great either."
   a. Why is everything going wrong at the same time in your life?
   b. Now that your girlfriend is gone, there is nothing to fill the void?
   c. It's just one rotten thing after another for you.
   d. You shouldn't feel so bad. At least you have a job to see you through these tough times.
   e. Let's focus on what happened between you and your girlfriend.

14. Your client lost her husband three years ago and is still depressed and withdrawn from her friends. She says, "Nobody knows what I have been through. They just don't understand my situation."
   a. What are your friends saying to you?
   b. You are entitled to your feelings. They are very real.
   c. Life certainly has its trying times.
   d. Your friends think you should get on with your life, but you still feel sad over the loss of your husband?
   e. Maybe you need to talk with somebody who won't tell you how to think and feel.

15. After two years of marriage, your client reports problems with his wife. He states firmly, "I try hard to please my wife. I buy her gifts and take her out to dinner when I'm not working. No matter what I do, it's never enough."
   a. You are frustrated that nothing you try satisfies your wife?
   b. Things always look worse than they are.

c. Your wife obviously wants more than presents. She wants your time.
d. Is the issue that your wife wants more time with you?
e. Perhaps you need to stop spending money and spend more time with your wife.

16. Your client is a 21-year-old single parent who has been on welfare for five years. She indicates that she wants more out of life than poverty. She sighs, "Where do I start? I don't even have my grade 12."
a. Let's review some realistic options for your future.
b. You want to make some changes for the better in your life, but the changes must be realistic?
c. Do you want to review some options for the future with me?
d. It's tough, even when you try your best, to see what options might be realistic.
e. A review of realistic options is the best thing to do.

17. Your client, a young woman in her early 20s sits across from you. She is very close to tears. When asked why she is seeking counseling, she quietly says, "I'm not really sure."
a. Keeping everything inside will only make matters worse.
b. It is difficult to talk about personal things.
c. What would you like to talk about?
d. Things don't seem very clear to you right now.
e. Sometimes if you start talking about something, it makes it easier to talk about what is really bothering you.

18. Your client is a secretary, about 40 years of age, who is about to lose her job because of a plant closure. She will have to relocate to a plant in another city or face unemployment. She laments, "After all these years with the same company, what am I to do?"
a. You feel unprepared to make such a tough decision right now?
b. That really is too bad. Sometimes things just take a while to work out.
c. Are you ready to review both options and make a choice?
d. Perhaps it will help if you look at why you feel unprepared to make such a decision right now.
e. Indecision doesn't help anyone. You'll feel much better once your decision is made.

19. Your client, a 30-year-old journeyman mechanic, has been laid off from his job at a local pulp mill. He talks briefly about the layoff and continues, "I know what I want, but I'm not sure I can get it without putting a strain on my wife and kids."
a. Your family's well-being is important to you?
b. What do you want?
c. Tell me what you want, and let's see if there is an option that won't put an undue strain on your family.

d. I admire your concern for your family. Finding a balance between work and home isn't easy.
e. You'll make it. Don't worry.

20. Your client, an unemployed teacher, does some substitute teaching for the school board but has not been offered a full-time job in the eight years that she and her family have lived in the community. She states with frustration, "They don't seem to want me on a full-time basis."
   a. What reasons has the board given you?
   b. The board likes your work but not enough to give you a permanent position?
   c. School boards have an obligation to keep others informed.
   d. Keep your chin up. You'll eventually get it.
   e. Give me an idea of what the board's reasons might be.

Counseling Communication Inventory Answer Sheet

In the spaces provided, rank order the five possible responses according to the following code:

1. I would be most likely to say something like this.
2. I would be somewhat less likely to say something like this.
3. I would be even less likely to say something like this.
4. I would be very unlikely to say something like this.
5. I would be least likely to say something like this.

1.	___ a	___ b	___ c	___ d	___ e
2.	___ a	___ b	___ c	___ d	___ e
3.	___ a	___ b	___ c	___ d	___ e
4.	___ a	___ b	___ c	___ d	___ e
5.	___ a	___ b	___ c	___ d	___ e
6.	___ a	___ b	___ c	___ d	___ e
7.	___ a	___ b	___ c	___ d	___ e
8.	___ a	___ b	___ c	___ d	___ e
9.	___ a	___ b	___ c	___ d	___ e
10.	___ a	___ b	___ c	___ d	___ e
11.	___ a	___ b	___ c	___ d	___ e
12.	___ a	___ b	___ c	___ d	___ e
13.	___ a	___ b	___ c	___ d	___ e
14.	___ a	___ b	___ c	___ d	___ e
15.	___ a	___ b	___ c	___ d	___ e
16.	___ a	___ b	___ c	___ d	___ e
17.	___ a	___ b	___ c	___ d	___ e
18.	___ a	___ b	___ c	___ d	___ e
19.	___ a	___ b	___ c	___ d	___ e
20.	___ a	___ b	___ c	___ d	___ e

Counseling Communication Inventory Scoring Sheet

Transfer the answers from your answer sheet to this scoring sheet, putting the number (1,2,3,4,5) you have for each letter (a,b,c,d,e) in the appropriate place. *Note that the letters (a,b,c,d,e) are generally not in the same sequence on the scoring sheet as on your answer sheet. Be careful in making the transfers.* Sum each column to obtain subtotals. Then sum the two subtotal scores for each communication-style column to get a total score for each style (grand totals). Each of the five communication styles covered in Part I is represented by its first letter: Listening, Questioning, Coaching, Inferring, or Supporting.

1.	a	b	c	d	e	11.	a	b	d	c	e
2.	b	a	c	d	e	12.	c	b	e	d	a
3.	c	b	d	e	a	13.	b	a	e	d	c
4.	c	b	d	e	a	14.	d	a	e	b	c
5.	a	b	d	e	c	15.	a	d	e	c	b
6.	b	d	c	e	a	16.	b	c	a	e	d
7.	b	a	d	c	e	17.	d	c	e	a	b
8.	b	c	d	e	a	18.	a	c	d	e	b
9.	c	b	e	d	a	19.	a	b	c	d	e
10.	c	b	e	d	a	20.	b	a	e	c	d
	___	___	___	___	___	**Subtotals**	___	___	___	___	___
	L	**Q**	**C**	**I**	**S**		**L**	**Q**	**C**	**I**	**S**

___	___	___	___	___
L	**Q**	**C**	**I**	**S**

GRAND TOTALS

When you try to interpret your profile for the Counseling Communication Inventory, the first thing to remember is that the inventory is not a rigorous psychological measuring instrument. It is a teaching instrument, designed to help you become more familiar with the concepts you are studying. It represents your opinions about specific situations as a "snapshot in time." Like all such questionnaires, it provides a partial basis for generalizing the styles you preferred on the questionnaire to your real life. But your responses in real life are likely to be more rich and less simplistic than was allowed in answering this questionnaire.

Another thing to keep in mind in interpreting your profile is that the Counseling Communication Inventory takes you only one tier into a transaction. You might not respond to subsequent statements in the same way. And don't forget that the inventory addresses what you think you would say in a hypothetical situation, not what you would say in an actual situation.

With these caveats in mind, it is still useful to study the results. It is particularly helpful to look for communication styles that you appear to use a great deal—or not at all. Depending too heavily on one or two styles might mean that you do not have the repertoire to bring different styles into play as flexibly as is desirable.

For each subscale (L, Q, C, I, S) scores in the range of 20 to 100 are possible. *The LOWER your score on each subscale, the HIGHER your preference for that style of communication.* For instance, you could receive a score of 20 on a subscale if you ranked the twenty responses representative of that style first ("I would be most likely to say something like this").

Pay particular attention to your scores on the listening style; this is one style that is often not well developed. As you will see throughout the text, able use of a listening style is fundamental to effectiveness as a counselor. Look at your scores on both listening and questioning—these are basic data-input skills, very necessary for good communication. Is your score on questioning much lower than listening? If so, you may be overinclined to ask too many questions—without convincing the client that you are listening to the answers!

Is your supporting score low? If so, be aware that using a supporting statement at the start of a transaction often results in an awkward break because the conversation must then be restarted. Are your inferring and coaching scores low, along with a high listening score? This might mean that you are overinclined to give directions and pass along inferences without taking what other people are saying into account as much as you should.

In interpreting your profile, try to think of real-life examples of where you have used each style, and the impact each had.

INDEX

To the owner of this book:

I hope that you have been significantly influenced by *Counseling for Results*. I'd like to know as much about your experiences with the book as you care to offer. Your comments can help me make it a better book for future readers.

School: ______________________ Instructor: ______________________

School adddress (city, state, and zip code): ______________________

1. What I like most about this book is ______________________

____

____

2. What I like least about this book is ______________________

____

____

3. The specific topics I thought were most relevant and important: ______________

____

____

4. Questions that occurred to me that the book ignored: ______________________

____

____

____

____

5. The name of the course in which I used this book: ______________________

____

6. In the space below—or in a separate letter, if you care to write one—please let me know what other comments about the book you'd like to make. I welcome your suggestions!

Optional:

Your name: ______________________________ Date: ______________________

May Brooks/Cole quote you, either in promotion for *Counseling for Results*, or in future publishing ventures?

Yes: ________ No: ________

Sincerely,

Edward H. Scissons

FOLD HERE

NO POSTAGE
NECESSARY
IF MAILED
IN THE
UNITED STATES

BUSINESS REPLY MAIL
FIRST CLASS PERMIT NO. 358 PACIFIC GROVE, CA

POSTAGE WILL BE PAID BY ADDRESSEE

ATT: *Dr. Edward H. Scissons*

Brooks/Cole Publishing Company
511 Forest Lodge Road
Pacific Grove, California 93950-9968

FOLD HERE

LOVING THE HIGHLANDER

BOOKS BY JANET CHAPMAN

Charming the Highlander
Loving the Highlander

Loving the Highlander

Janet Chapman

POCKET BOOKS
New York London Toronto Sydney Singapore

This book is a work of fiction. Names, characters, places and incidents are products of the author's imagination or are used fictitiously. Any resemblance to actual events or locales or persons, living or dead, is entirely coincidental.

An *Original* Publication of POCKET BOOKS

POCKET BOOKS, a division of Simon & Schuster, Inc.
1230 Avenue of the Americas, New York, NY 10020

ISBN: 0-7394-3364-4

Front cover illustration by Min Choi
Photo credit: Gail Shumway/Getty Images
Back cover illustration by Jon Paul Ferrara

Printed in the U.S.A.

For my two sons,

Ben and Nick,

who are as comfortable in the civilized world as they are in the woods. What remarkable men you've become. Thank you for the laughter, for keeping me grounded, and for constantly reminding me to trust you. It has definitely been an adventure.

Oh, and thank you for stacking the firewood.

Acknowledgments

As I travel along the pathway of my life, I realize that I've been blessed with the greatest of family and friends, as well as with the many dynamic people I find myself working with now.

And so, I would like to thank Grace Morgan, my agent, for guiding me (with energy and patience and just enough compassion) through the wonderfully exciting—and to me, mysterious—world of publishing.

And thank you to everyone at Pocket Books—especially Maggie Crawford, Selena James, and Micki Nuding. Your confidence in me, your enthusiasm, and your encouragement, has made my journey most rewarding.

And thanks also to the Publicity and Art Departments at Pocket, and to the enthusiastic Sales Team who did such a great job of making sure my books reached all corners of the country.

Blessings to you wonderful people.

Chapter One

Present day, deep in the Maine woods

The old wizard sat in reflective silence on the tall granite cliff, oblivious to the awakening forest around him, the roaring waterfall that shot from the precipice, and the churning pool of frothing water a good hundred feet beneath where he sat. Daar scratched his beard with the butt of his cane and sighed, his troubling thoughts completely focused on the lone fisherman below. He had done a terrible disservice to that young man six years ago. Aye, he was solely responsible for turning Morgan MacKeage's life into the mess it was now.

Daar had cast a spell that had brought Morgan's laird and brother, Greylen MacKeage, forward to the twenty-first century. It had been the wizard's greatest blunder to date. Oh, Greylen had made the journey safely enough, but so had six of his enemies, two of his men, and his younger brother, Morgan. Even their disgruntled war horses had managed to get sucked into the spell, catapulting them all on an unimaginable journey forward through time.

Daar blamed the mishap on his advanced age. He was old and tired, a bit forgetful on occasion, and that was the reason his magic sometimes went awry.

Morgan MacKeage should have been eight hundred years dead, having had the joy of a couple of wives and a dozen or so kids. Instead, the Highland warrior fishing below was now thirty-two, still unwed, and lonely. It seemed nearly a sin to Daar that his wizard's ineptness had caused such a fine, strong, intelligent warrior to be cast adrift without direction or purpose.

Daar hunched his shoulders under the weight of his guilt. Aye, that young man's malaise was all his fault, and it was past time he fixed things.

A woman might help.

Then again, a woman might only add to the young warrior's troubles.

Daar had discovered that twenty-first-century females were a decidedly peculiar breed. They were brash, outspoken, opinionated, and stubborn. But mostly they were simply too damned independent. They dared to live alone, they worked to support themselves, and they quite often owned property and held positions of power in business and government.

How was a man born in a time when women were chattel supposed to deal with such independent women? How was a virile twelfth-century warrior supposed to embrace his new life in such an outrageous time?

The MacKeages had lived in this modern world for six years. Six years of adapting, evolving, and finally accepting, and still Morgan MacKeage stood alone. Morgan's brother, Greylen, was happily settled with a wife, a daughter, and twins on the way. Callum was courting a woman in town, and Ian was secretly seeing a widow two nights a week. Even their sole surviving enemy, Michael MacBain, had fathered a son and was getting on with his life.

Only Morgan remained detached, not only from the company of females but also from the passions of life itself. He hunted, fished, and walked the woods incessantly, as if searching for something to settle the ache in his gut.

"Give a care, old man, lest you fall and become feed for the fish."

Daar nearly did fall at the sound of Morgan's familiar voice behind him. He stood and faced the young warrior and gave him a fierce scowl.

"You're a pagan, Morgan MacKeage, for scaring ten years off an old priest's life."

Morgan lifted a brow. "When I next see a priest, I'll be sure to confess my sin."

Daar attempted to straighten his shoulders and puff his chest at the insult but gave up as soon as he realized it made little difference. "You're seeing a priest now."

Morgan lifted his other brow. "What church ordains a *drùidh* into its ranks?"

"I was a priest long before I became a wizard," Daar shot back, pointing at the warrior. "And one is not contradictory to the other. Both roads lead in the same direction."

Morgan merely chuckled as he turned and started

up the path that led to Daar's cabin. "Come on, old man, if you want breakfast," he said without looking back.

Eyeing the string of trout swinging from Morgan's belt, Daar decided he'd school the warrior on his manners later. After all, this argument had been repeated often over the last two years, since Daar had been forced to reveal his wizard's identity in order to save Greylen MacKeage's wife from kidnappers.

And what thanks had he got? None. Not even an "I'm sorry" that his precious old staff had been cut in half and thrown into a high mountain pond. It was that same pond, by the way, that was the source of the waterfall shooting out the side of the cliff from an underground stream, creating the crystal-clear pool that had produced the tasty trout he was about to have for breakfast.

"Does that puny new cane have any real power yet, *drùidh?*" Morgan asked as he settled into a comfortable, unhurried pace toward Daar's cabin.

Daar snorted. "As if I'd tell you," he muttered, eyeing the leather-sheathed sword tied to Morgan's backpack. The sword was more than three feet long, extending from Morgan's waist to a foot above his head, the hilt cocked to the side for easy access. That sword was as large as Greylen's sword and just as capable of destroying Daar's new cane.

Morgan stopped and turned to help Daar over a fallen log in the path. "Can it even toast bread yet?" he asked.

"It's powerful enough to gather stars in your head if I smack you with it."

Apparently not worried by the threat, Morgan turned his attention to something he pulled from his pocket. "What do you know of these?" he asked, holding up a three-foot-long orange ribbon of plastic.

Daar squinted at the ribbon. "What is it?"

"I don't know." Morgan leaned his fishing pole against his chest and used both hands to stretch the ribbon to its full length to show off the writing on it. "I found this one and several like it tied to trees all over the valley. And each one has numbers written on it."

Daar dismissed the ribbon with a negligent wave, eyeing the trout instead. His stomach rumbled, loudly announcing his hunger. "It's probably surveyors marking ownership lines," he said. He started toward home again. He was hungry, dammit, and had no patience for puzzles right now. "That's what they do in these modern times to mark their lands," Daar continued. "A man's word that he owns up to a river or to the crest of a mountain is no longer enough."

Daar stopped when he realized Morgan was not following. "Hell, boy. Your own land has lines drawn on a map and marked in the woods. They're even written in the deed you got when your brother purchased TarStone Mountain. It's what makes things legal today."

"They're not borders," Morgan said, stuffing the ribbon back in his pocket as he moved to follow Daar. "They don't run in any line I can discern."

"Then maybe they're logging markers," Daar offered next, mentally planning what he would fix with the trout. He started scanning the forest floor as they walked, looking for edible mushrooms. "Maybe they're doing a cutting in the valley," he absently continued. "Those numbers could be directions for the cutters."

"No. I found some of the ribbons on MacKeage land," Morgan countered, moving ahead to block his path, forcing them to a halt yet again. "And we are not cutting trees in this valley. The loggers we've hired are working east of here."

Daar looked up into Morgan's intense green eyes. "What is it you're wanting that's so important you're letting a fine brace of trout grow old?"

"I want you to use your magic and tell me what's happening in my woods."

Daar lifted his cane and used it to scratch his beard. "Ah. So it's okay to cast spells when it's convenient for you but not me? Is that how it works now?"

Morgan's eyes darkened. "There are rumors of a park being built in this valley, and I want to know if they're getting ahead of themselves and presuming to start work."

"And if they are, what does it matter?"

"I don't want the park to be here. A quarter of this valley is MacKeage land, and I'm against selling any of it."

"Why?"

"It's ours."

Daar lost hope that he was going to get breakfast anytime soon, unless they simply built a fire here and roasted the trout on spits. He sat down on a stump, cupped his hands over the top burl of his cane, and stared up at the young warrior.

"What's a few thousand acres to you, when your clan already owns four hundred thousand?"

"They can build their park someplace else, as long as it's not near this gorge."

Daar finally got his mind off his belly and focused on the man standing in front of him. Was that a faint spark he saw in those usually indifferent spruce-green eyes? Had something in this forest finally captured the attention of Morgan MacKeage?

"What's so special about this particular gorge?"

Morgan unhooked the trout from his belt. "These," he said, holding them up. He waved his fishing pole to encompass the forest. "This entire ridge. The stream that mysteriously appears from nowhere out the side of the mountain, cutting this gorge down to the valley. These trees. Have you even noticed their size, old man? Or their health? And these fish," he said again, shaking them slightly. "They're brook trout the size of salmon."

Daar frowned as he slowly looked around the forest. Aye, the trees did seem rather overlarge when compared with the others of the area. "They are big," he admitted. "I never noticed that before."

"That's because they were just like the rest only two years ago."

That number pricked at the wizard's memory.

"It's when your staff was thrown into the pond," Morgan continued at Daar's look of confusion. "It's the mist," he added, waving his fishing pole again. "See? It boils up from the falls and covers this gorge."

Daar nearly fell off the stump he was sitting on. The mist from the stream that ran from the mountain pond where his old staff lay?

Well, hell. Daar knew the water was special in that

pond, since it held his magical staff, but he had never stopped to consider consequences such as this. Huge fish? Towering trees? A veritable rain forest where none should exist.

"It's magic," Morgan said in a whispered, almost reverent voice. "This entire gorge is the result of what happened two years ago. And I don't want it to become part of a park. Hundreds of people will come hiking through here and discover the magic."

Daar stood up. "And neither do I," he quickly agreed. "We must do something about this."

"You've got to talk to Grey," Morgan said. "And make him understand that our land must not become part of this park."

"Me?"

"He'll listen to you."

"He will not. He's mad at me right now. His wife just had some test for her pregnancy, and the blasted doctor told Grey that Grace was carrying twin daughters, not sons."

Morgan looked startled. "They can tell if an unborn child is a boy or a girl?"

Daar shrugged. "It seems they can now." He started walking back the way they had come, totally resigned now to missing his breakfast. He chose a path that would lead them above the falls to a ridge that overlooked the valley below. "Come on. Let's go see just how strong my staff has grown."

Morgan quickly fell into step beside him. "Will it tell me what the plastic ribbons are for?" he asked.

"Nay. It's not a crystal ball. It's only a conductor of energy."

As they walked along the path, Daar fingered the smooth, delicate cane he had been training since his had been lost. It sported only a couple of burls so far, which indicated that its power was not yet strong. His old staff, the one Grey had severed with his sword and thrown into the pond, had been riddled with burls, carrying the strength of fourteen hundred years of concentrated energy.

"Then what's the point?" Morgan asked. "If it can't do anything yet, why are we climbing the ridge?"

"Hush. I'm trying to remember the words," Daar instructed as they walked along. It was not that easy, reciting spells by rote. The last time he had tested the new cane for something more intricate than lighting a fire, it had rained dung beetles for more than an hour. He could only thank God that it had been dark outside at the time.

Surprisingly, Morgan obeyed his request, and they quickly reached the top of Fireline Ridge. Two miles behind them was the pond where his old staff lay on the bottom, and in front of them was the deep gorge that fingered its way to the vast valley below.

Daar was stunned. From this vantage point the stream's path was blatantly obvious. Large, lush hemlock and spruce and pine trees, draped in a mantle of mist, towered up from the forest floor in a carpet of vivid evergreen splendor.

The cane in his hand suddenly began to hum with delicate power. A warm, familiar energy coursed up his arm, and Daar closed his eyes to savor the distinct feel of his long-lost staff.

"What is it, old man? What's happening?" Morgan

asked, taking a step back, eyeing the humming cane as it twisted and grew in length and thickness.

"Here. Touch this," Daar said, holding out his staff. "Feel it, Morgan. 'Tis the energy of life."

"I'm not touching that accursed thing."

"It won't bite," Daar snapped, poking the warrior in the belly.

Morgan instinctively grabbed the cane to protect himself, his eyes widening as the warm cherrywood sent its vibrations up his arm and into his body.

"There. That's what it's about, warrior. That's the life force. Have you forgotten what passion feels like?"

Morgan let go and stepped back, rubbing his hand on his shirt as he did. "I've forgotten nothing, old man. Now, point that thing at the valley and say your words. Tell me what's happening down there."

Daar pointed his staff toward the valley below and began to chant his ancient language. The burls on his cane warmed. The breeze kicked into a wind, sending the mist into swirling puffs of chaos around them. Birds and squirrels scurried for cover, and the distant roar of the falls turned to a whisper.

Daar opened one eye to peek at Morgan. The man had his hands balled into fists, his eyes scrunched closed, and his head pulled into his shoulders, his jaw clenched with enough force to break his teeth. And the poor warrior appeared to be holding his breath.

"It would go much better if you helped," Daar said. "Grab hold of the staff with me, Morgan, and concentrate. Feel the energy first, then see it in your mind's eye."

Morgan MacKeage slowly laid his hand over the second burl on the cane, his grip tight enough almost to splinter the wood. Together they waved the staff, which had nearly doubled in length, over the valley.

"Now. Tell me what you see, warrior. Tell me, and I will interpret it for you."

"Light. I see blinding light, yet it does not hurt my eyes."

"What color is the light?"

"Can you not see it yourself, *drùidh?* It's white. I can feel the heat, but I don't feel burned. And yellow. I see yellow sparks."

"And what is the yellow light doing?"

"It's dancing through the white light in dizzying circles, as if searching for something."

"What else do you see?"

"There is green also, chasing the yellow light."

Daar swept the staff into an arc farther afield, then stopped, bracing himself for the jolt of energy he knew was coming. The light intensified, swirling the colors into a blinding rainbow. The staff jerked, tugging at their hands as the new energy hit with the force of a tornado.

The warrior was not prepared. He staggered back against the assault but did not let go of his powerful grip.

"Holy hell. What's happening, *drùidh?* There's a great blackness swirling through the light now, driving against the yellow sparks. The yellow light is disappearing."

"And the green, warrior? What is the green doing?"

"Chasing the blackness. But when it reaches it, nothing is there."

Daar released his grip on the staff and stepped back. The wind stilled, and the mist immediately returned, as did the roar of the falls.

Morgan turned to face him, still clutching the once again normal-sized cane in his hand. Pale and shaken, Morgan threw the now silent piece of wood to the ground.

"Few mortal men have experienced what you just did, warrior. What think you of my gift?"

"It told me nothing, old man. I saw only colors."

"It told you everything, Morgan. You just had a glimpse of the energies roaming this valley. The emotions."

"Emotions?"

"Aye. Did the green light not feel familiar to you? Was it not the same shade of green in the MacKeage plaid you wear?"

"If the green light represents me, then who is the yellow?"

Daar grinned. "Someone you have yet to meet."

"The ribbon planter? Is that the yellow light?"

Daar widened his grin. "Possibly."

Morgan frowned at his answer. "And the black?"

"Ah, the black. That is another life force. Something visiting your valley."

"Something? Or someone?"

Daar shrugged and bent to pick up his cane. "Evil usually takes a human form when it wishes to plague humans."

"So the black represents evil, then? And it's coming?"

"Nay, warrior. It's already here. And so is something good. Don't forget the yellow light, Morgan. That covered your valley as well."

"But I couldn't catch it, either."

"Because you became more busy chasing the black."

Morgan's sigh blew over Daar with enough force to make him take a step back. Morgan MacKeage looked ready to explode in a fit of frustration. Good. There was certainly no lack of passion now.

Daar held up his hand to stop Morgan's outburst. "Talk to your brother," he quickly suggested. "Ask Greylen's permission to claim this valley as your own. Then build your home here. He'll not deny your request."

That suggestion took the bluster from the warrior's expression. "A home? You think I should build a house here?"

"This is a good place to raise a family," Daar said, then added speculatively, "I'm guessing you've got two months at least, judging by the strength of the lights we saw, before you must truly become involved in this mystery. You should be able to have a house up in that time. And then your claim will be unmistakable. It will put an end to the threat of a park in this gorge."

Morgan's face reddened. "I'm not having a family," he muttered. "So I don't need a house."

Well now, Daar thought. He wasn't having children, huh? That was news. Very disturbing news, considering the strength of the passion Daar had seen in the lights just now.

Not that he intended to tell Morgan that. No, some things were better left discovered on their own.

Such as the gender of unborn children, to name one.

"But why?" Daar asked. "Every warrior wants sons."

Morgan rubbed the back of his neck with one large hand. "I'm not a warrior anymore, *drùidh,* thanks to you. I'm just a man who shouldn't even exist now. I'm nothing."

"That's not true. You are alive, Morgan MacKeage, whether you wish to be or not. You are a landowner and a member of this community now. You run a ski resort with your clan."

Morgan actually laughed at that. "I sit people's asses onto a ski lift by day and spend every winter driving a machine up and down the mountain, grooming perfectly good snow. You call that noble work?"

"And fishing and hunting is?"

Morgan actually growled. "I feed you, old man."

His growl was suddenly answered by another, coming from the mist just below them. Morgan pivoted and drew his sword in one smooth motion.

"You'll not harm Faol," Daar said, moving to place his hand over the hilt of the sword. "He's my pet."

"A wolf?" Morgan asked, recognizing the Gaelic name for the beast. He tried to peer through the rising mist, then looked briefly at Daar. "You have a wolf for a pet?"

"Aye, it seems I do now. He arrived on my doorstep just last week."

"There are no wolves in this land."

Daar shrugged. "Maybe they're just wise enough not to be seen."

Faol finally showed himself, stepping silently out of the mist, his head low and his hackles raised. Morgan grabbed Daar by the shoulder and quickly pushed the wizard behind him. Morgan raised his sword again.

The wolf growled.

Daar snorted. "Two warriors, each protecting me from the other. Now, cease," he said, stepping back between them. He faced Morgan. "Faol can help you."

"Help me what?"

"Your valley, remember? The lights? The blackness? Faol can help you discover what's happening."

Morgan looked incredulous. "He's a wolf."

"Aye, warrior, he is that. But, like you, he's without direction. He's wanting a good fight to stir his blood."

Morgan looked over Daar's head at Faol, then back at the wizard, his eyes narrowed in speculation. "Is he one of your spells, *drùidh?* Have you conjured the wolf to plague me?"

Daar raised his hand to his heart but cocked his head to keep one guarded eye on the heavens. "May God strike me dead if I'm lying. Faol is as real as the hair on my face. He just showed up at my cabin eight days ago."

Morgan still looked skeptical. He slowly lowered his sword until the tip touched the ground. With his free hand he ripped one of the trout from his belt and tossed it to the wolf.

Faol stepped forward until he was standing over the fish and growled again.

Morgan snorted. "Some pet."

Alarmed that Morgan was giving away their breakfast, Daar moved to gather wood for a fire. By God, they would eat now before he fainted. He quickly set several branches into a pile, touched his cane to it, and muttered under his breath.

The wood immediately caught fire.

"I'll be more civilized if you toss one of those trout to me," he said then. "Ignore the beast, and whittle some spits to roast our breakfast on. A man could starve to death in your company."

It took Morgan another good minute to move. Finally, satisfied that Faol was more intent on guarding his trout than on eating the two of them, Morgan sheathed his sword and drew out his dagger. He stripped a maple sapling of its leaves and fashioned two intricate circular spits, skewered the three remaining fish, and walked over to the now crackling fire. Not once throughout his chore did Morgan take his attention off the wolf.

"Will you lend me your dagger, please?" Daar asked, once the trout were roasting.

Morgan studied the hand held out to him. "What for?" he asked, darting another brief look at Faol.

"I've a chore that needs doing while breakfast cooks."

Obviously reluctant to give up his weapon, considering he was within lunging distance of a wolf, the Highlander hesitated.

"He's more intent on eating the trout than us," Daar assured him, still holding out his hand. He grinned at the warrior. "Or is it me you're afraid of arming?"

He was answered by a green-eyed glare strong enough to turn a man into stone. Daar had a moment's concern that true passion in this warrior might very well turn out to be a dangerous thing for anyone on the receiving end of it.

Morgan finally handed his dagger to Daar, then quickly drew his sword and laid it across his knees. Faol lifted his head at the motion.

"Have you noticed his eyes?" Daar asked, using the dagger to point at Faol. "And the way he cants his head slightly to the right? Does he not seem familiar to you?"

Morgan's and Faol's gazes locked, each seemingly determined to outstare the other.

"No," Morgan said, not breaking eye contact. "He's just a wolf."

Daar sighed and set the sharp blade of the dagger to the small burl in the middle of his cane. Morgan had been only a lad of nine when Duncan MacKeage had died. And nine-year-olds had no time for noticing things like the color of their fathers' eyes.

"What are you doing?" Morgan asked, his attention suddenly drawn from the wolf when he realized that Daar was using the dagger on his cane.

"I'm thinking you should have some help as you set out on this path you seem determined to travel," Daar said, prying at the stubborn knot. The cane hissed in protest and started to vibrate.

"I want nothing to do with your magic," Morgan said, quickly moving back to tend the trout. "Keep your precious cane intact. You need its powers more than I do."

Daar ignored Morgan. His snarling cane was trying to scorch his hand as it twisted and sputtered to avoid the blade of the dagger.

Faol whined and stood up, leaving his trout and backing away toward the woods. Morgan also stood, his sword at the ready in his hand. He, too, began moving toward the safety of the forest.

With the deep roar of a wounded animal, the burl suddenly popped free of the cane and rolled across the forest floor, igniting a path of snapping red flames. Faol yelped and disappeared into the woods. Morgan grabbed Daar around the waist, lifted him off his tree stump, and pulled him into the forest. They stood together behind a giant spruce and watched as the angry knot of wood rolled around in frantic circles, spitting and hissing a rainbow of sparks.

"Are you insane, old man?" Morgan whispered. "You shouldn't piss off the magic."

Daar wiggled himself free of Morgan's grip and walked back to the stump. He picked up his now maimed staff and stroked it gently. "Give me that cord from around your neck," he told Morgan as he soothed his trembling cane.

"Why?"

Daar looked up. "Because it's time you let go of that pagan charm. It's been a worthless crutch and does nothing for you."

Morgan grasped the stone at his neck. "It's been with me for years."

"Old Dorna was not a true witch, Morgan. See her here today, alive and practicing her black magic? The old hag is eight hundred years dead. She preyed on simple-minded men and desperate women for her living. The stone is useless."

"I am not simple-minded."

"Nay. But neither are you quite ready to let go of your old beliefs. Have you learned nothing in six years? This thing called science has disproved what Dorna practiced and what you call magic."

"Then how does science explain you?"

"It can't. Nor will it ever. Some things must simply be accepted on faith."

The Highlander did not care for that explanation, if Daar read his expression correctly. Morgan gripped his amulet protectively, then finally tore the cord from around his neck. "Here," he said, handing it to Daar.

The wizard let the smooth stone slide free and fall to the ground. "Hand me that burl, would you?" he asked, using his cane to point at the now silent knot of cherrywood.

Morgan paled. "You pick it up," he whispered.

The burl was sitting against a rock, softly humming. With a sigh of impatience, Daar pushed himself off the stump and picked up the burl. He closed one eye and squinted the other to thread the rawhide cord through the burl.

"There's no hole," Morgan said, coming up behind him. "You can't push a soft rope through solid wood."

The rawhide smoothly slipped through the swirling cherrywood. Daar quickly knotted the cord and turned to Morgan.

The warrior stepped back, holding up his hand. "Keep that thing away from me."

"It won't bite," Daar snapped. "Now, lean over so I can put this around your neck."

"I said I don't want your magic."

"And I'm thinking the time will come when you will need it," Daar countered. "If not for yourself, think of the valley. And the yellow light. Remember? The blackness was consuming it."

Daar pointed at Morgan. "And although you may have survived your journey six years ago, there's no saying you'll survive this one. You are a fierce warrior, Morgan MacKeage. But hear me well. You are not invincible. The blackness is a powerful life force void of goodness, compassion, or conscience. It will devour anything that gets in its way—you, the yellow light, and eventually this whole valley if it manages to get past you. This small piece of my cane will be your greatest weapon against it."

It took the warrior some time to digest Daar's words. Finally, Morgan leaned forward and bowed his head, allowing the wizard to place the cord around his neck. Daar then centered the burl over Morgan's chest as he straightened.

"If you want this to work, you're going to have to give it your faith," Daar told him, stepping back to admire his gift. "And your intelligence. This burl is not strong by itself. You must discover the best way to add to its strength."

Standing as still as the mountains themselves and holding his breath again, Morgan scowled at him. "How—" He swallowed hard. "How do I do that?"

Daar waved his question away. "You'll figure it out when the time is right."

He handed Morgan back his dagger. As if afraid any quick movements would fry him on the spot, the warrior carefully held out his hand and took his weapon, then slowly placed it back in his belt.

"Oh, one more thing, Morgan. You're not to whisper even a hint of what's happened here today. Especially not to your brother. Not one word about the unusual state of this gorge, your vision, or my special gift to you," Daar said, pointing at the burl. "I don't want Greylen knowing that any part of my old staff still exists, and I surely don't want him knowing that my new one is gaining strength."

The first hint that Morgan was beginning to relax appeared when one corner of his mouth turned up in a smile. "You have no worry I'll tell anyone about this, old man."

Daar's nose suddenly twitched. What was burning? He looked around. The small fires the sparking burl had started were gone. The campfire, however, was burning brightly.

"Dammit! The fish!"

The burl around his neck suddenly forgotten, Morgan rushed to the fire and pulled the trout free of the flame. He held them up and turned to Daar, grinning.

"No worry. They're only charred on the outside a bit."

Morgan kicked at the fire with his foot, dousing the flame to leave only the smoldering coals, then placed the trout above the coals to finish cooking more slowly. Daar joined him, and together they sat once again facing the fire.

Morgan looked off into the forest, in the direction Faol had run. "Do you think he'll return?" he asked.

"Aye. I doubt he went far. He's probably watching us now."

Morgan hesitantly lifted his hand to the rawhide cord at his neck and slowly closed his fist over the burl. His eyes widened.

"It's warm."

Daar nodded. "Aye. It was angry for being ripped from the collective energy of the staff," he explained. "But now it is content. If feels your strength, warrior. It will work hard to protect you."

Faol silently returned to the edge of the clearing, lying down beside his trout. Morgan did not unsheathe his sword this time or pull his dagger from his belt. Instead, both warrior and wolf turned their attention to the burl hanging around Morgan's neck. Faol watched as Morgan fingered it briefly before he tucked it out of sight beneath his shirt.

Daar smiled. It was good, all that had happened today. Morgan had found his passion for life again in a mystery that promised a battle worth fighting.

Faol had found a new purpose as well.

And Daar's guilt was somewhat assuaged.

After ten long minutes of waiting, the trout was finally ready to eat. Daar watched as the Scot expertly pulled their breakfast from the spits, and the wizard was reminded of a similar moment nearly eight hundred years ago. There had been another campfire then, with old Laird MacKeage teaching his two young sons how to cook their catch.

What would Duncan MacKeage think of his sons today, of their predicament and their incredible journey? Would he be proud of how they had comported themselves through it all and how they were coping with their new lives now?

Or did Duncan already know?

Daar looked over at Faol. The animal rested much as Morgan did, relaxed but ready to spring into action if need be. For the tenth time in the last eight days, Daar wondered what power had lured a wolf in from the wild to walk among humans. And for the tenth time, he decided he didn't really care enough to inquire.

Daar finally took his first bite of the delicious trout the warrior handed him, and not a moment too soon. His stomach rumbled with thanks. He leaned back against one of the magically tall pine trees and watched Morgan MacKeage eat his breakfast.

Should he mention the fact that there was a woman involved in this valley mystery? And that she had shiny yellow hair that sparkled with the sensuous promise of passion?

Nay, probably not.

Better to leave some things a surprise.

Chapter Two

Seven weeks later

Sadie Quill squinted through the brightness of the noonday sun, her attention focused on the opposite shore of the narrow cove of the cold-water lake. Holding her breath, careful not to make any noise, she watched the young moose calf slowly step into the water where its mother stood. The calf was only three months old and already had learned a few lessons about survival, judging by his reluctance to move into the open.

Mama moose lifted her head to watch his progress, water pouring from her mouth as she chewed on the succulent growth she had pulled from the lake bottom. Startled by the cold water dripping onto his face, the calf staggered backward and fell on his rump on the slippery bank. His angry bleat of protest was lost on his mother, however, as her head was underwater again.

Sadie stifled a chuckle and raised her camera,

pointing the long lens through the honeysuckle bush where she hid. This scene was priceless, exactly why she loved her job so much.

She was still in awe of her luck. She was being paid to help put together a proposal for a wilderness park. She was scouting locations for trails and campsites while cataloging both geographical areas of interest and animal activity. These last ten weeks had been a pleasant dream she never wanted to wake up from.

Well, most of it had been a dream job, except that some of her work was being sabotaged. But having her trail markers stolen was more of a nuisance than a setback. The orange ribbons were nothing more than a visible tool for her project. She had the coordinates written on the large wall map back at her cabin, and she still could locate them by satellite, using her handheld global positioning system device.

It was only an inconvenience that some shortsighted fool thought he could slow down the progress of a wilderness park by stealing the ribbons. Still, Sadie had turned her attention away from scouting trails for the time being, hoping the jerk would think he had won.

This week she had been exploring the flora and fauna of the valley, noting in her journal areas that future hikers would want to see.

At the urging of his mother, the calf again stepped into the shallow water of the protected cove. Sadie depressed the shutter on her camera, captured the shot, and advanced the film. No noise betrayed her position, thanks to her father's ingenious skill with equipment, which made the mechanics of the camera silent.

Sadie and her dad had walked these woods for years, taking pictures as she was doing now, and Sadie's heart ached with sadness that he was not here with her today.

Frank Quill had taught Sadie the fine art of moving silently among the animals and had instilled in her not only an appreciation of nature but a respect for it as well.

And now she was thanking him by the only means she could find, by helping to build a park in his memory.

The mother moose suddenly lifted her head and looked toward the open water of the lake. Sadie used the telephoto lens of her camera to scan across the calm lake surface. And there, near the opposite shore, she saw the movement.

Something was swimming toward them.

Sadie leaned forward to get a better view. The mother moose heard her, whipped her head around, and stared directly at Sadie. For a moment, their eyes locked.

There wasn't much in these woods that worried a full-grown moose, but a mother had to be more cautious of the vulnerability of her calf. Sadie's presence and whatever was swimming toward them were apparently more than the mother moose was willing to deal with. She gave a low grunt of warning and stepped out of the cove, pushing her baby ahead of her.

With a sigh of regret for scaring the moose, Sadie

turned her attention back to the lake. She couldn't imagine what was swimming directly across the widest expanse of water, when walking around would be much easier. Most animals were lazy by nature or, rather, more efficient with the energy they were willing to spend.

Whatever was swimming toward her was too small to be another moose and too large to be a muskrat or an otter. Sadie sharpened the focus on her lens and watched, until finally she saw the rise and fall of arms cutting a path through the water.

Arms? There was a person swimming across the lake?

Sadie could count on her fingers and toes the people she had run into this summer: kayakers taking advantage of the last of the spring runoff nine weeks ago, a biologist, a game warden, a small fishing party, and a middle-aged couple from Pine Creek searching for mushrooms to eat.

Sadie settled herself deeper into the bushes, making sure she was well hidden as he moved ever closer. Yes, she could see now that the swimmer was male. And that he had broad shoulders, long and powerful arms, and a stroke that cut through the water with amazing ease.

The cove she was hiding in, and that he was heading toward, was strewn with boulders. The swimmer moved with lazy, rhythmic grace, right up to one of the larger rocks. He placed two large hands on the rock and pulled himself out of the water in one strong, seamless motion.

Sadie blinked, then tore her eye away from the

viewfinder. She no longer needed the vivid clarity of the telephoto lens to see that the man was naked.

She looked through her camera again and adjusted the focus. He was as naked as the day he was born. He sat on the boulder, brushing the hair from his face and wringing it out in a ponytail at his back.

Well, heck. The guy's shoulder-length, dark blond hair was almost as long as hers. Sadie pushed the zoom on her lens closer, aiming it at the top half of the man. She almost dropped the camera when he came into focus. He was huge, and it wasn't an illusion of the lens, either. His shoulders filled the viewfinder, and when he lifted both hands to push the water away from his forehead again, his chest expanded to Herculean proportions.

Sadie noticed then that the guy wasn't even winded from his swim. His broad and powerfully muscled chest, covered with a luxurious mat of wet, dark hair, rose and fell with the steady rhythm of someone who had merely walked up a short flight of stairs.

Who was this demigod of the woods?

Sadie zoomed the lens of her camera even closer, on his face. She didn't recognize him from town. She'd been back in the Pine Creek area for only a few months now and had gone into town only six or seven times for supplies since returning, but she would have remembered such a ruggedly handsome face on a man his size. She definitely would have remembered such startling green eyes framed by such a drop-dead gorgeous face. His jaw, darkened with a couple of days' growth of a reddish-blond beard, was square, stern, and stubborn-looking. His neck was thick, with a leather cord around it that dangled an odd-shaped ball of some sort over his chest.

Sadie zoomed the lens out again until his entire body filled her viewfinder. His stomach was flat and contoured with muscle. He had long, powerful-looking thighs, bulging calves, and even his feet dangling in and out of the water looked strong.

The man could have been made from solid granite.

And he was turned away just enough to keep his modesty intact. Too bad. It wasn't every day she was treated to such an exhibit of pure, unadulterated maleness. And despite her own sense of shame for being a blatant voyeur, Sadie wished he would turn just a bit more toward her. She was curious, dammit, and made no apology for it.

She liked men. Especially big ones, like this guy. Sadie was six-foot-one in her stocking feet, and she usually spent most of her time talking to the receding hairlines of the men she knew. Since she had hit puberty and shot up like a weed, Sadie had wished she were short. Like the heroines in the romance novels she loved to read, she wanted to be spunky, beautiful, and petite. And she was tired of having only one of those traits.

About all Sadie could say for herself was that she did possess a healthy dose of spunk. She may have come close to beauty once, but a deadly house fire eight years ago had ended that promise. And no matter how much she had willed it, she hadn't stopped growing until her twenty-third birthday. She was taller than most men she met, and every bit of her height was in the overlong inseam of her jeans.

She'd bet her boots that the guy on the rock had at

least a thirty-six inseam and that he wore a triple-extra-large shirt he had to buy from the tall rack.

The vision in her viewfinder suddenly began to fade, and Sadie had a moment's regret that it had all been a dream.

Until she realized that the viewfinder had fogged up.

Well, she did feel unusually warm. And she was breathing a bit harder than normal.

Wow. Either she was having a guilt attack for being a peeping tom, or she was experiencing a fine little case of lust.

Sadie didn't care which it was, she wasn't stopping. She used the back of her gloved right hand to wipe the viewfinder dry before she looked through it again.

The man was now laid out on the boulder, his arms folded under his head and his eyes closed to the sun as he basked in its warmth like an overfed bear.

Sadie suddenly remembered that she was looking through the lens of a camera. If this guy was willing to parade around the forest naked, why should she feel guilty about a couple of pictures? She just wondered where in her journal of fauna she should place his photo.

Probably at the top of the food chain.

Feeling pretty sure that the man had fallen asleep, Sadie snapped the shutter on her camera and quickly advanced the film. She zoomed in the lens and snapped again.

But just as she advanced the film for another picture, the man leaped to his feet in a blur of motion. And suddenly he was looking directly at the bushes where she hid.

Dammit. He couldn't have heard that. Animals couldn't hear the damn thing, and their lives depended on their ears.

Sadie sucked in her breath and held it; she wasn't sure if she was doing so from fright or because she now had a full frontal view of the man.

She snapped the shutter down one last time and scurried backward to free herself from the bush. She foolishly stood up, then immediately realized her mistake when she found herself face-to-face with the giant, with only a hundred yards of water between them.

She couldn't move. He was magnificent, standing there like a demigod, his penetrating green stare rooting her feet into place.

"Come on, Quill," she whispered, her gaze still locked with his. "Move while you still have the advantage."

He must have heard that, too, because he went into action before she did. He dove into the water and began swimming toward her.

Sadie snatched up her backpack and headed into the forest. She broke into a run as soon as she hit the overgrown trail and set a fast, steady pace toward home.

She grinned as the forest blurred past.

The swimmer didn't stand a chance of catching her. He had to get to shore first and then find the trail as well as the direction she had taken. Sadie's long legs ate up the ground with effortless ease, and she actually laughed out loud at the rush of adrenaline pumping through her veins.

This was her strength; there were very few people she couldn't outrun. Especially a barefooted streaker who looked as if he outweighed her by a good sixty pounds. It took a lot of energy to move that much weight through the winding trail, ducking and darting around branches and over fallen logs.

Yes, her long legs would give her the edge this time, rescuing her from the folly of trespassing on a stranger's right to privacy.

Sadie slowed down after a while, but she didn't quite have the courage to stop yet. Only a maniac would have followed her, but then only a crazy person would be swimming naked in a cold-water lake.

So Sadie kept running, easing her pace to a jog.

Until she heard the branch snap behind her.

She looked over her shoulder and would have screamed if she could have. The man from the lake was fifty feet behind her. Sadie turned back to watch where she was going, the adrenaline spiking back into her bloodstream.

There was nothing like seeing a fully naked, wild-haired, wild-eyed madman on her heels to make a girl wish she had stayed in bed that morning. Sadie ran as if the devil himself were chasing her. She could actually hear the pounding of his feet behind her now, could practically feel his breath on the back of her neck.

She grabbed a small cedar tree to pivot around a corner, and that was when he caught her, hitting her broadside in a full body tackle. Sadie wanted to scream then, too, but he knocked what little air she had left out of her body. They rolled several times, and

Sadie swung her camera at his head. He grunted in surprise at the blow and grabbed her flailing arms as they continued to roll.

When they finally stopped, he was on top of her . . . and her wrists were being held over her head . . . and her back was being crushed into the ground . . . and she had never been so scared in her life.

Sadie thought about really screaming now, but her throat closed tight. She pushed at the ground and tried to buck the man off her, at the same time as she lashed out with her feet.

That was when he shifted from sitting on her to lying on her, trapping her legs with his own.

Sadie instantly stilled. This was going from bad to worse; she now had a naked madman on top of her—and she was wearing shorts.

Oh, God. Now that she had such a close look at him, he was no longer a demigod. He was a full-blown god, Adonis, maybe. His broad shoulders and amazingly wide chest blocked out the sunlight. His warm breath feathered over her face. Sadie could feel every inch of his muscled legs running the length of hers. And she could feel something . . . something else touching her bare thigh. Something firm.

He was excited, either from the thrill of the chase, their suggestive position, or the anticipation of what he was planning to do. Sadie didn't want to scream anymore. She wanted to faint.

She did close her eyes, so she wouldn't have to look at his triumphant, very male face. Why didn't he move?

Then she opened her eyes to find him staring at her hands, which he still held firmly over her head. She immediately opened her bare left hand and let the camera fall onto the ground.

Still, he kept staring over her head.

He reached up and tugged at the glove on her right hand. Sadie closed it into a fist, to keep her glove on. Momentarily deterred from his task, he turned his attention to her face.

She turned her head away.

He pulled her chin back to face him, then gently ran his thumb along her bottom lip, watching as if fascinated.

Good Lord. Was he going to kiss her?

His finger trailed down her face, over her chin, to her neck, and Sadie felt him touch the opening of her blouse. She twisted frantically and tried to bite the arm holding her hands over her head.

He lowered the full force of his weight onto her then, and Sadie fought to breathe. Well, heck. She hadn't realized he'd been holding himself off her before. She stilled, and he lifted himself slightly, allowing her to gasp for air.

Their gazes locked.

His long blond hair dripped lake water on her chin and throat. The heavy object dangling from his neck nestled against her breasts, causing a disturbing sensation to course all the way down to the pit of her stomach. Sadie could feel her clothes slowly sopping up his sweat, his hairy legs abrasive against hers, his chest pushing into her with every breath he took. The heat from his body scorched her to the point that she couldn't work up enough moisture in her mouth to speak.

Not that she could think of anything to say to the brute.

As if sensing her discomfort, he slowly turned up the right corner of his mouth, and his gaze broke from hers and returned to her right hand. This time Sadie was unable to keep him from pulling the glove off. She balled her now bare hand into a fist as she felt her face flush with embarrassment.

And that made her mad. Why should she care that this man found her disgusting? Her disfigurement could well be half of her salvation.

He sat up suddenly, still straddling her, and released her wrists. Sadie instinctively rushed to push down her twisted clothes and cover her stomach, but her hand bumped into his groin. With a gasp of dismay, Sadie jerked, hiding her scarred right hand in her shirt.

The other side of the brute's mouth turned up, setting his face into a cocky grin, his forest-green eyes sparkling with the pleasure of scaring her spitless.

Dammit. Why didn't he speak?

He leaned forward, and Sadie froze in anticipation of his kiss. But he only picked up her camera. He carefully lifted the rewind and popped it open. He was not so gentle, however, when he ripped the film from it. He tossed the exposed film and the camera onto the ground beside them.

He opened her pack next, spilling the contents onto the ground. He poked around in the mess he'd made and found her handheld GPS. He turned it over, pushed several buttons, and tossed it back onto the ground. He picked up her cell phone, flipped it open, then discarded it like trash.

Next, he picked up her roll of orange surveyor tape.

He stared at that tape for several seconds, turning it around in his hand as he looked from it to her. He pulled a three-foot section free and tugged it between his hands until it snapped in half. He threw both pieces down onto the ground next to the GPS and the cell phone.

And then he picked up the small roll of duct tape she used for emergency repairs.

Now, Sadie had heard that victims often were killed with their own guns. She suddenly understood that concept when the man freed a length of her own tape and grabbed her wrists. He stopped, though, when he saw the eight-year-old scars on the palm and wrist of her right hand.

He handed her back her glove. Sadie struggled to put it on, the chore made difficult by her uncontrollable trembling. He was still sitting heavily on top of her, he was still disturbingly naked, and he still hadn't uttered one single word.

He took both her hands as soon as she finished putting on her glove and taped them together. He slid down her body and started to take hold of her legs.

Sadie kicked him hard enough in the stomach that he grunted, then she rolled and scrambled up to run. She didn't make it past her camera before he grabbed her by the ankles and pushed her back to the ground, on her face this time. Sadie looked over her shoulder as he wrapped duct tape around her legs.

The damn crazy man was grinning again.

She kicked out at him again with her bound feet.

He smacked her on her fanny.

Sadie closed her eyes and gritted her teeth, burying her face in her arms. God save her, Adonis was a sadistic brute.

Sadie flinched when a sharp, carrying whistle suddenly rent the air. She snapped her head around to see what he was doing.

Was he calling a friend?

Sadie looked at the scattered contents of her pack. Where was her knife? She needed something, a weapon, to defend herself. She checked to see that he was still looking off into the forest, watching for someone, while she rolled toward a group of young pine trees. She found a lower limb devoid of bark and wiggled to sit up beside it. She looked up at the man again, only to find him looking over his shoulder at her, still grinning, not at all worried that she would get far being trussed up like a turkey ready for cooking.

Ha. This turkey was not going into the pot without a fight.

He turned back and whistled again, and Sadie broke off the small branch at the same time, his signal covering the sound of the snap. She quickly tucked the sharp little stick under her arm.

The ground started to rumble beneath her. A sound, faint at first, slowly gathered in volume until it was like thunder moving closer. A huge, solid black horse appeared suddenly, galloping through the forest and sliding to a stop a mere two feet in front of the man. Sadie had to shield her face from flying debris.

A horse?

Holy Mother of God. The brute had a horse?

Sadie also remembered hearing that a victim should

never let her assailant take her to a second location. She almost snorted at the absurdity of that useless warning. Where could he take her that was any more remote?

The horse was the largest animal of its kind she had ever seen. It had a funny-looking saddle on its back, and tied to that saddle was a bundle of clothes, a backpack, and a long, leather-wrapped stick that must be a fishing pole.

With an almost negligent look back to see that she was still there, the man patted his fidgeting horse and pulled the clothes free of the saddle. Turning to face her, he started dressing.

The jerk had no shame.

Once dressed, he pulled some socks and boots out of the pack and walked over to sit down beside her.

Sadie decided the man didn't look any less scary fully clothed. If anything, he appeared even larger. Still as silent as a mime—which was really starting to get on her nerves—he wiped off his feet and dressed them.

Sadie dismissed the fact that she hadn't exactly been a fountain of words herself. She was the victim here. She had a right to be scared speechless.

His chore finished, he stood up, put his hands around her waist, and picked her up to stand in front of him. Sadie pulled her stick free and drove it at the center of his chest.

She hit that odd-looking object he wore around his neck. It deflected her blow and allowed him to wrest the stick from her hands. Staring at her with forest-green eyes now laced with laughter, he snapped the stick in half and tossed it to the ground. He ducked and lifted her over his shoulder.

Sadie kicked and twisted as if her life depended on it.

And then she finally screamed at the top of her lungs.

Her assailant was so startled he dropped her onto the ground like a sack of wormy meal and covered his ears. His horse backed up a good five paces, shaking its head as if his own equine ears had been damaged. Sadie dug at the tape binding her legs.

"You bastard!" she yelled, pleased with herself for finally finding her voice. "You get the hell out of here, before I claw you to shreds!"

His hands still covering his ears, the man just stood there staring at her. He shook his head slightly, then turned and calmly walked over to his horse. He untied the fishing pole from the saddle and pulled it free of the leather case.

Sadie snapped her mouth shut. It wasn't a fishing pole, it was a damn big, scary-looking sword.

She kicked her feet and scurried back as fast as she could, until she bumped into a tree. The man advanced on her, his eyes narrowed, and stopped when his booted feet touched hers.

That was when Sadie realized their little game of cat and mouse had come to an end. She closed her eyes and waited.

But instead of the prick on her skin that she was expecting, Sadie felt his warm, tender mouth covering hers.

She opened her eyes and found herself staring into deep, evergreen eyes. The giant raised his hand and cupped the side of her face and pressed closer, his sweet-tasting lips compelling her to respond.

Sadie shoved him away.

He laughed as he fell backward, the sound a deep, boisterous rumble that echoed through the forest. He stood up, brushed himself off, and turned and walked back to his horse. Goose bumps shivered over Sadie's skin as she watched him walk away, that long sword held so casually in his hand, his stride almost swaggering. He vaulted into his saddle with effortless grace, then moved his horse closer. He brought his sword up to her hands and cut the tape.

"Take a care, *gràineag,* until we meet again," he whispered with a nod, swinging his horse around and thundering away in the direction of the lake.

Sadie sat in stunned silence as she watched horse and rider disappear into the woods. Holy Mary Mother of God and all the saints and angels in heaven. Who was that lunatic?

And that word he'd used—had he just cursed her?

And what did he mean when he said "until we meet again"?

Hell, not in this lifetime.

Not unless she was carrying a gun.

It took Sadie a good ten minutes before she could will herself to move. She was still trembling so much she had to use a tree to help herself stand. As she gripped the branch and fought to keep from falling, she brushed at her clothes, more or less patting herself down to make sure she really was okay.

She started walking back to her cabin.

For the first time in a lifetime of growing up in these mountains, Sadie realized how arrogant she had been to think she could protect herself from any danger the woods might offer. By the time she reached her cabin, she had worked herself up into a full-blown frenzy aimed more at herself than at anyone else.

She could have been raped or even killed. But instead she'd been chased down by a naked giant who was way too handsome to be real. He hadn't been angry, or even all that rough; he had just been determined to teach her a lesson.

And he'd succeeded, more than Sadie cared to admit.

For all of her own anger at having put herself in such a vulnerable position, she couldn't help but remember the feel of his rock-solid body pressing against hers, couldn't help but think about the sensuous touch and taste of his lips.

And she couldn't decide if her shivering was the lingering remnants of her initial fear or the awareness that she had found the encounter exciting.

She ran up the steps and shoved open the door of her small cabin, quickly moving to close the wood shutters on each window, locking them securely, throwing the interior into darkness. She threw paper and kindling into the huge stove that sat in the center of the room and lit a fire. She left the stove door open, sat on the floor in front of the fire, and held her hands out to the heat.

Ping, Sadie's gray tiger cat, came slinking out from

under the bed, yawning and stretching as she walked, and climbed onto Sadie's lap. Purring loudly enough to wake the dead, the cat stretched up and gave her a gritty lick on the chin. Sadie hugged the cat against her chest and buried her face in the animal's fur.

"Oh, Ping," she whispered against her rumbling little body. "You won't believe what happened to me today."

She couldn't stop shaking. Her naively safe little world had been shattered by the stone-hard body of a man who had held her very life in his hands.

Sadie already had a rather low opinion of men—all except for her father. She was twenty-seven, and she had never had a relationship that lasted more than two months. And that had been before the fire had scarred her in more ways than one.

But up until now, Sadie had never actually feared any man. Never again would she be able even to go out on a simple date without realizing that she might be tall and strong, but she was not invincible.

Even her ugliness couldn't protect her.

Or had it? Had the man felt so sorry for her that he had decided to let her go?

Now, that irked.

Perversely, Sadie got angry that the sinfully handsome man might have let her go out of pity.

She stopped rubbing Ping and lifted her hand to her lips. He *had* kissed her. And after he had seen the ugly scars on her hand. Had it been a sympathy kiss?

Oh, those were the worse kind, quick little pecks that said she was likable, just not in a passionate way. She'd had quite a few of those over the last eight years.

Ping protested the loss of affection by nudging

against Sadie's arm. Sadie absently began scratching the cat again as she tried to judge the kiss she'd received today against those sympathy pecks.

Naw, the guy hadn't felt sorry for her. He'd been too amused.

Had it been a mocking kiss?

That was just as bad. Sympathy or mockery, when the kiss was from an Adonis, both were equally humiliating.

Chapter Three

It was late afternoon when Morgan guided his horse, Gràdhag, through the magical mist of the gorge. He chuckled as he remembered the expression on the woman's face when she had realized he was right behind her, when she had tried to stab him with a stick, and when she had shoved him away when he'd kissed her.

Morgan simply couldn't quit smiling. If he had known the ribbon planter roaming his valley these last ten weeks had been a stunningly beautiful woman, he would have spent less time building his house and more time plaguing her instead.

Well, he certainly had plagued her today, and it would be a long time before he found any more ribbons.

His smile quickly faded, however, when he rode into the clearing and saw Daar sitting on the steps of Morgan's newly completed home. He ignored the *drùidh* and walked his horse to the small barn and dismounted. Daar came over, took the beast by the reins, and fed him a carrot.

Morgan shook his head. Gràdhag was as fierce a war horse as any warrior could hope for. But in the presence of the *drùidh,* the animal became as docile as a newborn kitten.

"Now what have you done?" Daar asked without looking up from his chore.

"What makes you think I've done anything? I always swim in the morning."

"You were grinning like the village idiot when you rode up, which tells me something pleases you greatly." The priest cocked his head, squinting at him. "And that usually means you've been up to mischief. How did you get that cut on your head?"

Morgan briefly touched the small cut on his forehead, then began unsaddling Gràdhag. "I am smiling, old man, because I have just put a good dent in the plans to build a park."

"How?" Daar asked, turning a suspicious eye on him as he fed another carrot to the horse.

"By scaring our ribbon planter away." Morgan chuckled again. "She probably hasn't stopped running yet, nor will she likely stop until she reaches Pine Creek. She'll not be back in this valley anytime soon."

"She?"

Morgan tossed the saddle over the rail of the paddock and picked up a brush to begin grooming his horse. "It's a woman who's been marking the valley with ribbons. I found the roll of orange tape in her bag."

"And how would you know what she was carrying in her bag?"

Morgan stopped brushing. "I looked."

"Did this woman see you look?" Daar asked, looking pointedly at the cut on Morgan's forehead.

Morgan grinned again. "Aye. I was sitting on top of her at the time."

"Sitting on her?" Daar's eyes widened. "What have ya done?"

Morgan tossed the brush into the bucket and took Gràdhag's reins away from the *drùidh*. He led the horse into the paddock and opened a bale of hay.

"Tell me. What did you do to her?"

"I scared her, okay?" Morgan said, turning to face the old priest. "I ran her down and scared her so badly she couldn't even speak."

"You accosted an innocent woman you found in the woods? Are you mad, Morgan? That's unforgivable, not to mention illegal."

"She's no innocent. She's the one laying out the park in the valley."

"So you caught her tying ribbons to trees, then?"

"Ah . . . no," Morgan said, walking toward the house.

His home was a sturdily built structure, two stories tall, made of timber he'd cut from the surrounding forest and had milled in town. The house wasn't that large and, with Callum's help, had taken only two months to build. There was a porch spanning the front and several large windows facing Prospect Valley, which offered a spectacular view whenever the mist was not too heavy.

Morgan walked onto the porch and through the door, into the large single room that served as both living room and kitchen.

Daar followed close at his heels. "Then what made you go after her?" the priest asked, moving to the cooler on the counter and helping himself to a can of soda.

Morgan watched the old man fight to open the flip top on the can. With a sigh of resignation, he walked over, took the can from him, opened it, then handed it back.

"She took my picture," Morgan told him. "She was hiding in the bushes with her camera, and she took my picture while I was sitting on a rock in the middle of the lake."

Daar lowered the can from his mouth. "You were swimming naked as usual, I presume?"

"Aye." Morgan found his grin again. "She'll certainly have something to dream about tonight."

"So you chased her because of the pictures?"

"That I did."

"While you were still naked."

"Well, I didn't stop to find my clothes, old man. She's a fairly fast runner. I swear the woman has legs all the way up to her ears."

Daar sat down and placed his soda on the finely crafted maple table in front of him. He turned the can with his fingers and absently watched the label spin around. Unable to decide if the old priest was angry or bemused by his tale, Morgan went to the cooler and took out a can of beer. He leaned against the counter and opened it, taking a long drink of the weak ale as he watched the *drùidh's* back.

"What did this woman look like?" Daar asked without turning around. "Her eyes. And her hair and skin. What color were they?"

Morgan frowned at the question. "Her eyes were blue," he said, as if that detail were unimportant. He wasn't about to reveal to the priest just how captured he'd been by the woman's eyes when he finally saw them up close. "What does it matter what color they were? She had tanned skin, blond hair, blue eyes, and she stood as tall as a man."

Daar twisted in his seat to face him. "Blond hair? A red-blond or a yellow-blond?" he asked. "Do you remember seeing that color before today?"

Morgan wondered what the old man was getting at. She was a blond, dammit. Lots of people had light-colored hair and blue eyes. His sister-in-law had blue eyes. Hell, the old priest had blue eyes.

But his ribbon planter did have a distinct honey-yellow shine to her hair and flawless golden skin that looked to be kissed by the sun.

Well, flawless skin but for the scars on one hand and those he saw peeking around the side of her waist from her back.

Morgan suddenly straightened away from the counter.

"It's not the same," he said, glaring down at the priest. "This woman is not the yellow light we saw in the vision. Her work will destroy the gorge."

"Then you saw the blackness around her?"

"Of course not. I don't practice your magic. But she did try to kill me. She tried to drive a stake through my heart."

Daar glared at him. "You didn't hurt her, did you?"

Morgan glared back. "Not unless a person can actually die of fright."

The priest's stare darkened. Morgan blew out a frustrated breath, rubbing his neck. "I left her whole and hearty, old man. Just shaken, I hope, enough to leave the valley and not come back."

"Ah, warrior," Daar said with a tired sigh, shaking his head and turning back to the table. He began toying with his soda again. "You may have just scared away the only goodness this valley has seen in more than eighty years."

"Explain yourself," Morgan demanded, moving to sit at the table. "How can anything that has to do with that park be good?"

"You've claimed this land now. If the park doesn't include your gorge, what can it hurt?"

"They don't run a fence around it," Morgan countered. "People will wander, and once the waterfall—and the magic—is discovered, nothing will keep them away."

The old man sighed again. "That is true. But there must be some way for both you and this park to exist in harmony."

"I've thought about that." Morgan leaned his arms on the table. "I had our lawyer check the registry of deeds at the courthouse. The lands of the valley are still held by many owners. They haven't been combined yet to form the park. What if I buy this south end of the valley? That will keep the people miles away."

"Buy it with what?"

Morgan warmed with the excitement of saying his plan aloud for the first time since thinking of it two weeks ago. He leaned closer. "You can put me in touch with the auction house where you sold Ian and Callum's swords and several pieces of our equipment."

"You'll not sell your sword! Your brother would kill you."

"Nay. I would die before I part with it. But my dagger is a gift from my father. It's nearly nine hundred years old now and is jeweled. It might bring enough money to buy the land."

Daar leaned back in his chair and scratched his beard. He didn't speak for a full minute.

Morgan grew impatient. "What are you thinking, old man?" he finally asked.

"I'm thinking it might work, if your brother agrees."

Morgan was surprised. "What has Grey to do with this?"

"He's still your laird."

Morgan waved that away. "That means nothing today, especially in this country. It's only a hollow title now."

It was Daar's turn to be surprised. "My, my. How you do like to cling to the old ways, Morgan MacKeage, and embrace the new ones only when it's convenient for you. You should not let your brother know your opinions if you value your skin. Grey is still determined to bring this clan back to the power it once was."

Morgan grinned. "With daughters?"

Daar nodded. "Aye. But also with the sons you will give him, warrior."

"I'm not having children," Morgan snapped.

"Sometimes children appear without warning," the old priest replied, a smirk lifting the edge of his mouth. "Sometimes they're wanting to be born so badly they sneak in when you're not looking. Or do you intend to live like a monk the rest of your life?"

"Babies can be prevented."

"Aye," Daar agreed. "And sometimes they can't, no matter how careful you are. Mother Nature is a formidable force to go up against when she's wanting something to happen."

Morgan stood up and got himself another beer. He wasn't liking what the old *drùidh* was saying. He didn't want children.

Then again, he didn't much care for the celibate life he was living now.

A vision of a leggy, blue-eyed blonde suddenly rose unbidden in his mind. He'd gotten hard lying on top of her, knowing he just had to use his knees to spread her legs apart. Oh, yes, he wouldn't mind feeling those long, lovely legs wrapped around his waist.

Hell, he wanted the woman.

Morgan turned to look out the window and adjusted the fit of his pants. Dammit, he wanted her gone from this valley.

But he also wanted to see her again.

"There's something that doesn't make sense in all this," Daar said from the table.

Morgan continued to look out the window, willing his male urges to go away. "What?" he asked harshly.

"I'm wondering why they would start work on a park if they don't even own the land yet."

That changed the direction of his thoughts. Morgan turned around. "I wondered the same thing," he admitted, "when I discovered the valley was owned by several different people. Two paper mills own most of it, but five individuals own the rest."

Daar turned in his seat to face him. "Can your lawyer find out *who* is building this park? Is it the government or a group of people?"

"I'll have him look into it," Morgan said, nodding. "Now, will you give me the name of that auction house?"

"You can't really mean to sell the dagger? It was a gift from your father."

"And the land I buy with it will become his legacy. It's metal and stone, old man. Selling the dagger to gain property will not diminish my father's gift. It will only strengthen my memory of him."

"Speaking of Duncan, have you seen Faol lately?" Daar asked.

Morgan had to shift gears mentally. How had they gone from Duncan to the wolf?

"Aye. The beast has been sneaking around here for the last seven weeks. Did you not notice the scratch marks on my door?" Morgan asked, irritation lacing his voice.

That damn animal had nearly ruined his woodwork.

Daar made no more mention of the wolf. He stood up and walked out onto the porch, his cane tapping the rhythm of his steps. "I'm wanting a ride home. And not on that damn rough-gaited beast ya call Pet," he complained, though Morgan knew he shared his affection for the beast. "I want to go on the ATV."

Morgan followed him out. The old *drùidh* was fascinated with mechanical rides—trucks, snowcats, ATVs, even the chair lift that climbed TarStone Mountain. Daar insisted on riding the lift at least three times a week from May to October. But when the snows came, he stopped. He thought only idiots would ride in the winter, in the freezing weather, with sticks strapped to their feet.

Morgan settled Daar on the back of the four-wheeler and climbed on in front of him. But before he could start the engine, the old man tapped him on the back with his cane.

"You've done a fine job with the house," Daar said, when Morgan looked back to see what he wanted. "Any woman would be proud to call it home."

Morgan swung back around and started the bike, the engine drowning out his muttered disagreement. Hell would freeze over before he ever brought a woman here.

Chapter Four

Both mentally and physically exhausted from her afternoon outrunning a gorgeous, nude maniac, Sadie spent a fitful night locked in her cabin. She tossed and turned as nightmares paraded through her mind. She was trapped inside a mountain of solid green that glowed with crushing malevolence. She was running without direction through a maelstrom of swirling black mist that sucked the very energy from her muscles. And she was trapped in a burning house, her only escape blocked by an apparition carrying a sword, mounted on horseback, laughing at her as she cowered in the corner of her smoke-filled bedroom.

Sadie woke with a scream lodged in her throat. Thunder shook the cabin with resounding force just as lightning flashed through the cracks of the shutters, splintering the wood and shattering the glass in one of the windows on the opposite side of the room. Rain flooded into the cabin, immediately soaking everything it touched.

Sadie struggled to free herself from the sheet twisted around her body. Ping shot from the foot of the bed, her snarl of displeasure lost in another crack of thunder and blinding white lightning. The cat disappeared under the table, and Sadie ran to the window to capture the banging shutter and lock it back into place.

Her heart pounding louder than the rain on the roof, Sadie slowly backed up until her knees buckled against the seat of a chair. She sat down, flinching as another shaft of pure light brought another deafening boom of thunder. She rested her elbows on her knees and dropped her head, forcing herself to take deep, calming breaths. Still bent over, she placed a hand on her chest, willing her heart to slow down before it cracked one of her ribs.

Holy hell, the storm was intense. The lightning seemed bright enough to penetrate the walls and continued to strike in rapid succession. Sadie could hear the sizzle of boiling sap when a nearby tree was hit. She sat in darkness broken only by intense flashes of light, hugging her soaked, shivering body as she waited for the storm to pass.

It seemed forever before the rain slowed to a drizzle and the thunder faded. Ping brought Sadie out of her trance by jumping onto her lap, forcing Sadie to open her arms and catch her.

"Ah, Ping Pong," she whispered, scratching the cat behind her ears. "Did the thunder scare you?"

Ping purred in answer, then moved from Sadie's lap

to the table. She sat down and promptly began cleaning herself. Sadie sighed. After the fire had burned down in the stove last night, she had simply crawled over to her bed, still fully dressed, wrapped herself in the sheets, and fallen into a fitful sleep—only to be awakened this morning by the storm.

The intermittent rumble of the retreating storm had a surprisingly calming effect on Sadie. Her energies slowly rebalanced, and the events of yesterday were finally washed from her immediate conscience.

She doubted she'd ever forget feeling that vulnerable, but this morning's storm had served to remind Sadie that nothing in this world was without risk. Such as how a candle left burning unattended in the study could spark a deadly house fire or how trespassing on a stranger's privacy could provoke him to violence.

But the green-eyed man hadn't turned violent, had he? He hadn't actually hurt her. He had only accomplished his goal of scaring the holy hell out of her, smartly teaching her a lesson she wasn't likely to forget.

Yes, the stranger had never meant her physical harm—she could see that now. Heck. What would she have done if she had discovered someone snapping pictures of her?

She might not have been quite so gracious.

Sadie started to stand up but winced at the pain in her feet. She immediately lifted one foot to her knee, saw the blood, and glanced at the shards of glass littering the floor in front of the broken window. She'd cut herself closing the shutter. She looked at her other foot.

Well, damn. Both feet were bleeding.

Sadie hobbled to the kitchen area, pulled down the first aid kit, then hobbled back to the table. She cleaned each small cut and examined her feet for any hidden shards of glass. Satisfied that there weren't any and pleased that none of the cuts was deep enough to need stitches, she bandaged both feet and covered the bandages with heavy wool socks.

She stood up and tested her work.

The salve helped, as did the cushion of the bandages and socks. And once she put on her hiking boots for support, the small wounds wouldn't even slow her down.

Sadie walked to the bathroom at the back of the cabin, stripping off her clothes and throwing them on the disheveled bed as she passed by. She checked the level of water in the overhead tank and decided there was just enough left for a lukewarm sponge bath.

Sadie turned to find a towel and caught sight of herself in the mirror. She almost screamed at the woman looking back at her. Her hair was a tangle of knots and actually had twigs and pine needles sticking out of it. There was dirt on her forehead and dried blood smeared on her cheek, and one of her little gold stud earrings was missing.

And then there were the scars. Always the scars, peeking over the top of her right shoulder, continuing down her back, and wrapping around the left side of her waist in a crazy quilt of raised patchwork.

Sadie lifted her right hand and turned it over to look at the ugly scars on her palm. The burning beam had nearly crushed her, and she had pushed at it frantically with her right hand, trying to free herself.

Frank Quill had died three years ago with both of his hands scarred—a testament to his strength and determination to leave the burning house with at least one of his daughters.

Sadie dropped her hand and turned away from the image that had been so much a part of her life for the last eight years.

She'd gone to bed that night eight years ago and left the lilac-scented candle burning in the study; her only thoughts had been of a long-dead trapper named Jedediah Plum, a camp cook named Jean Lavoie, and the obsessive dream of helping her father find Plum's gold.

Sadie soaked her washcloth in the basin of tepid water and scrubbed at her face, forcefully washing back her threatening tears. Eight years, and still the memories rose unbidden. Beautiful Caroline, teasing Sadie for locking herself in their dad's study instead of going out on dates. Frank Quill, focused on the new piece of evidence that reinforced his belief that Plum's gold really did exist. And Sadie herself, home for the summer between her second and third years of college, equally enthralled by the hunt for treasure.

Scrubbing would never wash the memories away. Regret would not bring her sister and her father back. And no amount of guilt would ever grant Sadie's wish that Caroline Quill had been the daughter her father had reached first.

Sadie fought daily to keep the demons firmly tamped down in the back recesses of her mind. And now she put her energies instead into building a park in Frank and Caroline's memory. A small measure, certainly, compared with the days, months, and years of missing half her family. But she hoped that establishing the park would bring her some semblance of peace.

Sadie quickly washed up and dried off, then walked back into the main room of the cabin and rummaged around in the bureau. She put on a pair of well-worn jeans, slipped a finely woven silk camisole over her head, and tucked it into her pants. She smoothed the wrinkles from the soft body sock until it fit like a second skin to protect her scars, before she put her bra on over it, fastening the clasp between her breasts. Over the bra she put on a simple, long-sleeved, and colorful cotton T-shirt.

She picked out a supple leather glove for her right hand from the pile she'd amassed over the years. She had another pile just like it packed in a box in the attic at home, but all of those gloves were left-handed. Sadie intended to donate the pile of unused left-handed gloves to a charity for people who also had scars they wanted to hide from the world.

Sadie walked back to the bathroom and took a brush to her hair. She worked out the twigs and pine needles and finished the job with a baseball cap, pulling her ponytail through the opening at the back.

She inspected her work in the mirror.

Not bad for having ten years scared off her life yesterday—a bit of distress showing under plain blue eyes that were too big for her face, a small scratch on her chin, probably from the tussle, and a golden tan that had grown darker over the summer. Sadie lifted her bare left hand and wiped at her face, as if she could rub away the crinkle lines at the corners of her eyes.

She needed to pluck her eyebrows.

And she also needed a haircut.

She'd neglected these rituals while living like a nun in the woods. Why bother? Ping didn't seem to mind that her roommate was beginning to look like a bag lady.

She'd get her hair trimmed when she went to visit her mom, and she'd have her eyebrows waxed while she was at it. Sadie sighed at her reflection. Heck, she'd even buy some makeup at the drugstore.

Sadie knew her mother would be telling her about the blind date she had already arranged the moment she stepped into the house.

Charlotte Quill did that a lot. Sadie visited her every week, and nearly every week there was another new man just dying to meet her. Sadie wondered where her mom kept finding them. Pine Creek had a population of sixteen hundred and twelve. Had Charlotte been placing ads in the county paper or something?

Upon returning to Pine Creek this spring, Sadie had resigned herself to humoring Charlotte's motherly need to see her daughter happily married. So she went on the blind dates without complaint. Sometimes they bombed, and sometimes they turned out rather nicely—until it came time to dance.

Five dates in nine weeks, and Sadie had danced a grand total of once. And then it had been a fast dance, not a waltz, and she really hated those. She had always imagined she looked like a cow moose on roller skates, all legs and arms and not a clue what to do with any of them.

Not one of the guys had called her again, even though she had given several of them her cell phone number.

Sadie wasn't surprised. She was taller than four of them, and the fifth guy, though taller than she was by a good inch, had been so shy it had been all he could do to shake her hand when he had left her at her front door.

Maybe this week would be different. Maybe when she went into town in two days, her mom would tell her that they'd spend a quiet evening at home instead. Just the two of them. She was even willing to spend the evening scrapbooking, if that's what her mom wanted to do.

Charlotte Quill was a scrapbook junkie. Every picture ever taken of her family, every fingerpainting or tattered ribbon won, every newspaper list of honor-roll students that had Sadie's or Caroline's name on it, every birth certificate, death certificate, marriage license, and fishing license was forever immortalized in one of Charlotte's scrapbooks.

Sadie turned when Ping gave a loud meow from the door. The cat was standing in the open doorway, her mouth full of feathers, grinning like a Cheshire.

"No," Sadie said, rushing over and picking her up. "You let that bird go. Give it to me," she insisted, using her fingers to pry open Ping's mouth. She squeezed the cat's ribs. "Spit it out."

With a low growl in her throat, Ping dropped the small bird into Sadie's hand. Sadie set the cat on the floor and carried the bird outside, rubbing its unmoving body. She set it up high on the old bird feeder and quietly stepped away to watch it. After a few minutes the tiny bird stirred, awkwardly sat up, and looked around in a daze. Ping rubbed against Sadie's legs. She picked up the cat and carried her back to the cabin.

"Here. You eat the food in your dish," she told Ping, setting her down on the porch. "I have to go for a little walk, but I'll be back by lunchtime. I'll give you some canned food then, if you promise me no more hunting today."

Ping blinked up at her, then lifted one of her paws and began cleaning herself. Sadie turned and faced the forest.

She had to go back in there this morning. Her father's camera was still in those woods, now soaking wet from the morning's storm, and nothing, not even yesterday's fright, would stop her from getting it back.

Chapter Five

For the entire three-mile walk to where her pack and camera were—which took longer than normal because of her tender feet—Sadie knew she was being followed. And now, as she stood and scanned the empty ground where her pack and camera should be, she still felt silent eyes watching her from the dense undergrowth.

She wasn't afraid. She knew it wasn't the stranger from yesterday, not unless the man had crawled on his hands and knees for the last three miles.

No. The presence out there just beyond her sight was four-legged, probably a bobcat or a fox, a black bear, or even a coyote. Although bears and coyotes usually shied away from humans, young ones were directed more often by curiosity than by their own good sense.

While growing up, Sadie and her dad had been followed like this on several occasions. Sometimes they caught a glimpse of their stalker but usually not. The animals hadn't been looking for a meal, they'd just wanted to see what was intruding on their turf.

Which was why Sadie ignored the eyes watching her now. She was too busy trying to decide what had happened to her stuff.

She couldn't find any signs anywhere—no pack, no GPS, no cell phone, no camera. Nothing. Not even the duct tape that had bound her hands and legs.

Sadie wanted to weep. She'd lost her father's camera, the one she had carried since his death three years ago. How could she have been so careless as to walk away from it yesterday?

But, more important, where was it now?

The stranger must have returned and taken it. He may have been merciful by letting her go, but that was probably the extent of his good will. She would never see her camera again.

A tree branch snapped in the woods behind her, and Sadie turned at the sound. Had she unnerved the animal by stopping here? Was it growing impatient for her to move on?

Sadie looked around the small clearing one last time, but when her things did not magically appear, she gave a sigh of regret and headed for home.

She walked for a good half hour before the bandages on her feet wrinkled enough that walking became impossible. She sat down on a fallen log and was just leaning over to untie her boots when she saw it.

The animal stepped silently out of the forest less than thirty feet from where she sat.

He was absolutely the largest, most magnificent, most regal-looking coyote she had ever seen. His eyes were two calm liquid pools of iridescent green. The fur around his face was full and fluffed out at the jowls, swept back against two large, alert ears. His shoulder blades would come to her waist if she were standing, and his long legs were placed solidly over huge, broad-toed feet. His dense, unruffled fur was the color of cedar sawdust sprinkled with hues of variegated grays.

He was truly the most beautiful animal she had ever seen.

Sadie didn't dare move a muscle. In fact, she nearly stopped breathing. What was he doing, showing himself to her? No coyote with even an ounce of instinct would dare approach a human this close. They were hunted animals, killed for the simple reason that they competed for the deer that humans prized so highly.

But coyotes simply weren't this large. Or this bold. A thought came to her then, that she was staring into the eyes of a wolf.

Sadie immediately dismissed that notion. It simply wasn't possible. Wolves hadn't been seen in Maine in more than a century. They'd been hunted to extinction and smart enough to never return. Until now?

Sadie didn't know if she should keep such direct eye contact with the animal, for fear that he might consider it an aggressive action on her part. Then again, she wasn't quite brave enough to look away, either.

The animal yawned, nicely showing off every one of his lethal teeth, and leaned back on his haunches, flexing his shoulders into a stretch. But instead of straightening up, he lay down right there in the middle of the path and began licking his paws.

Just as Ping did when she was bored with human company.

Sadie could only stare. He was acting as if he had stopped in for a friendly visit.

She didn't know what to do.

Could she just get up and quietly walk away?

Nope. He might consider that rude.

Unless he wasn't a coyote or a wolf at all but a domestic hybrid. There were often classified ads in the paper that offered half-wolf pups for sale. God, she hoped that was the case. If he were half domestic, he might not mind that she didn't return his desire to spend some quality time together.

Her sore feet forgotten, Sadie slowly stood up, careful not to make any sudden movements. The animal lifted his head from his chore and looked at her.

"Nice fella," she said in a calm and soothing voice. "I'm just going to continue my walk home now. You can keep cleaning your feet if you want. I can find my own way from here."

As she spoke, Sadie took small, guarded steps away from the animal, keeping her back to the trail and her eyes on him.

"That's a nice boy," she whispered, slowly turning around and widening her stride. She took at least ten steps before looking over her shoulder to see if she was being followed.

He was gone.

Sadie picked up her pace, not knowing if his disappearance was a good thing or not. A branch broke in the woods off to her left, and Sadie let out a shaky breath. It seemed they were back to the same routine as before, her walking the path and the wolf following in the shadows.

The final mile was the longest she had ever traveled before her cabin finally came into sight. Sadie decided that her career as a woodswoman was being sorely tried. The forest was suddenly crowded with all manner of beasts she wanted nothing to do with.

As if to prove her point that the valley had turned into Grand Central Station, Sadie spotted a strange-looking man, a hundred years old at least, sitting on her porch and scratching an ecstatic Ping under the chin.

"Aye, there you are, girl," he said, standing up and walking toward her.

He had a thin, delicate cane he used for support—probably to catch himself when his feet got tangled in his long black robe—and a wild mane of white hair and a perfectly trimmed beard. A crisp white collar peeked out above the top button of his robe.

A priest?

Wasn't this a bit remote for a parish call?

Sadie took the hand he offered and shook it, surprised by the strength of his grip, which was nothing compared with the direct stare of his crystal-clear, bright blue eyes.

"Are you lost?" she asked, taking a quick scan of the cabin grounds, looking for either a vehicle or a traveling companion.

"Nay. I'm right where I want to be, girl. And I apologize for showing up on your doorstep without notice," he said, not releasing her hand. "I'm Father Daar. And you would be?"

"Ah . . . Sadie. Mercedes Quill."

He cocked his head at her, his wrinkled face forming a smile. "I'd be knowing that name, Quill. Is your mother Charlotte, by any chance?"

He still hadn't released her hand. Sadie didn't really mind, though. She liked old people. She liked their old-fashioned manners, their straightforward talk, and their spit-in-the-eye attitude toward life.

"Yes. Charlotte's my mom. How do you know her?"

Tucking her hand into the crook of his arm, he began to lead her toward her own cabin. "We have a mutual friend. Callum MacKeage has been spending a wee bit of time with your Charlotte, I believe."

Yes, she knew that. As a matter of fact, Callum was all her mother had been able to talk about since Sadie had returned to Pine Creek. Charlotte had met Callum at a grange supper last winter, and the two had been dating ever since.

They climbed the stairs together, her hand still in the priest's possession, and stopped at the door. Ping rubbed up against Sadie's leg. Sadie pulled free and scooped up the cat, looking back over her shoulder at the forest.

"We should probably move inside, Father," she said, pushing open the door. "A large dog followed me back to the cabin, and I don't want him to catch sight of Ping."

"Ping, is it?" the priest asked, not stepping inside. He scratched Ping under the chin again, then looked out at the woods and grinned. "No worry, lass. Dun . . . er, I mean Faol has always had a soft spot for cats. The wolf will not hurt your friend."

"Wolf? You've seen him, then?" Sadie asked. Realizing he'd called the animal by name, she added, "Is he yours?"

The priest lifted his bushy eyebrows into his shaggy white hairline. "Wolves know no owners, girl. They're independent beasts."

The beast in question stepped out of the woods just then and sat down at the edge of the clearing, facing the cabin. The hackles on Ping's back rose in alarm, and four sets of claws dug deeply into Sadie's arms. Sadie all but ran into the cabin and pushed her frightened pet under the bed. She ran back, took Father Daar by the arm, and pulled him inside the cabin and closed the door.

"Ah . . . I just thought we'd be more comfortable sitting inside, out of the sun," she said lamely, peeking out through the broken shutter. "Have a seat, Father," she instructed.

He didn't sit down but walked over to the corner and stood studying the large four-by-eight-foot model of the valley.

"What would this be?" he asked, running his finger along the tops of the mountains.

"That's a model of this valley," Sadie explained, moving to stand beside him. "This is where we are," she said, pointing to a black dot near the center. "And this is Fraser Mountain, Pitts Mountain, Yawning Ridge, and Sunrise Peak," she added, moving her finger along the tops of the eastern range. "This side of the valley is nicknamed Thoreau's Range, made up of these six mountains," she said, pointing to the other side of the model. "And in the middle is Prospect River, running the length of the valley."

"Where's TarStone Mountain?" he asked, leaning closer and scanning the names taped onto the mountains.

"TarStone would be here," she told him, placing her hands just off the southeastern edge of the board. "It's not on the model because it won't be part of the park."

Still bent over the makeshift table, he turned his head to her and waved his hand over the valley. "This is all supposed to be a park?"

"Yes. That's why I'm here. I'm mapping landmarks and cataloging the various ecosystems, so that I can help put together a proposal for a nature preserve."

He straightened and turned fully toward her. "A proposal? So it's not really a park yet?"

Sadie shook her head, absently running her finger along the edge of the model. "No, not yet. I was hired by a group of people who are working up a feasibility plan to present to our state legislature. It's still in the early stages. Surveys have been done only on paper, not in the field yet. It's my job to propose a basic layout for the park, with suggestions on where to put the trails and campsites and roads, locate the best place for a visitor center, and highlight prominent landmarks."

"All by yourself?" the priest asked, looking back at the model. "It's a mighty large task for one person alone."

"I'm only the beginning of what will take years to develop," Sadie explained, walking toward the window.

She looked outside, and, sure enough, the wolf was still there, lying down now, grooming himself again.

"I'd be liking a cup of tea, Mercedes, if you have some," Father Daar said, heading back over to the door and opening it. "You got anything sweet to go with it?"

Sadie smiled as she moved to put the kettle to boil on the gas range in the kitchen area. "I have some brownies that my mother made," she told him, getting two cups down from the shelf and quickly rinsing the dust off them.

"Would you be having something Faol could eat?" he asked.

Sadie looked past Father Daar at the napping wolf. "I don't think we should feed him, Father. He might hang around if we give him free handouts."

He turned and smiled at her. "You would not care for a wolf as a pet?" he asked, lifting one brow. "You don't think a great beast like Faol would be handy to have around on occasion?"

"If he really is a wolf, then he's wild. And it's dangerous to endow him with human emotions."

Father Daar left the door open, returned to the table, and sat down. "You haven't much magic in your soul, have you, girl?" he said, taking a sip of his tea and setting the mug back on the table. His eyes suddenly lit with speculation. "How about this? What if I tend to those cuts on your feet and promise they'll be completely healed by tomorrow? Would that not seem magical to you?"

Sadie was dumbfounded. "But how did you know?" she asked, looking down at her boots.

"You're limping. And I see the glass on the floor," he said, using his cane to point at the broken window littering the floor. "And I see tracks of blood," he added, now pointing at the obvious path leading from the table to the counter and back.

Sadie sat down so she could untie her boots, thankful for the opportunity to straighten her bandages at last. They did hurt, but she had thought it would be rude to undress her feet in front of a guest.

"Thank you for the offer, Father, but I can tend myself. You sit back and enjoy your tea."

She used the table to conceal the mess of her feet and slid out of her boots. The socks did not come off quite so easily. They were stuck to the bottoms of her feet.

"Here, child. Let me do that," Father Daar said, slowly getting down on his knees in front of her.

Sadie was horrified. She hid her feet under the chair.

He looked up at her and grinned. "You're a mite shy when it comes to your perceived flaws, aren't you, Mercedes? I promise not to laugh if you have six toes."

"You're not tending my feet, Father. You're a guest in my house."

"The Son of God was not above washing a man's feet," he said, grabbing her by the ankle and pulling her foot out to inspect. "Besides, how can I make you believe in the magic if you don't let me do my work?"

Her face flooded with heat. Lord help her, she would either have to kick the man or let him clean and bandage her feet.

"Where's the salve?" he asked once he had the bandages off. "Ah, here it is," he said, seeing the first aid kit on the table. "And now for the magic," he whispered, opening the salve and ceremoniously dipping the head of his cane into the jar.

Sadie was fascinated as well as entertained. He was a funny old priest, making a production of magically healing her feet.

Well, if he'd wanted to put her at ease for his doctoring, it was working. She didn't mind so much anymore that he was doing this humble chore for her.

"Mercedes is a beautiful name," he said as he fingered the salve from his cane and worked it into the cuts. "Is it a family name? From a grandmother or great-aunt, maybe?"

"Yeah, something like that," Sadie said, tucking her crossed fingers under her thighs. She wasn't about to tell this man she was named after a car. Especially not the car she had been conceived in.

Frank Quill had had a warped sense of humor.

"There. How does that feel?" he asked, patting the last bandage into place and straightening up, giving her an expectant look.

"Hot. My feet feel warm as toast."

And they did. Warm and tingly and wonderfully soothed. Sadie wanted to hug him, they felt so good. She smiled instead.

"Thank you, Father. You really did work magic."

He narrowed one eye at her suspiciously. "You think I'm jesting about the magic, don't you?" He lifted his cane and showed her the salve-covered burl of wood at the top. "I wish I could be here to see your face in the morning, when you wake up and find your feet completely healed."

Sadie patted his shoulder. "Magic is the stuff of fairy tales, Father. I'll put my faith in modern medicine. And your kindness, too, because I know it helps."

Still kneeling in front of her, his eyes not quite level with hers, he gave her a fierce glare. "The magic isn't here," he said, touching her forehead with his finger. "It's here," he continued, touching her just below her collar bone. "It's deep inside, in your heart. It's the belief that anything is possible, against any odds, as long as you're open to the gift."

"You're very sweet."

"Nay. Never call an old man sweet, child, unless you're wanting to prick his temper. Even priests have pride," he finished, leaning on his cane to stand up. He walked around the table, sat back down, and took up his tea again.

Sadie ignored his scolding and sipped her own tea as she stared at the strange man sitting across the table. Where had he come from? And why was he here?

"Why do you call him Foul?" she asked, waving toward the wolf. "He doesn't stink."

"It's spelled *F-A-O-L,* and it means 'wolf.' "

"In what language?"

"Gaelic. I'm a Celt, girl, in case you haven't noticed."

The man did have a mean accent. Gaelic, huh? Maybe he would recognize the word the giant had used yesterday when he'd told her to take a care until they met again.

"Father? Do you know what 'gray-agch' means?"

He scrunched up his face. "What language would that be? You sound like you have a frog in your throat."

"I don't know what language it is."

"Where did you hear it? That might help me decide."

Well, now. What to tell him. She wasn't saying spit about yesterday's encounter. "It's just something I heard someone say," she prevaricated. She shrugged. "It's not important. I was just curious."

He finally put his brownie into his mouth, chewing and grinning and then taking a sip of his tea. He stood up suddenly.

"I've enjoyed our visit, Mercedes. And now I was thinking ya could give me a ride home in that comfortable-looking truck you've got parked out back."

Sadie stared up at him. What had been the point of his visit? And now he wanted a ride?

"Did you walk all the way out here from town?"

He started for the door, waving his cane in the air. "Nay. I live on the west side of TarStone Mountain."

"Good Lord. That's nearly ten miles away, cross-country. And a good fifteen miles by road. You walked?"

He turned to her and thumped his chest with his cane. "Walking is good for the heart, not to mention the soul. But then you already know that, don't you, Mercedes? You've covered every inch of this valley in the ten weeks you've been here, most of it on foot, I would guess."

Now, how had he known that?

Dammit. Who was this strange man?

He suddenly turned and was out the door and already down the steps before she could respond. The wolf—Faol—stood up and watched as Father Daar quickly walked around the cabin and disappeared from sight. Sadie heard the door of her truck open and then slam shut.

She could only stand there, immobilized with confusion, finding herself with many more questions than answers for a visit that had lasted less than an hour.

Chapter Six

Sadie wasn't waiting two days to visit her mother, she was going home tonight. She was taking a long weekend, hoping that was enough time for the green-eyed stranger to move on, the wolf to move on, and the priest to forget where she lived.

Talk about weird. The old man had eaten her food and drunk her tea, doctored her feet, urged her to make a pet of a wolf, and scolded her for hiding her scars. It hadn't been Sunday, but Sadie felt as if she had sat through a four-hour sermon.

So, with all her dirty laundry loaded in the truck and her empty cooler packed, all she had left to do was convince Ping that there was nothing ignoble about riding in a cat carrier.

Just as Sadie finally caught Ping and put her in the carrier in the front seat of the truck, another truck pulled up to the cabin. Sadie quickly closed the cage before the spitting-mad cat could escape and cursed her terrible timing. Heck. It was *worse* than Grand Central Station out here.

At least she knew this visitor. Eric Hellman, her boss, jumped out of the truck before it had fully shut off, his hand full of papers and his expression saying he was a man on a mission.

"You're still alive, I see," he said by way of greeting as he strode toward her.

Sadie looked down at herself in mock surprise. "I guess I am," she agreed, giving him a broad smile she hoped would disarm his obviously bad mood.

He stopped in front of her and glared at her answer. "I've been calling your cell phone since yesterday morning. Why haven't you answered it?"

"Because it's broken?" she offered, still forcing a smile but bracing herself for the outrage she knew was coming.

His face turned bright red. "That's the third phone in two months! What are you doing, chopping wood with the damn things?"

Sadie wanted to tell him that this last one wasn't her fault, but she remained mute. It was nobody's business what had happened in the woods yesterday—not the priest's and not Eric's.

"This is the last one," Eric told her angrily. "They said they would cancel the insurance the next time I brought them a smashed phone." He held out his hand. "Give it to me so I can get it replaced. But the next one you break is coming out of your paycheck."

Sadie looked at his hand, shifting her feet uncomfortably. Damn, she knew he needed the ruined phone to get the credit from the insurance.

"I don't have it. It's at the bottom of Prospect River, probably halfway to the Penobscot by now." She steeled herself for the next explosion. "And so is the GPS. I lost my backpack overboard when I dumped at Portage Falls."

Instead of the explosion, there was silence. Eric's gaze shot to the kayak strapped to the roof of her truck. His face incredulous, he looked back at her.

"You're a class four kayaker, Quill. You don't dump your boat on class two rapids."

She shrugged. "Hey, anyone can have a bad day."

"Why wasn't your pack in the dry hatch?" he asked, looking back at the nineteen-foot-long yellow kayak.

The boat was really an ocean or calm-water kayak, since Sadie usually traveled lakes and dead-water streams, but she did need to get down swift water on occasion, and she wasn't lugging around two different boats to do the job. This poor kayak carried the scars of rough use, but it was still an excellent vessel, a gift from her dad on her sixteenth birthday.

"The hatch popped," she said, straight-faced.

The bluster seemed suddenly to go out of Eric. He shook his head. "What were you doing at Portage Falls? Do you think Jedediah's gold is that far north?"

"I was mapping the river, looking for possible campsites."

"That kind of stuff can come later," he said, dismissing her work with a wave of his hand. "You need to find that gold, Quill. It's going to be the focal point of the park."

"I'm looking, Eric. Honest to God, every day I'm out there, I'm looking for it." She sighed and rubbed her forehead. "It was Dad's obsession to find Plum's gold, before the fire. You know that. I spent every school vacation and summer and every weekend looking for Jedediah's claim."

"And that's why I suggested the consortium hire you, Quill. You have the best chance of finding it. You know this valley, and you know your father's research. So why can't you find it?"

"It might not exist, you know. Even Dad was aware of that possibility. Maine is not a state known for gold."

"It exists," Eric said through gritted teeth. "Frank spent the better part of his life looking for that gold."

"As a hobby, Eric. He found some writings on Jedediah Plum, even unearthed an old journal. But it all could have been the romantic delusions of an eccentric old hermit. Jedediah claimed he'd found the source of Prospect River's placer gold, but the man died a pauper nearly eighty years ago."

Eric's face suddenly brightened, and he handed her the papers he was holding. "I've been doing some research of my own," he said as Sadie took the papers and unfolded them.

She gasped when she saw what they were. "Where did you find this?" she asked, leafing through the photocopies of an old handwritten journal. "This is the diary Dad found just before . . . well, just before the fire."

"It is?" Eric asked, moving to look over her shoulder. "Frank had this diary? I found this in an obscure little logging museum about sixty miles north of here and got permission to photocopy it. It's the journal of a logging camp cook who lived in Jedediah's time. It seems that just before the old hermit died, he came back out here one last time. The cook, Jean Lavoie, thought he was after some of the gold. But Jedediah disappeared a few days later. They found his body after the spring thaw."

"Yes. They also found that he had been shot," Sadie added. "That part of Plum's life—or, rather, his death—is well documented. I can't believe you found this." She looked at Eric, smiling sadly. "I tried cajoling Dad into gathering back his research, but after the fire he lost his passion for the hunt."

Eric moved back to face her, smiling sympathetically. "I'm sorry, Quill. But maybe now you can study this diary and finally come up with a location. I've read it at least a hundred times, but I don't know this valley as well as you do. Maybe you can find where these logging camps were, and that will tell you the vicinity of Plum's claim."

"I wish I had the rest of Dad's research. We'd been so close eight years ago."

"Everything burned?" he asked, tempering his voice with kindness.

"Yes. The fire started in the study where he kept his research," Sadie confirmed, turning away and walking to the driver's side of her truck. She opened the door and put the papers inside.

"You're going home? It's only Thursday," Eric said, seeing that the truck was packed with her belongings.

"I need a few days off. And I want to contact the geological people in Augusta."

"Why?"

"I've been studying my model and began wondering about approaching the mystery of Plum's gold from a different angle."

"A geological angle?" he asked, suddenly not looking so disgruntled about her self-approved vacation.

"Yeah. Instead of only trying to follow Jedediah's path, which is all but nonexistent, why not see where Mother Nature would most likely have set her gold?"

He looked skeptical. "Frank never tried that approach?"

"Sure he did. But all his maps and aerial photos burned with his research."

Eric got a far-away look in his eyes as he rubbed the back of his neck and stared over the hood of her truck. "I never thought of that. And I wasn't aware Frank had, either."

Sadie climbed into her truck and looked at Eric, still standing in the open doorway.

"Come by my store Sunday," Eric said. "I'll have a new cell phone for you. And you can pick out a new GPS while you're at it." He gave her a stern look. "You pick out a waterproof one, and you wear the damn thing tied around your neck. The budget we've allocated for this phase of the project is nearly spent. And until we can raise more funds, or you can find that gold, anything else you lose is coming out of your paycheck."

She gave him a salute. "Gotcha. I'll cherish my new equipment as I would my own child," she promised, reaching to close her truck door. Eric stopped her by grabbing the handle.

"Oh, one more thing," he said. "The Dolan brothers are in town. It seems they're actively looking for the mine again. You keep an eye out for them, Quill," he told her. "You also be sure you stay one step in front of them, not behind them. If they find that gold before we do, our plans for the park will be set back by several years. We're counting on that gold for funding."

That reminder given, he closed the door, walked back to his own truck, and headed back toward town as quickly as he had arrived.

Sadie was about to start her own truck when the wolf stepped out of the woods right beside her. Only he wasn't looking at her but in the direction Eric had gone. His hackles were raised on his back.

Goose bumps lifted on Sadie's arms. What had Father Daar said? Something about Faol protecting her from strangers?

Oh, she needed to get out of here. Now.

But even before Sadie realized what she was doing, she rolled down the window and actually spoke to the wolf. "Thank you, big boy," she said in a whisper.

Faol turned his head and looked up, his regal green eyes calm and direct, and whined.

Sadie gaped at the animal, then shook her head to clear it. She was acting more foolish than the priest, endowing the wolf with human emotions.

It was definitely time to go home.

But home had its own host of surprises, not the least of which was a very tall, very naked man standing in her mother's darkened kitchen. He was peering into the fridge, singing rather loudly and off key as he sorted through its contents.

Sadie yelped and nearly dropped the cat carrier on

the floor. The man's song turned to a shout, and he spun around as if ready to fight. His eyes wide and his mouth frozen open in shock, he suddenly grabbed one of the kitchen chairs and held it up in front of his waist. The man turned as red as his hair, from his forehead to his feet, as they stared at each other in silence so thick Sadie actually could hear her heart beating.

"Why did you yell, Callum? Did you drop the milk?" Charlotte Quill asked as she walked into the kitchen.

Sadie's jaw dropped. Her mother was dressed in the sexiest, most beautiful nightgown she had ever seen.

"Mother?" Sadie croaked. She looked back at the man. This was Callum? In her mother's kitchen? Naked?

She looked back at her mother, who had stopped dead in her tracks and was blushing to the roots of her blond tousled hair.

"Oh, dear," Charlotte whispered.

It was Callum who broke the triangle of stares. Still holding the chair like a shield to protect what modesty he had left, he sidled over to Charlotte, then backed through the doorway before disappearing into the darkness of the hall. Her mother walked over and closed the refrigerator door, then walked over to Sadie and took the cat carrier out of her hands and set it on the floor. Charlotte leaned up and kissed her still shocked daughter on the cheek.

"Hi, sweetie. I wasn't expecting you home tonight."

"I see that."

"He's a fine figure of a man, don't you think?"

Sadie stared at her mother, then suddenly broke into laughter. She gave her mother a huge hug. "Oh, Mom. Only you would ask your daughter what she thought of your lover's bod."

"Well, you did get a good look, I take it," Charlotte said into her shoulder, hugging her back.

"I guess I did."

Charlotte pulled away and took Sadie by both hands, absently running her thumb over Sadie's glove-covered scars. "He's so embarrassed, sweetie. He's probably dressing right now and practicing what to say to you when he comes back out here."

"Maybe I have something to say to him. Like asking what his intentions are toward you."

"I intend to marry your mother, lass," Callum said from the entrance to the hall.

He was fully clothed now and no less impressive for being dressed. He had obviously tried to smooth down his hair with his hand but had fallen quite a bit short of taming it. Charlotte let go of Sadie's hands and crossed the kitchen to stand at Callum's side.

"Hush, Callum. Now is not the time."

"Not the time, woman?" he asked in a growl, looking down at her with a gleam in his eyes. "Your daughter has just caught us in a compromising position. Her question is fair."

He wrapped one arm around Charlotte in an embrace that said he wanted no more interference from her. He looked at Sadie.

"I've asked your mother to marry me, lass, at least once a week for the last two months. But she's being stubborn about giving me an answer."

Sadie lifted her shoulders into a shrug. "Don't look at me. It took two years of coaxing just to get her to visit me in Boston."

"Two years!" he said, looking a bit sick in the face as he glared down at Charlotte. "I'm getting old, woman. I can't wait two more years."

Charlotte patted his shirt, then ducked out from under his arm to move away. "Well, Callum MacKeage, you're going to have to wait a while longer," she said, going to the kennel.

Charlotte's cat, Kashmir, had silently come into the kitchen and was standing with her nose pressed up against the kennel. As soon as Charlotte freed Ping from her carrier, both cats took off at a run to the nether regions of the house.

"Well," Sadie said into the awkward silence. She held out her gloved right hand. "It's nice to finally meet you, Callum. I'm surprised we haven't met before now."

Callum took her hand in a warm, gentle embrace. "I've wanted you and your mom to have some time alone together," he told her. "I know you've been living away since college." He looked at Charlotte and smiled. "She's glad to have you back."

"And I'm very glad to be back. I think I'm going to stay this time."

Callum looked back at Sadie, the rugged planes of his face softened by the warmth of his smile. "Good. Now, I must be going. You two have a good visit together."

"You don't have to leave," Sadie quickly assured him. "I can go down to Nadeau's and have a beer."

"Alone?" he asked, looking somewhat scandalized.

Sadie refrained from laughing out loud, but she couldn't stop a smile from escaping. "But I won't be alone once I get there, will I?" she said, holding her mirth in check. She didn't want to tease her mother's friend. At least, not until she knew if he had a sense of humor.

Charlotte groaned and came to Callum's rescue by physically pushing him toward the door. "I'll talk to you soon, Cal. Thanks for the . . . um . . . lovely visit," she said, standing on tiptoe and pulling his mouth down to meet hers, giving him a quick kiss on the lips and then pushing him again.

Only he wouldn't be hurried. He kissed her a bit more thoroughly and then straightened and smiled at Sadie. "It was nice to finally meet you, lass. I'll see you again this Saturday evening."

That said, he allowed Charlotte to send him out the door. Sadie moved to stand beside her mother, and they both watched Callum walk to the truck parked a short way down the street.

"What's happening Saturday night?" Sadie asked.

Charlotte turned to her, excitement lighting her already beautiful face. "We're going to double date."

"You, Callum, me, and who?"

"His cousin, Morgan." Charlotte clapped her hands together. "Oh, I don't know why I didn't think of the two of you together before now. Morgan is perfect, Sadie. He's taller than you. Well, actually, he's a lot taller than you. And he's handsome and well mannered, and he seems very interesting to talk to, the few times I've met him."

"If he's so perfect, why isn't he already taken?"

A worried frown creased Charlotte's brow. "He's—ah—Morgan is a bit of a loner, sweetie, from what Callum has told me. He's building a house someplace in the middle of the woods, and that's taken up most of his time."

"Great. A hermit. You've matched me up with a tall hermit this time." Sadie kissed her now fretting mother on the cheek and then walked to the table and sat down. "Don't worry, Mom. I'll go on a date with you and Callum and Morgan-the-hermit," she assured her once Charlotte had joined her at the table. "Why won't you marry him?"

Charlotte looked startled, if not a little confused, by the change of subject. "You wouldn't mind if I got married again?" she finally asked.

Sadie leaned back in her chair and stared at her mom for a full minute. "You've been holding the man off because of me?"

"Of course I have." Charlotte reached out and took hold of Sadie's hands. "You didn't just love your father, sweetie, you adored him. I always assumed you would never want anyone to take his place."

"Oh, Mom. No man ever will. But that doesn't mean I expect you to spend the rest of your life alone, as some sort of shrine to Frank Quill. You're only forty-three years old. You're not even halfway through your life yet."

Charlotte pulled back, fingering the folds of her gown nervously. "It's been only three years, Sadie. How can I live with a man for twenty-four years, then suddenly expect to move on with a new life so soon, as if he never existed?"

"Because Daddy is dead, and you're not. Because nothing says you stop feeling, or wanting, or needing human contact. Because even though you have me, I know that's not enough. If you love this guy, I say go for it."

"I still can't marry him," Charlotte said in a barely audible voice, still toying with her gown.

"Why not?"

"Because I'm pregnant," she whispered, looking up finally, her eyes two stricken circles of worry-washed blue.

For the third time in thirty minutes, Sadie was rendered speechless.

"I married Frank when I was sixteen because I was pregnant with you, Sadie. And even though I loved you and Caroline and your father with all my heart and have never regretted a day of my life, I just can't start another marriage that way."

Sadie still couldn't think of a thing to say.

"Oh, Sadie," Charlotte cried, burying her face in her hands. "I'm so foolish. How could I let this happen again!"

Sadie dove from her seat to her knees, wrapping her arms around her mother, hugging her fiercely. "You're not foolish," she assured her, lifting her mom's face and wiping her cheeks. She gave her a warm, affectionate smile. "You just have the damndest luck with men. What is Callum, the second guy you've dated in all your life?"

Wiping her tears with her gown, Charlotte nodded. "Can you believe it? Two boyfriends, and both of them knocked me up."

"But how?"

Charlotte blinked at her. "The usual way," she said, her face turning bright red. She wiped at her tears again, and Sadie let out a frustrated breath.

"I know how. What I mean is, weren't you using something? You're old enough this time to know about birth control. What did you and Daddy do all these years?"

"Frank had a vasectomy just after Caroline was born," Charlotte told her through a short round of hiccups. "In my entire life, I never used birth control. And I didn't even stop to think this time. It just . . . it just happened," she ended with another round of weeping, burying her face in her hands again.

Sadie let her mother cry instead of asking if Callum hadn't at least been bright enough to use something himself.

Sadie stood up and decided her mother needed a cup of tea. Personally, she needed something a little stronger. It was as she was getting the brandy down from the top shelf of the cupboard that Sadie suddenly realized what all this meant.

She was going to be a sister again.

The bottle of brandy forgotten on the counter, Sadie ran back to her mother, pulled her up out of the chair, and hugged her fiercely.

"We're going to have a baby, Mom. I'm going to be a sister again."

Charlotte looked up, blinking in surprise. Slowly, and with the immense power of love behind it, she smiled the smile of a woman coming to terms with her condition.

"You are, aren't you? You're going to be a sister again because I'm going to have a baby."

"This is wonderful, Mom," Sadie whispered, as if she could keep their precious secret just between them, not even wanting the house to hear it. "You can marry Callum if you truly love him, but you can also raise this baby yourself. You know I'll help you. No pressure. No history repeating itself. You're not a scared girl of sixteen this time. You have me."

"Oh, sweetie. You have no idea how hard it was back then and the struggles we faced, what with your father trying to finish school and working at his family's mill to support us."

Charlotte hugged her quickly and then moved to put the kettle on to boil before she placed the brandy back in the cupboard, taking down two teacups instead. She talked while she worked.

"I do love Callum. I've known that for months now." She turned and pointed a china cup at Sadie. "I wouldn't have gone to bed with him if I didn't," she said firmly. "I'm not that kind of girl."

Sadie took a seat at the table, recognizing her mother's need to be busy. She quickly nodded agreement as a dutiful daughter should.

"It's just that I don't want to *have* to marry him," Charlotte continued. "Your father loved me, Sadie. But I always felt that he could have gone on to greater things if he hadn't had us to slow him down."

"Dad loved running the lumber mill," Sadie quickly interjected. "And it never stopped him from pursuing his hobby of Maine history."

"He could have been a professor," Charlotte countered, turning to take down the teapot.

"He could have been," Sadie agreed. "But that would have meant leaving these woods, and you and I both know that never would have happened."

Her mother turned to her again, her tear-swollen eyes hopeful. "Do you really think that's true, Sadie? That I didn't hold Frank back?"

Unable to sit any longer, Sadie got up and went to her mother, taking the forgotten teapot from her hands and setting it on the counter with the cups. She took her mom by the shoulders and looked her square in the face.

"Dad loved you, me, Caroline, and his life here. How can you doubt that?"

Charlotte pushed the hair from her face with a trembling hand and let out a tired sigh. "I don't. It's just that I'm so confused right now. And scared. How am I going to tell Callum he's fathered a child? The man's forty-eight years old. He'll practically be on Social Security before our kid even gets her driver's license."

Sadie dismissed that worry with a chuckle. "I'll teach her to drive if Callum can't handle the stress. It's okay, Mom. People are having children later in life now. You won't be the only gray-haired lady at the PTA meetings."

"I'm going to have to tell him soon, aren't I?"

"Yes, you've got to tell him. But that does not mean you have to marry him."

It was Charlotte's turn to laugh. "Of course I do, sweetie," she said, patting Sadie's cheek and then moving back to pour the boiling water into the teapot. "Callum MacKeage is one of those old-fashioned men. Once he knows I'm having a baby, he'll probably drag me to the minister before I've even finished telling him."

Charlotte shot a grin over her shoulder that said she found that idea amusing. "If he doesn't have a heart attack first. The poor man is so *hung up* on proprieties. That's why he always parks his truck down the road instead of in my driveway, so people won't know he's visiting me so late," she said, waving at the window facing the street. "And he tried hard not to show it, but he was mortified that you found us together tonight." She winked at her daughter. "And naked, at that."

Sadie laughed. "Then he really would have keeled over if I'd arrived earlier and actually found you in bed together. And I would have, if Eric hadn't shown up at camp."

"Eric actually ventured into the deep woods?" Charlotte asked, tongue in cheek.

Everyone in Pine Creek knew that Eric Hellman hated the woods. And everyone thought it ironic that the man owned an outfitters store.

"He only took a few steps on actual dirt," Sadie assured her. "And he drove like the devil to get in and out as fast as he could."

"But why make the trip? He knows you come into town on the weekends."

"He found an old diary that belonged to a camp cook who knew Jedediah. And he couldn't wait for me to see it."

"I tried calling you today," Charlotte said, bringing the tray of tea to the table. She lifted one brow. "Did you forget to charge your cell phone again, or did you break another one?"

"I—ah—I sort of lost this one," Sadie admitted.

Charlotte sighed into her tea on the pretense of cooling it off. She looked over the rim of her cup, and Sadie could see that her mother was trying very hard not to laugh.

"Hey. It's physical work that I do," Sadie defended herself. "But the cell phone's nothing. You should have seen Eric's face when I told him I lost the GPS at the same time." She suddenly sobered. "I lost Dad's camera, too, Mom."

"Oh, honey, I'm sorry," Charlotte quickly consoled, understanding what the loss meant to Sadie. She reached over and patted her hand. "You still have the one Frank gave you for your tenth birthday."

"But it's not the same. And now I don't dare use it. I don't want to risk losing that one, too."

"Then I'll buy you a new one," Charlotte said, sitting up and smiling at her plan. "And you can have it fixed so it doesn't make a noise when you use it."

"Then I'll be worried about losing *your* gift." Sadie blew into her own tea. "I'm better off just buying my own. That way, I won't feel bad if something happens to it. I'm too damn sentimental."

"No, sweetie. You're too damned absentminded," her mother said, not unkindly. "You're always so busy being curious about everything that you keep overlooking the details of life. And that's why you need a husband."

Sadie didn't respond to that half-truth; she might need to work on getting her act together, but she sure as heck didn't need a husband to do it for her. So, instead of arguing the point, Sadie drank the soothing chamomile tea and basked in the warmth of her mother's kitchen.

Yes, this was why she had come home today. Charlotte's mothering was a balm to her soul. Her mom was grounded in reality, always able to put things in the proper prospective for Sadie, always able to give Sadie the confidence she needed to continue moving forward despite the guilt she wore around her neck like a granite tombstone.

It was her fault that Caroline and her father were dead. She had caused the fire that had killed Caroline and disabled her dad to the point that he had only lived five years, until he died from a weakened heart at the young age of forty-one.

Frank Quill had returned to the burning house, and it had been Sadie, not the innocent Caroline, he had pulled from the flames.

A preventable, senseless tragedy. And not once, ever, in the eight years since had her mother or father condemned Sadie for the loss of their younger daughter. In fact, they had both gone out of their way to convince her that they cherished the one child God had left them while they mourned the one they had lost.

Sadie loved them both so much for that.

And she loved her mom's friendship now. Charlotte Quill always met whatever life gave her head-on, since finding herself pregnant at the age of sixteen, through the tragedy eight years ago, through her husband's death three years ago, and now as she found herself pregnant yet again.

Sadie only hoped that someday she could be half the woman Charlotte Quill was. Because she needed very much to be the sort of big sister this unborn child could look up to.

Chapter Seven

Sadie was out of bed and halfway down the hall before she realized she should have been feeling bare feet touching the hardwood floor. She stopped in the doorway of the bathroom and stared down at the bandages covering her feet. She wiggled her toes, then shifted her weight from one foot to the other, testing for pain.

There was none. Not a twinge or even the memory of pain.

Sadie sat on the edge of the tub and lifted one leg to her knee, quickly unwrapping the bandage and twisting the bottom of her foot toward her.

Well, hell. There weren't even any scars.

She quickly unwrapped the other foot and examined it closely, stretching the skin and running a finger from her toes to her heel, looking for the tiny little cuts that should have been there.

There wasn't even any redness.

Sadie dropped her foot to the floor and stared out at the empty hall. Cuts didn't heal, much less disappear, in twenty-four hours. It wasn't possible.

And it sure as heck wasn't magic.

Sadie looked down and wiggled her toes again. If she hadn't pulled the small pieces of glass from her feet herself, she would say that it had all been a dream—or a really good advertisement for the salve she had used.

But it was not magic.

She had to see that priest again. She had to sit him down and make him explain how rubbing some over-the-counter medicine onto his cane could heal her feet. And she also would insist that he explain why he wanted her to believe it was magic in the first place.

"Sadie? What are you doing sitting on the tub and staring at nothing?" her mother asked, walking into the bathroom. She pointed at the floor. "And what are those?"

Sadie grabbed the bandages and tossed them into the trash by the sink. "They're just some padding to help prevent blisters on my feet," she quickly lied. "I've got to get some new boots this weekend. Do you remember that Dad used to own a small handgun? Do you still have it?"

Charlotte frowned at her. "A handgun? What's that got to do with blisters?"

"Nothing. It's just that I remembered Dad always carried a gun whenever we hiked. And I was wondering if you'd kept it."

Her mother's face wrinkled with worry. "Why?" she asked, sitting down on the closed toilet, facing Sadie.

"Are you having trouble at the cabin? Has someone been bothering you out there?"

Sadie shook her head. "No, Mom. Nothing like that. I just thought I should probably have some sort of protection with me."

"You can't mean to carry a gun, Sadie. Frank only kept that for emergencies."

"And that's all I want it for. What? You think I'm going to walk around with it strapped to my hip like a gunfighter? Mom, I'm miles from nowhere out there. I just want to know that I can take care of myself if a problem arises."

"But a gun, Sadie? Do you even know how they work?"

"Now, that's a sexist remark."

"You know what I mean. Gender has nothing to do with ignorance. You're going to shoot yourself in the foot."

"Dad taught me to use a gun when I was twelve." She grinned at her mother. "And he also made me promise never to tell you."

And she still shouldn't have told her, judging by the scowl her mother gave her just then.

"I don't have it anymore," Charlotte told her. "After Frank died, I gave it to Sheriff Watts to get rid of."

"Why?"

"Because I don't like guns."

Sadie rolled her eyes. "Mom, you're living smack in the middle of hunting country. Every damn pickup in town has a gun in the back window."

"That's different. Those are rifles, meant to put meat on every damn table in town," she shot back, standing up and glaring at Sadie. “And if you don’t feel safe in the woods anymore, then maybe you should move home and forget about that stupid park.”

Sadie also stood up, mostly from surprise at her mother’s outburst. “I thought you supported the wilderness park.”

“Not if it means my daughter has to live in the woods like a hermit and carry a gun in order to feel safe.”

Sadie blew out a frustrated breath and scrubbed her face with her hands. She pushed her hair behind her ears and forced herself to smile. “Well, jeez. If it bothers you so much, forget I even mentioned the gun. I am perfectly safe doing my job.”

“But that’s just it, Sadie. It’s not just a job to you. That park has become an obsession. From the time Eric Hellman called you in Boston, you’ve become a driven woman. You left a perfectly good career and all but ran up here in less than a week. And just look at you,” she said, grabbing Sadie by the shoulders and pivoting her around to face the mirror. “You’ve lost weight.”

“I’ve toned up,” Sadie countered, glaring at her mother in the mirror.

“And you’re not taking care of yourself,” Charlotte continued, as if she hadn’t spoken. “Your hair hasn’t seen a pair of scissors in six months. You’re not using any sunscreen, and you have two hairy caterpillars for eyebrows.”

“I’m going to the salon today.”

Charlotte lifted Sadie’s left hand and turned the palm toward the mirror. “Look at that,” she said.

"Calluses the size of quarters. Scratches. Bug bites. Broken nails." Her mother examined the fingers on the hand she was holding. "Or are you chewing your nails again?"

Sadie pulled free and stared into the mirror, unable to utter a word.

Charlotte spun her around to face her. "You're so obsessed with this park that you're ignoring the details of life again. You're not even thirty yet, and you're already becoming one of those addlebrained old spinster cat ladies."

Sadie could only gape at her mother. "I date," she snapped, pulling away.

"You go through the motions," Charlotte said fiercely, not backing down. She waved an angry hand in the air. "And you spend those dates systematically driving the poor guys away before they can even get to know you."

"Those poor guys are dorks. I gave three of them my cell phone number, and they never called."

"You gave them the number of a cell phone that is always broken." Charlotte waved her hand again. "It's those damn details, Sadie. You've got to start living in the present, not the past. And not in some future shrine to your father and sister. I want you to live in the *now*."

Deciding it was definitely time to end this conversation, Sadie moved forward and took her mother into a fierce embrace. "I will, Mom. I promise. Starting today." She leaned back and smiled. "I'll go to the salon, spiff myself up real pretty, and I'll even buy a new outfit for our date tomorrow night."

Charlotte's expression was skeptical.

"And I promise," Sadie said, placing a hand over her heart. "I'll be the epitome of charm and grace for Morgan MacKeage."

Morgan MacKeage tightened the knot at his neck with a severe jerk, then tugged at the front of his silk tie with an impatient hand. He lifted his chin to free his throat and scowled at his reflection in the mirror.

"Ya can't mean to wear those braids in your hair tonight," Callum said, walking up and looking pointedly at the small braids running down both sides of Morgan's head.

Morgan turned slightly and examined one of the braids. "And why not?" he asked, glaring back at Callum in the mirror.

"Because men don't wear braids in this time." Callum snorted and tapped the back of Morgan's head. "Nor do they wear their hair so long. You look like a heathen."

Morgan walked to the dresser and picked up a short leather strap. "I am a heathen," he acknowledged. He pointed at Callum. "And I've agreed to go on this accursed date only because you nagged me into it. But it will be a cold day in hell before I cut my hair for a woman."

Callum raised both his hands in surrender. "I appreciate the favor you're doing for me. And I'm not asking that you cut your hair. I'm just wishing you could be a bit more . . . well, more civilized. Just for tonight? Is that asking too much, Morgan, for you to dig out some of that charm you were once famous for?"

Morgan pulled his hair to the back of his neck and tied it with the leather strap. He grinned at his cousin. Poor Callum had definitely been bitten by the domesticating bug—and she was named Charlotte Quill.

"And what, pray tell, is wrong with Mercedes Quill, that she needs her mother to find her dates?" Morgan asked. "Does she have pointed ears? Or is she missing some teeth?" His grin turned into a scowl. "Dammit, she'd better not be five feet tall. I get a crick in my back dealing with short women."

Callum suddenly paled. Morgan watched, surprised, as his cousin nervously smoothed down the front of his shirt and looked every place but at him.

"Ah, no. Sadie—she prefers Sadie to Mercedes—is a comely lass," Callum said in a pensive voice. "And she's tall, Morgan," he added a bit desperately, taking a step forward and finally looking at him. "But there is something I want to warn you about."

Morgan slapped his hand down on the bureau. "Dammit, I knew you were setting me up. What woman reaches the age of twenty-seven and still needs her mother to find her a date?"

"A perfectly fine woman," Callum said, getting defensive. "But nobody is flawless."

"And this Quill woman? What is her flaw?" Morgan asked, feeling a bit defensive himself. He'd agreed to this date only because he owed Callum for helping him build his house. Hell, one evening out with a woman, even if she stood five feet tall and was missing some teeth, was well worth two months of free manual labor. Or was it?

Morgan was getting an ache in his belly.

"Sadie Quill is perfectly normal," Callum said, not looking at him again. His cousin began fidgeting with his own tie, tugging at the knot at his throat. "It's just that . . . well, she was in a fire eight years ago," Callum said to the floor. He looked up, his hazel eyes worried. "She has some scars."

"She's disfigured? From the fire?" Morgan asked, his defensiveness suddenly gone. It was replaced by suspicion. And a sudden thought. "Where are these scars?"

Callum waved a negligent hand in front of his body. "Her back, mostly, Charlotte told me," he said. "Her left side and the inside of one arm."

"And?" Morgan asked, his suspicion more focused.

Callum frowned at him. "And her hand," he added. "She wears a soft leather glove on her right hand to hide her scars." He pointed at Morgan. "You cannot back out on me now," he said, his expression threatening. "I promised Charlotte. And I swear I'll tear your house down board by board with my bare hands if you renege on our deal."

Morgan rubbed his own hands together and started for the door. "Don't worry. I've no intention of missing this evening." He looked back over his shoulder to find that Callum wasn't following. "What? We're going to be late."

"One more thing," Callum said, his eyes narrowed in suspicion. "When I introduce you to Sadie, don't offer to shake her hand unless she offers first. She may be self-conscious with you because you're her date, and I don't want her to be embarrassed."

Embarrassed? Hell. Morgan doubted embarrassment would be the first emotion the woman would feel. Shock was more likely. And a healthy dose of discomfort.

"Don't worry, cousin," Morgan quickly assured him, slapping himself in the chest. "There. I just put on my mantle of charm," he said with a smile. "For my date with your woman's daughter." He held his hand up in salute. "Long hair, braid, and all, tonight I will be a perfect gentleman."

"Are you sure Callum warned this guy about my scars?" Sadie asked for the tenth time in as many minutes.

Charlotte walked over and rearranged Sadie's newly trimmed, gently permed hair over her shoulders. She smiled with motherly satisfaction.

"Callum promised me he'd discreetly broach the subject," Charlotte warmly assured her. She straightened Sadie's new silk blouse next, undoing the button at her throat. "Here. You don't need to look as if you're being strangled. You have an elegant, long neck and a beautiful throat. Show them off."

Sadie automatically reached up and pulled the edges of the collar closer together, but she didn't redo the button.

Charlotte smoothed down her sleeves next, ending up by taking hold of Sadie's hands and smiling at her again. "The color of that blouse sets off your eyes. And that new camisole is much prettier than those old body socks you're always wearing. It was worth the drive to Bangor to go shopping for your outfit and find a professional salon. You're beautiful, Sadie."

Sadie felt her cheeks heat. She pulled her hands

free and finished her mother's job, smoothing down the front of her black linen pants. She tested the fit of her new shoes. It was the first time in her life she'd worn anything other than flats. Her mom had insisted that her blind date was a good bit taller than her, and so Charlotte had talked Sadie into two-inch heels.

She only hoped that she wouldn't break her long, elegant neck trying to walk in them.

And that Morgan MacKeage wouldn't turn out to be a dork.

Sadie couldn't explain it, but she was actually nervous about tonight. She would never in a million years admit it to her mother, but she was also worried that she was slowly becoming one of those addle-brained old spinster cat ladies. How many more frogs was she going to have to kiss before she found her prince?

The really sad part was, Sadie was starting to consider herself lucky if even the frogs wanted to kiss her.

"You're sure Callum prepared the hermit for what he's getting tonight?" Sadie asked again, suddenly filled with anxious energy. "I mean, not just my scars but that I'm a bit of a klutz sometimes?"

Charlotte walked to the kitchen door and snapped on the porch light. "You're not a klutz," she said fiercely, turning back to face Sadie. "You can be graceful when you want to be. You just refuse to bother most of the time."

"The point being?" Sadie asked, disgruntled that her mother had all but agreed with her.

"The point being that your abilities change in direct proportion to your interest in something. When you're kayaking rapids, you're not a klutz," Charlotte said more softly, coming to stand in front of her again. "When you're photographing wildlife, you never make a mistake." She fluffed the padded shoulders of Sadie's blouse. "And with the right partner, you could dance like Ginger Rogers."

Somewhat mollified, Sadie turned to present her back to her mom and used both hands to point at her body. "Does the camisole drape properly to hide my scars?" she asked, looking over her shoulder at her mother. "Does it give my back a smooth line?"

Charlotte gave her a critical inspection, her brows furrowed. "As smooth as a baby's bottom. All six-foot-one-inch of beautiful woman."

Sadie grinned and turned back to face her mother. "Did I just get all gussied up for another dork?" she asked.

Charlotte shook her head. "No, sweetie. You got gussied up for yourself. Because even if you and Morgan don't hit it off tonight, you can safely assume it's his shortcoming, not yours."

Sadie walked over and kissed her mother on the cheek. "And that's why I need you," she whispered. "You keep things in perspective for me."

Charlotte's smile was warm. She started to say something but stopped suddenly at the sound of a truck pulling into the driveway.

"They're here," Charlotte said, her face immediately lighting with pleasure. She turned and rushed to the door, opening it wide before smoothing down her own outfit.

Sadie followed at a more sedate pace, shaking her

head and smiling at her mother's excitement. Charlotte Quill really was in love again. And she positively glowed, not only from that love but from the promise of the secret little life nestled securely in her belly.

Sadie only wished she could be a fly on the wall when that secret was finally revealed to Callum MacKeage.

Truck doors slammed, and Sadie peeked over her mother's shoulder to see two men walking toward the porch. She sighed with relief. Morgan-the-hermit really was tall. That was one awkward obstacle out of the way.

He certainly wasn't a dork, if that manly swagger was any indication. Even from this distance, Sadie could see that the man carried himself with confidence, apparently not at all put off by finding himself on a blind date.

Sadie backed up to let her mother greet their guests, at the same time quickly smoothing her cuff over the hem of her glove, hoping to calm the butterflies now rioting in her belly.

Callum stepped through the door first, stopping in mid-stride to stare at Charlotte. "I swear, woman," he said, his voice gravely serious. "You get prettier every time I see you."

With that declaration, he swept Sadie's suddenly flustered mother into a bear of an embrace and kissed her soundly on the lips. Charlotte, her face flushed red, pulled away and quickly turned her attention to smoothing down her clothes again. She tried fussing with her hair then, but Callum pulled her under his arm and turned them both to face Sadie, Callum grinning like a cat who had just polished off a large dish of cream.

"Sadie," he said, "I'd like to introduce you to my cousin, Morgan." He turned slightly, moving a still flustered Charlotte with him. "Morgan, this is Sadie Quill."

Sadie barely heard what Callum was saying. Her feet were lead weights stuck to the floor. Her vision had narrowed and dimmed, her heart was trying to pound a hole in her chest, and the loud buzz of pumping blood rang in her ears. She couldn't work up a drop of moisture in her mouth, and a lump the size of a basketball was lodged in her throat.

She could only stare, open-mouthed, at her date.

The man stood just inside the kitchen door, his broad shoulders nearly touching the woodwork on both sides, his hands negligently thrust into his pants pockets, and his unforgettably familiar, forest-green eyes making Sadie think the butterflies in her stomach just might escape.

Her date wasn't a dork. He was the madman from the lake.

And she was supposed to spend the evening with him?

He took a step toward her.

Acting on instinct alone, Sadie took an equal step back.

His eyes suddenly lighting with unholy mischief, Morgan MacKeage took yet another step forward. He pulled a hand out of his pocket and held it out to her.

The jerk. The silently laughing, defiantly challenging jerk was just daring her to put her gloved right hand in his.

Callum gave a deep cough into his fist. Sadie looked over to find him glaring at Morgan MacKeage with enough force to knock the man over. She looked back at her date from hell. He wasn't paying any attention to his cousin. He was still staring at her, still holding out his hand.

Sadie looked at her mother then. Charlotte appeared horrified. But was her mother horrified *for* her or *at* her for not politely greeting her date?

Anger suddenly came to Sadie's rescue. Morgan MacKeage had been born a jerk and would likely die a jerk. But that didn't mean she had to let him be a jerk to her tonight.

He had no right to toy with her this way. Even if she had caught him swimming naked, he didn't have the right to continue punishing her for what was really no more than a minor indiscretion four days ago. It had been an innocent mistake that any person would have made given the circumstances. If their roles had been reversed, she'd like to have seen Morgan MacKeage simply turn his back on a naked woman swimming in a lake.

Which meant she had two choices here. She could shake the hand that he was still insistently holding out to her, or she could spit on that hand—if she could somehow get the glands in her mouth to work again—and run screaming up to her room.

Both choices made her stomach knot.

Lifting her chin and steeling herself for the feel of his grip, Sadie reached out with her right hand and firmly placed it in his. He gently closed his fingers over her glove and bent slightly at the waist.

"It is certainly my pleasure, Mercedes," he said in a soft brogue, his polite tone a stark contradiction to his laughing eyes. "I can't tell you how much I've been looking forward to meeting you. Again," he added in a soft whisper that only she could hear.

The right corner of his mouth turned up in a grin, and he looked at Callum. "You could have warned me, cousin, that she was beautiful enough to take a man's breath away."

Callum arched one bushy eyebrow. "I believe I did mention that fact," he said, smiling tightly.

Sadie gently tugged on her hand, hoping to get it back sometime tonight. Morgan MacKeage shot her a mischievous wink that silently said he clearly knew her discomfort. Instead of releasing her hand, he moved one long finger past the hem of her glove and rested it on the inside of her wrist, directly over her racing pulse.

Sadie flinched at the intimate contact and shivered at the fire that shot up her arm and into the center of her chest. She tugged more frantically to free herself.

His smile now decidedly wicked, Morgan MacKeage refused to release her. He moved instead to stand beside her, tucking her arm through his, anchoring her to his side.

"Shall we go, then?" he said to the room at large. "I believe our reservations are for eight o'clock."

"I need my sweater," Sadie said. She made another attempt to free herself.

He started walking to the door as if she hadn't spoken, her entire arm as well as her hand still entrapped. "You won't need it," he said as he all but dragged her along. "It's a perfect late-summer night."

He led her through the door and onto the porch, where he stopped briefly. "If you get chilled, lass, I'll gladly warm you up," he said in a lowered voice, for her ears only.

Sadie was already chilled, all the way down to her bones. She couldn't possibly spend an entire evening with this man, considering what she'd done to him four days ago. Especially considering that she knew exactly what Morgan MacKeage looked like without his clothes on.

A bead of sweat trickled between Sadie's breasts. How was she supposed to spend an entire evening with this Adonis and not make more of a fool of herself than she already had? How did a woman smile and talk and share food with a man when she knew that his tie and jacket were merely a civilized veneer covering the body of a god?

Then again, how could she bow out on her mother now?

She was smartly trapped—in more ways than one.

Her arm still in his possession, he led her off the porch toward the monstrous four-door truck he and Callum had arrived in. He finally did release her, but only after he had opened the back door of the truck. He let go of her arm, grabbed her around the waist, and lifted her into the seat. He then gently closed the door before she finished gasping in shock.

Sadie found herself sitting beside her mother. Charlotte quietly handed Sadie her purse, a bemused smile warming her face.

"Morgan seems to be one of those take-charge kinds of men," Charlotte said, approval obvious in her voice. She patted Sadie's knee. "Just what you need."

Sadie smiled at her mom. "You mean the kind of man who puts his date in the backseat?" she asked. She waved at the still empty front seats. "What is this, 1955?"

Charlotte smiled back, shaking her head. "I told you Cal was old-fashioned," she said. "And it's kind of sweet, when you think about it. Cal is always worried about getting into an accident when we go out and having the airbag hurt me if it deploys." Charlotte leaned over and said in a whisper, "He saw something on the news about them being dangerous to small people." She actually giggled. "Cal says I'm a tiny thing, and it worries him. Can you believe that, thinking me tiny?"

Sadie refrained from rolling her eyes. "You are small, Mom, compared with Callum."

Sadie shot a look through the windshield to see their two dates now standing at the front of the truck, exchanging words. She couldn't hear what they were saying, but both men wore darkened expressions. It appeared that Callum was scolding Morgan. Good. The arrogant jerk needed a set-down. And since Callum was more of a size to do it, Sadie basked in the hope that her mother's boyfriend was up to the task.

Chapter Eight

On the pretense of smoothing down his tie, Morgan petted the cherrywood burl softly humming against his chest. The *drùidh's* charm had started to warm and gently vibrate the moment Mercedes Quill had placed her hand in his.

And now the damn thing was still not wanting to settle down.

Morgan sat at the tiny table of the restaurant nestled on the shore of Pine Lake. The dining room was dotted with only a few late diners, as most of the people had already moved to the adjoining dance floor and bar. Morgan absently listened to the lounge music and idle chatter between his cousin and his cousin's woman, but his attention was definitely focused on his date.

The woman had cleaned up rather nicely from the woods sprite he'd encountered four days ago. He had almost forgotten how tall she was. But not how beautiful. Mercedes had shiny blond hair that fell in waves to the small of her back, golden skin that had been kissed gently by the sun, and an utterly feminine body that made his own skin tighten in response. She was arresting, and Morgan had noticed more than one man glancing at her during dinner.

Not that his date noticed. She seemed completely oblivious to her effect on men.

And that pleased him.

Morgan was also pleased that Mercedes was a woman of very few words. He'd gotten maybe a dozen sentences out of her all evening, and most of those had not been directed at him.

But what he really liked, what most drew him to Mercedes Quill, was the thing that most disturbed him: her eyes. They were the color of an autumn sky freshly washed by a fast-moving rain. Sparkling. Energized. Alive.

And he wanted to possess them.

To possess her. He wanted to wrap his arms around Mercedes, pull her lovely, supple body against him, and focus all five of his senses on her beauty.

Morgan stood up and held out his hand to Mercedes—his left hand this time. "I'd enjoy your company on the dance floor," he said, making sure his voice didn't betray his thoughts.

She appeared downright appalled by his invitation, her gaze darting from him to the dance floor, then swiftly back to him. She looked as if he had just asked her to take off all her clothes.

Now, that irked. Except for demanding that she give him her scarred hand back at the house, he'd been a perfect gentleman all evening. Hell, he'd set her in the backseat of the truck where she'd be safest, he'd ordered a delicious dinner of salmon for her, and he'd just ordered her a nice glass of sweet red wine, of which she'd only taken one sip.

He saw Mercedes suddenly jump as if she'd been kicked, and she snapped her gaze to her mother and scowled. Tired of standing there with his hand out and not getting the response he wanted, Morgan simply moved to the back of her chair and pulled it out. Mercedes shot to her feet as if he had pinched her and leveled her scowl on him.

"I'd rather not dance," she said.

He took her arm and guided her to the dance floor. "I promise not to step on your toes," he assured her, turning her into his embrace.

This was the nicest thing Morgan had discovered about modern society, the slow dancing. It was like courting in public. Perfectly acceptable. Encouraged, even.

Aye. He definitely liked dancing.

Except that dancing with Mercedes Quill was like wrestling with the ridge pole on the roof of his house. She was as stiff as a board and uncooperative. And Morgan soon discovered it was *his* feet that were in danger of being stepped on.

Holy hell. The woman didn't know how to dance. He would subtly guide her in one direction, and her feet would head off in another instead, trying to lead him. Morgan couldn't keep his smile from tugging free. And that little quirk seemed to deepen her scowl even more.

"Ah, lass. Just this once, just for five minutes, give me your trust," he entreated, firming his grip on her waist and moving them into a rhythm that matched the music.

"I don't like dancing."

"In general, or just with me?"

"Both."

He chuckled and pulled her closer, tucking her head under his chin. It was definitely nice to dance with someone he didn't have to bend over to hold.

"Maybe you'd enjoy yourself a bit more if you had drunk your wine," he suggested.

She snapped her head up. "I don't like wine."

Morgan blew a sigh over her head, praying for patience. It was difficult being a gentleman to a *gràineag.*

"Then why didn't ya say so?" he asked, trying his damndest not to sound disgruntled, shoving her head back down so she wouldn't see his own scowl.

"Because you didn't give me a chance," she muttered into his jacket. She popped her head up again. "Just like you didn't give me a chance to order my own dinner."

"You ate the salmon."

"Because I happen to like salmon."

"Then what's the problem?"

She blinked at him, started to say something, then suddenly sighed and returned her head to his shoulder. Morgan grinned. She was still having trouble finding her words. That was fine with him. Her body language was all that mattered.

The woman in his arms slowly began to relax, and together they moved to the soft music, slowly learning to sway in harmony.

He wanted her. That simply, that urgently; he wanted Mercedes Quill with the passion of a man long lost and needing the anchor of a special woman. But what Morgan really wanted was for Sadie's own simmering passion to ignite in his arms. Together they could probably light up the entire valley.

"Hey, Moose Woman!" someone hollered from across the dance floor.

His date's feet stopped moving, and Mercedes stiffened into a pole again. Her fingers dug into his back, and Morgan wasn't sure, but it felt as if she were trying to crawl inside his jacket.

"Moose!" the voice repeated, closer this time. "When did you get back?" the man asked as he and three other men and two women approached.

Mercedes stopped trying to hide and finally pulled free of his arms and turned around. The quick glimpse Morgan got of her expression told him that this was not a welcome reunion with old friends. Her entire face was scorched red.

"It is you," the man said. "I thought you had a job in Boston. What was it? Oh, yeah. Meteorology. You make it as a weather girl yet?"

"Ah, no. I've moved back home," Mercedes said, darting an embarrassed look around the room.

"Hey, that's good. That you've come back, I mean. We're just headed over to Nadeau's for a beer. Want to join us?" The guy looked briefly at Morgan, then back at her. "You can bring your friend if you want."

"No, Peter. We're here with my mom and her date," she told him.

"Aw, come on, Moose. We can catch up on old times," he said, aiming a cajoling punch at her arm.

Morgan stepped forward and caught the man's hand before it could connect with his date.

"Peter, is it?" he asked.

Peter nodded, trying discreetly and unsuccessfully to get his hand back.

"Well, Peter. My date's name is Sadie, not Moose. And if you try to punch her again, I'm going to break your hand," he finished softly, squeezing Peter's hand just enough to get his point across before he released him.

Now, as warnings went, Morgan thought this one had been nicely delivered according to modern rules. His date, however, appeared to take exception. She whirled on him, her eyes wide with disbelief.

Peter the idiot was even less believing. He actually took a step closer. So did the three men behind him.

Morgan gently pushed Mercedes behind his back. She stayed there all of three seconds before she came bounding back around to stand between him and the four now defensively postured men.

"I'm going to help them beat you up if you cause a scene," she whispered in a much more threatening voice.

"You want to go with them?" he asked, trying to keep his smile from escaping. His date was flaming mad—and obviously unaware of the scene she was creating all by herself.

"No, I don't want to go with them. And I don't want

a fight breaking out, either. It's an old nickname from high school," she said, leaning up to whisper her confession. "Peter didn't mean anything by it. And he didn't try to punch me to hurt me. Now, stop being a caveman, MacKeage."

He had two choices. He could shove the spitting-mad woman into the arms of his now approaching cousin and give in to his urge to punch Peter the idiot in the nose. Or he could finish dancing with his date.

What to do?

Both actions stirred his blood.

Both would be equally satisfying.

With a grin sent to Callum, Morgan reached out and pulled Mercedes back into his arms, turning them both so that his back was to the intruders, smartly dismissing them as a threat to his evening. He ignored her squeak of surprise and nodded his head to Callum, who had now stopped his advance through the dancers. But his cousin didn't return to his seat until the four men and two women, obviously confused by the sudden loss of a fight, simply walked away.

"Never issue threats you can't back up, lass," Morgan whispered into her hair. "It's a bad habit that might prove dangerous someday."

She popped her head off his shoulder and stared at him in silence. Her blush had calmed down slightly, but still her entire face glowed with lingering anger.

Morgan lifted his hand, entwining his fingers in her hair so she couldn't look away, while he gently continued to coax her body to sway with his to the music.

"If I apologize for terrorizing you the other day, will

you call a truce to our silent war?" he asked. "And maybe start enjoying yourself tonight?"

"No."

Why didn't her answer surprise him? "Will you kick me in the shin if I tell you how beautiful you look this evening?"

Her gracefully arched brows puckered together, and her eyes narrowed, as if she suspected he was toying with her. Morgan gave up trying to make pleasant conversation. Instead, he urged her head back down to his shoulder before he gave in to his own urge to kiss her—right here on the dance floor, in front of God and all these people.

It was damn prickly business, trying to possess a *gràineag.*

It was also damn fun.

Sadie didn't know what to make of her date. One minute he was pricking her temper, then defending her from an embarrassing nickname, and the next minute he was telling her she was pretty.

And he was a bossy date. The guy hadn't stopped manhandling her all evening. He was constantly leading her here and there, ordering dinner and drinks for her, then guiding her over the dance floor like a drill sergeant.

And now they were walking the two miles back to her home because Morgan had decided it was a beautiful evening for a moonlit stroll.

Sadie still couldn't understand why she liked him.

Can a man actually smell sexy? Sadie had been around plenty of men, but when she'd found herself in Morgan's arms on the dance floor, all she could think about was how sexy he smelled. Warm in a masculine sort of way, with just a hint of the woods.

And he felt the way he smelled—just as sexy and very inviting. Sadie couldn't believe she'd been able to relax enough actually to snuggle against him. Heck, what girl wouldn't be enchanted to find herself in the arms of a tall, powerful, very handsome god? She'd have to be insane not to take advantage of the moment, to rest her head on his broad shoulder and sway to the music as if she were a goddess.

Which was why Sadie had said her goodbyes to her mom and Callum and had gone along with Morgan's plan to walk her home.

She was in no hurry for this dream date to end.

Sadie sighed into the stillness of the peaceful night. She was going to have to admit her actions four days ago had been wrong. Morgan had proven himself a gentleman tonight, and she could at least act like a lady. She would have to apologize.

"I'm sorry I took your picture the other day," she said, keeping her eyes straight ahead on the road. "I had no right to invade your privacy that way."

Sadie stopped when she realized she was speaking to empty air. She turned and looked. The man was standing several steps back, staring at her. And he was not smiling.

"Dammit, MacKeage. I wasn't thinking, okay? It's just that you . . . well, you surprised me, and I didn't stop to think about what I was doing."

Without responding to her not-so-gracious apology, he slowly slipped out of his jacket and walked up to her. He swung the jacket past her head and settled it over her shoulders, gathering the lapels together and tightly entrapping her.

Sadie caught her breath as she stared up at him, just as trapped in the depths of his moonlit evergreen eyes.

"Did you like what you saw through the viewfinder, lass?" he asked, his gaze never wavering from hers.

She couldn't have answered that question if she dared.

He suddenly smiled and released his hold on his jacket. He touched the end of her nose with one finger and shot her a wink. "It doesn't matter if you did or not," he said, moving to continue their walk toward home. "It's the only body I've got, and you'll just have to get used to it."

Sadie blinked at his back, watching him walk away. She ran to catch up, tripped on her heels, and started skipping as she pulled first one shoe and then the other one off. She ran into him then, when he unexpectedly stopped and faced her.

"Ya can't be baring your feet," he said, reaching to take her shoes from her. "There might be glass or metal on the road."

Sadie quickly tucked her shoes into the pockets of his jacket she was wearing and moved past him, walking on the pavement now, once more leading the way home. "I went barefoot the first ten years of my life," she said over her shoulder. "Besides," she said as his stride quickly brought him beside her, "I know a priest with a magic cane who can heal me just like that." She snapped her fingers in the air.

She was suddenly brought to such an abrupt halt

and spun around that one of her shoes fell onto the road.

"What do you know of a priest with a magic cane?" he asked.

Sadie blinked again. Morgan had gone deathly pale and frighteningly still, but for the fire of inquest in his now emerald-black eyes.

"I . . . I met the old priest who lives up on TarStone Mountain," she said, not knowing what to make of his reaction.

"When?"

"The other day. Thursday. He came to visit me."

Morgan's hands on her shoulders tightened. "You stay away from Daar," he told her. He shook her slightly. "Understand, Mercedes? You stay away from that old priest."

She could only gape at him.

He shook her again. "You're not to believe anything he tells you."

And with that command issued, Morgan turned on his heel and started toward her house again. And again, Sadie found herself gaping at his back. His moods changed more often than the weather.

She ran to catch up. "Wait," she said, grabbing his arm. "There's something I want to ask you."

He stopped and turned to her.

"I want to know if you're the one stealing my trail markers."

"Trail markers?"

"My orange ribbons. You said so yourself, earlier tonight, that you didn't want a park built in Prospect Valley. Are you taking my ribbons, hoping to stop it?"

"And will taking the ribbons stop it?"

"No."

"Weren't some of those ribbons on MacKeage land?" he asked, crossing his arms over his chest as he looked at her.

Sadie dropped her gaze to the knot in his tie. "They might have been," she quietly admitted. "But stealing ribbons won't stop the park."

He took hold of her hand and started walking again, this time across the grass, in the direction of the town pier that jutted into Pine Lake. Sadie allowed him to lead her to a bench, aware that he hadn't answered her question and resigned to the fact that he probably would never admit to stealing her trail markers.

"Why a park in Prospect Valley?" he asked as he settled her on the bench and then stood across from her, leaning against the pier rail.

"Why not? It's a beautiful valley with plenty of recreational features. We have the opportunity to offer four-season use—camping, hiking, kayaking, snowmobiling, fishing. You name the sport, and the public can come here to do it."

"We? Who is this 'we' you speak of?"

"Right now it's a group of businessmen from around the state who have formed a consortium. Eric Hellman hired me to help work up a proposal to present to our legislature."

"These businessmen, what is their gain? Why have they come together with the hope of building a park here?"

Sadie frowned at his question. "Maybe because they

want to see this vast wilderness preserved for future generations."

"Or maybe they hope to profit?" he asked very quietly. "Will they donate all the land to this park, or are they intending to sell lots for vacation homes?"

"But that's the point," Sadie said, leaning forward to make her own point. "Not only will the park open a beautiful piece of land to the public, it will also help grow the economy of this area. Just as your ski resort has done. Look at all the shops and inns that have cropped up since you opened. The population of Pine Creek is nearly double in winter. With a new park, that economic boom could be year-round."

"And then what do you have, Mercedes? Another small city with hordes of people overrunning the wilderness, crowding the animals onto smaller and smaller tracts of land?"

Sadie stood up, pulling the lapels of Morgan's coat tightly around her. Morgan stepped away from the rail and took hold of her shoulders.

"I know why the businessmen have come up with this plan, Mercedes. But I don't understand your connection. What is it you hope to gain?"

"Nothing," she said, torn between pulling away and wanting to lean into his broad chest.

The man was making her angry.

But he still smelled sexy.

"Since I learned to walk, I've been hiking that valley," she continued, looking up into his serious, deep green eyes. "And I want to be part of preserving it."

"Has the valley not been happily existing all these years without your intervention? Can a person not hike and fish and hunt there now? And will turning it into a park not ultimately destroy the valley, if more and more people come here?"

Dammit. She hated that his argument made a certain kind of sense. Hadn't she had that very worry herself? Wasn't it still a concern?

"Why are you so against the park?" she asked. "Your family will likely profit the most. Your hotel will be full winter and summer. Your restaurant on the summit could be open year-round."

"It's already open year-round. And how much profit does one family need? Especially at the expense of the land."

Morgan suddenly released her shoulders, took hold of her right hand again, and started walking them toward her house.

"My camera. I want it back," she said, deciding it was time to change the subject and probably better to keep a line drawn between them.

He was too handsome and tall and masculine and . . . and too damned sexy to be attracted to her. She would bet that when Morgan MacKeage made love to a woman, they both got naked, sweaty, and completely consumed by each other. All the lights would be on. The covers would be stripped from the bed, with no place to hide. Everything would be exposed.

Well, if she lived to be a hundred, she was never getting undressed in front of a man.

Especially a man who could give Adonis a run for his money.

"What camera?"

"What?" Sadie asked, completely lost in her train of thought. "Oh. The camera I had with me the other day, that you took the film out of. I want my pack, my GPS, and my camera back."

"I don't have your camera. I left it on the ground."

"You must have come back later and gotten it, along with everything else." She squeezed his hand which was holding hers. "I want my stuff back."

"On my honor, lass. I didn't return and take your belongings," he said softly. "Did you go back and look for them?"

"Yes." Sadie sighed into the night. "I'm never going to see my stuff again, am I? Someone else must have come along and found it."

"I'll buy you a new camera, Mercedes. It's my fault yours got lost."

"It doesn't matter. The camera can't be replaced, anyway. It was my dad's."

He used his grip on her hand to stop them again. "I'm sorry," he said simply, staring down at her with serious eyes.

Sadie straightened her shoulders. "It was my fault. I walked away without even thinking about my stuff."

He raised a finger to her cheek and brushed a strand of hair off her face, tucking it behind her ear.

"We didn't get off to a very good start, did we, lass?"

Sadie balled her left hand into a fist and shoved it into her pocket, determined not to run her own finger over his cheek.

Lord, she was attracted to this man, and it had nothing to do with having seen every naked inch of him four days ago.

Well, maybe that had a little bit to do with it. But it was more than this unfamiliar stirring of lust she was feeling right now as she stared up into his warm, mesmerizing forest-green eyes. It was the warmth of his touch, the way he held her gloved hand as if it were a perfectly normal act, the way he looked at her, smiled at her, and made her feel . . . well . . . special.

"The start of what?" she asked.

"Excuse me?"

"You said we didn't get off to a very good start. The start of what?"

He tugged her forward, pulling her off balance toward him, and released her to wrap both of his arms around her. He hugged her to him tightly, and his chest heaved with another deep sigh.

"The start of a cautious but important friendship," he whispered over her head, his arms tightening around her.

Sadie wanted to bury her face in his shirt and weep.

Friendship.

Dammit. She was lusting after his body, standing in his arms in the middle of the moonlit road, foolishly hoping that he had been talking about starting a flaming affair.

And he was offering her friendship.

Sadie pulled away with a jerk. She shot him a good glare to let him know what she thought of his offer, then turned and started walking toward home again.

Morgan quietly fell into step beside his obviously angry date, not knowing whether to be amused or angry himself.

He did know he was damned frustrated. He wanted the woman with a fierceness that was almost painful. There was nothing casual about his feelings for Mercedes. He didn't just want to bed her, he wanted to possess her, to capture and hold on to that powerful energy he felt whenever she was close.

He rubbed the softly humming burl on his chest again as he walked along the dark road, keeping pace with the silent woman beside him. If he were a gentleman, he would not be starting anything with her tonight but ending things by taking her to her door, politely saying good night, and walking away and never seeing her again.

Aye, that is what he should do.

If he were a gentleman.

By the time they reached Sadie's front porch, she was dreading the sympathy kiss on the cheek Morgan likely would give her and his wan smile and false declaration that he'd had a nice time tonight, that maybe they'd see each other around sometime soon.

Well, not this time. And not with this man.

Sadie had actually had a wonderful evening. Morgan MacKeage had been a nearly perfect date—attentive, considerate, amusing, and entertaining. He had danced like Fred Astaire and made her feel like Ginger Rogers. Heck, even the near brawl on the dance floor had been invigorating.

She didn't want a peck. Not from a guy who could probably lay a kiss on a girl that would blow her socks off.

And she was not going to let this man ruin the first

truly wonderful date she'd ever had, because she was not going to let him kiss her at all.

But before Sadie could complete her thought, one of Morgan's large hands came around the back of her neck and slowly drew her closer. With his other hand, Morgan lifted her face toward his. "I've been wondering if you taste as good as you look," he whispered just before he touched his lips to hers.

Sadie stopped breathing as he completely engulfed her in his embrace, tightening his hand on her hair, wrapping his arm around her back with fierce intent. He canted her head and deepened the kiss, urging her mouth open, sweeping his tongue inside.

Sadie was so overwhelmed she completely lost all train of thought save one: she didn't want him to stop.

Because her arms were being held at her sides, she could only move her hands to grip the back of his waist. And, glory of glories, she actually had to stand on tiptoe to kiss him back.

The guy rumbled an earthy, approving growl at her tentative action and tightened his hold on her, taking her breath away again. Their tongues introduced themselves, forgoing the pleasantries and getting immediately down to business. Sadie kneaded her fingers into his back, wondering if she might simply crawl into his skin beside him.

He broke the contact suddenly and tilted her head to expose her neck. Sadie whimpered the moment his mouth touched her throat.

Light flashed in the back of her eyes, and she wiggled her arms free to reach up and grab his shoulders.

He lifted her then, bringing her feet completely off the ground, and stepped forward until her back was pressed against the side of the house. He moved even closer, nestling himself between her thighs.

With only the fleeting worry that she might burst into flames, Sadie wrapped her legs around his waist and welcomed the storm brewing deep inside the pit of her stomach.

His mouth trailed a path of fire down her throat, to the opening of her blouse. His teeth rasped against her skin briefly, and then a button popped. Sadie felt his hot mouth touching the sensitive skin at the base of her throat.

"Morgan," she whispered, closing her eyes, letting her head fall back against the house. She pulled at his hair, tugging it free of its ponytail, running her fingers through the length of it. She finally gave in to the urge she'd had all evening and fingered one of the small, thin braids that now ran loose down the sides of his face.

He lifted his head and stared at her, then took possession of her mouth again, just as deeply and far more intimately than before. The vision of evergreen eyes swam through Sadie's dizzily reeling mind.

Her hands trembled with building passion as she held Morgan to herself, savoring his taste. Their tongues sparred. Their lips molded together. And their pounding hearts beat against each other.

He tore his mouth free, taking a shuddering breath that rocked her like a small earthquake, and blew it out harshly as he rested his forehead on hers.

"Two choices, Mercedes. We make love right now,

right here on this porch, or you run like hell into your house and lock the door."

He thrust his hips forward, forcefully, backing up his ultimatum with hard, blatant evidence that clearly said which choice he preferred.

Heat scorched her cheeks, and Sadie couldn't decide if it was radiating from him or from inside herself, as she realized just how close she was to committing emotional suicide.

And just how much she wanted to.

She immediately reversed her grip on his shoulders and pushed at him frantically as she unwrapped her legs from around his waist and dropped her feet to the porch. She pushed him again when he continued to hold her tightly, staring down at her with a look that said he wanted to take the choice out of her hands.

He suddenly let go, dropped his arms to his sides, and took a step back.

Sadie shivered. With his hair loose and tangled in waves, his face harsh from lust denied, and his dark eyes unreadable, her date had lost his mask of civility.

He was that same madman again who had chased her through the woods four days ago.

And she suddenly felt just as vulnerable as she had then.

Sadie spun around and groped for the knob, twisting it violently and throwing her weight against the door until it opened and she could run inside and slam it shut behind her. And, as he had so kindly suggested, she threw home the bolt with a desperate twist and backed away into the safety of the kitchen shadows.

She stood there in the dark, breathing heavily, listening for his footsteps on the porch stairs. They were five minutes in coming, and in that time every touch, every sensation, every emotion his kiss had evoked ran through her head like sparks of energy gathering strength. Sadie touched her trembling fingers to her lips and shivered again.

Holy heck. That had been one hell of a sympathy kiss.

But it wasn't until she was lying in bed later that night, stark naked because every inch of her skin was super-sensitive, her heart still pounding in her chest and her mind still reeling with confused emotions, that Sadie realized Morgan MacKeage hadn't simply kissed her socks off—he'd blown them clean past the summit of Fraser Mountain.

Chapter Nine

It had taken Sadie most of the morning to wiggle gently out of her mother's clutches. Charlotte had wanted to know how Sadie could have lost one of her shoes, why Morgan's jacket had been found crumpled in a ball on the kitchen floor, and what she thought of her date last night.

Sadie still couldn't believe the lame excuses and raving praises she'd come up with to appease her mother.

She was glad she'd made Eric open his store early this morning, so she could pick up her new GPS and cell phone, backpack and supplies, as well as a new, overpriced camera.

Now she was finally back at her cabin. She was going to miss Ping, though. She had left the cat at her mother's house, afraid the wolf might return and decide Ping would make a tasty lunch. No matter what the priest had said, she wasn't trusting Faol with her pet.

Sadie opened her cabin door and set her new backpack and supplies on the table. She walked over to the model of the park and studied the eastern mountain range.

Morgan MacKeage had built his house halfway up Fraser Mountain, he'd told her last night. He owned a good chunk of land there that ran all the way down to Prospect River.

Which meant he owned the southeastern corner of the proposed wilderness park.

Sadie pulled out the map she'd been given the day she took this job. She spread it on top of the model and studied it again. The boundary of the park, traced in bright green marker, definitely included the western slope of Fraser Mountain. It was nearly five thousand acres—a small part of the park but a very important part. The south access road would be going across the MacKeage land, bringing people in through Pine Creek.

Sadie suddenly straightened from looking at the map, pushed her hair behind her ears, and listened. She heard it again, a gentle, barely audible *woof*.

She closed her eyes and dropped her head. Damn. She'd been hoping that damn wolf would be gone by now. Had he been hanging around for three whole days, waiting for her to return?

And now he wanted her to come out and say hello?

Sadie moved to the window and peeked out. And there he was, sitting just on the edge of the forest, staring at the cabin. With a gasp, Sadie ran to the door and threw it open.

He was holding her old backpack his mouth.

The one she'd lost.

And it looked to be full.

Faol stood up and took several steps forward, his tail wagging. Sadie slowly walked down the steps and stopped a good ten paces from the wolf when he let out another muffled *woof*.

"What have you got there, big boy?" she asked. "Where did you find that?"

He took a step closer to her, giving a soft whine.

Sadie took a step back.

Faol immediately sat down and gently laid the pack on the ground at his feet. He lifted his head, and this time his bark was stronger, almost demanding.

Not for all of Plum's gold would Sadie move an inch closer to the huge, powerful-looking animal. She was not bending down to take her pack, putting her face mere inches from Faol's teeth.

He wagged his tail as he sat there staring at her, sending a cloud of dust wafting into the air. He whined again, stood up, and took several steps back.

Keeping ten paces between them, Sadie moved forward, matching his retreat. But he stopped suddenly, only a few feet from the pack.

She darted a look at her pack and almost cried with relief when she saw the camera lens peeking past the zipper. Sadie looked back at the wolf. His tongue was lolling out the side of his mouth, his eyes—a crisp, iridescent green—round and sharply focused as he softly whined again, darting his own look from her to the pack, then back at her.

Sadie took another cautious step forward, then

waited, watching him. He lifted a paw and started to lick it clean.

She took another step forward.

He yawned, then walked his front legs forward until he was lying down, for all the world looking as if he couldn't care less that she was there.

Two more cautious steps, then Sadie used her toe to hook the strap on her pack and slowly pull it toward her.

Faol laid his head on his paws.

The pack now on the ground at her own feet, Sadie bent her knees and blindly felt for the strap, grabbing it and then slowly straightening. With her back to the cabin and her eyes trained on the still reclined wolf, Sadie retreated until she felt the porch touch her thighs. Then, keeping one guarded eye on her visitor, she sat down, opened the zipper, and looked inside.

The wolf completely forgotten, Sadie stared at the contents of the pack. She lifted her father's camera out, then dumped the rest onto the porch.

It was all there: GPS, cell phone, surveyor's ribbon, knife, water bottle, even the shredded duct tape she'd been bound with.

Everything. All there.

And all dry.

Sadie looked over at Faol. He was sitting up now, staring at her, his tongue lolling out again, his eyes unblinking, and his head cocked as if he were expecting her to speak to him.

And say what? *Thank you for returning my things, wolf?*

Sadie hugged her father's camera to her chest and

laughed out loud. She was going nuts, and she didn't care.

"Thank you, big boy," she said, waving the camera at him. "I don't know where you found this stuff or how you knew to bring it here, but thank you from the bottom of my heart."

She wiped at the unexpected tears that suddenly welled up in her eyes. Her daddy's camera. She had it back.

Sadie went into the cabin and rummaged around in her supplies on the table. She found the bag of beef jerky she'd bought from Eric this morning, tore it open, and grabbed a handful of the dried meat. She headed back outdoors and down the steps toward the wolf.

"This might go against everything I believe about feeding wild animals, you big, beautiful wolf, but I've never met anyone who deserves a reward as much as you do. Here," she said, tossing the beef onto the ground in front of him. "I promise there'll be more where that came from. Next trip into town, I'm buying you the biggest bag on the shelf."

Faol sniffed the food at his feet but didn't actually touch it. He lifted his head and looked at her.

"Hey. That's not the cheap stuff," Sadie told him. "That's prime beef."

He suddenly raised his nose into the air and gave a long, plaintive howl before he turned and trotted away, disappearing into the forest.

Shivers ran down Sadie's spine as the last echo of the haunting cry faded into the air around her. She stared at the spot where Faol had disappeared. He couldn't have known the pack belonged to her. He was just an animal who had found something in the woods and brought it here, the same way Ping brought hunting trophies to Sadie to show off.

That must be it. Faol didn't like the food because it carried a human scent. And he had just found the pack, and because it had *her* scent on it, he had brought it here.

Yeah. That was a perfectly logical explanation.

Morgan forced more power to his tired muscles and pushed his overheated body through the calm waters of the cold lake. He was on his second trip across the lake, and still he couldn't seem to outswim the emotions driving his thoughts.

Mercedes Quill. She was responsible for his mood this evening. He'd spent the entire day thinking about her. It didn't seem to matter that she was independent, prickly sometimes to the point of rudeness, and determined to open this valley to hordes of people who needed wilderness parks in order to play at primitive living.

Mercedes was beautiful.

Intelligent in a most challenging way.

He'd walked off her porch last night frustrated to the point of pain and decided on the point that he would have her—on whatever terms it took, by whatever means he could find.

Mercedes Quill was his. Morgan had declared that she belonged to him in the late hours of last night as he'd stood in the mist-shrouded moonlight overlooking the waterfall. He'd told God, the forest, and anyone who could hear him that the blue-eyed woman who walked this valley was his.

Morgan pulled himself onto the boulder in the middle of the cove and let the setting sun wash over his body. He wrapped his fist around the cherrywood burl hanging from his neck and watched the sky dance in a brilliant display of colors that arced from soft blue to a warm, vibrant red.

And somewhere in the middle he saw Mercedes.

Aye. After last night on the porch, aroused by his kisses, her eyes had been the same deep blue of tonight's sky. And Morgan made another vow then, that he would see that same color again, fired by the passion of their lovemaking.

But first he must find a way to explain to Mercedes that when she had walked into his valley and planted her first ribbon, she'd entered the world of an ancient and possessive man.

A world she would never be leaving again.

A gentle bark carried over the water toward him. Morgan turned in the direction of the sound and saw Faol standing on the shore of the lake, staring at him.

"Go away, you accursed beast," Morgan said, turning his back on the wolf. "I'm not in the mood for your company."

Faol barked again, louder this time, more urgently.

Morgan dove into the water, swimming back across the lake, away from the wolf. His stroke less rushed, his breathing barely labored, he thought again of the *drùidh's* vision and the blackness that had swarmed through the valley, chasing the yellow light.

He couldn't tell Mercedes that she was in danger,

because he couldn't explain to her how he knew such a thing. Nor could he let her discover his gorge. The woman was too intelligent, too curious, and too knowledgeable about this forest not to realize that something more than just the fickleness of nature was at work here. And she was too modern to comprehend that the magic of an aging *drùidh* was responsible.

His kicking feet suddenly touched bottom, and Morgan stood up, brushing the water from his face and wringing it out of his hair. He walked onto the gravel beach but stopped at the sight of Faol standing at the edge of the forest, staring at him.

"Dammit. Go away," he said, turning to walk down the beach towards Gràdhag. His horse took several steps back as he approached and began to prance nervously in place. Morgan stopped and looked behind him.

Faol was matching his steps, ten paces back.

Morgan pulled his sword from its sheath tied to the saddle and turned to face the wolf. He raised the weapon threateningly. "I want nothing to do with you tonight."

Faol lowered his head and dropped something out of his mouth. Morgan lowered the tip his sword and squinted at the ground. "What is that?" he asked, taking a step closer.

Faol whined, nosing it forward in the dirt.

Morgan bent down in front of the wolf, set his sword across his knees, and picked up the metallic object. A hot, wet tongue suddenly ran up the side of his face.

Morgan fell back in surprise.

"Damned beast," he said, wiping his face with the back of his hand. "You'd better not be seeing if I'll make a good meal."

Morgan reached out and touched the wolf on the side of his face, just below his right ear. Faol nosed the palm of Morgan's hand, then rumbled a contented growl deep in his chest. He took a step forward and nudged the forgotten object in Morgan's hand.

Morgan turned his attention to what looked like the ammunition clip of a hunting rifle. A powerful rifle, judging by the size of the bullets.

"Where did you get this?" he asked, turning it over in his hand. He looked at the wolf. "Where did you find this?"

Faol turned and started into the forest but stopped and looked back. Morgan stood up, placed his sword back in its sheath, and pulled clothes down from his saddle. He dressed quickly, tucking Faol's gift into his pocket, then mounted Gràdhag and turned them into the forest to follow the now running wolf down the narrow, darkening path.

Faol turned onto a tote road and headed north, deeper into the valley. Morgan followed Faol for several miles along Prospect River, then pulled Gràdhag to a halt when the wolf suddenly left the road and leaped onto the crest of a knoll. Morgan followed on foot, making no sound as he moved through the woods.

The voices of men carried softly across the stillness of the evening. The wolf abruptly stopped and lay down; Morgan did the same and watched the two men in the camp below.

"Jesus Christ, Dwayne. A bigger idiot was never born. How in hell can you lose an entire clip full of bullets?"

"I swear, Harry, I left the clip right here," the man named Dwayne said in a whine, pointing at the tarp spread out on the ground. "I was cleaning our guns and went to the truck for a polishing rag. But when I tried to put my gun back together, I couldn't find the clip," he continued, holding up the gas lantern as he scanned the ground. "It's got to be here somewhere."

The man named Harry also scanned the forest floor, using a flashlight. Morgan looked around the camp the men had erected. It appeared they planned to be in the valley for quite a while. They had boxes of supplies stacked against the outside wall of a large tent, several gas cans, backpacks, and a canoe strapped to the rack of their truck.

They'd set up camp near the river, just far enough back that anyone coming down the Prospect by boat would not see them.

Morgan didn't like this, that these men were here in Mercedes' valley, looking for all the world like a pair of poachers. Hunting season was not for several more weeks in this area, but there were two high-powered hunting rifles leaning against a tree near the tarp.

And poachers, in Morgan's experience—both from eight hundred years ago and from these last six years—were unconscionable men who thought only of themselves and were a danger to anyone who crossed their reckless paths.

Which Mercedes was bound to do, eventually, if she kept planting her ribbons.

With a silent sigh, Morgan retreated down the knoll and headed toward Gràdhag, leaving Faol to watch the men. And as he rode through the night, Morgan tried to decide how he could protect Mercedes while trying to protect this valley from her—and not let his wanting to possess her distract him from either duty.

Chapter Ten

When it came to the weather, September and March were transition months in Maine, and Sadie had decided long ago that they were also the most interesting. It had to do with the equinoxes, when the sun sat directly over the equator, equalizing the hours of daylight and darkness. It was the turning point of the seasons, the final push of the air masses that moved with the tilt of the earth, producing great battles between the warm airs of the south and the cold airs of the north.

And September, in Sadie's estimation, was the greatest time of year to be living in Maine, caught in the middle of those timeless meteorological wars.

So this morning she packed accordingly and filled her kayaking dry bag with shorts, T-shirts, jeans, and heavy sweaters. She also packed a pair of long johns, a full rain suit, a tent, and enough food for several days.

She checked her equipment next—GPS, cell phone, new camera, five rolls of film, matches, lighter, knife, water bottles, duct tape, two flashlights, and several lengths of rope. In another dry bag she placed her carefully folded maps and the copy of the diary of Jean Lavoie that Eric had brought her, as well as her own journal of the last ten weeks.

Finally, satisfied that she had everything, Sadie headed to the cabin door. She was driving to the headwaters of the Prospect, a good eight miles upriver past Fraser Mountain. Then she'd make the eighteen-mile run down the river, in three days if she didn't dawdle too much.

And if she were really lucky, she'd talk her mother into driving to the end of the valley to pick her up. If not, well, she'd have a mighty long hike back to her truck.

Sadie opened the cabin door with her foot and had just stepped onto the porch when she suddenly halted and dropped everything she was carrying. She stared at the note skewered to the nail on the porch post: DON'T GO INTO THE WOODS TODAY.

Sadie ripped the paper down and glared at the boldly scrawled letters of an obviously masculine hand: DON'T GO INTO THE WOODS TODAY. That was all it said. No name of the writer. No explanation. Only a dictate that she was expected to obey.

Morgan MacKeage was manhandling her again, from a distance this time. And, as in every minute of their date two nights ago, he was expecting her cooperation.

Sadie frowned into the forest in front of her cabin.

What was this about? The guy just leaves a note and expects her to obey meekly?

Sadie crumpled the paper in her hand, crushing it with angry force and then throwing it at the woods. Dammit. She was being paid to do a job here. Morgan couldn't expect her to change her plans simply because he was in the mood to test their *friendship.* She didn't care if she still hadn't found the socks he'd kissed off her feet; she was not playing his game.

He had plenty of nerve to leave such a note, instead of having the decency to knock on her door and explain his reasoning.

What to do? What to do?

If she stayed in camp today, what message would she be sending him? That she was a good, obedient little lass whom he could bend to his will on a whim?

Yet Morgan didn't strike Sadie as a man who issued idle orders. Nor was she a woman to ignore a sincerely given suggestion if there was sound reasoning behind it.

"Dammit, MacKeage!" she hollered, shaking her fist at the woods. "You're an arrogant jerk!"

Her echoing outburst unanswered, Sadie let out a frustrated breath and returned to her fallen gear. She picked up the dry bag that had her papers inside and took out Jean Lavoie's diary and her own journal. Then, still angry at herself for letting six simple words rule her day, Sadie stomped down the steps and strode to a pair of towering maple trees with a hammock strung between them.

She pretty nearly hung herself getting into the hammock. As it was, she ended up on the ground, creating a cloud of dust that made her cough.

She had to get a grip here before she did herself bodily harm. Oh, she would stay out of the woods today, but Morgan MacKeage would be getting a rather scorching lecture on *friendship*—if and when she ever saw him again.

It amazed Sadie the amount of work she could get done when driven by a healthy dose of anger. She had spent more than three hours lying in the hammock, completely engrossed in Jean Lavoie's diary, furiously scribbling notes in her own diary that would help her map out Jean's movements through the valley.

Now she was giving her old kayak a good waxing and replaying Jean Lavoie's diary through her mind. This entire valley had been heavily cut in the early 1900s. The logging camp where Jean cooked had slowly migrated upriver with the cutters. There seemed to be three camps at least, maybe four, she'd been able to discern from the diary, erected over a six-year period.

But all of this had taken place more than eighty years ago. The remains of the camps would be mostly rotted back into the forest by now.

And Jean Lavoie, for all his attention to detail, was not a very gifted writer, especially considering that the diary was laced with enough French-Canadian words to make the reading downright impossible in places.

Still, it seemed that Jedediah Plum had visited camp number three during the fourth year of Jean's stint as camp cook. And camp number three appeared to have been set someplace on the west side of Fraser Mountain, away from the banks of the Prospect River.

Sadie turned her kayak over on the picnic table and began rubbing wax on the top surface. She needed to find camp number three. That was the last known place Jedediah had been seen alive. And the west side of Fraser Mountain was also the area near which Frank Quill had suspected the gold was located.

Her daddy's years of research had only been able to pin the location down to about a two-thousand-acre area, however. And finding a small pool full of placer gold in two thousand acres was like trying to find one particular grain of sand in a desert. There were hundreds, maybe thousands, of tiny streams running down off these mountains, and any one of them could be the source of Jedediah's gold.

Sadie tossed the wax-covered rag onto the table, picked up a clean rag, and began wiping the kayak with strong, circular strokes. She would travel to the base of Fraser Mountain tomorrow and set up her camp there. She'd search not for Jedediah's stream, though, but for the site of the third logging camp. If she could find it, then maybe, just maybe, she could also find a clue that would lead her to the gold.

The sound of a fast-moving truck broke into Sadie's thoughts, and she looked up to see Eric Hellman arrive in a cloud of dust-laden gravel and pine needles, making a mess of her newly raked yard.

"It's Monday," he said as he jumped out of the truck and strode toward her. "Which means you're on the clock, Quill. Why aren't you out looking for Plum's gold?"

Sadie set her fists on her hips and glared at her boss. "Because I'm just now deciding where to look. And the question is, Eric, if you thought I was out hunting for gold, what are you doing here now?"

Her words, and quite possibly her posture, stopped him in mid-stride. "I . . . er, I brought the aerial photos you asked for," he said, lifting his empty hands and staring at them. He turned around and returned to his truck.

"I drove to Augusta this morning," he said over his shoulder. He opened the truck door, took out a cardboard tube, and walked back to her. "I didn't want to wait until they mailed them out. After you came by my store yesterday and told me which sections you needed, I decided it was easier simply to drive down this morning."

He held the tube out to her. "And here they are. I was going to leave them in your cabin."

Feeling a bit foolish for snapping at him, Sadie took the tube and pulled the photos out, unrolling them on top of her kayak.

"You take good care of these," Eric said, looking over her shoulder at the photos. "They cost a small fortune."

Sadie turned in surprise. "Didn't you tell them in Augusta that they were for the park? They shouldn't have charged you a penny."

Eric shook his head. "Not a chance, Quill. The consortium is footing the bill until the park is accepted. Then the state will take over the costs. Which is why you need to find Jedediah's gold, so we'll have all the funding we need."

"The gold might not exist," she shot back through gritted teeth, not liking what he was implying. "Dammit, Hellman. I was never told the consortium was counting on that gold for funding."

"How in hell do you think we intend to buy the land? Do you have any idea what productive timberland goes for?"

Sadie set her hands back on her hips and narrowed a level gaze on Eric. "Are you saying a group of intelligent businessmen is actually putting up the money for this proposal based on a legend?"

"Jedediah Plum is not a legend," Eric countered, getting angry himself. "The man roamed this valley for nearly sixty years. He knew every inch of it. And he did find gold. My great-grandfather saw it himself when the old prospector came into town. Hell, Jedediah bought beers for everyone that entire summer."

Eric suddenly sighed and sat down on the picnic table, looking up at her. "And the plans for the park are real, Sadie. It will help this area in countless ways. And we'll eventually pull together the funding we need to buy the land. But finding Jedediah's gold will make it happen that much sooner."

"But if we find an actual lode? We can't just walk in and take it if we don't own the land."

Eric grinned. "Even your daddy knew there's no mine, Sadie. Jedediah was a panner, not a digger. And if you pan for placer gold, you get to keep it. As long as it's not in the ground but in state waters, it's finders keepers. And that means we can legally keep the gold to build our park."

Eric stood, rolled the photos up, and stuffed them

back into the tube, then used the tube to point at her. "So if I were you, lady, I'd use every daylight hour available for hunting. If the Dolan brothers find the gold before us, it'll be years before we can raise the money we need."

"What's in it for you, Eric?" Sadie asked, remembering Morgan's accusations two nights ago. "Are you part of this as an environmentalist or a businessman?"

Eric rolled his eyes. "Get real, Quill. The consortium is made up of businessmen. It's a win-win situation. We profit from having a beautiful park in our backyard, and the land gets protected."

"If I find the gold."

"That's the plan," he agreed, tapping the tube of photos on her kayak. "So see that you keep ahead of Harry and Dwayne in this little race."

"The Dolans have been hunting nearly as long as I have," she told him. "They're no closer now than they were three years ago."

"Don't count on it," Eric said. "How do you think I got the diary?"

"How?" she asked softly.

"Harry and Dwayne actually discovered it and were foolish enough to brag about it. I snuck into their house one evening while they were out, made a copy, and returned their original."

He nodded in the direction of her hammock, where he could see her stolen copy, then used the tube of photos to point at it. "Just figure out the connection between Jedediah and the cook before they do."

But before Sadie could let him know what she thought of his business ethics, a low and ominous growl suddenly came from the woods just off to their right. Eric, a man not at home in the forest, turned in surprise, his eyes widening when he spotted the wolf standing at the edge of the clearing. Eric took a quick step back and to the side, placing first the table and then Sadie between himself and the large set of teeth the wolf was so nicely displaying.

But Faol wasn't the reason for the shiver that suddenly ran down Sadie's spine. No, it was the man standing beside the wolf that made her mouth go dry.

The note writer had returned to the scene of his edict.

Why wasn't she surprised that these two green-eyed, wild-looking males knew each other?

"Who the hell is that?" Eric asked out of the corner of his mouth. "The guy looks meaner than his dog."

"That's Morgan MacKeage," Sadie told him in a voice that wouldn't carry across the clearing. "And if you want this park to work, it's his land on Fraser Mountain that has to be purchased first. Without that acreage, there's no south access to the valley. And that's not a dog, Eric," Sadie added, just to rile him. "That's a wolf."

Eric stiffened and moved another step closer to her. Faol, apparently not liking the direction Eric had taken, stepped forward and growled again, hackles raised in warning.

"Jesus Christ," Eric said on an indrawn breath. "Get me to my truck, Quill. Now."

More from wanting him gone than from pity, Sadie moved around the picnic table and toward Eric's truck. Keeping herself between him and her uninvited guests, she tried not to laugh as Eric latched onto her side like a shadow. Together they walked the short distance, and Sadie opened the truck door. Eric quickly climbed in, slammed the door shut, and locked it, then started the engine and rolled up the windows.

Only then did he turn and glare at her. Sadie smiled back, waggled her fingers in a mock wave, and stepped away just as Eric sent the truck spinning backward, sending another cloud of dust into the air and leaving a groove in the gravel an inch deep.

Brushing herself off, Sadie turned and headed back to her cabin, completely ignoring her guests. She picked up her dry bag, her pack, and her tent and carried everything to her truck. She opened the back hatch and threw the gear inside, only to turn around and nearly run into Morgan MacKeage.

"I don't like your boss," he said, not moving out of her way.

"Neither do I, at the moment," she shot back, stepping around him. She went to the picnic table, grabbed her kayak, and hefted it onto her shoulder. She swung around, and Morgan barely had time to catch the nose of the boat before it hit him in the chest.

"Dammit, Mercedes," he said, lifting the kayak off her shoulder and setting it on his. "I'm trying to talk to you."

"The only talk I want to hear is your reason for leaving that note on my porch this morning."

He repositioned the kayak and grinned at her. "I can't believe you stayed put."

Sadie scowled at him. "Was it a test, or was there something in the woods that was dangerous?"

He sobered. "Poachers," he told her succinctly. "Or so I thought. But, according to your boss, the two men are your competition. And that makes them even more dangerous."

Sadie waved that away and headed for her truck again. "It's the Dolan brothers," she said. "Neither one of them is competent enough to tie his own shoes. They're more a danger to themselves than to anyone else."

She stopped at the truck and grabbed the end of her kayak, lifting it onto the roof rack. She left Morgan to slide it into place while she moved to stand on the running board to tether it down.

"And what do you know of this competition?" she asked as she tossed one of the straps to his waiting hands. "How long were you standing there, listening to Eric and me?"

"Long enough to know that this park you're so determined to build might not happen."

Sadie glared across the roof at him. "It will happen. Because I'm finding that gold and giving it to the consortium. The Frank Quill Wilderness Park will be built if I have to turn over every rock in this valley."

He stopped working and rested his arms on the roof, staring at her. "But why? Why a park, of all things, and why here?"

Sadie tightened the last buckle on her side of the boat into place. She also rested her arms on the roof and looked at him. "Because this is the valley my father loved. This is where I spent every summer, every weekend, and every vacation with him. Frank Quill's soul still roams these woods, searching for Jedediah's gold."

With a frown at her answer, Morgan finished fastening his side of the kayak down, then walked around and stood in front of her. Sadie got a good look at his face, and her toes instantly curled in reaction to what she realized was coming.

"I'm mighty impressed you stayed put this morning," he said just as his arms came around her and his lips made contact with hers.

Sadie stiffened, kept her mouth firmly shut, and tried not to notice how nice he smelled or how his powerful body pressed so intimately against hers made her heart race. He couldn't kiss her whenever he wanted.

But, more important, she couldn't want him to. Responding to Morgan MacKeage's kisses, she had learned on their date Saturday night, could very quickly lead to intimacy. And intimacy would mean getting naked.

And that could never happen.

Sadie felt herself spinning through space, and it wasn't until her back touched the hood of her truck that she realized Morgan had just picked her up and was all but lying on top of her.

Damn. He was pure alpha male when it came to kissing.

Sadie felt the hem of her T-shirt being pulled from her pants. She tore her mouth away with a gasp, at the same time grabbing his hand to stop its advance. She gave his shoulder a mighty shove to push him away.

It was like trying to push a mountain. Sadie found herself staring into solid green eyes, as dark and as swirling as the forest during a storm.

"That's far . . . I don't . . . you can't . . ." Sadie snapped her mouth shut and glared at him.

Morgan simply watched her for the longest time, then threw back his head and laughed out loud. He straightened and pulled her upright to stand against him, hugging her tightly.

"Someday, lass, your mouth will catch up with your brain," he told her, still laughing, still hugging her. He pulled on her hair to tilt her head back and kissed her soundly but briefly on the lips. "But you have my permission to postpone that day for several more years yet."

She tried to pull away, but he wouldn't release her.

"Now, lass. Where is it we're going in such a hurry this afternoon? Will I be needing my own boat?" He darted a look at her kayak, then back at her. "Because I'm telling you now, that's a mighty odd craft you use, and I don't have one like it."

"I'm going to the Prospect and setting up camp. You're going home and staying the hell out of my business."

He shook his head and grinned at her. "Ah, Mercedes. Haven't you figured it out yet? When you stayed put today, you gave me your trust."

"I *stayed put* because I had things to do."

Sadie wiggled free, went to the hammock, and picked up the stolen diary and her own journal. She turned to find Morgan sitting on her porch, watching her. Faol was sitting beside him. The wolf's head was cocked at an inquisitive angle, his eyes following her every movement.

And if Sadie didn't know better, she would think the two arrogant fools were grinning at her.

She strode to her truck, ignoring the male parade that silently fell into step behind her. She climbed in, but before she could shut the door, Morgan had one hand on the roof and one arm resting on the inside handle, effectively stopping her from leaving.

Sadie glared at him.

He grinned at her. "Until later, *gràineag,*" he said as he softly closed her truck door.

Sadie rolled down the window. "What does that mean?" she hollered to his retreating back.

He stopped, only turning his head, and shot her a wink. "It's a term of endearment, lass. And one that fits you much better than that glove you wear on your right hand."

He walked into the woods with that nonanswer, and Sadie watched as Faol ran to catch up. The wolf stopped, though, just before he entered the forest and looked back at her. He gave a single bark, then turned and also melted into the landscape.

Sadie heard the sound of pounding hooves traveling through the woods then, and she listened until only their fading echo remained. Morgan MacKeage and his odd band of animals were gone, disappearing as suddenly as they had arrived.

Sadie turned and stared out the windshield at the road ahead of her. "An endearment, huh?" she whispered to herself. "I'm thinking of a few of my own for you, MacKeage. And I doubt you'll like them any better than I like mine."

That said, she twisted the key in the ignition and put her truck into gear. She was heading into the great woods herself, with the hope that this valley was big enough for her to avoid the Dolan brothers, her boss, the wolf, and Morgan MacKeage while she searched for Jedediah's gold.

Chapter Eleven

The problem with lust, as Sadie saw it, was that raging hormones knew no sense of discretion. They were just as happy to target the first handsome male—suitable or not—who had the unfortunate luck to step into their path. And it was exactly that sort of recklessness that was causing Sadie such worry now.

Because her hormones definitely liked Morgan MacKeage.

Sadie absently tossed another stick onto the dying fire and took a sip of chamomile tea as she watched the wood catch and flare into flame. The air was heavy with summer-tropical moisture, pregnant with the promise of thunderstorms. That was why she had positioned her campsite away from the threat of suddenly rising river water, towering trees that might attract lightning, and the path of falling rocks that might suddenly slip down from Fraser Mountain without warning.

The same way her heart might suddenly slip, also

without warning, over the spell of Morgan's unforgettably deep, mesmerizing, forest-green eyes.

And that was the problem. How could she casually let Morgan know that friendship was not what she wanted but that a lusty affair was more to her liking? And how could she orchestrate it all without taking her clothes off?

Her hormones didn't seem to understand that she simply couldn't undress and hop into bed—not if she didn't want Morgan hopping right out and running away in horror.

Sadie set her mug of tea on a rock near the fire and slowly worked the glove off her right hand. She flexed her fingers and turned her palm up, staring at the maze of scars that patterned the smooth skin like white lines of spider silk.

Whenever she tried to look at her scars with detachment, Sadie could almost make herself believe they weren't that ugly, nothing more than damaged skin that had done a very efficient job of healing.

She still had use of her hand. The skin, although tight and somewhat more leathery than its original version, was still nicely functioning to protect the bone and muscle and cartilage beneath it.

Sadie splayed her fingers wide. It was the romantic view of herself that made her put her glove on every morning, made her wear a body sock and long sleeves, and made her sometimes wish that her father had never reached her in time.

"Do you wear your glove so much you forget what your own hand looks like?"

Sadie fell off the log she'd been sitting on, landing

on the ground with a yelp of surprise. Her foot hit the mug of tea, sending it into the fire. The liquid hissed as it evaporated on the embers, and the plastic cup burst into colorful flames.

The laughter of a highly amused male wafted into the campsite, followed by the forms of two shadowed bodies—one impressively tall, the other short and fur-covered.

"Dammit, MacKeage. You travel these woods like a ghost."

He laughed again and hunched down in front of her. Sadie caught her breath. He appeared more formidable than the old-growth pines that towered over these woods, more solid than the mountains, and far more wild than the river that ran in rapids just a hundred yards away.

His wavy blond hair was loose, with two thin braids holding it off his face. His shoulders were broad enough to make her heart race, his hands on his knees large enough to make her mouth dry. He wore a pack on his back, the straps pulling his shirt taut against his chest, nicely showing off every muscle a man would need to make a girl's head spin.

"Come on, lass. Let me help you up."

Sadie stared at the hand he held out to her. What was it with this man, that he always insisted on taking her right hand? Ignoring his offer, a bit peeved that she was having lustful thoughts and he seemed totally oblivious, Sadie rolled over and got to her feet without his help. She immediately put some distance between them, at the same time tucking her bare right hand into her pocket.

Morgan pivoted on his haunches and sat on the log she had been occupying. He reached down, picked up her glove from the ground, and held it up to examine it in the light of the setting sun.

"It's made of fine soft leather," he said as he rubbed the glove between his fingers. He looked up at her. "Do you need it to protect your skin, Mercedes?"

She balled her hand in her pocket and gritted her teeth to keep from growling in frustration. "No," she told him succinctly, lifting her chin and holding out her left hand for the glove.

He tossed it to Faol. The wolf immediately snatched it up and looked at her, the glove dangling out of his mouth like a dead rat.

"Then why do you wear it?" Morgan asked, drawing her attention again.

Sadie glared at the man. "What is it with you people? Is it a Scottish thing, this need you have for being rude? First that nosy old priest, and now you. Why I wear a glove is my business."

He shook his head, and the corner of his mouth lifted in a crooked grin. "Ever the *gràineag,*" he said, shrugging out of his pack and letting it fall to the ground behind him.

"What does that mean?"

"I'll tell you if you come sit with me," he said, patting the log beside him.

Sadie immediately became suspicious. She held her position, crossing her arms under her chest and burying her right hand in the folds of her fleece.

"What are you doing here, MacKeage?"

He picked up his pack. "I'm thinking a hunt for

gold might be a nice adventure," he said, undoing the buckles and opening the top flap. He shot her a grin. "And I'm also thinking it might be the most fun with you."

Sadie could only gape, speechless, as he then turned his attention back to the contents of his pack. He wanted to hunt for Plum's gold? With her? As in their traveling together, sharing a boat and meals?

And a campsite?

He pulled a bottle of wine from his pack, set it on the ground, then picked up the pot of tea she had set by the fire to keep warm. He sniffed the pot, made a face, and dumped the tea onto the ground.

Still unable to find her voice—not sure if it was from the shock of his stated intentions or from curiosity about what he was doing now—Sadie could only hug herself and watch. He set the now empty pot on the grate over the fire, then rummaged around in his pack again, pulling out a corkscrew. He quickly opened the bottle of wine and poured nearly all of it into the pot.

Something bumped against her thigh, and Sadie flinched in surprise. She looked down to discover Faol standing beside her, her glove still in his mouth, his iridescent green eyes unblinking as he stared up at her. Sadie quickly moved away, putting several feet between them.

"He'll not harm you, Mercedes," Morgan said, drawing her attention again. He shot her another grin. "I'm thinking the beast has taken a liking to you."

"And I'm thinking you think too much. You're not hunting for Plum's gold." She waved to encompass her campsite. "You can't just waltz in here and say you're joining me. I'm not on an adventure. I'm building a park."

"A park that will only happen if you find the gold, according to your boss. I can help." His grin broadened, and his already impressive chest puffed out a good six inches more. "I'm a very good hunter."

Sadie wanted to screech in frustration and maybe walk over and smack him on the side of the head. She rubbed her hands up and down her thighs instead. She was not sharing a campsite with him, not even for one night. She'd probably do something foolish, like throw herself on top of the man the moment he fell asleep.

"Hunting for gold is not like hunting for supper," she explained patiently. "It's tedious, frustrating work that depends on luck more often than skill."

He wasn't paying attention to her. His nose was buried in his pack again. This time, he pulled out a small silver tin, which he opened. He took a pinch of something out of it, which he tossed into the pot of now steaming wine.

"Morgan, you have to leave," Sadie said, somewhat desperately. "You can't come with me. And you sure as hell are not sharing my camp."

It was Faol who answered, since Morgan was busy ignoring her, rummaging around in his pack again. The wolf, her glove still in his mouth, walked over to the back side of the fire, lay down as if settling in for the night, put his head on his paws, and closed his eyes.

Morgan pulled two tin cups from his pack.

Sadie spun on her heel and walked into the forest.

She stopped just beyond the light of the fire and let her eyes adjust to the darkness of the woods. Once she could see, she headed for the river.

They were both denser than dirt, bullying their way into her life, fraying her emotions, neither of them heeding her petition to leave her alone. Faol, apparently, had decided he liked the company of humans and was trying to worm his way into her affections. And Morgan was much too handsome and far too self-serving for her peace of mind.

That was probably why he had accepted the blind date with her in the first place. Knowing her mother, Charlotte likely had mentioned Plum's gold to Callum, and Callum likely had mentioned it to Morgan. So the man had dated her, kissed her senseless in hopes of worming *his* way into her affections, and now he thought he could search beside her and claim his share of the gold so that she wouldn't have enough left to fund the park he was so much against.

Sadie suddenly tripped and landed facedown in the moist dirt of the river bank. She turned into a sitting position and stared back at the dark green canoe lying keel-up on the gravel.

The boat hadn't been there an hour ago.

Sadie crawled on her knees to the canoe for a closer look. It was an old boat, strongly built of cedar and canvas, at least twenty feet long. It was also heavy. It took all of her strength to turn the boat upright, exposing the canvas pack that had been stashed beneath it.

She immediately reached for the long, leather-sheathed sword lying beside the bag. She settled down on the gravel and rested her back against the canoe, then pulled the heavy sword across her lap. She undid the leather stays at the top and awkwardly slid the great weapon out of its sheath.

Moonlight glinted off the blade.

"Have a care, lass, not to slice open your hands."

Sadie looked up to find Morgan standing not ten feet away, holding two steaming mugs. He came over and sat down beside her, placing one of the mugs in her hand.

"You're thinking a sword is a strange thing to be carrying around," he said just before he took a sip from his own mug.

Sadie lifted her steaming cup to her nose, sniffed it, and involuntarily shuddered. "Whew. What is this?"

"Mulled wine. Or the closest I can get to mulled wine. Drink, lass. It tastes better than it smells."

Not wanting to hurt his feelings by refusing his gift—although she couldn't imagine why she should care about his feelings—Sadie took a small, tentative sip. And, again, every muscle in her body uncontrollably shuddered.

Morgan chuckled and took another, heartier drink of his wine. Sadie absently fingered the blade of his sword. "It is a rather odd thing to be lugging around the woods. It's very heavy. Why do you carry it?"

He stilled her fingers by covering her naked right hand with his own. "Because it is a very efficient weapon," he said, lifting her hand to his lips and kissing the palm of it softly.

Sadie sucked in her breath and held it.

He had just kissed her scars.

She didn't know what to do. What to say. How to act.

So, without thinking, she took another drink of her wine.

Tears immediately came to her eyes, and her throat closed up in defense of the powerful taste. It was all she could do not to break into a fit of coughing.

The man beside her chuckled again and set down his mug so that he could take her right hand in both of his. Ignoring her tug to get free, he turned her hand palm-up and traced a finger lightly over her scars.

"Will you tell me about the fire?" he asked, his voice soft and low-timbered, sending a shiver down Sadie's spine.

"No."

"About your sister, then. And your da."

"No."

He laughed softly and let go of her hand. He lifted his sword off her lap, set it on the ground beside him, and reached over to take her mug of terrible wine and set it beside his sword. And then he grabbed her by the waist and picked her up. In the blink of an eye, Sadie found herself straddling his thighs, her eyes level with his.

She stopped breathing again.

"Then, if you're not in the mood for conversation, what should we do with the rest of our evening, lass?"

With all the hormones in her body suddenly zinging around like sparks from a wildfire, Sadie pondered her options. She was all alone in the woods with a very handsome man, miles from nowhere with nothing to disturb them, and it might be nice to feel that tingling sensation deep in her chest again.

"I'm not asking you to solve the world's problems," he said through a grin, giving her a squeeze. "I'm only looking for suggestions on how to occupy our time."

We could kiss until the cows come home, she thought.

She truly did love the taste of Morgan MacKeage. She liked the way he smelled, the way he felt, and the way he made all five of her senses come alive.

But she just couldn't work up the nerve to start something that would end with her taking off her clothes.

Morgan answered his own question, not with words but with action. He cupped the sides of her face and pulled Sadie into his kiss, canting her head to access her mouth fully.

Her resistance faltered under the siege of his sensual, enticing lips. His hands sent shivers down her spine as they wrapped around her back and pulled her against his solid body.

Sadie quit fighting—both Morgan and herself. She trailed her mouth over his jaw, tracing the edge of his beard with her lips. She felt his groan rumble through every inch of her own trembling body, felt his muscles tense, heard his indrawn breath.

She dropped her hands to his shoulders, then his chest, digging her fingers into his shirt. *She* groaned this time, as she followed her fingers with her mouth, kissing his neck and throat. She worked at the buttons of his shirt. One came open. The next one popped off. And God bless the rest, they retreated without a fight.

Sadie pushed his shirt aside and caught her breath again. He was magnificent. Better than she remembered.

He still wore that strange-looking object around his neck, dangling from a leather cord over his breast bone. It looked to be made of sandstone or wood, swirling lines that appeared to be in constant motion.

An illusion of the disappearing sun.

Or her own emotions, maybe.

"Why couldn't you have been a dork?" Sadie asked with a sigh of resignation.

He pulled back and looked at her though narrowed eyes. "What is a dork?"

Sadie gave him a slow, warm grin. "It's a term of endearment," she whispered, curling her fingers into the mat of hair on his chest. "One that fits you better than that sword you carry around like some medieval warrior."

So quickly that she didn't even have time to scream, Sadie found herself flat on her back on the ground, one very unamused male lying on top of her.

"Don't throw my words back at me, Mercedes."

Pleased to have her brain back in charge of her hormones, Sadie gave him a huge, satisfyingly smug smile.

Morgan did not respond. He had gone suddenly tense, his face raised to the sky, his head cocked to the side as if he were listening for something.

"Do you hear that?" he whispered.

Sadie held her breath and listened, too. And she heard what he had, far off in the distance, the low rumble of an approaching storm.

"That's thunder," she said, turning her head to the western sky. "The front's moving in." She looked back at him and smiled. "We're in for a good soaking, judging by the heaviness of the air. Did you bring a tent?"

He still wasn't listening to her. He released her so suddenly, and scrambled off so quickly, that Sadie couldn't stifle a grunt of surprise. He stood over her, facing west, his hands clenched into fists and his entire countenance as fierce and foreboding as the churning sky.

Sadie scrambled to her own feet and took hold of his sleeve. "It's just a thunderstorm, Morgan. A cold front is moving down from Canada tonight, washing away the humidity."

He shrugged her off and took several steps back. Sadie could only stare at him. This great big bear of a man was afraid of thunderstorms? Lightning flashed on the other side of the valley, and she saw Morgan flinch violently.

She also saw his expression clearly for that one brief moment. Tightly controlled, stone-cold terror was etched into every line of his face.

"Morgan," she said, moving toward him again.

He took another step back, holding up his hands to stop her advance. "Don't come near me, Mercedes," he said, his voice harsh with warning.

Lightning struck high on a mountain across the valley, sending a wave of rumbling thunder toward them. Another flash, farther north, then another, the strikes echoing like cannons along the length of the river. A west wind kicked up, pushed ahead of the arriving storm, sending a flurry of leaves into the air around them. The rain arrived with surprising force, beating more leaves from the trees and adding to the chaos.

Morgan suddenly pivoted on his heel, strode to his canoe, and picked up his sword. Sadie ran after him.

He whirled back toward her. *"Falbh!"*

She stopped on the spot at the sight of that sword pointed at her.

"Begone!" he shouted, waving his weapon toward the woods. "Go back to your camp."

She could only stare at him in shock and confusion. He suddenly slid his sword back into its sheath and settled it over his shoulders onto his back. Lightning flashed again, closer this time, sending the smell of ozone through the air as thunder shook the ground with resonating force.

Sadie blinked against the brightness of the lightning and the driving rain, then blinked again when she realized she was staring at nothing.

Morgan MacKeage was gone.

Chapter Twelve

Daar paced the length of his cabin porch, then stopped suddenly to frown at the darkening sky. Lightning flashed in the distance, creating a halo over the mountains to the west.

Another storm was visiting the valley.

There was something happening here, more than just Morgan and Mercedes' conflict over a park being built. For eighty years the balance of good and evil in the valley had been uneven, since the death of Jedediah Plum. The restless prospector still roamed this valley, waiting for justice finally to be served. And in that time the darkness had been building, gathering strength for the inevitable confrontation.

Daar had spent the entire summer trying to learn the reason for this impending clash of powers. Why here, in Mercedes' valley? And why now of all times, just when he was finally getting Morgan settled into a new and promising life?

Daar rubbed the back of his neck and blew out a tired sigh. As best as he could tell, the violent death of Jedediah Plum had gone unpunished, and the murderer's spirit of greed was still alive today in his descendants. An evil had gone unavenged eighty years ago, tilting in its favor the balance of energy in this valley. The blackness Daar and Morgan had seen earlier this summer had been entrenched here since that long-ago murder.

And just recently, in this generation, Daar had learned through his spells that the darkness had gathered even more strength. Other murders, somehow connected to Jedediah Plum, had again gone unpunished.

The yellow light, which symbolized not only Mercedes but also her family, seemed to be equally involved. It was possible that Caroline Quill had been the second victim of the darkness and Frank Quill the third.

And Mercedes might be in danger of becoming the fourth.

Daar had tried many spells over the last few weeks, attempting to vanquish the blackness. But the churning powers would not be budged. It was happening here, now, and to the folly of all who stumbled into its path. The energies needed to be rebalanced. Grievous wrongs had to be righted. A simple, lonely prospector wanted peace.

That Mercedes and Morgan were sitting smack in the middle of this war was beyond the wizard's power to control. He had done what he could to protect them. It was now up to the warrior to unite with the woman against the darkness and lead them both safely through the coming maelstrom.

Daar's delicate cane began to hum in his hand, and he lifted it skyward and waved it at the valley beyond. He saw the glow of a familiar green light, charged with energy, running through the forest, desperate, driven, aimlessly searching for safety.

Daar shook his head. No words of assurance could convince Morgan that he was not in danger of being sent on another journey through time. For two years the wizard had made promises to all the Highlanders, but only Greylen seemed to believe him.

Probably because Grey thought that Daar's banished staff had left him powerless.

The humming grew louder. Insistent. Daar fought to control his staff as it pulled against the turbulence of the approaching storm. Yellow light, as bright and vibrant as the sun, sparked through the wizard's mind.

Daar smiled. Such passion from one so innocent. Such determination and potent vigor. If anyone could capture and hold the interest of Morgan MacKeage, it was Mercedes Quill.

She was a fine match for the warrior—strong, intelligent, and possessing the courage it would take to fight by his side. And for that Daar was glad, because if he understood the signs he'd been reading these last few weeks, Mercedes Quill's search for the gold was sending her deep into the middle of a violent war.

Morgan ran without direction save one: away from Mercedes. He had to protect her from the storm, from the terror of a journey that could send him, and possibly anyone near him, through time.

As much as he wanted to run to Mercedes, not from her—to bury himself in her soft strength and hold on tightly until the storm had passed—he could not endanger her that way.

But if he were gone, who would keep her safe from the darkness that roamed this valley now?

Morgan stopped his flight abruptly on that thought and squinted through the driving rain to get his bearings. Though it seemed like a hundred, he'd traveled less than half a mile from the river. Lightning flashed again, followed almost immediately by ground-shaking thunder. The storm surrounded him. Wind bowed the tops of the taller trees and drove the autumn-turned leaves from the branches of oak and maple and beech.

A voice, high-pitched and insistent, came through the echoing thunder, faint at first but moving closer.

Morgan dropped his chin to his chest and closed his eyes. Mercedes, the maddening little *gràineag*, was searching for him.

He was torn between continuing on for her safety and returning to her for his own selfish reasons. Dammit. They belonged to each other.

He could protect her, be they in this time or another; he could face any challenge as long as they were together.

But did he have that right yet, to choose Mercedes' destiny for her? She'd been about to give herself to him, but did she fully understand what that giving meant?

And was he desperate enough—and selfish enough—to wait until after he possessed Mercedes to explain to her the age-old laws of claiming?

He did not care for this modern society's rules of mating. Once he made love to Mercedes, there was no turning back. She would be his until eternity.

Morgan moved into the shelter of a giant spruce tree. The sound of her calling him was closer now, echoing from several directions and carried on the wind. Her voice rang with desperation and concern—and maybe just a touch of anger.

Morgan couldn't keep from smiling. His little *gràineag* was nothing if not tenacious. She'd drown herself searching for him, or possibly catch pneumonia. But she would not give up, he knew, because she was proving herself to be just as possessive as he was.

And for that reason alone, he stepped into her path.

As quickly and mysteriously as he had disappeared, Morgan was suddenly standing in front of her, a dark, formidable specter visible only in the strobe of lightning that pulsed through the sky.

His shirt was still unbuttoned, the leather strap of his sword lying across his chest. Water ran in steaming rivulets over the harsh planes of his face, down his neck, over his powerful body that could have been carved from granite.

For one brief moment, in one particularly blinding flash of light, Sadie saw clearly the danger she was in. Morgan MacKeage would not negotiate. Would offer no concessions. Accept no excuses.

He would demand her complete surrender.

And then he would demand even more.

The air between them crackled with electricity. The object hanging around his neck seemed to sparkle and hum with energy, taking on an ethereal glow of its own. The nerves covering every inch of Sadie's skin came alive. She didn't know if it was the storm crashing around them or the blood rushing through her head, but she was having a hard time keeping her balance. Her heart wanted to jump out of her chest. Her knees wanted to buckle. And she couldn't stop shaking.

Morgan suddenly stepped forward and swept her into his arms, lifting her against him and burying his face in her neck. "Too late, Mercedes," he growled into her hair. "It's happening now. And we both live with the consequence."

She couldn't have denied him even if she understood what he was talking about. She wrapped her arms around his neck and clung to him fiercely. He carried her deeper into the forest, until he found an outcropping of ledge that would protect them from the storm. He stood her on her feet, pulled off his sword, and set it on the ground, then gathered the grass that grew at the base of the ledge, fashioning a soft bed.

He worked quickly, in silence, keeping one guarded eye on her as if he were afraid she'd bolt. Sadie stood rooted in place, unable to look away.

He straightened and turned and took her back in his arms, kissing her with a passion that bordered on desperation. Sadie kissed him for their entire journey to the ground, smelling the rain heating his skin, tasting the woods he was so much a part of, feeling the tension gathering in every one of his muscles.

He covered her with his body, surrounding her completely.

And Sadie welcomed the onslaught of emotion that overloaded her senses. She sent her hands exploring, touching, kneading his flesh. She opened her mouth to him, suckled his tongue, and tugged on his hair in an attempt to get even closer.

His hands were everywhere, pulling at her clothes, rubbing exposed skin that felt to be on fire. In a frenzy of movement, with time suspended despite her urgency, Sadie helped him tear away all of their clothes. The storm receded from her mind, her focus narrowed on just the two of them, sharpening inward until only warmth and light and feelings were left.

He laced their fingers together and lifted her hands above her head, using his mouth to trace a path across her face, down her neck, to between her now exposed breasts. Searing heat followed his lips; shivering anticipation preceded them. He kissed the nipple of her right breast, taking it into his mouth and sucking. Sadie shivered and cried out and arched her back with pleasure.

His mouth moved on, over her breasts, his teeth rasping her skin and sending shudders throughout her. Sadie wrapped her legs around his waist and arched her back again, feeling his erection pushing against her belly.

He lifted himself off her slightly, just enough that he could stare down at her face. The swirling, now brightened glow of his necklace exposed harsh features and eyes sharp with intent.

"Do you take me, Mercedes?" he asked in a low, guttural voice. "And all that I have to offer—do you take me?"

Her mouth suddenly desert-dry, she could only nod.

He pressed himself forward against her belly, then retreated again. "Say it, Mercedes. Say it out loud, so all can hear. Do you take me?"

"Yes, Morgan. Everything you offer."

Some of the tension eased from his face at her words. His muscles relaxed slightly, and it felt as if he all but melted against her. His mouth returned to hers in a kiss that was different this time. More possessive.

"Take my shoulders, lass, and hold tight," he whispered. "It will be unpleasant for only a moment, I promise."

Unpleasant?

How could anything that had to do with this be unpleasant? Sadie was shaking with the need to feel him inside her. "Get on with it, Morgan," she whispered huskily.

A slow, maddening smile lifted one corner of his mouth. "So you can find the words when you need them, huh, *gràineag?*" he said, moving back and reaching one hand between them, guiding himself between her thighs.

Sadie sucked in her breath and held it as he slowly pushed against her. His mouth returned, his hands trapped hers, and his hips finally moved in the direction she wanted.

Weighted tension. Unbelievable pleasure. An awareness of stretching, filling, spiraling heat. The moment he had spoken of lasted a lifetime measured in seconds.

And suddenly he was completely inside her.

It was Sadie who moved then, lifting her hips to accept him, digging her nails into his shoulders, and reaching up to capture his mouth again. She swallowed his moan that came the moment he began to move, rocking them both in a rhythm that shot repeating currents of fire throughout her.

The pleasure doubled. Tripled. With a cry of pure joy, Sadie turned her mouth onto his shoulder, feeling his straining muscles against her teeth as she tightened around him.

Morgan stopped and reared up and threw his head back with a shout.

Her eyes widened when, she saw the stone at his neck suddenly flare to life as if struck by lightning, blinding her to everything but feeling. And what she felt now was Morgan, so very deep inside her, pulsing against the throbbing of her womb.

With a groan like that of a wounded bear, Morgan dropped his full weight to his elbows, brushing back her hair and kissing her tenderly on the nose. His heart pounded against hers. His breathing was labored. And she became aware of every steaming inch of him that touched her naked skin.

The storm returned to her consciousness. The rain continued, but the thunder was moving away now, the flashes dulling to mere hints of light. But it was enough for her to see clearly the gleam of triumph dancing in Morgan's eyes.

Chapter Thirteen

He had one hell of an apology to make.

No better than a rutting animal, he had just taken his woman in the woods, in the middle of a damned storm. What should have been the most pleasant experience of Mercedes' life had most likely been her greatest disaster.

She was frighteningly still but for the faint trembling he could feel coursing through her body beneath him. The apology would have to wait. He needed to get her warm, get her up and dressed and hustled back to their camp in a hurry.

As carefully as he could, Morgan lifted himself off Mercedes and rose to his knees. She immediately scrambled away, crossing her hands over her chest, frantically searching for someplace to hide.

Morgan was stricken by the sight. Much more was needed than a damned apology. He would gladly give up his sword arm for this not to have happened.

He groped on the ground until he found his shirt, shook it out, and attempted to put it on Mercedes.

She flinched, rose to her knees, and almost scrambled away before he could catch her. He wrapped one arm around her waist and hugged her to his chest, feeling her shiver. He closed his eyes and silently prayed for forgiveness, and then he whispered those same petitions to her.

"I'm sorry, lass, for what I've done. But you've got to let me get you dressed. You're going to catch cold."

"I can dress myself."

Her voice was faint. Distant. And without emotion. Morgan grew alarmed. Her shivering had turned violent now, her whole body as cold as snow.

"You can rail at me tomorrow, *gràineag,*" he said, returning to his chore of dressing her. "You even have my permission to use my sword, if you still have the strength to lift it," he added, hoping like hell she did have the strength, that she wouldn't catch pneumonia.

She was amazingly strong now and fought him, trying to squirm out of his hold. But it wasn't until he wrapped his hands around her back that Morgan fully understood why Mercedes was so frantic to escape him. She immediately twisted away and kicked out with her feet.

It was those damned scars she was trying to hide from him. Mercedes was horrified that he might see them and be disgusted.

He immediately moved away from her. "Easy, Mercedes. I'll let you dress. Here," he said, gathering up her soaked pants and shirt. "Here's your clothes.

They're wet, but I'll have you back in front of a warm fire in minutes. Just get dressed."

Morgan then stood, shaking out his own pants and stepping into them. He shuddered as the wet cloth grated against his skin. He put on his boots and set his sword over his shoulder before he shook out his shirt and held it up to Mercedes once again.

"Here. It's wet, too, but it's wool. It will add some warmth to your own clothes."

She was only half dressed. She had thrown her shirt on with haste and had buttoned it crooked. Her pants were pulled up, and she was now fighting with the zipper. Her trembling hands were making the chore nearly impossible.

Morgan lost what patience he'd been trying to hold on to. He wrapped his shirt over her shoulders and swept her into his arms.

Her first reaction was to squeak.

Her second was to take a poorly aimed swing at his head.

"You're going to kill us both," she grumbled. "I'm too heavy."

He couldn't stifle a laugh. "Ah, *gràineag.* When the day comes that I can't carry you, I'll be three years in my grave." He hefted her slightly, settling her comfortably. "Now, be quiet and save your strength," he added, giving her a quick kiss on her dirty forehead. "Because tomorrow, Mercedes, we are having a much-needed talk about the rules of this match."

He was planning a lecture, most likely.

Sadie lay in the warmth of Morgan's embrace and

stared up at the ceiling of her tent, most of which Morgan MacKeage was filling.

It was quite nice, she decided, to wake up and find herself snuggled securely against a sleeping bear.

It was also a bit disconcerting.

The guy was completely naked.

It seemed she'd fallen in love with an exhibitionist. She'd probably seen Morgan naked more often than dressed.

She was just the opposite, wanting to keep herself covered up to the chin.

Hence the upcoming lecture.

She expected Morgan was planning to scold her for acting so insanely modest, even to the point of foolishness. She knew he had been worried last night that she'd been wet and cold.

So she'd shut up, let him carry her back to camp—that had been an experience in itself—and then she had washed, dressed in layers of dry clothes, and crawled into bed. She had even remained silent when Morgan had crawled into the tent and settled beside her.

Now she was staring at the dawn-lighted ceiling, wondering how she was going to extricate herself from both his embrace and the mess she'd made of their flaming affair.

But first there was the matter of her body sock. It was lost in the forest someplace, muddy and wet, along with her bra. She had other bras with her, but that was her only camisole, and she wanted it back.

Holding her breath, Sadie carefully lifted Morgan's arm off her waist and gently set it beside her. With painstaking care, she pulled the zipper on her sleeping bag down, cringing at every metallic click it made. She moved first one leg and then the other one free of the bag and silently rolled to her knees and backed her way to the door.

She stopped, though, caught by what she was seeing. The man was lying on his stomach, completely naked. His entire body was tanned, sprinkled with a downy coat of sun-bleached hair. There was a wicked-looking scar just above his right buttock, crossing his waist in a six-inch raised welt of light-colored skin. And another one on his right shoulder, not as long but obviously just as old.

His feet were dirty, thick-skinned with calluses. He apparently didn't wear boots any more often than he wore clothes. And at his side, almost as tall as he was, lay his sword. Sadie stifled a snort. Why wasn't she surprised he slept with the thing?

She continued her study.

His hand rested relaxed on the spot where she'd been lying. It was a large hand, strong-looking, blunt. His huge body took up most of the tent, his feet touching the door and his head all but touching the end. He had to be nearly six and a half feet tall. Beautiful. Magnificent. Completely naked but for the leather cord he always wore around his neck.

Sadie shook off her lusty thoughts, turned, and slid down the tent zipper just enough to crawl through. She continued to crawl all the way to the now smoldering fire Morgan had rekindled last night. She stood, only to realize that she wore only socks and that her boots were someplace in the woods with the rest of her clothes.

Damn. She walked to her dry packs sitting beside her tent and picked up one of the bags and carried it back to the fire. Then she pulled out her spare sneakers and slipped them on. One minute later she was back on her feet and running through the forest, trying to remember where in these woods she might have left her most intimate clothing.

Morgan took his time dressing. He was pretty sure he knew where Mercedes was going, and he suspected it would take her some time to find her way. She hadn't been paying much attention last night to where in the woods they had made love.

She'd been too busy being appalled.

He would set Mercedes down today, once he got her back to camp and filled her belly with food, and have a nice little talk with her about this new and hopefully peaceful life they had begun last night.

He would be understanding but firm.

Patient but insistent.

Calm but determined.

She would get over her modesty.

She would respect his authority.

Morgan snorted to himself. Aye. Mercedes would accept his dictates with all the grace of a *grâineag*.

With that thought lifting the corner of his mouth, Morgan set his sword over his back and headed into the woods at a trot. In less than a minute he picked up her trail and followed its aimless wanderings for nearly a mile.

He heard her sneeze before he actually saw her.

Dammit. She was catching a cold.

He stopped a good twenty paces away and watched as Mercedes scattered leaves with the toe of her shoe. She'd already gathered her boots, their socks, and both of their underwear into a pile. She was now pushing at the leaves and sticks littering the ground but stopped suddenly and reached down to pick up a thin shirt that looked more like a rag than clothes.

She suddenly stiffened and whirled toward him, hiding both her hands behind her back like a guilty child. Morgan pulled away from the tree and walked toward her.

She took a quick step back, realized what she'd done, and stepped forward again, her chin lifted at him. Morgan made sure his smile didn't show what he thought of her actions.

"What's so important that you felt the need to sneak off this morning and come here?" he asked.

Her chin went up another notch, and her beautiful blue eyes narrowed. "Nothing. I didn't sneak off, I walked."

"Then what was that you picked up from the ground just now?"

Her entire face flushed red, and her chin lowered slightly. "That's my business. I came here alone because I wanted some privacy."

He slowly shook his head at her. "Privacy no longer exists between us, Mercedes," he said, stepping closer. "It ended last night." He reached out a hand. "Show me what you're holding."

She took two steps back. "You don't understand!"

Ah, but he was quite sure that he did. "My hands covered every inch of you last night, woman. I know exactly what you look like under your clothes. And exactly how you feel."

Her eyes widened, and her blush paled—and Morgan continued with a determination grounded in truth. "I also know that you have no reason to feel vulnerable with me, Mercedes. Because I don't see scars when I look at you. I don't feel them when I touch you. I only experience your beauty."

He pounced on her then, before she had time to realize his intent. He had to tackle her to the ground to keep his shins from being bruised, and he had to grab her hands before she pummeled him to death. In the end, he was a bit muddy but victorious. He turned them both until he was sitting on the ground, Mercedes was on his lap, and the rag she'd been hiding was in her hands being held by his.

And seeing it close up, he was also quite sure what it was.

Morgan sighed and rubbed his forehead with his free hand. Damn. They were going to have their talk on an empty belly.

"This has to stop, Mercedes. There is no room for modesty or shyness between us." He pointed at the finely knit shirt she usually wore like a second skin, now clutched in her hand. "And it is a sin for a wife to keep secrets from her husband."

Her gasp was expected.

Her sharp little elbow driving into his ribs was not.

Before he could catch her, Mercedes was off his lap and standing over him, her hands balled into fists at her sides, her eyes snapping fire, and her complexion so red it was a wonder she didn't explode.

"That's a sick joke, MacKeage."

He slowly stood up and carefully brushed the mud from his pants, not once taking his gaze off her indignant face. "Joke? What are you talking about, a joke?"

"I'm talking about what you just said. A wife not having secrets from her husband, as if that pertained to us. Well, damn you, when I find a husband, I'll be sure to remember your advice."

It hit him then, like the blow of a mace, that this spitting-mad woman was actually the confused one here. Morgan rubbed his forehead again and closed his eyes while he prayed for strength—and plenty of patience.

"Mercedes," he finally said, in as calm a voice as he could manage when he looked at her again. "I wasn't making a joke to you just now, because you already are my wife."

"I am not."

He nodded. Curtly. "Aye, you are. The ceremony took place right here," he explained, waving his hand at the ground. "I remember asking you, quite clearly, if you took me. And," he continued more forcefully when she opened her mouth to protest, "you quite clearly said that you did."

"I wasn't marrying you! I was trying to get an affair started between us."

"It's done. We're husband and wife."

"But there was no minister. No witnesses, for crying out loud! It won't hold up in a court of law."

"It will damn well hold up to God's law. You're my wife, Mercedes. You are no longer a Quill but a MacKeage. And God save anyone who thinks different."

He stepped forward and firmly took hold of her chin, getting close enough so she would feel the finality of his words all the way down to her toes. "And that includes you, wife. Because this will not be one of your modern-day marriages. You will defer to your husband and respect my word. And to that end we will have a peaceful union if I have to take the flat of my sword to your backside."

That said, Morgan pivoted on his heel and strode away from the scene of his dictate, leaving Mercedes to come to terms with what she had just heard. Because, like it or not, he was holding Mercedes to her words of last night and keeping her as his wife.

And he'd even be generous, dammit, and allow her a few days to get used to the idea.

Holy spit. What had taken place here last night? How had they gone from friendship to marriage in less than a week?

And what had happened to her flaming affair?

Sadie folded her knees and sat down on the ground, clutching her camisole to her chest. The man couldn't be serious. Married? As in setting up housekeeping and living together?

Naw. The guy must be touched in the head. He was like his cousin, Callum, a bit old-fashioned was all. Yeah. Morgan was acting like a Neanderthal, being possessive and maybe feeling guilty for last night, and he was trying to make her feel good about the whole fiasco.

Naw. That wasn't it, either. He was just insane. Because there hadn't been one ounce of compassion in him just now, only a menacing threat lacing his whisper-soft voice and snapping in his forest-green eyes.

Take the flat of his sword to her backside?

The man was a throwback.

Either that, or she had fallen down a rabbit hole.

Sadie suddenly realized she was being watched and looked up to find Faol sitting just ten feet away. He was holding a stick in his mouth this time, her favorite glove nowhere to be seen.

The hulking wolf whined like a puppy and stood up and stepped toward her, wagging his tail as he advanced. Sadie scrunched her knees up to her chest and held her breath. She was in no shape right now to deal with another arrogant male.

Faol stopped just in front of her, opened his mouth, and let the stick fall onto the ground at her feet. It sounded like metal striking rock, and Sadie flinched.

And she flinched again when the wolf's tongue suddenly shot out and touched the hand she had wrapped protectively around her knees. The sensation of moist heat sent a tingle straight to her heart.

Faol stared at her, not backing off, not advancing. Tentatively, with great trepidation, Sadie slowly reached out and touched the side of his face. His tongue immediately shot out again and washed her hand.

He bent his head again to pick up the object he'd dropped.

It wasn't a stick but something metal. A large spoon, it looked like. Sadie took it from him, and Faol backed up several steps, lay down, and started washing his paws.

Sadie turned the spoon over in her hands, examining it. It appeared to be an old mixing spoon with half of the bowl rusted off. She pointed it at the wolf.

"This is not a fair trade for the glove, big boy."

He stopped his chore in mid-lick, his tongue looking stuck to his paw as he lifted his canine eyebrows at her. Satisfied that she understood that he didn't care, he went back to washing his feet.

Sadie went back to examining his gift. Using her sleeve, she rubbed some of the rust from the spoon and squinted at what looked like initials scratched into the bowl.

J.L.

Sadie stretched out her legs and straightened her spine. *J.L.?* Jean Lavoie? Was this the old cook's spoon from one of the logging camps? She looked back at the wolf.

"Where did you get this?" she asked, waving it at him again, not wanting to question the fact that she was talking to a wolf. "Can you show me?"

He stood up, wagging his tail as he stared at her. He suddenly turned, trotted down through the woods, and stopped and looked back at her. He let out a sharp bark, took several more steps, and whined.

Her worry over finding herself married suddenly forgotten, Sadie hastily folded her damp camisole and scrambled to her feet. She quickly picked up her boots and forgotten clothes and ran after the wolf.

But she slowed to a walk the moment she realized the treacherous beast had led her back to her own camp. The one where Morgan MacKeage was waiting, sitting by the now roaring fire, cooking breakfast. She stopped at the edge of the clearing and frowned at her gear sitting beside her tent. How was she going to pack her things without having to face the delusional man?

"You should have something to eat before we leave," he said without taking his eyes off his chore.

Sadie stormed into camp and walked past him to her tent. She crawled inside and quickly rolled up her sleeping bag, backed out, then zipped the door closed and carried her gear to her dry bags.

She continued to pack in silence, all the time feeling two sets of piercing green eyes watching her every move. Sadie willed her frazzled nerves to settle down; she needed for her hands not to shake, her throat not to close, and her eyes not to blur with tears.

Sadie MacKeage.

Mercedes Quill MacKeage.

She made a fist and hit the clothes in her bag, driving them deeper. Dammit. She didn't care if it sounded nice. She was not that man's wife. They couldn't be married just because he said so.

Sadie snapped her bag closed with a violent jerk, picked it up and tossed it over her shoulder, and headed to the river.

Morgan MacKeage stood up and blocked her path.

She stared at his feet.

"You'll eat breakfast first, wife."

She brushed the hair out of her face and glared at him. "Stop calling me *wife!*" she shouted, shaking her fist at him. "And stop telling me what to do! I'm not a child, we are *not* married, and so help me," she hissed, taking a step back and pointing her finger when he advanced toward her. "If you tackle me again, I'm going to bloody your face."

Morgan dropped his head so she wouldn't see his smile and was careful not to hurt her when he pounced on her again, twisting so that he took the brunt of the fall when they landed.

And he held her tight as she cursed him again, all the time thinking he must have been drunk on her kisses the night he'd stood on the mist-shrouded cliff and claimed her as his.

He could see now, this was not going to be a peaceful union.

Morgan grabbed at her flailing arms, buried his face in her neck, and smiled again. Who the hell cared if life was peaceful? He was just pleased she was no longer looking as if she wanted to cry.

He pinned both her hands between their bodies, holding her firmly on top of him with his arms wrapped around her back, and let her struggle in vain until she finally tired herself out.

Only then did he gently brush the hair off her face. "You're making threats again, *gràineag,* that you can't back up." He kissed her flushed, angry cheek. "This recklessness must come from not having older brothers who plagued you as a child."

"Let me go," she whispered, trying to get free again.

Morgan rolled them over and sat up, pulling her onto his lap. "As soon as we negotiate a truce," he promised, settling her comfortably but still keeping her trapped.

"You don't negotiate."

"This once, wife, I will try." He touched the end of her nose. "But if you wish my cooperation in the future, don't make me sorry this time. Now, which one of my sins would you like to begin with?"

He felt her take a giant, shuddering breath, and when Mercedes finally lifted her face to look at him, Morgan realized she was trying very hard to appear calmer than she was feeling.

"This married thing," she started, her voice trembling.

Morgan fought the knot in his gut. "What about it?"

"You can't just decide that we're married, just like that," she said, trying to snap her trapped fingers. "It takes two people to make a marriage. Two *aware* people."

"I asked you," he countered. "Do you not remember saying the words to me?"

"I thought you were asking for permission to . . . to . . . well, to do it," she ended on a faint whisper, looking down at his chest. "Not if I wanted to marry you."

"Then I'll ask you now. Will you marry me, Mercedes?"

"No."

He didn't think so. Morgan lifted her chin to look at him. "Then we have a bit of a problem, lass. I consider the deed done."

Her eyes widened, then suddenly narrowed. "And if I don't?"

He gave her a huge grin and once more touched the end of her nose. "I'll give you the answer to that in one week."

Her eyes widened again. "What happens in one week?"

"We will sit down and discuss this marriage then. But for the next seven days," he said quickly, before she could examine his plan too closely, "you will consider yourself my wife."

He gave her a gentle squeeze. "I'm sorry for last night, Mercedes. It shouldn't have happened."

Her head snapped up. "It shouldn't?"

"Not that way," he clarified. "Not under a ledge in the middle of such a violent storm. That was not well done of me."

"I started it," she blurted out. "I mean, I followed you. And I . . . I wanted it, too."

"Ah, yes. This affair you spoke of."

She gave him a frown. "What's wrong with a good oldfashioned flaming affair? Most men would jump at the idea."

"But not most women," he countered. "You demean yourself."

"Yeah, well. How many frogs have you had to kiss?"

"What is it with you and frogs?"

"Never mind. I have another question. Why are you so hell-bent on us being married, anyway? Do you want to sabotage the park so badly that you're willing to get married to do it?"

"Sabotage?"

He felt her exasperated sigh move through both of their bodies. "That's the only reason you're here, isn't it?" she said. "You went on a blind date with me because you knew I was building a park. And you're here now, demanding to be my husband, so you can stop me from finding the gold that will fund it."

Holy hell. The woman had a warped mind—and a

very low opinion of him. No, this was not going to be a peaceful union.

"There will be no park," he replied. "And the gold has nothing to do with it, because I'm not selling my land to your group of people. And without that land, there will be no park," he repeated, just in case she hadn't heard him the first time.

He gave her a less than gentle squeeze. "And the park has nothing to do with our marriage," he continued fiercely. "I want you, and now I have you. It's that simple."

"Well, I don't know why," she said, her voice quivering. "I can't even do it right."

"Do what?"

"M-make love," she whispered. "When you stopped," she said, somewhat louder this time.

Morgan could only stare at this poor, confused woman. She really did know nothing of men. Without thinking how she would react, he threw back his head and let out a deep laugh.

"It's not funny. I'm apologizing here."

"Ah, lass. I'm not really laughing at you," he said with a lingering chuckle. "Well, I am, but mostly I'm laughing at myself. I stopped because I was done, Mercedes."

"Done what?"

Well, hell. He could see that he was going to have to be blunt. "I was done making love to you. The shout you said I made was really a sound of pleasure and fulfillment, when I poured my seed deep inside you."

"You poured your . . ." She suddenly snapped her

mouth shut. Her eyes crossed, and her face sort of turned green—just before it went completely white.

"You . . . you didn't use any protection, did you?" she asked in a whispered squeak.

"No."

Her face turned green again. Morgan leaned back when he saw her hand go to her belly, afraid she was about to be sick.

"I could be pregnant." She looked at him, her glare angry enough to make him lean back even farther. "Dammit to hell. I will not get pregnant."

She jumped off his lap, making him grunt in surprise and cup himself protectively. She whirled and pointed her finger at him.

"I will not make my mother's mistakes!" she all but shouted, her anger flushing her face back to a flaming red. "And I'm sure as hell not making my baby sister an aunt before she's even three months old."

She stomped off after that outburst, in the direction of the river. Morgan leaned back and scrubbed both his hands over his face, attempting to wash away the still lingering echoes of their anything but successful truce. But then her last words finally caught his attention. What baby sister? He counted nine months forward on his fingers, then subtracted three.

And finally it dawned on him what her words meant.

Well, hell. Charlotte Quill was pregnant.

Chapter Fourteen

Charlotte Quill paced the length of Sadie's cabin porch, the concern obvious in every taut line on her face. Callum stood in the door of the ransacked cabin, watching his woman work herself into a fine state of worry.

She stopped in front of him. "Who would do such a thing?" she asked with motherly outrage. "And where's my daughter? Callum, there was blood on the floor," she whispered, digging her nails into his arm.

Callum reached out and pulled her into a mighty embrace. "It's old blood, Charlotte," he assured her. "And Sadie is fine, I promise you," he added. He pulled back and leaned down to look her in the eye. "I know for a fact that Morgan was coming out to see her. And this was the act of only one man, so you've nothing to worry about."

Charlotte pulled free, took a step back, and stared at him. "How do you know that?"

"The muddy footprints he left. This happened this morning, after the storm."

She resumed pacing, rubbing her hands up and down her arms, but stopped again and whirled to face him. "I'm going to find my daughter," she suddenly announced. "I won't have any peace until I see for myself that Sadie's okay."

Her tone was that of a woman expecting resistance, and Callum kept his smile to himself. Charlotte was almost as predictable as the sunrise. In fact, he'd already been mentally planning their camping trip into the valley since the moment he'd seen the destruction to Sadie's cabin.

The first sign of trouble had been the door torn from its hinges. The second thing had been the odor of freshly opened food emanating through the gaping hole. The family of raccoons, whiskers caked with crumbs, had come running out of the cabin the moment Callum's boots had hit the steps.

Charlotte, ignoring his command to go back to the truck, had silently followed him inside and silently looked around at the destruction. Furniture was overturned, a window was smashed, the bed slashed by a knife. But it wasn't until Charlotte had seen the model of the valley that she had helped Sadie build that she had finally found her voice. She'd become a mother on a mission then, to avenge the violation of her daughter's home. She was mad, worried, and just daring him to contradict her plan.

Callum reached out and pulled Charlotte back into his arms. "I'll drop you off at home so you can pack your gear," he told her, freeing his smile when she gasped in surprise. "I'll get my own things together and then pick you up again." He pulled back and looked at her. "Any idea where Sadie might be headed?"

Still looking shocked that he was being cooperative, Charlotte could only shake her head.

"Doesn't she carry a cell phone?" he asked.

Charlotte nodded but scowled. "She does. But I haven't been able to reach her on it once in these last ten weeks. She's either misplacing it, breaking it, or letting the batteries run down."

She pulled away from him, her motherly outrage returning threefold. "I swear that girl has the sense of a pine cone sometimes. She spends her time walking around with her mind in either the past or the future but never in the present. If she's not wallowing in guilt, she's planning absolution for her imagined sin." She angrily waved at the woods surrounding the cabin. "Like this stupid park she's trying to build. It's not a work of joy for her but an obsession to obtain her father's forgiveness."

"Forgiveness for what?" Callum asked, trying to follow the woman's logic.

"For killing Frank and Caroline."

Callum was stunned. "Sadie didn't kill her da," he said. "Or Caroline. I thought it was a house fire."

"That she started. Sadie went to bed and left a candle burning in the study."

"But Frank died only three years ago."

"From a weak heart," Charlotte explained, worry and lingering grief etched into the lines of her face. "The fire damaged his lungs, and he never fully recovered."

Standing stone-still and staring at his woman, Callum was appalled. "Do you blame your daughter, Charlotte?" he asked.

Outrage returned, and Callum watched as she balled her fists against her sides, as if restraining herself from striking him.

"Of course not," she snapped. "I love my daughter."

Charlotte's anger suddenly deflated, and she threw herself into his arms, burying her face in his shirt with a loud wail of anguish. "Oh, Callum. I don't know how to help her. She's lived so long with this guilt, and nothing I say or do will change her mind. And now this obsession has turned dangerous. Somebody ransacked her cabin," she ended with another wail.

Callum clutched her to him and rocked her back and forth. "Ah, woman," he soothed. "There is nothing you can do. This is Sadie's journey to take." He pushed Charlotte back, wiped her hair from her face, and gave her a warm smile. "But she's not traveling alone anymore, little one. Morgan is with her. He'll keep her safe from whoever did this."

He gave her a quick kiss on the forehead and then smiled at her again. "And if I know my cousin, he'll have your daughter so distracted she won't have time to dwell on either the past or the future. She'll be too busy trying to cope with the present, and with his undivided attention."

She looked as if she wanted to believe him, as if she wanted to put her faith in Morgan MacKeage. Callum kissed her again, this time on the lips, this time much more passionately.

Aye, but he loved this woman who'd come storming into his life just six short months ago when she'd accidentally dumped an entire bowl of baked beans in his lap at the grange supper.

He hadn't been looking for love at the time. Hell, he hadn't even thought it possible. Since the storm had brought them all here six years ago, Callum had tried to keep himself detached from this strange new world, to stay strong in the face of fear and uncertainty and the loneliness that came with both.

Charlotte Quill had scattered every one of his vows to the wind when her dinner had landed in his lap. Charlotte had thrown a fit of worry. She had been like the blow of a mace to his chest that night. Which was why Callum had taken Charlotte up on her offer and had taken his soiled clothes to her home the next day for her to clean.

Now he would use this camping trip to his advantage. Hell, he just might keep Charlotte out here until she agreed to marry him.

He wasn't worried about Sadie, because Callum knew for a fact that Morgan was with her. He knew because his cousin's dangerously spoiled war horse was staying at Gu Bràth while Morgan was away. Callum just hoped that Ian wouldn't finally give in to his urge and shoot the contrary beast.

Reluctantly, Callum pulled away from Charlotte and set her firmly from him. "Don't tempt me, woman," he said through a tight smile. "We have a trip to plan and gear to put together."

It seemed the woman had lost her tongue. Charlotte was just staring at him, starry-eyed and disheveled.

Aye. This was going to be a most rewarding adventure.

Sadie wasn't sure how it had happened, but it seemed she had agreed to be Morgan's wife for the next seven days. Of all the foolish notions a man could have, where had he come up with the idea that they were married?

Sadie dipped her kayak paddle into the water with lazy strokes, letting the current of the river do most of the work. Her attention was divided between the wolf jogging along the river bank and the man paddling his canoe in front of her.

The more she got to know Morgan MacKeage, the more she couldn't figure him out. He was simply strange. She didn't care what lame excuse he'd come up with, carrying a sword everywhere he went was a damned odd thing to do.

And this married thing. What kind of medieval notion was that, that two consenting adults making love constituted a lifelong commitment?

But more important—and the thing that scared her the most—was that she had so easily agreed to go along with his outrageous plan.

Was she in love?

No. But she was in lust. And for that reason alone, she had decided to spend the week pretending they were married, if that was the only way she'd get to have an affair with Morgan.

Which brought her right back to where she'd been last night before the storm had arrived, back to trying to figure out how to make love and still keep her shirt on.

☆ ☆ ☆

And Morgan was trying to figure out how to get Mercedes to talk. Her silence worried him. He'd bungled things last night, claiming her the way he had. And this morning he'd managed to dig the hole he was standing in deep enough that he might never be able to crawl free. Mercedes Quill was not a woman who liked being told what to do or how to do it—even when it was for her own good.

She was determined to build her park.

And he was determined to stop her to protect his gorge.

That damned wolf was not helping his cause. Faol had brought Sadie a tool of some sort and was now leading them to the place where he had found it.

And that place was near the mystical stream that ran through his gorge.

Morgan looked to the east, to Fraser Mountain, trying to decide if the tall trees were visible from this vantage point. He decided they were, but only because he knew to look for them. The gorge itself was deep, and because of that the tall trees appeared nearly level with the neighboring forest.

The mist, however, rose like the smoke of a smoldering fire before it slowly dispersed on the northwest breeze. But it was autumn, it was cold this morning, and mist was also rising from the river they were on.

Morgan absently trailed his oar in the water to guide the boat around a bend in the river. And that was when he found himself bow-to-nose with an equally startled bull moose.

Now, in his experience, moose of either sex did

not care for surprises. And this hulking bull was no exception. The great beast reared upward, churning the water with his front hooves, and charged toward him.

Cursing the lumbering weight of his loaded canoe, Morgan dug his oar deeply into the river and tried to power his way against the current, out of the path of the charging bull. The hit, when it came, struck with enough force to send the boat backward, splintering wood and knocking the oar out of his hand. Morgan grabbed the gunnels for balance and rode the storm of choppy water.

The bull reared again and charged a second time. Morgan dove for his sword, rolling in the bottom of the boat as he scrambled to unsheathe it. Mercedes' cry of alarm came to him over the sound of more splintering wood and the snorting of the enraged moose.

He was getting a little enraged himself.

A large antler appeared over him, just as two large hooves smashed down on the gunnel. The damned moose was trying to climb into the boat and kill him.

Morgan lifted his sword, grabbed the antler, and pushed it away. He drove his weapon deep into its neck. The bull jerked violently and bellowed in anger. His wife's shout ended abruptly and turned to a blood-curdling scream.

The bull kicked out, slashing a razor-sharp hoof into his thigh. Morgan twisted his sword, driving it deeper, feeling it slip past the shoulder blade until it found the animal's heart.

Now in its death throes, the shuddering, heavy

moose slowly slipped into the water, its only triumph that of finishing the destruction of his canoe. The boat snapped in half and rolled over, pulling Morgan and all his gear into the river.

Still holding the hilt of his sword, Morgan kicked his feet and pushed at the now dead moose, guiding them both toward the river bank. His feet touched bottom, and he turned, dragging the moose by the antlers. Once the animal scraped gravel, he let it go, pulled his sword from its body, and threw himself onto dry ground.

He lay on his back with his eyes closed, exhausted, breathing heavily, his muscles still quivering with battle-tense energy, reciting a list of curses that might have God striking him dead. He suddenly felt the coolness of a shadow fall over his face. Still he kept his eyes closed, loath to look up, not wishing to see the accusing glare of his obviously tender-hearted wife.

A warm tongue suddenly licked the side of his face, lapping the river water dripping from his hair. Morgan snapped his eyes open and sat up, shoving Faol away with another curse, this one out loud. The wolf backed off and went instead to inspect the kill.

Morgan looked around for Mercedes. She had beached her boat and was standing beside it, staring at him with eyes wide and her face completely drained of color.

Morgan closed his own eyes and cursed again out loud. His woman had just witnessed a violence that she didn't understand and might never be able to forgive.

"I cannot show mercy to anything bent on destroying me," he said across the twenty paces separating them.

She continued to stare in silence.

Morgan wanted to howl.

But it was Faol who lifted his nose into the air and let out a primeval cry that echoed up the sides of the valley.

Morgan looked back at Mercedes, only to find her suddenly standing just two feet away. Her dark blue eyes still huge and unblinking, her face drawn and pale, she continued to stare in silence. He followed the direction of her gaze to the bloody sword he still held in his right hand.

He opened his fingers and let it drop to the ground as he looked up at her. She took a step back. He rolled and stood up, and Mercedes quickly took another step back.

He wiped the blood from his hands on his wet pants as he moved toward her, matching her every retreating step with one of his own. He reached out and took her shoulders, ignoring her flinch, and held her firmly.

"Say what you're thinking, Mercedes," he instructed. "Give voice to your thoughts, so I can respond."

He watched her swallow and saw her eyes move to the carcass of the moose. He shook her, making her look back at him.

"When God gave man intelligence and free will," he told her, "he was giving us the means to survive in this world. Killing an animal for food or in self-defense is an act of nature, Mercedes, not malice."

Unable to look at her stricken expression any longer, Morgan pulled her into his embrace and hugged her fiercely. “That bull acted according to his own law, lass, set down by the blood of his ancestors,” he continued more gently. “That the two of us clashed today was nothing more than the journey of life playing itself out.”

He squeezed her tightly when he felt her begin to tremble. “Say something, Mercedes,” he entreated once again. “Give me either your anger or your hurt.”

“Will you be just as ruthless when you protect this valley from me?” she asked into his shoulder, her voice void of emotion.

Morgan closed his eyes on the realization that this woman knew him more than he cared for her to, that she now understood he would never compromise when it came to protecting his home.

He tugged on her hair, forcing her to look at him. “When the time comes, wife, I will do what I must to keep this valley safe. And also to keep you safe,” he quickly added when she tried to pull away. “Because you and this land are all that is important to me now. Without either, I am nothing.”

“Who are you, Morgan MacKeage?”

“Your husband.”

She tried to pull away again, but he held her firm. “I'm also your greatest ally, Mercedes. Give me your trust now, and we will find a way through this.”

Well, it seemed she needed to think about that for at least a minute. And in that time Morgan saw emotions flash in her eyes that ranged from hope to suspicion—before anger finally won the battle.

"Dam—"

He kissed her before she got the curse out, canting her head and covering her lips with his, swallowing her words as he swept his tongue inside. She made a mewling noise, and he couldn't decide if she was welcoming him or protesting. Nor did he care, as he found himself spiraling downward, deeper into the magic of her spell.

She tasted sweet, fresh, and so wonderfully alive. She felt vibrant in his arms, strong enough to possess his heart, solid enough to anchor his wandering soul.

He had traveled eight hundred years to find her, and he would let nothing come between them.

His spirit soared when she suddenly melted against him, raised her arms, and tugged on his hair to deepen their kiss.

Morgan flinched as pain suddenly shot through his body.

They pulled away at the same time, Mercedes with a gasp of surprise, Morgan with a groan. He shot a hand to his leg, covering the gaping hole in his jeans.

"You're hurt," she said, pulling his hand out of the way. She gasped again. "You're bleeding."

In a frenzy of movement, Morgan suddenly found himself sitting on the ground, Mercedes unfastening his pants at the waist. Unable to keep from smiling, he leaned back on his elbows and let his now distraught wife tend to his wound. He lifted himself up enough that she could pull his wet pants down to his boots, where she suddenly stopped and frowned. She grabbed his hand, making him fall completely flat, and slapped it over his bleeding thigh.

"Keep pressure on it," she hissed, now beginning to work on the laces of his boots.

It took her a few minutes to strip his legs bare, and then she carefully lifted his fingers and examined his wound. She looked up at him then, her eyes dark with concern against her pale complexion.

"It . . . it needs stitches," she whispered, as if the news might undo him.

He wanted to laugh but didn't dare. Mercedes was the one beginning to panic. Her hand covering his was shaking, her quivering jaw was making her teeth chatter, and her eyes were glistening again with unshed tears.

"Do you have a needle and thread, then?" he asked, stilling her jaw by clasping it with his hand, into which she slowly nodded.

He nodded back and gave her a reassuring smile. "I promise not to howl like the wolf, lass, when you sew me up. Now, do you think you can find my pack before you go looking for your thread? There's a nice bottle of Scotch in it that just might make the job a bit easier."

"I have painkillers in my first aid kit," she said. "But you can't mix them with alcohol."

Morgan lifted a brow. "The Scotch is for you, wife. I prefer your hands steady when you take a needle to my flesh."

He gave a grunt of surprise when she suddenly pushed herself to her feet, and another grunt—this time of approval—when she balled her fists on her hips and glared down at him.

"It's not funny, Morgan. Stitching a wound like that

is nothing to joke about. You belong in a hospital."

He scanned the river bank they were on and let his gaze stop on their one remaining boat before he looked back at her. "Any suggestions on how we get to this hospital?" he asked.

"My cell phone," she said, suddenly brightening. "I can call my mother to come get us."

She ran to her kayak and rummaged around in the front hatch. She straightened with her cell phone in her hand, but her smile suddenly disappeared.

"It doesn't matter, Mercedes," he quickly assured her. "I'm not needing a hospital. Sew me up and bandage my thigh, and I'll be good as new in a few days."

She still refused to look at him. She bent over and rummaged around in the hatch again. She straightened, a small red bag in her hand, and finally returned to him.

And, like the idiot he was, Morgan just couldn't seem to keep himself from asking, "What's wrong with the phone?"

"The battery is dead."

Morgan started undoing the buttons of his soggy shirt. He stripped himself bare, except for his wet and now muddy boxers, keeping them on only because he didn't want his wife distracted when she sewed him up.

She handed him two small pills. She looked up and down his now nearly naked body, then suddenly reached into her bag, took out one more pill, and placed it in his hand with the others.

"These are for pain?" he asked, examining them.

"They will dull it."

"And my head? Will they dull my thinking, too?"

"If I'm lucky."

He handed them back to her. "Keep them, then. I can't afford to be slow-witted right now."

She tried to give them back. "You need these. I can't sew you up without them." She lifted one perfectly arched brow. "Afraid I'll take advantage of you?"

He tapped the end of her insolent nose. "Nay, lass. That worry never crossed my mind." He looked upriver and then back at her, suddenly serious. "We're not alone in this valley, Mercedes. The Dolan brothers are here, looking for the gold. And I have no wish to be drugged should they suddenly appear."

"They're harmless," she said, waving his concern away. "They've been searching for Plum's gold as long as I have. It's a hobby for them. Almost a game."

"They're also armed with powerful rifles," he countered. "And last I knew, gold was not a dangerous prey to hunt."

"How do you know they've got guns?"

"I've seen them."

"You've met Harry and Dwayne?"

"In a way," he said, nodding. "I met them, but they didn't meet me."

"You spied on them?"

"I thought they might be poachers," he said. "That day I asked you to stay out of the woods, I was trying to learn their purpose here."

"Did it ever occur to you just to ask?"

Morgan gave her a broad grin. "What fun is there in that?" He reached up and ran his finger down the side of her cheek. "Why don't you go find my gear before it floats any farther downriver?" he told her. "I really could use a drink of that Scotch."

She hesitated, looking torn between getting him a drink and wanting to stab the needle she was holding into his thigh.

"I'll be fine, Mercedes. I'll keep pressure on it until you return."

She finally stood up, started for her kayak, but stopped and looked back. "I'm sorry you got hurt, Morgan. I thought the moose would just bump your boat and run off."

"I know, lass. I expected that, too. And don't worry about my hurt, Mercedes. I've had worse. I'll be fine in a few days."

Her expression suddenly brightened, and her eyes sparkled. "You stay put," she said, pointing a threatening finger at him. "Or I'll come up with some consequences of my own."

He solemnly nodded, then waved her on her way, watching her climb into her odd little boat and expertly guide it into the current.

He leaned back on his elbows again, letting the weak autumn sun warm up his skin as he watched Mercedes slowly disappear past the bend in the river. He couldn't quit grinning. He liked that she wasn't afraid to throw his words back at him. He liked her sassiness and her determination to match both wit and will against him.

But mostly he liked her ass. Mercedes had the nicest, firmest, most delectable bum—and the longest legs he'd ever seen on a woman. Aye, she pleased him in all ways, with her body as well as her spirit.

They'd make great babies together. She'd give him strong sons who would grow to love and cherish this land as much as their parents did. He was glad now that the old priest had talked him into building a home here. He was also glad that Grey had had the foresight to banish Daar's cane into the pond.

Because, like his brother, Morgan was now decided that he never wanted to leave this suddenly interesting new world.

When Mercedes finally disappeared around the river bend, Morgan set the needle and thread to his flesh and quickly repaired his wound—before his wife could return and make a mess of the job.

Chapter Fifteen

You need to stay off your leg."

"No. I need to keep it from stiffening up."

"Faol is eating your moose again."

Morgan muttered a few Gaelic words as he threw a rock at Faol to drive him away from the moose carcass still lying on the river bank. Faol gave a snarl of protest, then trotted off into the brush.

"We need to find a game warden and report the kill," Mercedes said from the campfire, drawing his attention. "And you need to put some clothes on. The sun's setting."

Morgan stopped tugging on the antler of the now gutted moose and scratched his bare chest as he looked at his clothes drying by the fire. He had pants on, but they were covered with moose blood. He had already carried the entrails far enough away that they wouldn't be bothered by scavenging animals, and he was ready to wash up. The problem was, all his clean clothes were still wet from their dunk in the river.

He looked at Mercedes' dry packs sitting by the tiny tent she had already erected so that it would be dry by nightfall. He needed to get himself some of those bags, since he'd likely be spending time camping with his wife and children in the future.

Mercedes seemed so at home here in the wilderness, so comfortable sitting on logs, cooking over an open fire, and sleeping on the ground. She guided her boat as if she had been born with a paddle in her hand and hiked these woods with the confidence and excitement of a wanderer determined to embrace life.

Morgan realized how lucky he was to have found such an old soul in this modern time.

"Why do we need to find a game warden?" he asked, walking over and picking up one of his still damp shirts.

"Because it's illegal to kill a moose out of season. And even then you need a permit."

He slipped into his shirt and sat down across from her. "But I'll have it quartered and carried to Gu Bràth by tomorrow afternoon. No one need even know about it."

Her eyes narrowed. "That makes you a poacher."

He didn't care for that title any more than he cared to hear it coming from his wife's mouth. "I am not. The animal is dead through no fault of my own. I didn't go hunting for it. But that doesn't mean I intend to let the meat go to waste."

"The warden will probably let you keep the moose,

once we explain what happened. He won't want to see it go to waste, either. What's Gu Bràth?"

"It's my brother's home," he told her.

"I thought it was called TarStone Mountain Resort?"

"That's the business name. Our home is called Gu Bràth."

"Is it Scottish? What does it mean?"

"Forever," he told her. "It means that we're here now, forever."

"But you don't live with your brother anymore?"

"No. I built my home on Fraser Mountain just this summer."

She scooted closer, suddenly interested. "Does your new home have a name?"

Morgan leaned back against a rock, crossed his arms over his chest, and grinned at her. "I thought I'd leave that chore up to my wife."

She frowned and scooted away, giving her attention back to the food she was preparing. She stirred the powdered soup she had dumped out of a foil pack and added more water.

Morgan stood and picked up his sword and a few clean clothes, then took the water bottle from her. "I'm going to find a place to wash up and refill our drinking water," he said. "Before it gets too dark."

"You need to stay off that leg."

He took hold of her chin and lifted her face up. "What I need is for you to spread our sleeping bag at the base of that ledge over there and stuff a thick bed of dry grass under it."

He watched her eyes suddenly widen. "What . . . what's wrong with the tent?" she whispered.

"I don't like tents," he said succinctly. "They keep me from seeing into the woods."

"They keep you dry when it rains."

He bent down and gave her a quick kiss on her arguing mouth. "Nature provides our shelter. That ledge will keep us dry tonight. Now, are you gripping my leg because you don't want me to go or because you're looking to leave another mark on me?"

She swatted his knee and pulled her chin free, glaring up at him. "I want you to tell me why you're always so guarded. You act as if the entire world is out to get you."

Morgan settled his sword over his back as he looked down at her. "I didn't come all this way to die at the hands of fools." He bent at the knees so he was level with her and took hold of her chin again. "And you must be on guard as well, Mercedes. There is a storm brewing in this valley, and it has nothing to do with the weather. There is danger here."

She tried to pull away again, but Morgan wouldn't let go. "I'm not jesting, Mercedes. The Dolan brothers are not to be trusted. You need to be just as guarded as I am."

"You expect me to trust you without question, don't you?"

He grinned and spread his fingers to encompass her entire face. "I expect obedience, *gràineag,* when it comes to your safety."

She suddenly leaned forward, grabbing his shoulders and pushing him off balance. They both ended up on the ground, Mercedes stretched full-length on top of him. She kissed him, her tongue slipping inside his mouth as she sensually wiggled her sexy body against his.

Morgan immediately placed both of his hands on her luscious bum, pulling into his erection with a groan of frustration. He wanted her again.

But not like this, with nothing but dirt for a bed.

Going against every urge he possessed, Morgan took hold of her shoulders and lifted her away. His teeth clenched in restraint and his gaze locked on her swollen lips, he set her on the ground beside him.

"Tonight, wife, we will finish what we began last night."

She blinked at him, then scrambled away. With another curse, Morgan stood up and walked into the forest without looking back.

And Sadie couldn't decide if she had just been rejected or threatened. Or if she should be insulted or scared.

And she couldn't decide if Morgan kept calling her wife to rile her or if he thought she needed to be constantly reminded of that disconcerting fact.

She would like to be his wife. Maybe. She could imagine what it would be like waking up beside Morgan every morning for the rest of her life, her in her nightgown buttoned up to her neck, him buck naked and beautiful.

Sadie snorted, went back to the fire, and stirred the soup. She was weaving a dream fantasy for herself. But she hadn't felt this alive, this excited about what the future might hold, since before the house fire.

And that was the one thing keeping her from realizing her dream. That stupid fire. She had killed two people she loved. Her carelessness, her inattention to detail, had resulted in a tragedy so horrific she could never be forgiven. Her scars were nothing compared with their deaths. She deserved every horrible one of them.

What she didn't deserve was a husband as beautiful as Morgan MacKeage. But that didn't mean she couldn't at least love him, couldn't be married to him if he continued to insist on it.

It didn't mean he couldn't eventually love her back.

Sadie caught a glimpse of movement out of the corner of her eye and turned to see a canoe come into sight, two men paddling it toward the shore where her kayak was beached. She stood up, scanned the woods for signs of Morgan, then slowly walked over to greet Harry and Dwayne.

Morgan began to limp the moment he was out of Sadie's sight. He rubbed his throbbing thigh and cursed his bad luck for getting hurt.

But then, better him than Mercedes. His chest tightened at that thought. She could have been in the lead boat, battling the moose, and him not able to reach her in time.

Or she could have been out here all alone, as she had been this past summer. Anything could have happened to her. She could have fallen during one of her ribbon-planting hikes, have drowned running some of the more violent rapids on the river, or simply have taken a fever with no one to tend her.

He knew from experience that Mercedes was reckless. She didn't always think before she acted. Hell, what if it had been some other guy she'd taken pictures of, instead of him? What dangers might she have faced?

The woman needed a keeper.

Morgan stopped at a stream that ran into the river and looked down into the crystal-clear water that slowly disappeared into the slightly brackish Prospect River. He turned and started upstream, lifting his gaze to the mountains ahead.

He knew where he was, and he didn't like it. This was the same stream that flowed from the cliff, through his gorge, then eventually into this valley. And he and Mercedes were camped not half a mile away.

He didn't want her to see this stream. Didn't want her to realize that it was special. Once he had her allegiance, then he could show her the waterfall.

Faol silently stepped into his path, planting his feet and curling his lips into an almost human smile.

"You scavenging dog. You leave that moose alone, or I'll have your hide tacked on the wall beside it."

Faol dropped his head, stepped into the stream, and began to lap the water, not the least bit bothered by the threat. Morgan remembered he was supposed to be looking for drinking water himself. He moved above Faol and knelt on the bank, submerging the bottle and letting it fill. He capped it, set it on the grass, then leaned down to take his own drink.

A sharp, crackling sensation shot through his body the moment his lips touched the water. Morgan grabbed the burl dangling from his neck into the stream that was now vibrating with the force of a thousand bees taking flight. He straightened abruptly as heat seared through his body and sparks of green light danced in his eyes.

The wolf gave a yelp of alarm and shot past Morgan, knocking him backward onto the river bank. The tingling lessened, and the burl settled into a soft hum.

Morgan lifted it from his chest to see it better. The cherrywood was swirling, pulling against his hand in the direction of the stream.

Well, hell. The magic was seeking its own. It felt the lure of Daar's old staff coursing through the water. Morgan lifted the burl over his head, gripped it in his fist, and touched his hand to the water again.

Needles of energy shot up his arm, through his chest, spreading to every inch of his body. The wound on his thigh throbbed as heat gathered around it like the touch of a hot poker.

He pulled his hand back, and it stopped.

He opened his fist and stared at the swirling, vibrating burl that glowed with intense light. What had the *drùidh* said? That this burl carried the magic and that Morgan must find a way to add to its strength?

Well, it seemed he just had.

Not that he understood it. He'd gotten the burl wet many times since receiving it, but this was the first time it had touched this particular water. And that was the secret. This magical stream that the towering trees drank from, that grew big fish, and that now sent energy coursing through his body.

Morgan slipped the burl back over his head and stood up. He unbuttoned his shirt and threw it on the ground, then stripped off his boots and pants and tossed them beside the shirt. He ripped the bandage off his thigh and examined his wound.

The skin around it was pulsing, pulling against the stitches he'd set. The jagged edges of flesh were tingling, swelling, throbbing together as if trying to become one again. The knots of thread suddenly snapped, sending pain shooting all the way to his teeth.

Morgan waded into the stream up to his waist, then sat down until all but his shoulders were submerged. The burl dangled in the water. Sparks shot from it in every direction, scattering bubbles of light around him. He closed his eyes and let the energy course through him, leaning back until only his face remained exposed to the air.

Color swirled through his mind. Warmth wrapped his skin in a blanket of heat so intense that breathing was difficult. The humming grew louder. The water boiled, bubbles exploding around him like sparks from a bonfire.

Morgan sank below the surface, twisting and kicking his feet in an attempt to outswim the chaos. He felt as if he had the strength of a legion of men, as if he possessed the power to bend the laws of nature.

And the ability to heal himself.

He twisted again and sat up, brushing the hair from his face and letting the water cascade down his back. He grabbed the burl into his fist and pictured his wound in his mind's eye, sending the heat there, willing his flesh to seal itself up. He flexed his left knee, pulling against the skin on his thigh.

And he suddenly felt no pain.

Nothing but the warmth of pliant flesh.

Morgan opened his eyes and looked around. The sparks had disappeared. The water was calm again, gently making its way down to the river. His body was cool, his breathing even, his muscles relaxed.

And he felt wonderfully alive.

He opened his fist and looked down at the burl. It, too, was calm, softly humming in his hand. But it felt different to his touch now. Smoother. Smaller.

Dammit. It was smaller. He'd used up some of the magic.

Morgan stood up, let the burl fall back against his chest, and waded over to the bank. He threw himself onto the ground and lay face-up, staring at clouds colored red by the lowering sun. He stayed there motionless for several minutes, trying to come to terms with what had just happened.

He sat up suddenly and looked down at his thigh. There was no wound, no stitches, not even a scar. He rubbed the balls of his fingers over the smooth, hair-covered flesh.

Well, hell. How would he explain this to Mercedes?

Faol came slinking out of the brush much more silently than he had left and nudged Morgan in the back. The wolf let out an agitated whine and trotted several paces down the stream bank.

The animal stopped, turned back to him, and growled, his head lowered and his hackles raised in an aggressive posture. He lifted his nose in the air, sniffed, and took several more steps toward the river before he stopped and let out a bark.

Morgan grabbed his clean clothes and quickly dressed. He snatched up the water bottle and his sword and trotted after the wolf. Keeping in the shadows of the tall brush that lined the stream, he stayed alert to whatever was making Faol travel with the stealth of a hunter.

They both worked their way back upriver to where he'd left Mercedes, and Morgan heard the voices as he neared camp. He hunkered behind the protection of an outcropping of ledge, behind a dense bush, and watched as his disobedient wife strolled to the river and warmly greeted the very men he had told her to avoid.

"Why, if it ain't Sadie Quill," Harry said, waving his paddle at her. "Haven't seen you in a year of Sundays. I thought you'd gone off to the big city to be a weather girl."

Sadie grabbed the bow of their canoe to keep it from hitting a rock, then stepped back when Harry stepped out. Together they pulled the heavily packed boat halfway up onto the beach, pulling a grinning Dwayne with it.

"Hi, Sadie," Dwayne said, nodding and smiling and shaking a finger at her. "You trying to beat us to Plum's gold?"

"And I'm winning, too," she shot back. "I'm a full day ahead of you two lazy prospectors."

Dwayne giggled and scrunched his shoulders. "Not this time, missy," he said with another giggle, his eyes nearly disappearing into his grin. "We got something better than a map this time."

"Dwayne," Harry snapped. "Get out of the boat before you roll it."

Dwayne scrambled up the length of the boat until he found himself unable to get past their gear. He solved his problem by simply stepping into the water and wading ashore. Sadie moved back, worried he might shake himself dry like a dog, and smiled when she saw his gaze drift down the shore and his eyes suddenly widen in surprise.

"You got a dead moose!" Dwayne said, pointing at the moose. He started running toward it. "You killed a moose, Sadie!" he yelped as he ran, stopping at it so suddenly he almost fell. He looked back at her and pointed his finger again, this time waggling it like a mother lecturing a naughty child. "You ain't supposed to kill these, missy. It's illegal."

Sadie ambled after Harry, who had followed his brother to view the moose. "I didn't kill it," she told Dwayne. "My husband did." Now what on earth had made her say that? "The moose attacked his boat, and he was defending himself."

"You got a husband?" Harry asked, first looking at her in surprise, then scanning the campsite for signs of the man. He looked at her again, his eyes narrowed. "You bring back one of them city fellows from Boston?"

Sadie slowly shook her head, still reeling from the thought that she had just told these men that she had a husband. "No. He's a local. Morgan MacKeage."

"We heard of them MacKeages," Harry said, his eyes still narrowed. "They own the ski resort."

"They're an odd bunch," Dwayne piped in, though

he appeared more interested in the moose than in the conversation. He suddenly stopped handling an antler and looked at her, his grin still in place. "What made you go and get hooked up with one of them, Sadie?" he asked. "I heard they're a big, mean-looking group of fellows that keep to themselves."

"They are big," Sadie agreed, unable to keep herself from grinning back. Dwayne's unflappable cheeriness was always contagious. "That's probably why I married Morgan. He's taller than me."

Dwayne's gaze scanned her from head to toe. He suddenly straightened to his nearly six-foot height, puffed out his chest, and shot her another crooked-tooth grin. "Well, hell's bells, Sadie. If I'd known you was looking for a husband, I would have offered to marry you. I don't even care about your scarred hand or nothing. I think you're right pretty just as you are."

God save her, Sadie could feel her heart melting at his sincere offer. "Thank you, Dwayne," she replied, nodding with gratitude. "But Morgan beat you to it. You're going to have to let a girl know sooner that you find her pretty."

Dwayne bobbed his head, his face flushed red as he nervously darted a look around the perimeter of her camp. "I hope your husband didn't hear that," he whispered. "I don't want him thinking I was poaching on his property."

Sadie waved Dwayne's worry away, then tucked her arm through his and led him toward the campfire. "He won't take offense," she assured him as they walked. She guided him to a rock and sat him down, then motioned for Harry to take a seat on the log. "Now, how about a trade, gentlemen?" she said.

"What you needing, Sadie?" Dwayne asked. "You running low on supplies?"

"No," she told him, shaking her head while she quickly scanned the woods herself, looking for Morgan. She hoped he had walked a fair distance to find a spring and that he wouldn't suddenly come barging in waving his sword like a heathen. All she needed was another twenty minutes, and then she could send Dwayne and Harry safely on their way.

"I was thinking of trading you two some supper for a peek at what you've got that's even better than a map," she said, hunching down and stirring the soup, sending the delicious smell toward them.

Both sets of eyes staring at her narrowed, and the smile finally disappeared from Dwayne's face. He waggled his finger at her again. "We ain't telling you spit, missy."

"Why you still looking for the gold, anyway?" Harry asked. "You don't need it none. Them MacKeage fellows are rich."

"They are?" she asked, lifting one brow.

Both men nodded. "They own most of the land in these parts, all the way up to Canada," Harry continued, waving toward the west side of the valley. "And they got that fancy resort."

"I'm still after the gold," Sadie told them, "because it never was for me. You know that. Dad was hunting for it only to prove the legend. He intended to donate the gold to a good cause." Sadie lifted her other brow. "What are your plans for it?"

Dwayne was suddenly smiling again, rubbing his hands together. "We're going to buy ourselves some wives," he said, nodding to show he was serious.

"Some what?" Sadie asked with a gasp. Of all the things she'd been expecting—like a new truck or maybe fixing up their house—wives were the last things she thought these two old bachelor brothers would want.

"Wives," Harry echoed, frowning at her shocked expression. He resettled himself on his log and gave her a defensive glare. "We found this catalog where you can buy women. They even sell trips to Russia, so you can meet them."

"We get our pick," Dwayne added, leaning forward, excitement lowering his voice to a whisper. "They throw this fancy party, and all the women come, and we get to meet them and then choose."

"But you gotta marry them," Harry explained, also lowering his voice in reverence. "They ain't whores or nothing. They're respectable women."

"They're down on their luck, is all," Dwayne added. "And so they're wanting to marry rich men and move to America."

"And once we find that gold," Harry said, straightening his back, puffing his chest, and running his thumbs under his suspenders, "we'll be rich Americans. We'll have enough money to go to Russia, buy our wives, and bring them here to look after us in our golden years."

"And we'll get to diddle without having to pay for it," Dwayne interjected, only to slap a hand over his mouth suddenly and turn beet red, realizing what he'd just said to her.

Sadie snapped her own mouth shut, realizing she was gaping like the village idiot. She felt heat rush into her cheeks. These two old goats were buying wives? From Russia?

"All this time . . . you've been hunting for . . . ? You think to actually *buy* wives?" she finished with a squeak.

She snapped her mouth shut again, took a deep breath, and fought to hold her composure.

"We'll make good husbands," Harry said defensively. "We'll take right good care of them women."

Sadie held her hands up in supplication. "I don't doubt you will," she quickly agreed. She looked from Harry to Dwayne. "All these years you've been searching for Plum's gold," she started again. "This has been your reason the whole time?"

Both men nodded, but it was Dwayne who spoke. "We never could stomach our own cooking," he admitted. "And we get lonely sometimes, especially in winter."

"And that's why we ain't sharing our secret," Harry said, drawing her attention again. He shook his head. "We ain't getting any younger, and we need to find that gold this fall."

"Why now, after all these years?" she asked.

" 'Cause we want children," Harry explained impatiently, sounding as if she should have figured that out by herself. He puffed up his chest again. "A man wants to leave a bit of himself when his time comes to depart this earth."

Sadie had to cough to cover up the fact that she was choking. Children? Heck. Both brothers were nearing sixty years old.

"Ah, Sadie?" Dwayne said. "I don't suppose that if you find that gold first and are wanting to donate it to a good cause like your papa intended, you would think Harry and me are good causes?"

"You wouldn't have to donate all the gold to us," Harry said, warming to his brother's idea. He leaned forward and rubbed his hands together. And she'd swear that she could almost see the beginnings of an idea forming behind his puckered brow. "We could pool our information and hunt for the gold together. Then split it."

Dwayne was shaking his head, frowning at his brother. "We already tried that with her papa, remember?" he told Harry. He looked at Sadie. And damn if he didn't waggle his finger at her again. "No offense, missy, but since we're wanting to buy two wives, it's going to take all the gold. We gotta have some left for when we come home, so we can take good care of them."

Harry frowned back at his brother, not liking that his plan was so quickly shot down. He darted a look at Sadie, then suddenly stood up. "We gotta go now," he said, prodding his brother to get him moving. "We need to make camp before it gets dark."

"Why can't we just stay here?" Dwayne asked, once he was standing. "She's already got a fire going."

Harry shook his head and nudged Dwayne toward their canoe. "She's got a husband," he reminded his brother. "She might want some privacy."

Dwayne, suddenly grinning again, turned a dull shade of red. "Oh," he whispered to Harry, not intending for her to hear. "You mean they might want to diddle."

This time Harry's nudge was not so gentle. He gave his brother a mighty shove into the river. Dwayne caught his balance by grabbing the canoe, then continued to wade out and climb into the stern. Harry grabbed the bow and shoved the boat toward deep water, then quickly climbed in and picked up his oar.

Dwayne waved his paddle into the air. " 'Bye, Sadie," he said. "We'll let you know where Plum's claim is after we take out all the gold," he said as they turned into the current, letting it carry them away. He twisted in his seat, still waving his paddle, still grinning. "We might even give you a nugget, just so you won't be skunked."

They began to slip toward the bend in the river, but still Dwayne kept waving and talking. "Say hi to your husband for us!" he hollered. "And remember, missy. If he don't treat you right, you come see me and Harry. We ain't afraid of them MacKeages."

Harry, apparently not liking his brother volunteering him for such dangerous service, slapped the water with his oar, soaking Dwayne. Dwayne sputtered something under his breath while wiping the river off himself.

The last Sadie saw of them, both men were paddling furiously, Harry determined to outrun his brother and Dwayne determined to catch him, apparently forgetting they were both sitting at opposite ends of the same boat.

Chapter Sixteen

Staring at the spot where Dwayne and Harry had disappeared, Sadie fought the bubble of laughter that was threatening to burst from her belly.

Buying wives. For all these years those two old goats had been hunting for gold because they were sure they had found a way to make the long winters less lonely.

Shaking her head in disbelief, Sadie walked back to her camp, continued past the fire, and stopped just in front of a giant boulder. She crossed her arms under her chest and smiled at the tall clump of brush beside it.

"Now do you understand why they're harmless?" she asked the dense honeysuckle.

Morgan emerged from behind the honeysuckle to stand in front of her. And he didn't appear anywhere near as amused as she was.

"Do you suppose a man can *sell* a wife in this catalog they spoke of?" he asked, his eyes gleaming in the last light of the setting sun. He suddenly sighed and rubbed the back of his neck. "Not that I could get very much for you," he added tiredly. "A disobedient wife can't be worth a hundred dollars."

"They're good men, Morgan," Sadie continued, deciding to ignore his not so subtle threat. "Between the two of them there isn't a mean bone in their bodies. Either of them would give the shirt off his back to someone in need."

"I will admit they do appear more a danger to themselves than to anyone else." He took hold of her shoulders. "But when it comes to gold, even the most timid of men turn lethal, Mercedes. They become blinded by the promise of riches. They act without thinking."

"Not Dwayne and Harry." Sadie shrugged free and walked to the campfire, pulled the now boiling soup off the grate, and set it on the ground to cool. She picked up her spoon and pointed it at Morgan.

"They're my friends," she told him, accentuating her words by poking the air with the utensil. "And you will trust my judgment," she added. "Marriage is supposed to be a partnership, Morgan. Tell me, do you think I'm stupid?"

"What?"

"Do you think I'm stupid?" she repeated. "That I'm a simple-minded woman who needs a man to look after her?"

His eyes narrowed at her question, and his jaw flexed while he thought about his answer. Sadie almost laughed out loud. The poor guy looked like one of those men who'd just been asked by his wife if her pants made her ass look fat. He understood that any answer he gave would be the wrong one.

Sadie stopped pointing her spoon and used it instead to stir the soup, hurrying the cooling process along. Their overcooked dinner was starting to look like mush.

"I don't think you're stupid," he finally said, his voice guarded. "I just think you're too trusting."

Sadie slumped her shoulders. Wrong answer. "Too trusting," she repeated. "As in the way I'm trusting you?"

She watched Morgan take a deep breath and let it out with a harsh sigh. He rubbed his hands over his face before he looked at her again. He slowly shook his head.

"What is it you're wanting from me, Mercedes?"

"I want you to respect my judgment when it comes to Dwayne and Harry. Until either of them does something that proves different, I want you to treat them kindly. And," she said, pointing her spoon again when he started to speak, "I want you to trust me."

He snapped his mouth shut and started thinking again. Sadie took a careful sip of the soup and nearly gagged. She turned the pot upside-down and dumped their ruined dinner onto the ground, then rummaged around in her dry pack, pulled out two granola bars, and tossed one to Morgan.

He caught it, examined the bar with a critical glare, then turned that glare on her. Sadie lifted her shoulders.

"Hey. You probably wouldn't get fifty dollars for me. You beginning to rethink this marriage thing?"

"I'm beginning to think it's time to go to bed," he

said, standing up and tossing the granola bar on top of her dry pack. He walked toward the sleeping bag she'd laid out by the ledge, pulling his sword off his back as he went. Sadie quickly scrambled to her feet.

"There's one more thing I want, Morgan."

"And what would that be?" he asked, turning his head to look at her, lifting one arrogant brow.

Well, damn. She didn't know how it had happened, but she was pretending to be this man's wife for the next seven days, and she assumed that included sleeping with him. Not that she minded. Truth told, she kind of liked the idea. But they needed to get a few things straight first.

"A-about our sleeping together," she started, nervously wiping her hands on her thighs. "I want to . . . but . . ."

He turned fully to face her, and Sadie nearly lost her nerve. But she squared her shoulders and lifted her chin. By God, this gorgeous, hulking, perfect example of man was not going to intimidate her.

"I want to set some ground rules," she finally told him. "I keep my shirt on, and my back is off limits."

Instead of an argument, Morgan simply shrugged his shoulders and nodded in agreement before turning back to their bed. He set his sword down beside it and began taking off his clothes. Sadie tossed her own granola bar onto her dry pack and walked into the darkness toward the river.

She took her time washing up before she rolled her bra, body sock, panties, and glove into her jeans. Then, wearing only her flannel shirt, she headed back to camp—and her waiting husband.

☆ ☆ ☆

Morgan gritted his teeth as his wife crawled under the covers beside him and stifled a groan as her long naked legs slid against his. Sweat broke out on his forehead. Blood rushed to his groin. And with only the barest bit of control, he kept his hands to himself.

"What is your necklace made of?" she asked, her hand going to the burl at his neck. "Is it covered with some sort of glow-in-the-dark paint? It seems to always be shining."

He wanted to jump her beautiful bones, and the woman wanted to talk. Morgan took a calming breath. Maybe talking was not such a bad thing. She obviously needed some time to get used to sharing a bed with him, and he could use the distraction to get his urges under control.

"It's made of cherrywood," he told her, lifting it from her hand and holding it up between them. "And I don't know why it swirls like that. It must be a play of the light," he said, ignoring the fact that the light had left with the sun.

"Why do you wear it?"

"It's a gift from an old friend."

"It looks just like the cane Daar was carrying," Sadie mused, frowning at the burl. "It was cherrywood and had knots in it just like this one."

"It is from Daar," Morgan admitted. "That crazy old man said it was a good luck charm. I think he's touched in the head."

"Yet you wear his gift."

"He's old. I have no wish to hurt his feelings."

She patted his chest, apparently pleased by his

answer, then left her hand there, her fingers lightly caressing his left breast. Morgan closed his eyes and prayed for patience.

Then snapped them open the moment her lips touched his.

The cagey little vixen had managed to capture his hands and was holding on to them with the desperation of a woman determined to have her way. She pushed his arms over his head, kissing him senseless as she wiggled to maneuver her body on top of his.

As she had promised, she was wearing only her shirt and was completely naked from the waist down. Every inch of her exposed skin touching his made the muscles in his body tighten in response. She weighed nothing, but still he was having a hard time catching his breath.

His manhood jutted into her belly, and Morgan was unable to keep from lifting against her. She squeezed her knees into his thighs and rubbed against him in slow, sensuous motions.

He groaned into her mouth and pulled his hands free in order to grasp her hips, hoping to slow her down.

She tore her mouth away from his, then placed her lips along his throat, and lower, where she lightly kissed back and forth over his chest.

He groaned again as Sadie straddled his lap. She was being so passionate, so honest about her desire for him, and he didn't want her pulling away with worry that he wouldn't keep to their bargain.

Dammit. He just wanted to make love to her.

"Slow down, Mercedes," he said between clenched teeth.

"But I want you. Now," she said, squirming against him. "I want to feel you inside me again," she added in a husky whisper, feathering her fingers over his shoulders.

He held back a groan when her hands moved down the insides of his arms, along his ribs, and stopped to stroke his hips.

Had he really expected his disobedient wife to listen? And why was he second-guessing his luck? He liked her aggression, her honest and unskilled passion. He especially liked that she seemed to have forgotten her shyness with him.

She moved restlessly above him and kissed him with open-mouthed abandon. Morgan simply gave up then, taking her with him as he rolled them over until he was on top. He nudged her thighs open and settled between them and captured her hair so that he could still her wandering lips just long enough to kiss them.

He rocked his hips in sensual circles, using his arousal to build her desire. She groaned into his mouth, dug her nails into his back, and wrapped both of her legs tightly around his waist.

He leaned up and stared down at her, barely able to see her expression in the pale moonlight. "Do you trust me, Mercedes?" he asked. "To the point that I can touch you anywhere but your back?"

"Yes," she whispered, nodding as she strained against him.

He rolled so that he lay beside her, cradling her against him. He started with her belly button, gently stroking and teasing with his fingertips, waiting for either her resistance or her acceptance. She lifted herself into his touch, making a sound of pleasure that sent a shiver coursing through his body. He splayed his hand wide, spanning over her belly from hip to hip, and moved lower, laying pressure with his palm on her most sensitive place.

She dug her fingers into his chest, raised her head to meet his lips, and kissed him.

Morgan moved his hand lower, cupping her, curling a finger inside her. He swallowed her gasp, captured her restless knee between his, and used his thumb to send waves of pleasure spiraling through her. He felt her tighten against his hand, felt her lift her hips in search of more.

He pulled away and reached under the edge of their sleeping bag, remembering her worry about getting pregnant. He was in no hurry to start a family, not until they both agreed to it.

He found the foil packet he had stashed there while she was washing up and quickly placed the protection between them. Then he rose up over her, spread her thighs with his knees, and slowly slid into her welcoming warmth.

He'd just found his guaranteed spot in heaven. She was so warm, so perfectly built, so well matched to him. He covered her face with kisses as he slowly moved back, then thrust forward, then back, creating a rhythm that had her tightening again.

Morgan lost what was left of his control. He thrust deeply into her, more forcefully, and withdrew only enough to do it again. He brought her with him this time to that blinding place of white energy he had found last night. Mercedes convulsed around him, shouted her pleasure, and sent him spiraling into the maelstrom with a rewardingly arrogant shout of his own.

He dropped his head to her shoulder, only to find himself touching the flannel of her shirt instead of soft skin. He lay unmoving, breathing heavily, savoring the feel of her lingering tremors.

Reluctant to move but knowing she needed to breathe, Morgan finally rolled onto his back, welcoming the cold night air rushing over his damp skin. She immediately followed, tucking herself up against him, wrapping one arm around his waist and settling the other one near his head so that she could run her fingers through his hair.

And he lay there. And he waited.

It was a good five minutes before she spoke.

"That was wonderful," she whispered, squeezing him.

He grunted in answer, rubbing his hand up and down her flannel-encased arm. Aye, it was wonderful but somehow not quite as fulfilling with cloth standing between them. And that was the reason for his sudden black mood. He wanted nothing between them. Not cloth, and especially not her scars.

She needed time. And patience. That is what it would take to cure her shyness.

"And because we're married, we can do this whenever we want?" she asked.

"Yes," he told her, wondering where her thoughts were headed.

"And as often as we want?"

He tilted his head just enough to see her expression

and almost burst into laughter, his dark mood suddenly gone. Mercedes looked quite pleased with the idea of making love to him as often as she wanted. He tapped the end of her nose, then tucked her firmly against him so that her head rested on his shoulder. He pulled the sleeping bag over her back and used it to swaddle her tightly.

"Not quite that often, wife. A woman is weak after making love. She needs at least until morning to gather her strength."

She fell silent again, and he couldn't decide if he should be glad or worried. She suddenly yawned, apparently accepting his ridiculous statement as truth, and snuggled against him like a contented, well-fed cat.

"Morgan?" she sleepily whispered into the silence.

"Aye?"

"When I find the gold, I'm giving some of it to Harry and Dwayne."

Chapter Seventeen

There were advantages to this marriage thing, one of which was having such a large, very warm body to snuggle against.

"Good morning, wife."

Yes, it was morning—the morning after, to be specific. What does a woman say to a man she was intimate with just a few hours ago?

Sadie decided to follow his example.

"Good morning, husband."

His grin broadened. "Have you regained your strength?" he asked, his voice husky, his eyes dark with obvious intent.

"It—it's daylight."

He nodded. "Aye. It is daylight."

"We can't . . . we shouldn't . . . no, Morgan, I'm still quite tired."

He stared at her for another overlong minute, then suddenly brushed back the covers and stood up, picking up his pants as he straightened. “Too bad,” he said as he slipped into them. “I was planning to take you to the site of an old logging camp I know of that’s not too far from here.”

He shrugged again and began to put on his shirt. “I thought it might be the one you’re looking for and that Faol was leading us to. But if you need more rest, then go back to sleep.”

Sadie shot upright and was standing before she remembered that she was naked from the waist down. Her cheeks—on her face and her backside—threatened to blister with embarrassment. Sadie jerked down her shirttails to cover herself. This time their state of dress was reversed. Now she was the exhibitionist, and he was the one looking on with interest.

“Turn around.”

“No.”

Why wasn’t she surprised by his answer? “Don’t you have a moose to cut up or something?”

“The job would be easier with a good morning kiss.”

“No.”

Unlike her, he seemed sincerely surprised by her answer. “Why not?” he asked, crossing his arms over his chest and glaring at her.

“Because if you kiss me, one thing will lead to another, and I’ll be flat on my back in less time than it takes to sneeze.”

One corner of his mouth kicked up in a smile. He uncrossed his arms and tucked both hands behind his back. “I promise not to lay a finger on you, lass. Just my lips.”

"I'm not kissing you. Not until we are both fully dressed and I've had some breakfast to build up my strength again." She shot him a seductive smile to let him know that she hadn't been fooled by last night's claim that women were weak. "Although I'd bet my boat that you're needing the nourishment more than I am."

Apparently not caring to have his words thrown back at him, Morgan spun on his heel and headed downriver, disappearing into the brush.

Sadie breathed a sigh of relief. She brushed the hair off her face and smoothed down the front of her shirt. She suddenly smiled. Well, spit. She had just survived a second night of sleeping with Morgan MacKeage.

And she thought things had gone quite well. Heck, she was actually feeling proud of herself. She had managed to make love to the man without embarrassing them both, she hadn't bitten him again, and she had just won an important battle of wills. She was feeling quite wifely this morning and beginning to think this marriage just might work out after all. She could survive living with Morgan.

She could even get used to the idea that he was strange. So what if the man carried a sword everywhere? He obviously knew how to use the weapon. He had skillfully killed that moose yesterday afternoon. It shouldn't matter to her why that was his weapon of choice, only that he didn't choose to use it on her.

A breeze suddenly kicked up, lifting her shirttail and sending a shiver past her bare bum and up the length of her spine. Sadie realized she was still standing on her sleeping bag, still naked but for her flannel shirt.

There was actually frost on the ground this morning. She hurried to find her clothes, then hurried even more to get them on. Only after she was finally dressed did she straighten from tying her boots to look around the tiny meadow she was in.

Leaves rained from the trees and wafted through the air like drunken butterflies, having given up the battle to hold on to their branches. The frost and then the abrupt heat of the rising sun had snapped their stems and left them to fall to their inevitable end, to become fodder for next year's growth of new flora. The cycle of life was playing itself out.

"I see breakfast isn't looking any more promising than last night's supper."

Sadie spun on her seat and shot Morgan a smile. She grabbed one of the granola bars, now frozen solid, and tossed it to him.

"When I'm traveling I only make one hot meal a day," she explained, her smile widening as she watched him frown at his breakfast. "Mostly I just graze on trail mix, granola bars, or jerky until supper."

Voices traveled in on the breeze just then, and both Morgan and Sadie looked upriver to discover the source of the sound. Sadie shot to her feet the moment she recognized her mother's voice. Charlotte Quill was sitting in the bow of the approaching canoe, paddling and smiling and talking to Callum sitting in the stern.

Sadie's mood took a sudden dive into the dirt. She slapped her hands over her face to cover her gasp and could only stare in mute shock through her fingers.

Dammit. Her mother was here.

She spun on her heel and ran to Morgan, grabbing him by the shirt and standing on tiptoe to get her eyes dead level with his.

"Not one word about our being married," she whispered urgently, clutching the front of his shirt. "Understand? No kissing in front of my mother. No calling me wife. And hide that damn sword!" she finished on a whispered shout, pushing away and running to their bed.

She quickly rolled up her sleeping bag, ran to her unused tent, and threw it inside. She went back to the ledge, kicked around the matted dry grass she'd put there for padding, and frantically scanned the campsite for any other telltale signs.

Dammit. What in hell was her mother doing here?

Morgan still hadn't moved one muscle, much less done as she'd instructed and hidden his sword. She did that for him, running back to the ledge and kicking some of the dry grass over the weapon. Then she smoothed down the front of her shirt, took a calming breath, plastered a smile on her face, and sedately walked to the river to welcome her mom.

Morgan just didn't have the heart to tell his wife that no amount of deception would ever disguise the guilt she was feeling at the sudden arrival of her mother. Mercedes' face was blushed red; she was embarrassed to the soles of her feet despite her efforts to appear otherwise. She didn't seem to realize that any person in her right mind, especially her mother, would consider finding her daughter sharing a campsite with a man anything but innocent.

Morgan mimicked Mercedes' amble and slowly made his way over to Callum and Charlotte. He grabbed the canoe and pulled the boat sideways to the bank, then reached in and lifted Charlotte out so she wouldn't get her feet wet.

Charlotte squeaked much the way her daughter was prone to do and blinked up at him with eyes the mirror image of Mercedes'.

Morgan stepped onto the bank and carefully set Charlotte down, then shot Mercedes a grin. Quickly recovering from her fluster, Charlotte ran to her daughter and gave her a motherly hug.

"I've been so worried," Charlotte whispered loudly enough for everyone to hear. She pulled back and took her by the shoulders. "Your cabin was ransacked."

Mercedes reversed their positions, taking her mother by the arms. "Someone broke into my cabin? When?"

"Yesterday morning," Callum said, straightening from pulling the canoe onto the beach. He looked at Morgan, then at Mercedes. "We were coming out to visit you, lass, when we discovered the destruction. And your mother," he said, waving a hand at Charlotte, "would have no rest until she knew you were safe."

Mercedes turned her shocked gaze back on her mother. "Who would do something like that? I had nothing worth stealing."

"It looked to be more vandalized than robbed,"

Callum said before Charlotte could respond. "It appeared as if the man was looking for something."

"The Dolan brothers were a half day behind us," Morgan interjected. He looked at his cousin. "You said one man."

Callum shrugged. "There might have been more. I could find only one set of footprints. They belonged to a small but heavy man, maybe two hundred pounds."

"It was not Harry and Dwayne," Sadie said, glaring at Morgan. "It was a stranger."

"What makes you so sure?" he asked. "Do you have any idea who would have done this? Other than the Dolans, is there anyone else looking for this gold?"

Sadie shook her head. "Not that I know of. For years the only people who even believed Jedediah's mine exists were my dad, the Dolans, and Eric Hellman."

Morgan walked over to her. "Now you will take my warnings seriously, Mercedes?"

Before she could answer him, her mother was poking her in the arm, trying to get her attention again. "There's a dead moose over there," Charlotte whispered, pointing down the beach.

Sadie quickly looked back at Morgan, nodded, then turned and led her mother over to see the moose. As Morgan and Callum followed, Morgan let his gaze scan the area. Morgan suspected that the danger he had seen in the *drùidh's* vision was coming closer.

Callum nudged Morgan's shoulder and motioned with his head that he wanted to speak to Morgan alone. Morgan looked to see that the two women were deeply engrossed in a discussion over the dead moose.

Satisfied that they would have some privacy, Morgan walked a short distance away, and his cousin followed.

"Tell me how I can help," Callum said quietly, keeping a small part of his attention on the women. "I've brought guns if you need them."

"What makes you think I need a gun?" Morgan asked.

Callum grinned. "It's been more than eight hundred years, cousin, but not so long that I've forgotten that look."

"What look?"

"You're guarded, Morgan. Feeling hunted. And you're wearing the look of a man who is about to turn the tables and do some hunting of your own." Callum rubbed his hands together, suddenly looking downright cheerful. "And I wish to help. Nay, I demand to help. I could use a rousing fight just now."

"I am not hunted," Morgan snapped, darting a look at the women to make sure they hadn't heard him. They had moved back to the canoe Callum and Charlotte had arrived in and were rummaging through the gear. He looked back at Callum.

"It's Mercedes who's being hunted. That her cabin was ransacked is proof enough. And I think the gold is the reason she's in danger. Either that, or someone doesn't want the wilderness park to be built."

"Besides you?" Callum drawled.

"That's different. I can stop the park from happening without endangering Mercedes."

"Why are you so against this park to begin with? It's only a small part of our land."

"My land," Morgan shot back. He let out a tired sigh

and attempted to rub away the tension slowly building in his neck. He needed to make Callum understand.

"That gorge is special," Morgan told him, deciding it was time to reveal his secret to Callum. Only then would his cousin be able to comprehend the scope of the problem.

"The waterfall comes from that mountain pond where Daar's staff was thrown," Morgan continued. "And everything around it has changed somehow. The trees have grown taller, the trout are the size of salmon, and even the granite of the gorge itself has been altered."

Callum took a step back. "By the *drùidh's* magic?" he whispered, his face drawn pale.

Morgan nodded. "Aye. From his old staff. But Daar has no wish for Grey to know this. He fears what my brother might do."

"Grey will likely dynamite that pond," Callum said, nodding agreement about their laird's determination that Daar's staff never reappear. "So this is why you asked Grey for that land? To protect the old priest?"

"Something like that," Morgan muttered, looking back at the women. They were unpacking the canoe, and by the looks of the gear, Charlotte was planning to stay for a month. He turned back to Callum. "People would wander out of the park and discover the gorge. And that would bring even more people."

Callum could only shake his head. "If Charlotte ever discovered that something like this was connected with us, she would never agree to marry me."

"You don't intend to tell her about our past?" Morgan asked.

Callum looked downright appalled. "Hell, no," he ground out, shaking his head again. "You saw what happened when MacBain told Mary Sutter. The woman ran away and got herself killed."

"Grace knows," Morgan reminded him. "And she still married Grey anyway."

"Grace is a scientist," Callum said, getting defensive. "And scientists are used to discovering wonders. They understand that there is something driving the forces of nature that can never be explained. Tell me, are you intending to tell Sadie about your past?" Callum asked quietly, turning the question back on Morgan.

"I do not like deception," Morgan said. He sighed and kneaded the muscles in his neck again. "I don't know," he said more calmly. He grinned. "I thought about getting her pregnant first," he admitted.

Callum looked appalled again. "And you don't think that's deceptive?"

"It might be a good plan. I've already claimed her. A babe would only bind us together more tightly." Morgan broadened his grin. "Are you saying you haven't thought that maybe a bairn would hurry your courtship along?"

Callum actually looked sick. "I could never do that to Charlotte," he whispered. "She had to get married at sixteen when she became pregnant with Sadie. I could not force her into another marriage that way."

Morgan didn't have the heart to tell Callum that it was too late, that Charlotte already carried his child. Besides, that was Charlotte's duty.

"I could use your help," Morgan said, changing

the subject. Telling their women they were eight hundred years old was a personal decision that each of them eventually would have to make. But not today. "I need to get that moose taken care of," Morgan continued. "And it seems I have to notify the authorities that I killed it. If you could help me do that, I would be grateful. I have no wish to leave Mercedes unguarded right now. Not with the news you've brought us."

"You killed the moose with your sword?" Callum asked, knowing full well that Morgan rarely carried a gun. "Tell me, what does Sadie think of your weapon?"

Morgan shrugged. "She seems to be getting used to it."

"I swear I'd give all my teeth to have my sword back," Callum said. "I've felt naked for six years." He suddenly grinned. "Although there is something to be said for a good rifle. You needn't get close to an enemy to dispatch him."

Morgan let his gaze scan the landscape again. "That works both ways," he said, looking back at Callum. "Neither does your enemy need to be close." He rubbed his neck again, the tension having suddenly doubled. "Hell. Someone could be watching us right now, with his gun trained on Mercedes."

"Do you honestly believe there is that kind of danger?"

"The *drùidh* warned me there was a presence roaming this valley. Something dark," Morgan carefully explained without coming right out and telling Callum about the vision he had seen. "Mercedes might be in danger. This is why I'm with her now. I want that damn gold found, and then I want to settle this park thing between us."

"In a way that won't expose your gorge?" Callum surmised.

Morgan nodded. "She's going to have to be content with just owning the land and not opening it up to people."

Callum gave Morgan a staggering pat on the shoulder. "For an ancient man, you can be foolishly young sometimes, cousin. Living with a woman who's had her dream taken away does not bode well for a peaceful union. Hell, it can be downright dangerous."

"Yeah, well," Morgan said, pivoting on his heel and heading back to Charlotte and Sadie. He hoped Charlotte was a better cook than her daughter. There had to be breakfast fixings someplace in all that gear she'd brought. "You'd better start putting some of your own long-lived wisdom to work," Morgan said quietly over his shoulder as he walked off. "You've got your own female problems to deal with, and I'm thinking they might turn out to be just as troubling as mine."

Chapter Eighteen

There was another advantage to having a husband, Sadie decided later that morning. He carried the bulk of their gear.

Sadie slid her unusually light backpack off her shoulders, absently letting it drop to the ground as she studied the old logging camp that lay before her like a slumbering beast forgotten by time. This was it. Camp number three.

The last place Jedediah Plum had been seen alive.

Sadie could easily make out the remains of what must be the cookhouse. The roof was gone except for the rafters, the door and several of the windows were broken, and good-sized poplar trees were growing inside, spilling the last of their leaves like yellow flakes of unmelted snow. Rotting into the forest floor just to the right of the cookhouse, not twenty feet away, were two bunkhouses running perpendicular to the cookhouse. Both were long and narrow and set low to the ground with the rusted remains of a stove pipe jutting crookedly against the middle rafter of one of them. Several of the giant logs that made up the walls had come free of their moorings, the ravages of time and nature working them into peat dust to litter the ground around the cabins. Young spruce grew in the acrid peat, reaching for the sunlight filtering through the few towering trees that had escaped the woodcutter's blades.

The building that housed the saw was far off to the left, set away from the living and eating area. Probably so that one group of men would be able to sleep in relative peace while another group worked.

Sadie knew from her years of studying journals and history books that the sawmill usually ran around the clock in ten-hour shifts. Maintenance was done during two-hour breaks; the saws were changed and sharpened, the machinery oiled, and the bark and debris from the previous shift cleared away to make room for the next round of sawing.

Sometimes the trees were sawn on sight and the lumber hauled to town over the frozen ground, and sometimes the whole logs were simply driven downriver in the spring. This site, apparently, had been a portable mill. Which meant it would have been a small, self-sufficient town unto itself.

Sadie slowly turned in a circle, studying the site, unable to believe what she was seeing, shaking her head in wonder.

"I bet my daddy's mill processed some of this timber," Sadie said, finally looking at Morgan. "Only it would have been Grampy Quill who ran it then."

Morgan was shaking her head. "It was more likely your great-grandfather," he corrected with a smile. "This site is at least eighty years old."

Sadie looked around again. "I can't believe this has been sitting here like a ghost town all these years, its location never documented."

Morgan shrugged. "Why would anyone bother? They moved in, harvested the trees, then got out. There was nothing here to lure people to settle, other than the timber. And once that disappeared, so did the camps."

He turned her to face him. "You can properly thank me now, wife, for finding this camp for you," he said, an arrogant smile lighting his eyes.

Not one to deny a person his due, Sadie leaned up on her toes and kissed Morgan the way she had wanted to since morning. His tongue swept inside her mouth, his body hardened against her, and that shivering tingle returned to her chest as Sadie melted against him.

Yeah, husbands definitely had their advantages.

She was trembling like a poplar leaf when she finally pulled back, still making sure that she stayed within his embrace. Her heart was threatening to fly out of her chest, and she was quite pleased to see that Morgan was equally affected.

"Thank you for bringing me here," she said, toying with a button on his shirt. She looked up. "And thank you for getting rid of mom so diplomatically. She's pregnant and doesn't need to be in the middle of this. Having her and Callum take the moose back for you was a brilliant idea."

"Ah. So you do believe you're in danger."

"I believe that someone besides us and the Dolans might be out here and that they might be looking for the gold."

"So, if I were to ask you to stay here with Faol today and explore only this camp, you just might obey me?"

Sadie thought it was past time Morgan's vocabulary got an adjustment. "*Obey* is one of those words women don't really care for, Morgan. But I might be inclined to go along with your *suggestion,*" she offered instead.

He pulled her back against him, tucking her head under his chin and rocking her gently. His laughter made her chest tingle, and Sadie closed her eyes and leaned into his strength. Yeah. She really liked being married.

"Ah, Mercedes. I'm starting to have hope for us," Morgan whispered, kissing the top of her head and squeezing her tightly. "You can spend the rest of your life making me into a modern husband, if that is your wish." He lifted her chin. "While I work just as hard to make you into a suitable wife."

His eyes darkened, sending her heart racing again, this time with anticipation. Now that she knew what making love could be like, she wanted to experience it again. Tonight. Just as soon as the sun set, she was going to attack this man like a woman possessed.

"You enjoyed yourself last night, wife?"

Sadie had to look away from his intense gaze, so she turned her attention to fingering the cherrywood knot hanging around his neck. "That depends," she whispered to his chest. "Did you?"

All she got for an answer was silence.

Sadie felt heat climb to her face. Dammit. He'd better give her the right words. She tugged on the cord that held the cherrywood knot. "Did you?" she repeated.

"Almost," he said quietly.

Sadie snapped her head up. "Almost? What does that mean?"

He tapped the end of her nose, dropped his arms to his sides, and stepped away. "I'll tell you what it means in six days," was all he said before he pivoted on his heel and strode off through the woods.

Sadie stared at his back until he disappeared around the cookhouse. Almost? How can someone almost enjoy something? Either he did or he didn't.

She was almost ready to scream.

It amazed Sadie how quickly she had grown accustomed to sleeping with Morgan. And as she set up their new camp, she thought again about her decision to pretend to be Morgan's wife for the week. Had she managed to sabotage her heart, making it impossible to walk away in six days?

For the first time since the fire eight years ago, Sadie had the hope of a future that included a husband, children, and a cozy home of her own. If nothing else—if she did have to walk away at the end of the week—Morgan had returned that possibility to her. He had made her realize that the fire may have taken half her family, but it had not taken her future.

She could still hope.

She could still dream.

She could still love.

But could she *be* loved?

Sadie finished spreading out their sleeping bag and stretched out on it and stared up at the tops of the trees. Morgan hadn't once mentioned the word *love,* for all his peculiar vocabulary. Sadie dismissed the fact that she hadn't exactly brought the word up, either. He was the one talking about marriage; he should be the first one to say it.

He acted possessive, like a caring husband.

He worried about her safety.

And he *almost* enjoyed having sex with her.

Sadie touched the fingers of her right hand together, feeling leather touch leather. Would he *completely* enjoy their lovemaking if she had no scars? What would it be like, to go to Morgan fully naked, flawless, and beautiful?

Would he say the words to her then?

I love you.

Sadie closed her eyes and let her escaping breath turn into a smile, letting those three little words echo though her mind like a promise. And she decided then that she was not walking away from Morgan MacKeage in five days.

Sadie woke with a start, unable to orient herself for several seconds. As the treetops towering over her head came into focus, she realized that she'd fallen asleep. Feeling a bit embarrassed for having a nap in the middle of the day, she sat up and scanned the area for Morgan.

He was nowhere to be seen. Sadie decided this was

her chance to have a bath while she still had some privacy. She gathered her toiletries and some clean clothes and looked around the logging camp. There had to be a water source nearby, a spring or a small brook. She hadn't seen any signs of a dug well during her exploration of the camp earlier.

She headed into the forest, hiking north along the west side of Fraser Mountain, figuring that if she walked far enough, she would eventually run into a stream.

She ran into Morgan instead.

He stepped from behind an outcropping of ledge and used his impressive body to block her path. Sadie's heart started to race at the sight of him. He was so incredibly handsome. So large and solid. And so damned sexy, standing there like a god of the woods.

She smiled at him.

He didn't smile back.

"I stink," she said, her smile rising a notch at the incredible look he gave her. "And I'm not kissing you until I wash my hair and change into clothes that can't stand up by themselves."

"You'll catch a cold."

"I don't care. I'll catch fleas if I don't have a bath."

He actually took a step away from her at that possibility. Sadie walked up to him, tapped him on the nose, and continued past him with an insolent sway of her hips. Morgan fell into step beside her. And as they walked in companionable silence, Sadie thought about the history of this area.

Jean Lavoie's diary mentioned that Jedediah Plum

had visited camp number three for several days and had taken to wandering off at night. But he was always back in his bunk each morning, which meant the prospector hadn't traveled far.

Jean had followed him once but had lost his trail when Jedediah's footprints had become mixed with the tracks the horses had made that day hauling logs. Jean also mentioned that he hadn't been the only one stalking Jedediah that night.

But on the fourth morning the prospector had not returned. His body had been discovered sticking out of a snowdrift about a mile north of the logging camp.

"That's it," Sadie said, pulling Morgan to a stop so abruptly he stumbled backward.

"That's what?" he asked.

Sadie brushed the hair from her face and shifted her bundle of clothes to her right arm. "I was thinking about Jedediah's gold mine," she said. "And when he died." She looked around the forest they stood in. "It was near here, according to the cook's diary I have. Someplace just north of the logging camp."

Morgan also looked around, frowning. "North? How far?"

Sadie shook her head. "The diary said about a mile or so but wasn't specific. But I remember from my dad's research that Jedediah's body was found near the base of a cliff that was at least a hundred feet high. Only we were never able to find that cliff because we never knew where the logging camp was."

She shot Morgan a bright smile. "Until now. Thanks to you and Faol, I can discover exactly where

Jedediah's body was found. And I'd bet my kayak that the old prospector died close to his gold mine."

"A tall cliff?" Morgan whispered, looking north. "About a mile from camp?"

Sadie dropped her bundle of clothes and threw her arms around Morgan's shoulders. "Forget our swim," she said with a laugh of excitement, hugging him tightly. "Let's go north and look for that cliff."

Morgan slowly untangled her arms from around his neck, setting her away from him. He bent down, picked up her clothes, and gently placed them back in her arms. He smiled at her, but his face was drawn, his expression tight.

"We have the rest of the week to look for that cliff," he said, his voice even-toned. "After our swim."

Sadie could only stare at Morgan, confused by his reaction. Why wasn't he excited about this?

Morgan took hold of her hand again and started them walking down the mountain, west, away from where she really wanted to go. Sadie followed along meekly and thought about her pretend husband's sudden change of mood.

With Mercedes' hand firmly tucked into his, Morgan headed to where his magical stream ran into the Prospect River. Sweat broke out between his shoulders and ran in a trickle down his back. His right hand involuntarily curled into a fist, and his feet felt like stones as every step he took led him closer to the magical stream he wanted to keep secret from Mercedes.

Of all the hundreds of square miles in this valley, why did Plum's accursed mine have to be located in his gorge? And why now, after all these years of searching with her father, did Mercedes have to be the one to find it?

The *drùidh's* vision rose in his mind, and Morgan started to shake with the force of his thoughts. He released Mercedes so she would not feel his trembling. He walked ahead in silence, holding back branches for Mercedes when the trail became thick.

They broke from the woods and stepped onto a sandbar jutting into the magical stream. Upstream the water rippled with gentle current over gravel worn smooth by time. But the stream's path bent around the sandbar and eddied into a deep pool of calm water—perfect for swimming, Morgan decided, and for making love to his wife.

Mercedes wasted no time. She dropped her bundle of clothes onto the sand and quickly followed it down, immediately unlacing her boots.

"Go away," she told him succinctly, pulling off her boots and then her socks. Her hands went to the snap on her pants. "Find your own swimming hole farther downstream."

Morgan pulled his sword from his back and set it on the ground, then unbuttoned his shirt and took it off, letting it fall beside his sword. Mercedes turned her head to discover he had not obeyed her order. She frowned at him.

He smiled at her. "I stink, too, wife," he said, wrinkling his nose. "And I like this swimming hole," he added, unbuckling his belt and pushing his pants down to his ankles.

His wide-eyed wife suddenly squeaked and turned

to face the stream. "It's broad daylight, Morgan. You can't . . . we can't just . . ."

Morgan ignored her flustered sputtering and stripped naked, setting the rest of his clothes neatly beside his shirt. He hesitated, then took the cherrywood burl from around his neck and set it on top of his pile.

He didn't need its help today to froth up the water. He and Mercedes could do that all by themselves.

Stretching his muscles against the cool autumn air, Morgan strode past his speechless wife and waded into the stream. He slipped under the water and kicked his way to the center of the pool before he turned and resurfaced. He let his feet sink to the bottom and stood facing Mercedes, the water only as deep as his chest. He brushed back the hair from his face and smiled at his still gaping wife.

"Hide in the trees to change," he told her. "And wear only your shirt if you feel you must hold on to your modesty."

He sent a splash of water toward her. "It's not cold, Mercedes. Hurry up and join me." He bobbed his eyebrows and spider-walked his fingers through the air. "I'll wash that beautiful hair of yours if you want."

She darted a nervous look up and down the length of the stream, then suddenly jumped up and ran for the forest. Morgan lay back in the water and floated, smiling up at the deep blue sky. For all of her shyness, Mercedes seemed to be a willing wife, playful and energetic and eager.

And so comfortable here in these woods.

Now, if he could only get her comfortable with him.

Morgan watched from the corner of his eye as Mercedes silently tried to sneak into the water. The little *gràineag* had emerged from the forest a good fifty paces from where she'd entered. Now she was tiptoeing up the stream toward him, trying not to make any noise or ripple the water.

Morgan closed his eyes, smiled, and waited.

Strong feminine hands—both of which were naked, he was pleased to feel—landed on his shoulders with surprising force and drove him under the water. Morgan twisted and reached for the tails of Mercedes' shirt, pulling her down with him.

His mouth captured her squeal under the water as she wrapped her arms around his neck and pulled their bodies together, snaking her legs around his waist and trapping him tightly. Morgan shouted, still underwater, the moment his groin came into contact with the naked, delicate, down-covered folds at the juncture of her thighs.

He ravaged her mouth while she stole the breath out of his body. Her hands tugged at his hair and dug into his shoulders. She wiggled her hips, further arousing him, setting him on fire as he hardened to stone.

They needed air.

Not that he cared at the moment. But Morgan had a thought that Mercedes' eagerness might drown them both.

He planted his feet and stood, keeping his very passionate wife firmly locked against him. They both tossed their heads back the minute they surfaced, taking in large gulps of air. But before he could catch his breath, the little *gràineag's* mouth was covering his. Morgan fell forward, sinking them both to the bottom, placing Mercedes between the gravel and his now rock-solid manhood.

And that was when Morgan suddenly remembered the foil packet that was still in his pants. On the beach. Much too far away right now. But Morgan simply didn't care at that moment. This woman was his. He was hers.

He kicked his feet just enough to bring them to the edge of the pool, lifting Mercedes' head above water and resting it on the shore. Still covering her, still locked in the embrace of her legs, he slid down just enough that he could touch the tip of his manhood to her feminine center.

Her eyes opened, blinking the cascading water away, and Mercedes smiled in anticipation of the passion he offered. Her hands dug marks into his shoulders as she used the heels of her feet to lift her hips against him, opening herself to receive him inside.

But he hesitated and pulled back.

"We don't have protection, wife," he said, closing his eyes against the urge to drive forward. "I need to go to my pants."

"I don't care," she whispered, lifting her hips again and trying to pull his mouth back down to hers.

Morgan held fast. "Well, I do, *gràineag.* I will not have you crying foul in two months. You'll say the words in front of a priest before I put a babe in your belly."

She gave him a fierce shove. And before he could right himself, Mercedes was up and running toward his clothes. Morgan didn't know if she was going for his pants or his sword.

"Why didn't you bring it into the water?" she growled as she knelt down and rummaged around in his pockets, making a mess of his neatly stacked clothes.

Morgan stood up and backed deeper into the pool while he appreciated the view of her beautiful backside. Soon she had the foil packet in her hand and was running back to the stream, her wet flannel shirt clinging to every delectable curve of her body, her long legs making short work of the distance between them.

Morgan heard the rifle shot the instant Mercedes lunged into his arms. When she landed against his chest, she was dead weight. He dove them both into the water, holding on to her with desperation. He covered her back with his hand and sank to the bottom of the pool, feeling the warmth of her blood against his palm as she lay limp and unmoving against him.

Morgan rose to the surface and frantically waded to the sandbar, turning to shield Mercedes from the direction of the sniper. He crossed the sandbar in less than three strides and ducked into the forest just as another shot cracked through the air, hitting the dirt at his feet.

Morgan kept running deeper into the woods, heading downstream toward the sniper, hoping the villain wouldn't expect him to move in that direction. Morgan ran a few hundred yards, then finally stopped and set Mercedes gently on the ground.

She was a bloody mess, nearly all of her flannel

shirt soaked red, both front and back. The bullet had gone straight through her body.

With shaking hands, Morgan popped all the buttons on the shirt and spread it open, revealing a small wound just below Mercedes' right breast. Her breathing was labored. She was unconscious, her face as pale as a winter's moon, her eyes already sunken beneath eyelids that were blue with the promise of death.

Morgan forced his hands to remain steady as he worked the shirt off her shoulders and held her in a sitting position. He wrapped the blood-soaked flannel around her back and over her breasts and the wound, using the sleeves to tie it as tightly as he dared.

Swiping his forehead with a trembling and bloody hand, Morgan looked up and cocked his head, listening for sounds of the sniper moving in for the kill.

He took a deep breath, trying to calm his racing heart. They were miles from nowhere, and Mercedes would bleed to death before he could get her to civilization. He had to get to Daar's magic burl and the stream to heal her before it was too late.

He heard a sound then, on the other side of the valley, the distinct shout of a man being surprised. A wolf's growl was followed by another shot, but this time the muzzle was pointed in another direction.

Confident that the sniper was now occupied elsewhere, Morgan gently picked up Mercedes and ran through the forest again, back upstream. He kept to the woods and passed the sandbar, running until a bend in the stream concealed him from the other side of the valley. He set his wife down gently on the gravel and then ran back to the sandbar.

With only a negligent look across the valley, Morgan stepped onto the sand and gathered up his clothes and his sword, quickly draping the cherry-wood burl around his neck as he ran back to Mercedes.

He tossed everything onto the ground beside her and picked her up, wading into the stream until it was deep enough for him to sit down. The moment the burl got wet, it started to hum against his chest. The water began churning, frothing around them and sparking to life with thousands of bubbles that rose to the surface as exploding green light.

He untied the shirt and pulled it from around her waist. Mercedes moaned, arching her back in pain. Morgan clasped her to his chest and lay back, sinking deeply into the stream. His body felt on fire as blinding green light blazed around him. He tightened his arms around his wife's limp body and held her head just above the surface for a good ten minutes, gritting his teeth against the heat assaulting him.

He sat up finally and looked at her wound. It was still bleeding, frothy red bubbles oozing from it. She'd grown paler, more limp.

Morgan roared. The magic wasn't working. "Dammit! I command you to work!" he shouted, grabbing the burl and tearing it from his neck.

Supporting her with his knees, Morgan tied the leather cord around Mercedes' neck and straightened his legs to lower her into the water.

The green bubbles suddenly turned yellow, snapping with angry pops that filled the air with steam. Morgan lifted Mercedes just enough to see her wound.

It wasn't throbbing as the cut on his thigh had, but the bleeding seemed to have slowed.

It still wasn't enough.

She was still dying.

Faol stepped out of the woods but stopped at the edge of the water. Morgan looked up to see the panting wolf frantically dancing from foot to foot, as if agitated. Faol whined, then barked, then trotted several paces upstream.

Morgan turned his attention back to his dying wife. Faol barked again, louder. He stepped into the water, then retreated, trotting upstream again, his bark turning into a keening howl.

Upstream.

The waterfall.

Nearer the *drùidh's* magic.

Morgan stood up and gently settled Mercedes against his chest. He waded out of the water and followed the wolf, who was now trotting quickly up the edge of the stream.

The desperate journey seemed to take forever before he finally reached the waterfall. Morgan simply kept walking until he was standing shoulder-high in violently frothing water.

This time the light snapping around them was neither green nor yellow but a pure, blazing white that forced Morgan to close his eyes or be blinded. Heat radiated from Mercedes in waves so intense his arms and chest felt scorched.

The mist rising around them warmed the air with summerlike heat, making sweat break out on his forehead and scalp. Morgan stood solid against the assault, reciting prayers he'd all but forgotten since he had been a lad on his mother's lap.

And he prayed, willing the *drùidh's* magic to save Mercedes' life, to heal her wounds and bring her back to him whole and hearty and spitting mad. He stood until his muscles trembled with fatigue, willing Mercedes to live.

"I had a wonderful dream."

Morgan snapped open his eyes and stared down at the woman in his arms. She was smiling sleepily up at him, her face flushed pink around heavy-lidded blue eyes.

"And what was it you dreamed about?" he whispered, his voice shaking as violently as his legs.

"I visited Daddy and Caroline. We had a picnic high up on a mountain overlooking a beautiful valley."

Sweat broke out on his forehead again when Morgan realized that Mercedes had actually died for a while. She'd been with her father and sister and very well could have ended up staying.

"Caroline doesn't blame me," Mercedes whispered, drawing his attention again. "She told me the fire wasn't my fault."

"I'm glad you saw your family," Morgan whispered. He shook her slightly. "Don't go to sleep again, Mercedes," he softly commanded when she closed her eyes.

"I'm so tired, Morgan. My muscles feel like jelly," she mumbled, turning her face into his chest. She smiled again, snuggling comfortably against him.

Morgan waded to shore and fell to his knees on the sand, still clasping Mercedes tightly, finding himself unable to set her down. He knelt there for several minutes, silent tears rolling down his face. Over and over he repeated his thanks to God that his wife was alive.

Faol suddenly appeared and quietly padded up to them and nuzzled Mercedes' hair, his tongue washing the entire side of her face. Morgan didn't send the wolf away but let the animal see for himself that Mercedes was okay.

And still Morgan couldn't put her down.

Faol started to whine and dance from foot to foot again, turning in circles, trotting to where the pool emptied out of the cliff-surrounded grotto they were in. He barked sharply and sat down, whining as his tail thumped the edge of the stream.

"I don't care," Morgan said softly to the wolf. "I will find our sniper and deal with him later. Mercedes needs my attention now."

Faol yipped again, standing and looking nervously downstream.

"Go, then," Morgan told the wolf. "Stand guard."

Without further urging, Faol whirled and shot out of the grotto, his tail disappearing from sight in a blur.

Morgan looked down at Mercedes.

She was still sleeping, her eyes no longer sunken into her head, her cheeks a warm, healthy pink. He looked around for a soft place to set her down, inching forward on his knees just a bit before he gently laid her on a carpet of thick green moss.

He straightened, brushing back the hair from her face, feeling the heat of life on her skin. He traced the shape of her cheekbone, letting his finger trail over her chin, then down the length of her throat.

He halted and stared at the empty piece of leather tied loosely around her neck.

The cherrywood burl was gone.

Morgan turned to look at the pool. The waterfall dropped from the cliff at the far end, sending a cloud of mist into the air that settled over the entire grotto. The water gently rippled with floating stardust that glittered and winked in the unearthly light that scattered its rainbow through the mist.

The magic was spent, the burl destroyed.

And Mercedes' life had been saved in the process.

Morgan turned back to his wife, continuing his inspection with a still trembling hand, needing to assure himself that she really was okay. His gaze went immediately to where the gaping wound had once been, but he saw only smooth, milky-white flesh that carried just the hint of a blush from her own inner heat. His hands settled around her waist, and Morgan closed his eyes with relief.

She was perfect. Flawless. Completely healed.

With a sharp intake of breath, Morgan pulled back, staring at Mercedes' body. He reached out, lifted her right hand, and turned her palm toward him.

No scars. Nothing but pink, healthy skin. He looked back at her left arm, then turned her just enough to see her back. There was no puckered skin. Nothing but flawless flesh.

Mercedes was completely healed.

Completely.

Morgan sat down on the ground and scrubbed at

his face, shaking his head and grinding his palms into his eyes.

Now how in hell was he supposed to explain this?

His wife was going to wake up to find herself lying in this magical gorge, completely naked and flawless. It was bad enough he wouldn't be able to explain why she hadn't died from her bullet wound. But her old scars?

Morgan twisted to see the scar he had on his shoulder from a battle that had been waged more than eight hundred years ago. And he turned more, to feel for the long ridge of flesh on his waist, where a sword had nearly cut him in half.

They, too, were gone. Disappeared.

He looked out over the still shimmering water and shook his head again. Was he dreaming? Why hadn't the *drùidh's* magic taken his old scars away the other day in the stream, when it had healed his thigh?

The light had been green then, not the pure, blinding white of today. The magic was more powerful here. Special. The strength of Daar's thick old staff flowed into this grotto and was soaked up with the mist to nourish the towering trees.

It also had nourished both himself and Mercedes and given them perfect bodies.

And now he was left with the task of explaining to this modern-born woman just what had happened to her. And to do that, he would have to explain his own magical existence here.

Chapter Nineteen

She was dead.

She remembered the force of the bullet slamming into her back. Remembered falling against Morgan. Remem-bered the disbelief, the pain, and the regret that she would not get to spend a long and happy life with this man.

She'd died instead.

But Sadie didn't know if she'd landed in heaven or hell.

Or maybe this was the purgatory she'd heard about.

It was hot. She was hot. But she was in the most beautiful place she'd ever seen. Towering cliffs of gray-speckled granite formed a half-circle around her. Mist hung overhead in a suspended cloud, blanketing her in muggy summer heat. The roar of water falling from a great height echoed off the tall granite walls, and she was bathed in a fog-amplified white light.

She still had all five of her senses. She could hear,

see, feel the tickle of moss beneath her, smell the warmth of the mist-soaked spruce mingled with pine. And she could even taste Morgan lingering in the back of her mouth.

Sadie slowly rolled over to face the sound of the falling water and widened her eyes as her gaze traveled up and up and up, following the stream of crystalline water that appeared to be shooting out of the side of the cliff like a giant faucet turned all the way on.

She scrambled to her knees and stood up, turning in a circle with her head thrown back, looking at the cathedral-like room surrounding her. Spruce and pine and oak and cedar rose so high over her head that their tops disappeared into the mist. Ferns grew so lush in long-feathered spikes that they looked prehistoric. The moss she'd been lying on was as thick as sheep's wool and so green it was almost fluorescent.

It should have been dark from the abundant canopy of growth, but there was light shimmering everywhere, the source coming from the water instead of the sky.

Sadie raised her right hand to brush the hair off her forehead, only to halt with her hand suspended in front of her face. She stared at her palm, at the perfect flesh that should have been covered with ugly scars.

She looked down at her body and gasped again at the realization that she was naked. She instinctively covered herself, folding her hands over her breasts.

And that was when Sadie noticed her arm.

The scars on the inside of her left arm were gone.

She twisted enough to see her back. The wide, jagged patchwork of skin grafts was gone. She tucked her chin and peered at her right shoulder. There was no scar peering back at her. Pink, flawless skin covered her back from her shoulder to her waist.

Sadie folded her legs and sat down, covering her face with her hands.

She *was* dead.

She would never see Morgan again. He was back in their valley—all alone, mourning her, cursing his inability to protect her.

Sadie pulled her hands from her face just enough to look down at her hand. What was the point of having such a perfect body if Morgan was not here to enjoy it with her?

Sadie threw herself facedown on the sand and burst into tears. She didn't care anymore that she'd been scarred. Better to have flaws and have Morgan than to be perfect without him.

Sadie cried loud, wrenching tears, mourning all that she'd lost. She'd come to this beautiful place, becoming beautiful herself, to spend eternity alone.

And that was when Sadie decided she'd landed in hell.

She lifted her head at the thud of something hitting the ground. She looked up to see Morgan, fully clothed, standing beside where the pool spilled out between the towering trees. At his feet was her bundle of clothes and her boots, his pack, and his sword.

Sadie jumped up and ran toward him but came to a stop several paces away when she noticed the look on his face.

He was as pale as snow, the skin drawn back on his cheeks in tight lines of tension. His eyes were the color of winter spruce, and his fists were clenched at his sides.

Sadie threw herself at him. She kissed his face, his hair, his mouth, whimpering her approval when his arms tightened around her.

"I think we're dead," she whispered into his ear. "I'm sorry, Morgan, that we've died, but I'm so happy you're here with me. I love you so much," she continued, kissing him again.

It took Sadie a full minute to realize he wasn't kissing her back. And that he'd gone even stiffer the moment she'd started to speak.

He didn't know yet, that they'd both died. He didn't understand what had happened to them.

She unwrapped her legs from his waist and stood, dancing away from him and twirling in circles with her hands out.

"Look, Morgan. I'm whole. I'm as naked as the day I was born and just as perfect." She spun to present her back to him, showing off her flawless skin. "The scars are gone, Morgan. I'm me again," she said with a laugh over her shoulder.

He didn't move. Didn't speak. He didn't so much as blink.

Sadie rushed back to him and unbuckled his belt. "Let me show you," she said, unsnapping his pants and pulling them down to his knees. "You're going to be perfect, too."

Sadie took his fisted left hand and set it over the spot on his thigh where he'd stitched up the wound from the moose. "There. See? It's gone," she said, looking up at his face.

He wasn't looking at his thigh. He was staring at her. Sadie gave him a huge smile, straightened, wrapped her arms around his neck again, and kissed him soundly on the mouth.

"I truly am sorry we died, Morgan," she whispered. "But we're together, my love." She rained kisses over his face as she spoke. "I was so afraid I'd lost you forever."

Sadie felt him reach down and pull his pants back up before his arms came around her again. Morgan swept her off her feet and carried her back to her spot by the pool. He set her down and then sat beside her, unbuttoning his shirt, shrugging out of it and handing it to her.

"Put this on, lass," he said softly, his gaze quickly roaming over her naked body before he turned his head and looked out over the pool.

"I wish you'd take your clothes off instead," she said, disgruntled but doing as he asked. She slipped into the shirt and buttoned it up to her neck but stopped at the feel of something dangling over her collarbone.

Sadie lifted the leather cord and gasped, sending her gaze to Morgan's chest. "This is the cord you wear." She tucked her chin and pulled the leather out to see better, feeling for the wood that should have been there. "Oh, no. I lost the cherrywood knot that was on it."

She turned, frantically searching the ground for the wood. Morgan grabbed her by the shoulders, then leaned them both over until he was lying on top of her. He brushed the hair back from her face.

"We're not dead, Mercedes," he said, his mouth mere inches from hers, his eyes dark and unreadable as he stared at her. "We are both very much alive."

Sadie blinked at him, pressing her head into the ground to focus better on his face. "We . . . we can't be, Morgan. I don't have any scars. And neither do you."

"You're alive, Mercedes."

"But I remember the bullet. The pain. I remember falling against you. I was shot, Morgan. I . . . I died."

He slowly nodded his head, his eyes never leaving hers. "Aye, lass, you did die," he whispered, bringing one hand up to finger the leather cord on her neck. "But the old priest's magic brought you back to me."

"M-magic?"

He nodded again. "Aye." He let go of the leather and waved at the air around them. "This place, the mist, the very water that flows from the cliff. It's special, Mercedes. It comes from a pond where the *drùidh's* staff was thrown two years ago."

"D-drùidh?"

Sadie pushed at his chest, struggling to get up. He rolled off and sat up as she scrambled to her feet and turned to stare down at him.

"What are you saying?" she whispered, fighting the fear that was rising inside her. She took a step back. "Are you . . . are you saying you're a . . . a witch or something? A warlock?"

He shook his head and then quickly stood.

She took another step back.

"I'm only a man, Mercedes," he said, keeping his distance. "I know nothing of magic."

"Then how . . ." She fingered the leather cord at her

throat, swallowing the lump that had lodged there. "Then how did you heal me?" she finished on a disbelieving squeak.

He nodded in the direction of her neck. "The priest's gift," he said. "The cherrywood burl and this water healed you," he told her, waving at the pool behind her.

Sadie darted a cautious look at the water, turning just enough so that she could see it without losing sight of Morgan.

"Wh-where is the burl now?"

He waved his hand again. "Gone. Dissolved. The magic was spent saving your life."

Sadie dropped her chin and toyed with the button on Morgan's shirt that she wore. What he was saying was fantastical. But, more important, why was he saying it?

Could he not accept that they'd died?

"Morgan," she said, looking at him, taking a small step closer, and holding out her right hand, palm up. "Do you see this?" she asked. "The scars are gone. And that's not possible. There's no such thing as the kind of magic you're talking about. A person can't get shot and then just . . . just heal. And eight-year-old scars can't disappear as if they never existed."

"Then explain to me what has happened," he softly demanded, his eyes now piercing points of solid green flint.

"We died. Both of us, or you wouldn't be here with me now. That cut on your leg wouldn't be gone. It's the only logical explanation, Morgan. We're dead." She suddenly smiled. "And we've landed in heaven."

He took a step toward her. "Mercedes."

Sadie beat him to it. She ran and jumped into his arms, laughing up at him. "And we're going to make love now, husband, before God realizes his mistake and kicks us out of here," she finished, planting her mouth on his. She pulled him down to the ground until she was sitting and straddling his waist.

Morgan let out a sigh that all but filled her lungs and settled his hands under his head. "That still might happen," he said, smiling up at her, only to sober suddenly as he softly feathered a trembling finger across her cheek. "I was so afraid I'd lost you, wife," he whispered.

Sadie covered his hand on her face. "Me, too. I love you so much, Morgan. I couldn't live without you." She shot him a smile. "I couldn't die without you, either."

She leaned down and kissed the frown on his forehead. She stretched out full-length on top of him and wiggled until her nose was even with his beautifully naked chest, grinning again when she heard him moan.

Sadie traced circles with her fingertip through the furry mat of hair covering his chest. She had a fair amount of area to cover and let it tickle her palm as she ran a lazy path over his muscles. She stopped and explored a nipple, heard him moan again, and ran her tongue over the silky-smooth circle. Hair tickled her lips as she gently suckled, and Morgan sat bolt upright and held her away.

Sadie smiled at his ferocious scowl, patting the spot she'd just licked.

"I promise to let you do the same to me in a minute," she told him. "But I want my wicked way with you first."

"I'll disgrace myself," he said through gritted teeth.

She pushed him back and leaned over him again, her nose inches from his. "We've got an eternity to practice, husband," she said, sitting up and unbuttoning her shirt.

She watched his eyes go from her face to her breasts, and his scowl relaxed. He set his hands behind his head again as she slid the shirt off her shoulders and let it fall to her back.

Sadie cupped her breasts, pushing them together as she leaned forward and let them dangle over his chest. She slowly brushed them back and forth, only to find that now she was the one building with a tension that started in the pit of her stomach and spiraled outward and down to the very center of her femininity.

Sweat broke out on Sadie's forehead. She felt flushed and wet between her thighs, and she couldn't seem to stop shaking with the need to feel Morgan inside her.

His hands came to her breasts, replacing hers that were now digging into his shoulders. He gently fondled her, setting her completely on fire. She may have cried out, Sadie wasn't sure, but she did know that she couldn't make her hips stop moving against him.

His hands left her breasts but were quickly replaced by his mouth. Sadie shouted then, louder than the roar of the waterfall. Morgan lifted her and pushed off his pants, and suddenly there was nothing between her and her husband's rock-hard erection.

Searing heat pushed against the folds of her womanhood, and Morgan's strong hands grabbed her hips and lifted, settling her more intimately onto him.

Sadie felt herself stretching, accepting, taking Morgan inside. She moaned this time, loud and deep and keening, when she felt his mouth cover her breast. He used his hands on her hips to set them into a rhythm, suckled her nipple until she thought she was going to explode.

And she did, gloriously, shouting her pleasure to the granite walls of their wondrous heaven, gasping as each rocketing spasm took her spiraling upward. Morgan shouted his own pleasure, tightening his grip on her hips to help her ride out the light storm they'd created together.

Sadie sprawled on top of him, tucking her head into the crook of his neck, feeling the lingering pulse of her pleasure still throbbing around him.

And they lay together that way, both breathing hard, until their racing hearts stopped trying to out-thump each other.

"It kind of sneaks up on you, doesn't it?" Sadie mumbled into his chest.

"What does?"

Sadie tilted her head back and opened one eye to the sleepy laughter she heard in his voice. "The passion. I thought I was going to spend an hour driving you insane. But I was the one who didn't last five minutes."

He patted her bottom affectionately. "I'm guessing we'll calm down in about thirty years," he said with a chuckle. He rolled them both over until she was beneath him, then kissed her on the forehead. "We'll practice until we get it right."

He brushed the hair from her face with repeated, gentle strokes, staring down at her with shining eyes.

"I love you, Mercedes," he whispered. "As God is my witness, I love you more than life itself, lass. Will you marry me, Mercedes? Just as soon as I find that crazy old priest, will you do me the honor of making our vows legal?"

Sadie stretched her arms over her head like a lazy cat and thought about making Morgan wait for her answer. But she was too sated, too happy, and too much in love with him to let him suffer one more second.

"There must be a priest somewhere around here," she told him. "And as soon as you find him, I'll marry you, Morgan. Do you think we can make babies in heaven?"

He rolled off her and stood up, then leaned down and picked her up. He waded into the shimmering pool until the water reached his waist and dropped her without warning. Sadie sank to the bottom, retaliating by touching him intimately and kissing his erection.

She could hear his shout even under the water.

They practiced getting it right three more times, moving from the warm, shimmering water to the sandy shore to the far side of the pool under the thick spray of the waterfall.

Sadie lay exhausted on top of Morgan on the rocks, not even possessing enough strength to let out a respectable sigh. Morgan, though, could still manage enough energy to stroke her bottom gently with a lazy hand.

He lifted her chin to look at him. "You're a scary woman, wife, when you lose your shyness."

She wrinkled her nose and tiredly patted his chest. "You ain't seen nothing yet, husband."

Sadie didn't know where the man found the strength, but he lifted her away from him and gently set her on the rocks beside him. She looked out over the waterfall. They'd ended up underneath it somehow, and the unusually warm water ran in a curtain that sparkled like sun-washed glass before it crashed into the pool at their feet.

Sadie's stomach rumbled, and she laughed. "I guess you can get hungry in heaven," she said, rubbing her belly. "But I'm simply too tired to eat."

"And I'm too tired to hike back to the logging camp right now and get our stuff," he said, standing and holding out his hand. "How about a small nap first, then I'll go get our stuff?"

She took his offered hand and stood up, looking around the water-walled chamber they were in.

"Oh my God!" She gasped, shaking off his hand and walking in small circles, staring at the ground.

She was walking on small pebbles of gold.

"This is it, Morgan!" she squeaked, whirling to face him. "Jedediah's mine. We found it!"

He scuffed at the ground with his bare toe, bending down and picking up one of the nuggets so that he could hold it up to the light of the waterfall.

"It seems we have," he said softly, his voice barely audible over the noise of the falls.

Sadie walked back to him and examined the nugget in his hand, letting out a weary sigh. "Fat lot of good it does me now," she grumbled. "The park will never be built."

Morgan looked at her, his smile sad and his eyes dark. "What would happen if we were not dead, Mercedes? What if you were alive and had all this gold at your disposal? What would you do?"

"I'd build the park."

"And then what would happen to this magical place?" he asked, dropping the gold and turning her to face him. "If we're alive, and this place really exists, then what will happen to it when all the tourists come to visit your park?"

She frowned at him. "It's a moot point. We're dead."

He shook her slightly. "But if we weren't," he persisted. "What would happen to this gorge?"

She had to think about that, and she didn't like what she was thinking. "It would be ruined," she told him. "Once it was discovered—and it would be—then the people would trample over every square inch of this ground, trying to get to the gold."

He nodded and released her shoulders. "That's right, they would. Your park, your father's legacy—it would all be forgotten, overtaken by the mystery of this special place."

"But we're dead, Morgan," Sadie insisted. "Simply based on the fact that nothing like this can exist in the real world. It isn't possible."

Morgan said nothing more. He took her hand and led her around the edge of the waterfall and along the shore of the pool until they were back on the sandy beach. He picked up the shirt she'd discarded and settled it over her shoulders, wrapping her up and grasping it closed over her breasts. He kissed her nose.

"Let it go for now," he softly entreated. "There will be plenty of time to worry about this later. We both need some sleep first. Then I'll find us something to eat, and we'll deal with our problems on full bellies."

He used his grip on her shirt to pull her down as he spoke, and Sadie happily let him. She cuddled into his embrace the moment they landed, closed her eyes, wrapped her arms tightly around him, and quickly fell asleep.

Chapter Twenty

Sadie awoke to the strong odor of a wet dog. She opened her eyes and reached up to push Faol's tongue away from her face, but her hand stopped in mid-reach and changed direction to poke Morgan in the shoulder.

"We've got company," she whispered, quickly wiggling to sink farther behind him. "Father Daar's here," she squeaked a bit louder, poking him harder.

Good Lord. She and Morgan were as naked as the day they'd been born, her shirt thrown off and lying behind her. And if they weren't dead already, the scowl on the old priest's face likely would kill them.

"Ya have two minutes to get up and get dressed," Father Daar snapped, pointing an age-bent finger at them. "Or you'll be saying your wedding vows naked."

Morgan sat up and used his body to shield Sadie from the scandalized gaze of the priest. She took advantage of his broad back and quickly found his shirt and slipped it on, buttoning it all the way up to her neck.

"Turn around, old man," Morgan growled. He waited until the priest complied, then looked to see that Mercedes was modestly covered. He grinned at her furiously blushing face.

"Are you ready to say the words, lass?" he asked, feathering a finger over her red-hot cheek.

Mortified beyond any ability to speak, Sadie nodded.

Morgan stood up, sauntered past the still waiting priest, and gathered the clothes he'd dropped by the end of the pool. Sadie scrambled to her feet and made sure she was decently covered to her knees, thankful that Morgan's shirt had long tails.

Her soon-to-be-for-real husband wasn't the least bit shy about his own state of undress, nor did he seem worried that they'd been caught sleeping together—naked—by the priest. He carried her bundle of clothes back to her, frowning at Father Daar as he passed him.

Sadie quickly dressed, pushing Faol out of the way several times in order to tie her boots.

She suddenly gasped. "Faol was killed, too!" she yelped, just now realizing what the wolf's presence meant. She gasped again. "And Father Daar. You're dead!"

The priest turned and looked down at himself. "I am?" he echoed in dismay.

Morgan sat beside her, putting his own boots on, but he stopped and looked at her.

"You're not dead, old man," Morgan said impatiently. He waved one large hand in the air. “Mercedes thinks she’s died and gone to heaven,” he explained. “Thanks to your magic.”

Looking more confused than relieved, Father Daar turned his attention to Sadie. “What makes ya think we’re all dead, girl?” he asked.

Sadie held up her right hand, palm toward him. “I’m healed, Father. All my scars are gone. And I was shot. I felt the bullet rip through my body, but I don’t hurt, I’m not bleeding, and I don’t have any scars anymore. So I’m dead.”

The priest darted a quick look at the still shimmering pool, then turned his penetrating gaze to Morgan as he lifted one bushy white eyebrow. “Ya used the burl again, didn’t ya?” Father Daar said in a low voice, waving at the water. “Ya exposed our secret to save your woman’s life.”

Sadie looked at Morgan and saw him nod.

“And being a modern, she don’t believe this is possible?” the priest continued, drawing Sadie’s attention back.

She looked at Morgan, and he nodded again.

Sadie stood up, deciding she could speak for herself. She walked up to the priest and pulled her shirttail from her pants, lifting it high enough to expose her stomach.

“The bullet went into the middle of my back,” she told him. “And came out my side,” she added, turning and pointing at her back. “And I should be covered with old scars here, from the fire that killed my sister.”

She dropped the shirttail and crossed her arms under her breasts. “I’m completely healed, Father.”

She heard Morgan sigh again right beside her and looked to see him rubbing a hand over his face.

"We can't say our vows until she understands," Morgan said to the priest. "She has to realize what she's getting for a husband."

"Then explain it to her," Father Daar said. "And be quick about it." He pointed at Sadie's middle. "At the rate you two are going, your firstborn will be sprouting teeth before ya're properly wed."

Sadie stepped back, covering her belly with her hand. "What firstborn? What are you talking about?"

"Are ya telling me it was an innocent nap you two were just having?" Father Daar asked.

Sadie felt her face heat to near flaming.

"We'll say our vows as soon as she understands," Morgan repeated.

"You'll say them now before me and God, or I'm going home and washing my hands of ya. There's a terrible storm brewing in this valley that's needing your attention. But not until you're properly wed."

Still unable to raise her mortified eyes above Morgan's belt, Sadie waited for him to decide if he really wanted to marry her or not. If they were all dead, what did it matter?

And if they were really alive?

"If—if you don't want to get married, we won't," she said to his chest, still unable to raise her eyes any higher, fearing what she might see in his. "We'll forget the rest of the week and just go our separate ways now."

She was suddenly hauled up against Morgan's side, turned to face the priest, her ribs crushed so fiercely it was a wonder they didn't crack.

"Begin!" Morgan snapped to Father Daar.

As a declaration of love, that one word sounded magical to Sadie. Yes, they would begin their life together right now. And they'd have the most blessed union heaven had ever seen.

Their vows would be real this time, in this wonderful place that was more beautiful than any church Sadie had ever seen. They would have a storybook marriage that would last for eternity.

Father Daar had taken a small book out of his pocket and had already begun reading their vows. Sadie smoothed down the front of her flannel shirt and decided she probably should pay attention. But the moment she started listening, she realized she didn't understand a word the priest was saying.

She squinted and leaned forward to see the book he was reading from, and she didn't recognize any of the words. She covered the page with her hand, making him frown up at her.

"What language is that?" she asked.

"Gaelic," Daar said, moving the book from under her hand and holding it up again.

"But I don't know what you're saying," she interrupted, making his frown deepen. "Can't you translate it into English? And why are you using Gaelic to begin with?"

He cleared his throat, turned his frown into a glare, and shot it at Morgan, then back at her. "Because it's our language, girl," Father Daar said impatiently. "And since we outnumber you two to one, we get to choose the vows."

Sadie waved at the book. "Then say them. But we're going to add our own vows—in English, so I know what I'm promising."

With a lift of his eyebrows at her impertinence, Father Daar raised the book up and began reading again. The words sounded more like curses than pledges to Sadie, with sharp consonants and guttural vowels that were more spat than spoken.

Faol had come to view the proceedings and was sitting beside Sadie, leaning on her leg, his tongue lolling out and his eyes a sappy iridescent green as he stared up at her. Morgan, disturbingly silent beside her, had her right hand clasped so tightly Sadie thought he was afraid she'd change her mind before the service was over.

Father Daar suddenly quit speaking and turned expectant blue eyes on her. Sadie guessed she was supposed to say "I do."

She took both of Morgan's hands into hers, straightened her shoulders, and started her vows.

"I love you, Morgan MacKeage. And I promise to be your wife for all eternity, to cherish you, to honor your spirit, and to guard with my soul this love that we've found."

She squeezed his hands. "And we'll have lots of babies together and raise them in a house overflowing with love. We'll teach them the wonders of nature and bring them up . . . bring them up . . ."

She couldn't go on. Her heart was near to bursting,

she was getting all mushy inside, and a lump the size of a basketball was caught in her throat. She shook her head and swallowed and forced herself to continue.

"And I promise to love you forever," she finished on a choked whisper.

That finally said, Sadie sucked in her breath and waited for Morgan to say his vows.

"You're mine," he growled, pulling her so forcibly into his chest that the air rushed out of her lungs with a gasp.

You're mine?

That was it?

Morgan's mouth covered hers with that same downright possession she'd seen in his eyes. He kissed the outrage right out of her before it could gather a foothold. And he kissed her some more, until the impatient coughing of a scandalized priest broke them up.

"It's done, then," Father Daar said with finality, rather loudly. "Now, let's eat. We'll have us a wedding feast of nice tasty trout. Stop mauling your wife, Morgan, and catch us some supper."

But her husband wasn't paying the priest any mind. Sadie pinched Morgan in the side to get him to come up for air.

"Go catch us some trout from one of the cooler pools below, Morgan," Father Daar said, taking Sadie by the arm now that she was free of Morgan. "We'll build a fire, cook your catch, and then you and I will set our minds to convincing your wife that we all have many years left before we finally see heaven," he added, walking her toward the sandy beach by the pool.

He looked back over his shoulder at Morgan and crackled with laughter. "Not that you have any chance of getting there yourself, warrior. They rarely allow pagans through the gates."

Sadie didn't know what surprised her the most, that the priest had called her husband a pagan or that he'd called him a warrior.

Morgan picked up his sword and settled it over his back, his glare fierce enough to fry Father Daar where he stood.

"You may begin the explaining without me, old man," Morgan said. "Faol. *Tàr as. Falbh,"* he added, waving the wolf toward the exit of the pool, then walking through the towering trees himself.

Staring at the spot where he'd disappeared, Sadie posed her question to the priest. "What did he just say?"

"Tàr as?" Father Daar repeated. "It means 'move off' or 'go.' And *falbh* means 'guard.' " He started walking around the cathedral-like grotto and picked up small pieces of wood. "He's set the wolf to guarding the entrance," he said as he continued his work, putting the branches into a pile. He straightened and looked at her. "I told you befriending Faol would come in handy one day."

Sadie put her hands on her hips and faced the priest. "So you're saying this Maine wolf knows Gaelic?" she asked. "A language that's been dead for hundreds of years?"

He sat down on the moss near the pile of branches he'd made and looked up at her. "It's not dead, girl. Gaelic's still spoken in some parts of Scotland." He suddenly grinned. "Now, watch," he said, touching the branches with his skinny cane while he muttered some words under his breath.

The wood erupted into flames, and Sadie stepped back. She quickly stepped closer, glaring at the now crackling fire.

"That's not magic," she said. "Not in heaven. Anything's possible here," she said, waving at the tall granite walls.

Father Daar sighed loudly enough to be heard over the noise of the waterfall and rubbed his hands over his face. He looked up at her and patted a place beside him. "Come. Sit with me, Mercedes, so that I can explain what has happened to you."

With a sigh of her own, Sadie sat down beside the crazy old priest and stared at the softly crackling fire.

"Do you remember my visit last week?" Daar asked, using his cane to push more wood onto the fire. "And your feet? Were the cuts not healed the next morning when you woke?"

"They were gone," she admitted, frowning to herself.

"And were you not alive when that little miracle happened?"

She looked at him. "It wasn't a miracle," she disputed. "Miracles are big things that happen to deserving people."

"And you're not deserving?"

"That's not the point. God wouldn't trouble himself with small cuts on my feet. He has much more important things to worry about."

Daar harrumphed and scrubbed his face with his

hands again, shaking his head. He finally looked at her, his expression confounded. "The whole world is still sitting out there, Mercedes, just beyond those trees," he said, pointing at where Faol and Morgan had disappeared. "Your valley, your mother and Callum, your two simple-minded friends, and the man who shot you. All are still there, all still waiting for you."

Sadie looked toward the trees. She hadn't even thought about trying to leave. "Then, if I'm not really dead, will my scars return if I leave here?" she whispered. "Will I be ugly again?"

"Ya can't be what you never were," Daar snapped. He blew out a tired breath. "But no, the scars are gone for good." He frowned. "Which will be hard to explain to your mother, I'm guessing. She's a modern, too, and won't be able to understand any better than you can."

"What do you mean, 'a modern'? You say that as if you and Morgan are ancient or something. And Morgan's not in the military. So why did you call him a warrior?"

Daar kneaded the back of his neck and finished by scratching his beard. "Because that's what he is. Or, rather, what he was," he said. "I had a little mishap with the magic six years ago and brought Morgan eight hundred years forward in time."

"You *what?*"

He frowned at her incredulousness. "I made a mistake," he said, lifting his hairy-white chin. "I was only wanting to bring Morgan's brother, Greylen, forward, but nine other men came with him, including Callum and Ian and Morgan. And MacBain," he added with a scowl.

"Callum?" Sadie squeaked. "Are you saying the man my mother is going to marry is like . . . like Morgan? That he's old . . . and also a warrior?" Sadie scrambled to her feet and balled her hands into fists. "What are you saying?" she shouted.

Father Daar lifted his cane into the air and began muttering words softly to himself again. Sadie's eyes widened as she saw the cane grow to nearly double its size and start to hum with gentle vibrations.

"Take hold of this, Mercedes," Daar said, holding it out to her. "If ya want to understand, hold this, and I'll show you."

She stepped back. "No."

"Aw, come on, girl," he cajoled. "Where's your spirit of adventure? Do ya not want to know who your husband truly is?"

She didn't understand any of this. What he was saying was impossible. But her scars were gone, she was in a veritable rain forest that shouldn't exist anywhere near Maine, and the old priest's cane was now glowing like a finger of lightning.

Hesitantly, but with more curiosity than fear, Sadie reached out and took hold of the surprisingly cool cane.

Light entered her head, flashes of brilliance that should have blinded her. But she was able to see something slowly appear in her mind's eye. A scene out of a picture book. Men on horseback, carrying swords and dressed strangely. Actually, some of the men were naked. They were fighting a mighty battle.

She could smell the dust being kicked up by the trampling feet of the horses. She could hear the clash of the swords striking each other. Sadie immediately recognized Morgan. And Callum. She could see Callum trying to unseat a man whose face was covered in paint. Lightning flashed over their heads. Thunder boomed. The very air around them became charged with the energy of a quickly descending storm.

A torrential rain suddenly blanketed the chaos, darkening her vision. There was an intense explosion of light, the detonation making Sadie flinch in surprise. She tightened her grip on the priest's cane. Suddenly, there was only silent white light as pure as the center of the sun, muted spectrums of color shading the edges.

The men reappeared, no longer fighting but scattered in dazed disarray on an earth that was the same but different. It was more lush. Greener. There were buildings. Cars and trucks were zooming by.

Sadie looked for Morgan. He was first holding his head, covering his eyes with his hands, then suddenly patting his body as if he didn't believe he existed. She cried out at the fear she saw on his face, the confusion, the very terror of what had happened to him.

Horses lay scattered around the men, dazed with terror and screaming, trying to stand. Sadie watched Morgan run to one of them and recognized the horse he'd been riding the first day she'd met him.

"What's its name?" she softly asked the priest standing and watching beside her in her mind's eye.

"Gràdhag," Daar answered. "It means 'pet.' "

Sadie let go of the cane and stepped back. The

vision left as mysteriously as it had come. She turned and stared out over the still shimmering pool made by the waterfall.

"That's why Morgan is afraid of thunderstorms," she said. "He was caught in one and ripped from his home and brought . . . brought here."

"Aye. He did not care for the journey," Father Daar said from right beside her, also looking out at the waterfall. "Nor has he cared much for the new life he's found himself living."

He took hold of her shoulder and gently turned her to face him. "Until now, child. He's found you, Mercedes. And he's not going to let anything come between the two of you. Not my magic, not the blackness visiting this valley, not even your own inability to believe. He's said his vows before God and man and claimed you as his. You belong to each other now. So accept what I have shown you for the gift that it is."

"Morgan called you *drùidh*. What does that mean? Who are you?"

"I'm what your modern language would call a wizard, and I'm nearly fifteen hundred years old."

"A wizard?" she repeated, taking a step back.

He frowned at her. "And a priest," he said defensively. "And a hungry one at that," he tacked on, looking toward where the pool spilled into the valley. He walked back to the fire and sat down again, working it back into flames.

Sadie stared at the cane he used as a poker. What he was saying, what she had just seen, it was . . . it was the stuff of fantasies and ancient legends that continued to survive despite modern science explaining it away.

But science couldn't explain her missing scars or the very fact that she was alive right now. And neither could she. Her dead theory made more sense, but she hoped with all her heart that she was alive. She had a new baby sister coming soon, and she wanted to be here when she was born. She wanted to see her mother get married. She wanted to have babies of her own.

So, yes. She wanted to believe in the magic.

Morgan stepped through the towering trees just then and stopped and stared at her. There were several trout hanging from his belt, his sword was still on his back, and if she looked hard enough, she could see that same warrior from the vision the priest had given her.

And Sadie knew then, no matter what means had brought them together, that she loved Morgan.

She launched herself into his arms, breaking into overjoyed laughter, confident that he would catch her and hold her safe—forever.

"We're alive, Morgan." She laughed into his startled face, which she couldn't stop kissing over and over. "Wonderfully alive, thanks to a wizard's magic."

He held her so tightly that her last words were squeaked rather than spoken. He buried his face in her neck, his whole body trembling with what she suspected was relief.

"I swear you two spend more time cuddling than looking to practical matters," Father Daar called from the fire. "Ya have a lifetime for that foolishness, Morgan. I want my supper."

Still crushing her tightly to him, Morgan carried

her over to the fire and set her down by the priest. He tore the trout from his belt and tossed them at Father Daar's feet.

"Eat, then, old man," Morgan said, darting a look at Sadie and then back at the priest. "I haven't the time right now. I've got to go find our sniper before he finds us again."

Sadie was standing before she finished gasping. "You will not! The man has a gun, and all you've got is that . . . that sword," she said emphatically, waving a hand at the inadequate weapon sticking up past his head. "You're staying right here."

Morgan took hold of her shoulders and pinned her with his eyes. "As beautiful and warm as this place is, we cannot hide here forever, *gràineag*. We have to leave eventually, and we cannot do that until I'm sure we'll be safe."

He pulled her against him gently and cupped the back of her head into his shoulder. "I'll be careful, wife. He won't even see me coming."

"It—it's not Dwayne and Harry," she muttered into his shoulder, trying to wiggle back to look at him. But he wouldn't loosen his hand. "Don't hurt them. It's someone else."

"I know, Mercedes. I will not hurt them." He finally leaned back to look at her, now holding her hair in his fist, his grip emphasizing his words. "In return, you must promise to stay here with Daar. You'll be safe with the *drùidh*."

He was holding her so tightly she couldn't even nod. His entire body was filled with tension.

"I'll protect Father Daar," she told him instead.

Father Daar snorted at her response.

The right corner of Morgan's mouth curved in amusement. He kissed her soundly on the lips, then stepped back.

"Wait." Sadie turned to the priest as she untied the leather cord she was still wearing. "Father Daar. Give Morgan another cherrywood knot to take with him," she said, handing the leather to the priest.

Father Daar clasped his cane to his chest protectively, fingering the empty leather cord now in his hand. "I can't," he said, darting a look from her to Morgan. He lifted his shoulders in a shrug. "I've only one decent-sized burl left that would have enough power to do any good," he explained. "And if I take it off, my staff will be useless."

"Then give him your whole cane," Sadie insisted, reaching for it.

"Nay!" Daar yelped, quickly tucking the cane behind his back. "He's liable to set this entire valley on fire. The magic's too powerful for mere mortals."

"Well, he needs something."

"I have you, wife," Morgan said, turning her to face him. "Nothing can stop me from coming back to you, Mercedes."

"You'll have your clan's help," Daar interjected. "Callum and Charlotte stopped by my cabin yesterday on their way to Gu Bràth. Callum said he'd return with Greylen and Ian." He waved in the direction of the valley. "They're probably already out there, hunting for whoever broke into Mercedes' cabin."

Morgan gave Sadie a reassuring smile. "See? You have nothing to worry about."

"Does your brother or Callum or this Ian fellow have guns?"

"Aye. We all do."

"Then where's yours?"

"Home in my gun cabinet. I'll be okay, *gràineag*. Now, make our priest some supper," he said, kissing her quickly on her still protesting mouth. "And try not to kill the man with your cooking," he said as a parting shot, turning and loping into the darkness at the end of the pool. He disappeared before Sadie could tell him at least to take Faol.

She turned back to Father Daar.

"Did you know that burned trout is an acquired taste?" she asked the man of the cloth who was still eyeing her suspiciously, still guarding his cane behind his back.

"I do know what that word is now, that you asked me about the other day," the old priest said instead, his clear blue eyes suddenly sparkling with mischief.

"Gray-agch?" Sadie whispered, stepping closer. "What? What does it mean?"

The old man rubbed his beard with the end of his cane and sent her a satisfied smirk. "Well, girl. *Gràineag* is Gaelic for 'hedgehog.' "

Chapter Twenty-one

Morgan stepped through the towering trees that protected the pool and out into the cold night, letting his eyes adjust from the bright glow of the grotto to the darkness of the forest. Faol whined beside him and stood up, his tail wagging and his eyes glowing green with their own inner light. The wolf was licking his lips, finishing off the trout Morgan had given him earlier.

"You be ready, my friend," he told the wolf in Gaelic. "I give Mercedes only an hour before she comes sneaking out here. Guard her, and keep her from wandering off the side of this mountain and getting herself killed."

He hunched down and ruffled the wolf's fur. "It seems we've gotten ourselves a *gràineag,* wolf, who has more heart than common sense sometimes. Nothing else can explain her acceptance of us."

Morgan smiled into the night as he thought about the afternoon he'd just spent with Mercedes. She'd been so playful and passionate when they'd made love. And so open with her now perfect body. Not an ounce of shyness did she possess, now that she felt beautiful. He would give his sword arm to have possessed her that way before she'd been healed. He'd never have that chance now, thanks to the magic. He would never be able to prove to Mercedes that love did not come with conditions.

Morgan stood up and let his gaze scan the quiet forest. "I'm going to find Greylen and the others," he told Faol. He reached into his pocket and pulled out a fistful of gold nuggets he'd taken from the pool. "I won't go after Mercedes' sniper. Grey and Callum and Ian can do that. I'll set out bait and wait for them to push our prey into my trap."

He gave Faol one final pat and a warning. "Be alert," he told the wolf. "And keep our woman away from the river."

And then Morgan walked into the night, towards the dark force that roamed his valley.

Though Sadie didn't know it, her husband's prediction was off by a good two hours. Sadie paced to the edge of the pool and stared down at the shimmering water which continued to glow with magical intensity. It appeared to be daylight within the confines of the granite cliffs, but when she looked skyward, the mist rose into blackness. It was the deep of night outside her own little heaven, and Sadie couldn't stop thinking about her shooter and the danger Morgan was walking into.

Sadie wished she had bought a handgun. But even

if she had, it most likely would be back at the old logging camp, with the rest of her stuff.

And that was another thing that was bothering her. The logging camp and her backpack. Jean Lavoie's diary was there as well, with the section pertaining to this cliff, and its approximate location, circled in red ink. If whoever shot her stumbled onto it, he would know where to look for the gold.

And he would find this mystical gorge.

Sadie skirted the edge of the pool, walking beneath the waterfall and scooping up a handful of gold. She turned and looked out over her small piece of heaven.

If this place were discovered, it surely would be destroyed.

In order to keep this magic a secret, she would have to build the wilderness park farther down in the valley and find another way to access it instead of through MacKeage land.

But she would have to worry about solving that problem later. Instead, Sadie set her mind to the bigger problem at hand now. She had to go to the logging camp and retrieve that diary before it was found.

Sadie tucked the handful of gold into her pocket and walked over to the slumbering old priest. She eyed the cane in his hand. She needed some sort of weapon that could protect her if she ran into trouble. It was only two miles to the logging camp and back. With luck, she'd be gone less than an hour. She'd have Father Daar's cane safely tucked back beside him before he woke up, and she'd be sitting here like a dutiful wife long before Morgan returned.

Being as careful as she could, Sadie slowly slipped

the cane from the sleeping priest's hand. She quickly straightened, clasped the warm wood to her chest, and turned and set off at a jog through the magically giant trees.

She nearly ran over Faol when she stepped into the darkness of the forest. The wolf jumped to his feet, whined, and started wagging his tail.

"Shh. You're going to wake Father Daar," she said, giving him a pat on the head. "Feel like a hike, big boy?" she asked, blinking her eyes at the darkness.

It took her a few minutes to locate the North Star and get her bearings and another few minutes for her eyes to adjust completely to the night forest. And then Sadie started south along the edge of Fraser Mountain, toward logging camp number three. Faol trotted ahead of her, his bushy tail wagging like a flag leading the way.

In less than half an hour they reached the camp, and Sadie ran toward the tent her mother and Callum had left standing in wait for her and Morgan's return.

She heard Faol's warning growl at the exact moment a gunshot cracked through the air, the muzzle blast flashing from a tree beside the tent.

Faol's yelp of pain was drowned out by her own scream of surprise. There were several shots in rapid succession, and all Sadie could see was the scurry of moving shadows where Faol had been standing. Another yelp, then the growl of an enraged beast, followed by another crack of gunfire.

Sadie screamed and threw herself toward the tent. She unzipped it and dove inside to find her pack and the knife she usually carried. She pushed around her sleeping bag and dry packs but couldn't find her backpack.

"Looking for this?"

Sadie whirled at the sound of the familiar voice. The beam of a flashlight sliced over her face. She held up her hand to see beyond the glare and gasped.

"Eric!"

He dropped her pack and grabbed her by the hair, pulling her out of the tent. With a yelp of her own, Sadie scrambled on her knees until she could stand up. She watched as Eric quickly scanned the forest with his flashlight, looking for Faol.

"Where's the MacKeage guy that dog belongs to?" Eric asked, turning the flashlight back on her.

"H-he's dead."

"He's not. I saw him carrying you from the water. You were the one I shot." He sent the beam of light over her body.

Sadie gasped, trying to step back, but was pulled up short by his grip on her hair. "You were the one shooting? But why?" she cried, struggling to get free.

He held her tightly. "I was aiming for MacKeage. I wanted him out of the way."

"Out of the way for what?" she whispered, holding herself perfectly still.

"He was distracting you from your hunt for the gold. I'm sure I shot you by mistake," he said, giving her hair a vicious tug.

"You just grazed me. Th-that's why I have this cane," she said, pointing at the cane on the ground by the tent. "But the bullet went into Morgan, and he used up the last of his strength getting me to safety."

"You wouldn't be here if MacKeage were dead. You'd be in town." He tugged her hair again. "Where is he?"

"O-okay, he's not dead. But he's wounded. I have him tucked down by the stream. I'm here to get my phone so I can call for help."

"The phone's not in your pack, Quill. I checked."

"It's got to be." She pulled from his grasp and bent down to her pack, pretending to look for the phone. "I know it's in here."

"No, it's not. And neither is your knife," he said, jerking her upright again. "I have it now. And I also have the diary, including the page you circled."

He released her and pulled his gun out of his belt. "You found the gold, didn't you? That's where MacKeage is now."

"No. No, we didn't find anything. He really is hurt."

Eric shoved her in the direction she'd come from. "The diary says the gold is north of here. So let's just go see."

Sadie bent, picked up Daar's cane, and pretended to use it as a crutch. With a final look over her shoulder at where Faol had disappeared and a prayer that the wolf wasn't too badly hurt, Sadie started limping back toward the stream.

"Why are you doing this?" she asked as she set a course slightly northwest of where Father Daar was. "I want this park as much as you do. I would have told you the moment I found Jedediah's gold."

Eric laughed. "The park's not important to me, Quill. Granted, I'll make a good chunk of money off my land once the park's in operation, but I'd much rather find the gold. Why in hell do you think I talked the consortium into hiring you?"

Sadie stopped and whirled on him. "You shot Morgan over some gold that might not even exist? Are you nuts?"

He aimed the beam of his flashlight down the trail behind them, then poked her with it to get her moving again. "My great-granddaddy wasn't nuts," he said, walking behind her, keeping his beam scanning the woods. "Old Levi Hellman financed the store I now run with what gold Plum was carrying on him when he died."

"Your great-grandfather? Did he . . . was he the one who murdered Jedediah?"

Eric shrugged. "Who the hell knows? Or even cares now? I just know that the Hellmans came into a good chunk of money eighty years ago, and there were stories passed down in our family that speculated about where it came from. And I'm guessing your daddy had heard the rumors, too. That's why he never would discuss his search for the gold with me. And I know he was close to succeeding when the fire destroyed all his research."

"How do you know that?"

"I knew he had Jean Lavoie's diary. I saw his copy."

"When?"

"The night of the fire," he said, his voice low and angry. "And if your sister hadn't caught me, I would have gotten it then."

Sadie whirled on him again, stumbling back when he bumped into her. "What are you saying?"

She could just make out Eric's sneer in the glow of

his flashlight. "I'm saying that your sister didn't burn in the fire, Quill. She was already dead."

She lunged at him with a shriek of anger, one hand coiled into a claw, the cane raised to strike in the other. They went tumbling to the ground, and Sadie tried to reach for his gun as they fought. He hit her on the side of her head with the flashlight, momentarily stunning her with the blow.

Eric rolled to his feet, his gun back in his hand, and kicked her. "After the fire, I spent the next five years trying to talk Frank into resuming his research," he continued as if nothing had happened. "But he'd lost his passion for the hunt. He wouldn't even tell me where he'd found the diary when I alluded to it. I couldn't come right out and mention the diary, because I wasn't supposed to know he had it."

"Then how did you?" Sadie asked, rising onto her hands and knees, clutching the cane in her fist.

"I only knew Frank had found something important. He couldn't wait for you to get home from school. He was like a kid with the key to the candy store."

Sadie glared at him past the flashlight beam. "So you broke into our house and tried to steal what he'd found."

Eric nodded. "But then Caroline came into the study. You really had left a candle burning, Quill," he continued derisively. "Your sister was covering your ass. But we struggled, and that's how the fire started. We knocked over the candle, and Lavoie's diary burned before I could get to it."

Sadie stood up, and Eric took a guarded step back, raising his gun.

"You're a murderer," she said in a low voice. "You killed my sister eight years ago, and you tried to kill me yesterday."

She could just make out that he was shaking his head. "No. It was Morgan MacKeage I was aiming at. Why in hell would I want to kill you?" he asked incredulously. "You're the only one who knows this valley."

"And now I know you're a murderer."

He nodded. "That doesn't matter now. Where's the gold?"

Sadie realized then that he intended to kill her. And that she needed a way to stall for time until Morgan could get here. Surely he'd heard the gunshots. "So where did you really find the diary you gave me?"

He laughed again, somewhat insanely. "I searched every museum in this state for eight years. But those bumbling Dolans managed to find it first. They came into the store last winter bragging their fool heads off that they had the next best thing to a map. And that's when I started making plans to get you back here."

"Why didn't you just work out a deal with Dwayne and Harry?"

He scoffed, waving the gun in the air. "With those two? Between them they don't even have a full brain."

"They found the diary."

"And I found a way to get it from them. Now, where's the gold, Quill?"

"It doesn't exist," she said. "I've already searched this entire side of the mountain. I found the cliff mentioned in the diary, but there was nothing there."

"You're lying." He took a threatening step toward

her, his face twisted in anger in the beam of his flashlight.

"But I did find placer gold in a stream near here," she quickly amended, taking a step back.

He stopped and was silent for several seconds, apparently trying to decide if he believed her or not. Sadie held the cane up in supplication and reached into her pocket with her other hand. She slowly drew out one gold nugget and held it up for Eric to see.

"This is what I found," she said in a voice that belied the anger she felt, handing him the nugget. "It's large, Eric. It must have been close to the source. You could probably be rich just panning that stream. I don't think there's an actual mine, Eric. I think Jedediah found only this heavy placer gold."

He put the nugget into his shirt pocket, then took his flashlight and waved it at the trail. "Then let's go, Quill. Show me."

Sadie turned and started them back in the direction of the stream, frantically thinking of what she should do next. Where the hell was her husband?

And where should she lead Eric? To Prospect River? Or to the stream? She could buy a couple of hours waiting for Morgan to show up by taking Eric to the stream well below the pool and then pretend to search for the exact spot where she'd found the nugget.

Sadie clasped Daar's cane protectively to her chest, then remembered it was supposed to be her crutch. She started using it like a cane and tried to think of a way to make the magic work for her without blowing them all to kingdom come.

What had the old priest mumbled to the cane when

he started the fire? She needed to be able to speak to the cane. And the only word she knew in Gaelic was *hedgehog.*

Morgan snapped his head up at the sound of gunfire echoing down the mountain. It was coming not from where Mercedes should have been waiting safely for him but from the old logging camp, where she'd probably gone.

He knew she wouldn't stay put.

Morgan turned his gaze down the mountain to where Grey and Callum were trying to drive anyone lurking in the woods toward him. But they probably still were a couple of miles away. Ian had been posted at the river, protecting everyone's back.

Sweat now covering his forehead, Morgan abandoned his post and started running upstream at an angle that sent him toward the logging camp, hoping to intercept whoever had fired those shots.

As they finally neared the stream, Sadie began speaking to Eric again, her voice loud enough that she hoped it would warn Morgan of her presence and that she was not alone.

She hoped Morgan had heard Eric's gunshots. An hour was enough time for Morgan to run to her rescue, wasn't it?

And Sadie worried about Faol. Was the wolf fatally wounded? Dead? Or was he quietly following them?

"How did you find the logging camp?" Sadie asked, still walking with a pretend limp, still trying to stall for time.

"That pack you picked up last Sunday," Eric said. "I sewed a transmitter into the bottom of it."

Sadie stopped and looked back. "A transmitter?"

"I sell them for hunting dogs," he told her, nudging her shoulder to keep her moving. "They're good for more than two miles."

"But why, Eric? Why leave me alone for ten weeks and then suddenly start interfering?"

"Because the Dolans arrived. And I heard about your date with MacKeage, and I didn't like the distraction he was making for you. So I decided it was time I intervened."

"Why ransack my cabin? It was you, wasn't it?"

"Because you always keep a journal, and I hoped you had made notes from Lavoie's diary. That day I brought you the photos, I was going to look for it."

They finally reached the stream, and the anger of knowing she'd been forced to walk and talk calmly with the man who had murdered her sister threatened to boil over. Sadie stopped beside the water and turned, forcing herself to be calm.

"This is it," she said in an even tone, using Daar's cane to point at the stream. "This is where I found the nugget."

"Where?" he asked, scanning the rippling water with the beam of his flashlight.

"Just up there." Sadie pointed at where she could hear the water churning over a sharp drop of ledge. "There's a tiny bowl that forms an eddy just below that ledge. And the bottom of the pool is littered with nuggets."

She led him to the small eddy. Sadie turned so

that Eric wouldn't see her reach into her pocket and palmed a handful of the nuggets, hiding them in her fist as she made her way to the edge of the small pool over the falls.

"There!" she yelled over the noise of the rippling cascade, throwing the nuggets into the churning water. "Shine your light there, at the eddy."

As she had hoped, Eric took one last cautious look around and tucked his gun into his belt. He scrambled over the strewn boulders to the edge of the eddy and shone his flashlight into the pool of water.

Faint bits of gold sparkled back at him.

Sadie took a small step away from him, into the blackness of the forest, but stopped when Eric turned his flashlight on her.

"Get down here," he said. "Hold the light for me."

Taking a look around, Sadie sighed and climbed down to Eric. Where in hell was Morgan? She may have foolishly gotten herself into this mess, but he was supposed to get her out of it.

She crouched beside Eric. The moment he tried to hand her the flashlight, Sadie took Daar's cane and smacked him over the back, putting all the force of her anger behind the blow. She heard Eric splashing in the pool as he tried to get back to his feet in the water. He shouted for her to stop, but she continued to run until gunfire erupted and tree bark exploded beside her. Sadie stopped and slowly turned around. Eric was standing in the pool, water dripping from his hair and clothes, the beam of his flashlight glinting off the barrel of his gun. He cocked the hammer to fire again, and aimed the weapon at her chest.

"Wait," she said, "I lied. This is nothing," she added, waving at the nuggets in the water. "There's more gold upstream than you could carry in a lifetime. But it's hidden. I can show you were it is."

Eric was silent for several seconds, then suddenly he waved the gun. "Then let's go. But if you run again, Quill," he added in a snarl as he stepped out of the pool, "I won't miss next time."

Chapter Twenty-two

Sadie led the way toward the magical pool, where she hoped Father Daar and his Gaelic words would make the cane do something magical to save them.

Where was Morgan? And Callum and the others? Why wasn't this mountain teeming with warriors, dammit?

Sadie saw the glow of the grotto ahead and breathed a sigh of relief.

"What's that light?" Eric asked from behind her.

"It must be coming daybreak."

"We're on the west side of the mountain," he countered, moving up beside her and peering through the tall trees. "The sun won't reach here for hours."

"It's a very high waterfall. Hear it, Eric? It sends up a mist that the sun's rays must be touching. It's filtering the light down."

Sadie led him through the trees until they reached the edge of the large, shimmering pool. She inconspicuously searched for Father Daar, but the priest was nowhere in sight.

Suddenly, she spotted him on the far side of the pool, just to the left of the waterfall. He was frantically tugging on the branch of a cherrywood tree. Sadie immediately led Eric to the right side of the pool and spoke loudly, trying to warn Father Daar of their presence.

"Wait until you see it, Eric. The entire floor of the cave is covered in gold nuggets."

She saw Father Daar shoot upright and whirl to face them. And then the old priest ducked behind the tree he'd been tugging on. He quietly pulled on a back branch instead.

"Where is it, Quill?" Eric asked, stopping and staring up at the towering cliffs surrounding them. "Where's the gold?"

"It's there, hidden by the falls," she said, using the cane to point to the far end of the pool. "Just walk behind it."

He nudged her forward with his gun. "You go first."

"I can't," she said, leaning heavily on the cane. "Just let me rest here for a minute."

She started to sit down, but Eric grabbed her arm and pulled her along after him. There was a loud snap from Daar's direction, and Sadie watched in horror as the branch he'd been tugging on broke free and fell on top of him.

"Who the hell is that?" Eric hissed, turning his gun toward the priest.

Sadie rapped Eric's hand with her cane, but he didn't drop the gun, instead whirling to pull her off balance. At the same time, an angry roar came from the lower end of the pool. Sadie saw Morgan standing with his sword in his hand at the entrance to the grotto.

And Faol was standing just in front of Morgan, his hackles raised and his teeth bared. Blood slowly oozed from where Eric's bullet had grazed his chest, but the wound didn't keep Faol from growling at Eric.

With his arm now firmly around her neck, Eric started backing away, pulling her deeper into the pool. "I'll kill her, MacKeage!" he shouted, touching the barrel of his gun to her head. "Slowly walk over to your right, to the cliff wall."

"Tàs as," Morgan hissed at Faol, using his knee to push him to the right. In unison, Morgan and the wolf moved toward the cliff.

"Remember the magic, girl!" Father Daar shouted.

Having forgotten about the priest, Eric whirled in his direction, spinning Sadie with him.

Father Daar pointed a finger at her. "Use it!"

Sadie was violently turned around again at the sound of a growl, and a gunshot rang out beside her head. Sadie screamed when she saw Morgan, running toward her with his sword raised, fold in half and fall to the ground. Faol lunged from the edge of the pool, and Eric stepped back and fired again.

Sadie slammed her cane into Eric's ribs. "No!" she screamed, striking him again, struggling to get free and reach Morgan.

Faol knocked them both off balance enough that Sadie was able to push Eric away and scramble to the edge of the pool. She reached Morgan just as another gunshot sounded, the bullet ricocheting off the ground beside them. Morgan rolled in a blur of movement, pulling Sadie with him as he grabbed the cane out of her hand.

He rose to his knees with his back to her, one hand grasping the cane, the other hand covered in blood pressed against his side. He held the cane over his head, pointed it at Eric, and shouted something in Gaelic.

Lightning suddenly cracked with blinding brilliance through the air, charging the mist with a rainbow of colors. The ground beneath them began to tremble. The cliffs began to groan and rumble. Large chunks of granite broke from the towering walls and fell into the water with thunderous splashes.

Eric's gun fired several more times. Light swirled through the grotto, and Sadie could no longer see Eric as he became surrounded by black whorls clawing at him through the mist.

Sadie screamed, not understanding what was happening.

Morgan continued to shout, the cane in his hand sparking with blinding energy. The mountain groaned louder, violently shaking as if trying to shrug off the chaos. Huge blocks of granite fell around them. Uprooted trees came crashing down, vibrating the earth with deadly shivers.

Black fingers chilled with the stench of death swirled past her, the howl of their rage making Sadie's ears hurt. She saw Eric clearly for one blinding moment, running to where she had told him the gold was, as the fingers reached him, clawing menacingly. She could hear his screams.

And her own. She could hear the mountain growling as it crashed around them. Morgan turned and pushed her, telling her to run.

But Sadie couldn't move.

Morgan slammed into her, throwing them both back against a large piece of the fallen granite wall. He used his body to cover hers as chunks of debris rained down around them with such relentless violence that she could no longer hear her own screams. The air detonated with the percussion of a sonic boom, and the cane in Morgan's hand whispered a mournful sigh before it simply dissolved into ash.

And the chaos suddenly stopped.

Silence replaced it. The air was still. The earth no longer rumbled, and the sound of the waterfall had ceased.

Sadie blinked in the dim light of dawn breaking over the summit of Fraser Mountain and looked past Morgan's shoulder. Destruction lay everywhere like a volcanic eruption. A gaping hole had opened several hundred yards deep into the mountain, and the sharp cliffs that had formed the grotto now lay crumbled into talus. The waterfall had been sealed off, the gold and most of the pool now deeply buried beneath boulders. The giant trees, most of them uprooted, some of them still standing but with their tops snapped off, littered the ground like discarded toothpicks.

The destruction was complete.

"Morgan!" she screamed, grabbing his shoulders and wiggling out from under his limp body. "Morgan!" she repeated, shaking him. "Answer me!"

There was a cut on his head, but his side was bubbling red with blood from one tiny hole from Eric's bullet. More blood spread at the ground beneath him, soaking his shirt all the way down to his pants. His eyes were closed. His breathing was shallow. His face was pale as death.

Sadie dug at the boulders pinning his legs, whimpering with frustration when she couldn't budge them.

Father Daar stumbled over and knelt beside them.

"Do something!" Sadie shouted at him. "Use your magic!"

"I have none!" Daar snapped back, adding his own weight to hers. "It was used up in the destruction."

Sadie spotted Morgan's sword lying beside him. She grabbed it and started prying at the boulders.

The sword suddenly broke, sending both Sadie and Father Daar stumbling backward. Sadie lifted the hilt that she was still holding, staring in horror at what she had done.

"Oh my God. I broke his sword."

She scrambled back and knelt down to cup Morgan's face. "Hold on, my love," she whispered, touching her lips to his ear. "You hold on," she ordered when he didn't respond.

Sadie was suddenly grabbed by the shoulders and pushed away so violently that she swallowed her gasp. A tall, dark-haired giant with eyes the exact same color as Morgan's replaced her at Morgan's head, running a large hand over her husband's face.

"We'll have you out in a minute," the stranger said, putting his shoulder into the larger of the two boulders.

Callum suddenly appeared and set his own shoulder to the rock, both men grunting and straining and cursing. Sadie sat on the ground and placed her feet just below their hands to add her own strength. Even Father Daar used smaller rocks to hold up the boulder each time it moved.

The stranger stopped, catching his breath, and looked at the situation. He walked to the back of the rock and started working, throwing debris out of the way. Callum found a stout branch and set it to pry against the boulder, only to stop suddenly and lift out the broken tip of Morgan's sword.

"I hope ya can run fast," Callum said. "Because just as soon as Morgan is well enough to stand, he'll come after you."

"Oh, please hurry," Sadie whispered. "He's bleeding to death." She turned to the priest. "Isn't there something you can do?"

Both Callum and the stranger—Sadie realized he was Morgan's brother, Greylen MacKeage—looked at the priest with Sadie. Father Daar slowly shook his head. "My staff was destroyed, and so was the waterfall. There's nothing left."

Faol suddenly appeared, limping over and washing Morgan's face, whining and pawing at the boulder.

"Get that beast away from him," Greylen said harshly, moving to kick the wolf.

"Nay," Father Daar said. "He's only worried about his son."

"His son?" Greylen whispered, his face paling as he snapped his eyes back to the priest.

Daar turned red in the face. "I'm guessing, MacKeage. But I have a notion Duncan's been visiting us this summer," he said, waving at the wolf.

All four of them turned to stare at Faol, who was now looking at them with unblinking green eyes. He whined again and pushed at the boulder with his nose.

Greylen and Callum went back to work. They were suddenly joined by another pair of large, strong-looking hands, and Sadie looked up to see an older man, with red hair and graying beard, putting his weight into the boulder.

"Ian," Greylen said. "Be ready to pull him out the moment there's room. Woman," he snapped, looking at her. "Help him."

Sadie quickly moved more debris out of Ian's way, making room for Morgan to be pulled free. With a lot of grunting and another fair amount of cursing, Callum and Greylen put their backs into the task. The boulder moved mere inches, and Ian roughly pulled Morgan free of his prison, continuing to drag him until his feet were clear of the boulder.

Sadie immediately crawled to Morgan and ripped open his shirt. Blood gushed into her hands.

Greylen grabbed her by the shoulders again and roughly set her to the side. "You've done enough to him. Get her out of here, Daar."

There was such anger emanating from Morgan's older brother that Sadie backed away on her own. She wiped her husband's blood on her pants and turned to Father Daar.

"There has to be something we can do. What about the magical water? Th-that puddle's still shimmering."

The priest slowly made his way to the puddle, bent down, and stuck his finger in the water. He looked up to where he'd been standing when she and Eric had arrived. Sadie followed his gaze. The cherry tree he'd been trying to break was splintered into a thousand pieces. He looked back at her.

"You can get there better than me, girl," he whispered. "Go look for a cherry burl in that mess. The tree's been growing in blessed water for more than two years now. Maybe some of the magic is hiding there."

Sadie crawled over the rocks to the far edge of what had once been the pool.

"Find a big burl!" the priest shouted. "From the root if ya can."

It took all of her strength, but Sadie was able to dig a knot free from the roots of the cherry tree. She hurried back to Father Daar and handed him the small piece of wood.

"This is all I could find," she whispered, anxiously glancing toward Morgan.

Greylen had taken off his shirt and wrapped it around Morgan's wound. He was now checking Morgan's legs for broken bones. Sadie looked back at the priest.

He was frowning. "I don't think it's enough," he said, sadly shaking his head. "It's wanting the strength of the water and my old staff. Already I can feel it losing its vitality."

Sadie reached out and touched his arm. "Please. We have to do something. We'll never get Morgan to town in time."

The moment she touched him, Daar's eyes widened in surprise. He covered her hand with his own, his mouth suddenly lifting into a smile.

"It's in you, girl," he said in a voice filled with awe. He turned to face her and touched her with both hands, holding the knot of cherrywood against her skin. "There's magic left. It's here," he said, turning her right hand palm up. "In you."

"What do you mean?"

"When ya were healed," he told her, rubbing her unscarred palm with his finger. "The burl dissolved because its energy went into you."

"And—and I can give it back?"

"Aye," he said, looking into her eyes. "Ya can."

"And I can heal Morgan?"

"Aye. I'm thinking it should be possible."

That was all she needed to know. Sadie jumped up and ran to her husband, pushing her way past his lethal-looking brother. Greylen stood up, took hold of her shoulders, and shook her.

"Ya've done enough," he snapped.

"I can do more!" she shouted, giving him a direct glare. "I have the wizard's magic in me."

He released her as if burned, stepping away and looking at the priest who had walked up beside them. Father Daar nodded.

"She has, MacKeage," Daar confirmed. "Your brother healed her with my own magic. She's carrying the energy of my staff in her body."

Greylen looked torn between wanting to believe it was possible and not wanting to let her anywhere near his brother.

"Please. Bring him over to the water," she entreated, taking the small cherry knot from Father Daar and walking to the water herself. "At least let me try," she added, holding out her hand. "He—he's my husband."

Again, Father Daar nodded confirmation to Greylen. "Aye, MacKeage. I married them myself just yesterday."

Greylen scanned the destruction around them, then looked down at his dying brother. He bent and picked Morgan up and carried him to the small puddle of water. Callum and Ian quietly followed. Faol trotted past her and around the puddle and lay down with a whine, his nose touching the water.

Sadie stepped into the puddle and sat down, holding open her arms to receive Morgan. Greylen gently settled him on her lap.

Father Daar came over and crouched beside her. "There's just one wee little problem, Mercedes," he whispered.

Greylen and Callum and Ian leaned closer to hear what the priest was saying.

"What's that, Father?" Sadie asked, not caring if they did hear.

"The magic . . . well . . . I don't know what will happen to ya, when ya give it up to your husband."

Sadie snapped her gaze to his. "Will I go back to when I was shot?"

Father Daar nodded hesitantly. "Aye, that is possible. But I don't really know." He shrugged. "I can't predict what the energy will do when passed through a mortal."

Sadie realized all three men standing over her were collectively holding their breath, waiting for her decision. They couldn't know that there simply was no decision to make. She didn't care if she bled to death right here in this puddle. She was not letting Morgan die.

She took the cherry knot and held it against Morgan's chest, brushing the hair back from his face with her other hand.

"No, girl. Hold the burl with your right hand," Father Daar instructed. "That will have the most powerful energy."

Sadie switched hands but hesitated, holding the knot just off Morgan.

"Wh-what will happen?" she whispered. "How do I know I won't kill him? Look what happened to this beautiful place when Morgan had your cane. What if all I create is just more destruction?"

Father Daar was shaking his head before she finished her question. "The wood is only a conductor of energy, Mercedes. Morgan was desperate and angry when he held the cane, and it was his wrath the magic brought down on us. But you're yearning for something good. Ya won't kill him."

Sadie set the knot of cherrywood over Morgan's wound, closed her eyes, and wished with all her heart for him to be healed.

The palm of her right hand suddenly started to warm. Light arced around her, filling her head with colors. She started to tremble as her whole body tightened with prickly heat. She could hear the blood rushing through her veins, feel it pulsing down her arm and into her hand, smell the halo of ozone that suddenly wafted around her.

Her belly churned. Her back felt on fire, the intense heat shooting through her middle. A sharp pain stabbed down the length of her left arm. Her lungs and ribs felt crushed.

She could feel her flesh burning, almost smell it.

A hand touched her shoulder, and a voice whispered beside her ear. "Send it into him, Mercedes," Father Daar instructed from a great distance. "Push, girl. Send the energy to Morgan."

Sadie concentrated on moving the heat. She held her palm fiercely against Morgan's side, pushing the knot of wood into his wound. Fire shot through her body. Her muscles trembled. Sadie fought not to lose consciousness, to keep the energy flowing to Morgan.

And slowly, ever so slowly, his heartbeat grew stronger.

And that made *her* stronger.

Sadie focused her thoughts. She pictured Morgan being healthy in her mind's eye, saw him laughing, glowing with the fire of passion as he made love to her. She saw him swimming naked in the lake, felt his patience even when he was angry with her. And she heard him calling her *gràineag* in a tone that was anything but endearing.

And Sadie sent him her love.

The green light that had faded in the destructive storm suddenly flashed and throbbed around her, sparking to a brilliant white before settling back into the gentle and steady glow of winter spruce.

"I had a dream," came Morgan's whispered voice.

Sadie pulled the sleeve of her shirt over her right hand and brushed the hair from his face as she smiled down at him.

"Did you see your mother and father?" she asked softly.

"My mum," he answered. "Da wasn't there."

Because he's here, Sadie thought to herself, peeking at the wolf who now had his nose tucked firmly against Morgan's arm.

"I'm so sleepy, wife," Morgan muttered, closing his eyes.

"Then sleep, husband," she whispered, stroking his chest in comforting circles. "And know that I love you."

Chapter Twenty-three

Daar sat on a rock in the middle of the destroyed and deserted grotto and glared at the rubble created by Morgan's desperate attempt to save his wife's life.

It seemed all the magic was not gone. He could still feel something quietly humming, energizing the air. The wizard kicked the splinters of cherrywood at his feet. A small branch from one of the trees that had grown here must have escaped the destruction. He just couldn't find the damned source of the hum.

With a weary sigh, Daar sat down on one of the smaller rocks and stared at the dig marks Morgan had made. When the warrior had awakened from his sleep and had been told that Mercedes had run away, Morgan hadn't flown into a rage as they'd all been expecting. No, he'd simply gotten up, stared at the destruction he'd wrought, and asked what had happened to Eric Hellman.

Greylen had silently pointed to the pile of rubble

that had once been the cliff at the far end of what had once been the pool. Morgan had walked over, pushed a few rocks out of the way, and started digging until he had amassed a small pile of gold nuggets. He'd tied the nuggets up in his shirt and then climbed the rubble, using his considerable strength to finish the destruction. Morgan had rained a final avalanche of boulders down over Hellman's grave, then dusted off his hands and walked away.

Daar continued to search for that small hint of magic that seemed to have survived. He needed a new staff, and it would be nice if he could find a branch from this place. The cherrywood growing here had soaked up the magical energy from the waters that had flowed from the high mountain lake. This was blessed wood, and a cane from here would be much easier to train.

Daar wanted one now more than ever. He didn't care to be powerless when it came to dealing with the MacKeages. For mere mortals, they were proving themselves powerful enough in their own right.

Faol suddenly stepped into sight, trotting over to one of the small remaining puddles. He took a drink, lazily lapping at the water for several minutes, before he lifted his head and stared at Daar.

"Duncan, ya old warmonger," Daar said, not unkindly. "Your sons have found themselves good lives here. There's no need for ya still to be hanging around."

Faol rumbled a growl from his chest and turned and started climbing over the rubble. The wolf briefly disappeared from sight. He reappeared just off to

Daar's right, holding a two-foot-long stick in his mouth.

With a shout of surprise, Daar jumped to his feet. "That's my old staff!" he yelped, quickly scrambling over the rubble to reach the wolf. "The half Grey threw away two years ago. Give that to me!"

Faol trotted toward the valley.

"Hey! Get back here, you damn dog!" Daar shouted, awkwardly following him. "That's my staff!"

His tail wagging like a banner of victory, Faol picked up his pace and continued down the winding and now dry streambed, Daar's staff held in his mouth like a prize of war.

The aging wizard ran until he was out of breath and couldn't go on, bending over with his hands on his knees, tiredly panting, overjoyed to know his old staff had shot free of the waterfall before it had closed, and frustrated that it was still out of his reach.

A howl came to Daar then, climbing up the side of the valley toward him in maddening echoes of triumph.

Daar sat down on a nearby log, pulling his white collar from his frock and undoing three buttons. God's teeth, but he was reaching the end of his patience. He kept losing his magic.

He shook his weary head in dismay. He'd had that old staff with him for more than fourteen hundred years, a gift from his mentor when Daar had been a young man of seventy-nine. And in only two years the MacKeages had managed to destroy not only it but the new staff he'd been training for Greylen and Grace's unborn daughter, Winter.

All that remained of his magic was now being

carried away by a mean-spirited wolf. And just what was Daar going to tell Grey's seventh daughter, Winter, when she came to him a grown woman ready to become a wizard?

Daar stood up finally, having caught most of his breath back. He needed that two-foot piece of his old staff. Faol couldn't actually take it with him when he went back to wherever he came from. Spirits crossed over; material things did not.

With a disheartened sigh filled with self-pity, Daar stopped chasing the wolf and started walking instead in the direction of Michael MacBain's home. Perhaps it was time he got better acquainted with MacBain and his young son while he searched for his old staff, which he was determined to find. Until then, he was staying the hell away from the MacKeages.

It took Sadie two hours to make it to the logging camp, and for every step of the way, she wished she had the old priest's cane. Not for its magic but for the help it would give her to walk.

She had sneaked away from the MacKeages and Father Daar like a thief, not wanting to face Greylen's wrath any longer—and definitely too cowardly to face Morgan when he woke up.

The beautiful gorge he'd tried so hard to protect was completely destroyed, thanks to her. He'd revealed its location and its magic in order to save her life and then had destroyed it saving her life a second time.

And she had nothing to give him in return. She didn't even have her beauty anymore, which he had so greatly enjoyed yesterday when they'd spent the afternoon making love.

Even the gold was out of reach now.

But for that she was glad.

Morgan was right. Gold made people do terrible things. It turned them into murderers.

Sadie unzipped the fly on the tent to pulled out her sleeping bag, which she tied to the pack Eric had left discarded on the ground. The pack, the sleeping bag, and the food would allow Sadie to survive for the next few days, until she could decide what to do.

For the entire next day, Morgan quietly followed his wife, patiently waiting for Mercedes to get over her bout of self-pity. He was anxious to bring her home and finally start their peaceful union, but he was keeping his distance for now, for her sake. It appeared she needed this time to think about everything that had happened over the last couple of days.

And so he sat in the shadows of the night, watching her sleep. He'd seen her bathe this morning, and his worry had lessened that the magic she had given him to save his life would take hers. He had seen the scars from the house fire covering her body again and the place where Eric Hellman's bullet had pierced her skin. And Morgan had silently thanked God that not all the magic had been pulled from Mercedes' body. Enough had been left to make healing only a matter of time. Already she had gained back most of her strength.

But the scars that had killed half of her family would always remain. Morgan didn't care as long as she was well.

She cared, though, he feared. She'd been so open with him that day in the pool after the magic had healed her body. Morgan sighed, wondering if Mercedes would ever be that free with him again.

He would demand that she be.

No. He would beg.

He loved her more than he loved life and was growing tired of this directionless pilgrimage his strong-minded wife insisted on traveling. How the hell long did it take to realize her heart belonged to him?

Morgan settled himself more comfortably against the tree, pulled his plaid more warmly around him, and closed his eyes with another sigh. If she didn't soon come around, he'd have to give Mercedes a bit of a push and see what sort of results he got. His *gràineag* would either run deeper into the valley or come up spitting and swinging and cursing.

He hoped with all his heart it would be the latter.

Sadie rolled out of her sleeping bag and quickly danced to the fire and stirred it up, adding first kindling and then large branches to coax it back into flames. She set her battered pot full of water on the grate, willing it to hurry up and boil as she rubbed her hands together and held them over the stingy fire.

It was time that she quit sulking. She would go to Morgan today and explain to him that no matter what had happened, they belonged together.

But first she had to find the Dolan brothers. She still had a bit of gold left in her pocket, and she'd give them the nuggets and let them know there was nothing left.

Sadie drank her coffee, broke camp, and headed south along the bank of the Prospect. Her resolve to set Morgan straight on how things would be between them added momentum to her pace.

But within ten minutes, Sadie realized she was being followed. And within another three minutes, she recognized her stalker.

"Come out here, big boy," Sadie cajoled with an eager laugh, clapping her hands to call him.

Faol stepped into her path not five paces in front of her, his big green eyes looking sappy, his tongue hanging out of his mouth, his ears perked forward, and his tail wagging a mile a minute.

"I'm so glad you're okay," Sadie said, walking forward and patting his broad head.

Sadie continued along the bank of the Prospect with her silent traveling companion, until she finally came to a large green canoe pulled up onshore. She stopped to signal Faol to stay back, only to realize the wolf had disappeared. Sadie turned from the river and traveled inland about a hundred yards.

"Hello the camp!" she called out. "Don't shoot. It's me."

"Missy Sadie Quill—oh, I mean Mrs. Sadie MacKeage," Dwayne said excitedly, bolting to his feet and running to greet her, waving like crazy. "What brings you out here today? I thought you'd be home cooking dinner for your new husband." He waggled his finger at her. "Feeding Morgan is going to be a full-time job."

Sadie narrowed her eyes at Dwayne. "It's Morgan now? What happened to 'that MacKeage guy'?"

Dwayne reddened in the face slightly. "He said we could call him Morgan, Sadie." He suddenly grinned. "I like your new husband. He ate my stew and belched loud enough to wake the bears."

It was Sadie who got red in the face all of a sudden, and it wasn't embarrassment. "Morgan was here? When?"

"Yesterday," Dwayne told her, frowning. "Didn't he tell you he was coming to see us? And what he was doing?"

"Ah, yeah. He did mention it," she quickly prevaricated.

Dwayne suddenly snapped his mouth shut, his frown turning into a glare as he waggled a finger at her again, this time scolding. "You just never mind, missy. I don't know nothing."

"Where's Harry?" Sadie asked, looking over Dwayne's shoulder at the camp behind him.

Dwayne stepped to the left to block her view. "Harry's in town buying us some supplies."

Sadie sighed and rubbed her forehead. "It's okay, Dwayne. The reason I'm not home cooking for my husband is that I'm checking to see if Morgan really did come visit you and that he did what he said he was going to do."

Her convoluted words nicely confusing him, Dwayne frowned again. He thought for a minute, shook his head, and suddenly smiled at her.

"I guess I can show you. Since the gift's really from you and all," he whispered, as if afraid even the trees might hear what he was saying.

He shot a suspicious look around the rim of his

campsite, then excitedly waved Sadie over to some boxes stacked by a honeysuckle bush. He put his finger to his lips for her to be quiet and looked around again just before he crouched down on his knees.

Sadie took a look around herself and then bent to see what he was doing. Dwayne pushed several of the boxes out of the way and started digging in the dirt.

"We hid it good, didn't we?" he whispered, pawing the sand away like a groundhog.

"You surely did," Sadie quietly agreed, shrugging her pack off her back and kneeling beside him.

Sadie gasped when Dwayne pulled a quart-sized Mason jar out of the ground and brushed the sand off it. "You hid it real good," she whispered in awe, blinking at the jar full of gold nuggets.

Dwayne continued to pet the jar, reverently cleaning every speck of sand off it with a slightly trembling hand.

"Morgan told me and Harry this was all the gold," he said, his voice still quiet and reverent. He looked at her, clutching the jar to his chest and grinning like a child at the circus. "That you and him found Jedediah's gold, Sadie, and that you want us to have it. That you don't need it none, being you have a rich husband now."

Unable to speak, Sadie nodded, feeling her face heat again. Dwayne suddenly grabbed her around the neck and noisily and very wetly kissed her shocked mouth.

And then he scrambled back, the gold still clutched to his chest, his own face as red as a sunset. He shot a look around his campsite with wide, horrified eyes.

"I—I didn't mean to do that!" he yelped, his entire

neck and face now blistering red. "I mean, I . . . but . . ." He looked around the campsite again. "I don't want your husband to think I was . . . that I was . . ."

Sadie patted his arm and stood up, finally gathering her wits enough to smile at him. "It's okay, Dwayne. Morgan understands that you and Harry are my friends. He wouldn't take offense even if he were here. Which he isn't," she assured the still worried man.

Sadie reached a hand into her pocket and curled her fingers over the two gold nuggets she still possessed. She had planned to give them to Harry and Dwayne, but now the gesture seemed lame, considering she had apparently already given them a fortune.

Why had Morgan brought this gold to them?

And just where had he gotten it? Everything had been destroyed. The gold had been buried under thousands of tons of granite.

"Did Morgan tell you why he—I mean, why we gave you the gold?" Sadie asked, waving her hand at the jar Dwayne was still clutching.

"Because you don't need it none," he repeated, crawling on his knees to the honeysuckle bush. He put the jar back in the ground, carefully covered it up with sand, and set the boxes back over it.

"Did he tell you where we found the gold?" Sadie asked.

Dwayne looked at her and frowned. "No. We asked, but he wouldn't tell us nothing. He just said this was all of it, that there weren't no more."

He stood up and brushed off his hands, suddenly narrowing his eyes in suspicion. "Was he telling the truth, Sadie? Is this all of it?"

She nodded. "Best as we can tell, Dwayne. There wasn't really a mine. Jedediah had only found a large deposit of placer gold, not the source."

"Where?" he asked, cocking his head and squinting one eye. "Was it close to a logging camp? Say, about a mile or so north of the camp?"

Sadie shook her head. "Nope," she lied, smiling while she did, having already decided it would be best to guide the Dolans to look elsewhere. "It isn't even in this valley, Dwayne." She pointed toward the mountains. "It's in the next valley over, almost in Canada."

"The next valley!" Dwayne shouted, only to look quickly around himself again. He stepped closer, lowering his voice. "You mean, we've been searching the wrong valley all these years? Even Frank?" He narrowed his eyes again. "Your daddy thought it was near the Prospect. And Harry and me even found flakes of placer gold here."

Sadie shrugged. "We all thought it was here, Dwayne. But if you were to look in the valley to the west, you'd probably find several old logging camps."

"Where?" he whispered, taking another step closer. He set his face into a puppy-dog look of pleading. "Can you at least give me a hint, Sadie?"

"Why? It's all gone, Dwayne."

"But there might be more."

"Why do you need more?" she asked, waving toward the honeysuckle bush. "There's enough there to go to Russia and bring back a dozen wives if you want."

Dwayne was startled by the idea. "We don't want a

dozen," he said, looking horrified again. "We only need two." He suddenly grinned. "Morgan helped us pick them out."

"He what?"

Dwayne strode over to his tent, picked up a magazine, and came running back to her, leafing through the pages as he ran.

"Here," he said, slapping the page with his dirty, callused finger. "Morgan said I should pick this one."

Sadie leaned away to focus on the page that was now being held in front of her face. A fortyish woman was smiling back at her, looking shy and a whole lot scared.

Dwayne suddenly pulled the magazine back and turned to another page. He held it up to her again. "He said Harry should pick this lady," Dwayne said, pointing to another woman.

This one was a bit older, a bit more worn-looking, also smiling with what appeared to be . . . hope.

Sadie smiled at her old friend. "They're pretty, Dwayne," she said. "They look like they'll make you and Harry fine wives."

Dwayne moved beside her, held out the magazine, and leafed through it again. "I liked this one," he said, showing her the picture of a twenty-something woman. "I think she's beautiful."

"She is."

Dwayne looked over at Sadie, his mouth lifted at one corner, his dusty gray-hazel eyes shining with wisdom. He was shaking his head at her.

"Morgan said she wasn't beautiful," Dwayne told her with authority, nodding his head in agreement with her husband. "Morgan said beauty isn't here," Dwayne elaborated, tapping the young woman's face. "That's it's here," he explained, quickly turning the page to the woman Morgan had chosen for him. Dwayne touched his finger to the older woman's eyes, then let it trail down to stop just below the photo, where her heart would be.

"Morgan said me and Harry have to look really deep below the surface to find beauty in a woman. That if we're wanting good wives, we won't be tricked by a pretty face." Dwayne squinted one eye at her, letting the magazine drop to his side. "Like you, Sadie," he said.

"Like me? Morgan said like me?"

"Naw," Dwayne said, shaking his head again. "I'm saying it. Look at your hand," he told her, waving toward her gloved right hand. "And I know you got other scars. But that didn't stop Morgan none from picking you." He smiled and touched her hair. "Because you got yourself a wise husband, Sadie. He looked real deep and saw your beauty."

A lump the size of a boulder got stuck in Sadie's throat.

Dwayne let his finger slide down her hair until he could tug on the end of it, his grin warm and his voice tender. "You're a beautiful lady, Sadie," he said in a whisper. "I only hope my new wife is half as pretty as you are."

Sadie threw herself into Dwayne's arms and struggled to hold back tears born of the fear and uncertainty of the last three days. Her old friend wrapped his arms around her, squeezing her tightly, and frantically apologized.

"Hell's bells, Sadie," he growled. "I didn't mean to make you cry!"

"You didn't," she said. "Morgan did."

Dwayne quickly set her away from him and scanned the bushes surrounding the campsite.

"I—I wasn't saying you're pretty because I want to steal you!" he shouted, backing away from Sadie as he spoke. "I was only trying to explain myself."

Sadie couldn't keep from smiling. "Oh, Dwayne. I didn't mean Morgan was here," she said. "What you said made me think of him, and that made me cry."

Dwayne relaxed slightly and lifted his brows at her. "Just thinking about your husband makes you cry?" he asked incredulously. He took a step closer. "What happens when you actually see him in person?"

"I smile."

Her answer confounded him. He scratched his dirty hair and squinted one eye at her.

"Does Morgan tell you you're beautiful?" Dwayne suddenly asked.

"Every day," she told him truthfully. "Without words."

"How's he do that?" Dwayne wanted to know, stepping closer.

"By his actions," Sadie explained. "By caring and worrying about me. By scolding and lecturing and bossing me around. By making me so mad sometimes I want to spit. He also teases me every chance he gets. He carries all the heavy supplies in his pack, lightening my load when we hike. He also makes sure I'm warm at night. And safe. And by doing all that, Dwayne, Morgan is telling me every minute of every day that I'm beautiful."

"Hell's bells, Sadie. Am I going to have to do that kind of stuff for my wife?"

Sadie wiped another threatening tear away and nodded. "You are. And you're going to love doing it, Dwayne. Because your wife will understand by your actions how much she means to you. Each small deed will tell her you think she's beautiful and that you cherish her and are glad she's agreed to share your life."

Dwayne suddenly frowned at the ground. "I probably will have to show her instead of tell her, like your Morgan does." He looked up, his expression confounded again. "Because I don't know Russian, Sadie. Me and Harry got us some tapes to listen to, but we just can't get the hang of the language. And, according to the book that came with the tapes, their alphabet is missing some letters and has some other ones that look mighty weird."

"The language of love is universal, Dwayne," Sadie assured him, walking to her pack and slinging it onto her shoulders. She walked back to Dwayne and touched his arm. "It's also timeless, I've discovered. Don't worry. You and Harry are going to do all right. Because," Sadie whispered, leaning over to kiss his blush-heated cheek, "*you* are beautiful, my good friend, deep down inside where it counts."

Sadie walked out of Dwayne's camp then and decided it was time she found her husband.

Chapter Twenty-four

Sadie knew the first rule of searching for someone was that the searchee had to stay put in order for the searcher to find him. If both parties wandered around in the same hundreds of square miles of forest, they likely would pass within yards of each other and not even know it.

But that theory only worked if the searchee really wished to be found, and it depended on how determined and tenacious the searcher was.

Sadie was very determined.

After wasting most of the afternoon hunting for Morgan, wearing out her boots and getting a sore throat from hollering his name over and over, Sadie finally conceded defeat. She knelt in front of Faol, who had suddenly appeared when she walked out of Dwayne's camp, and held his big head between her hands and pleaded with the animal to help her.

"You've got to find Morgan, big boy," she entreated,

getting her nose within inches of his. “Before he finds me first. It’s important that I go to him with my heart in my hand and remind him again that he loves me.”

Faol whined, darting out his tongue and lapping her chin, his wagging tail shaking his whole body. Gripping the tufts of hair on the sides of his face, Sadie held him away.

“Can you do that? Can you find Morgan for me?”

He tried to wash her face again, then barked when she wouldn’t let him. Sadie let go and stood up, waving her hand at the forest.

“Go on, then. Go find Morgan,” she told the wolf, giving him a nudge with her knee.

Faol barked again, spun on his feet, and took off at a run down the trail. Sadie tightened the waist belt of her pack and started jogging after him, the thrill of the chase lifting her spirits until she was laughing out loud.

Sadie lost sight of Faol but heard him bark someplace to her left. She turned off the trail and ducked under limbs, slowing to avoid getting poked in the face by low-hanging branches. She couldn’t see Faol anymore, but the wolf was making enough noise to wake the dead.

Sadie broke onto a narrow game trail, this one obviously used by moose more than deer. She was able to stand upright and pick up her pace again, and within twenty minutes Sadie realized exactly where Faol was leading her.

And she laughed again, at the irony of what was happening. Because it wasn’t all that long ago that she had been running down this very same trail—only away from a madman instead of toward him.

Faol had stopped at the edge of the lake. He was sitting down, his tail wagging the ground clean, and looking over his shoulder at her. He darted a look at the lake and then back at her, whining and standing up and padding over to touch her fingers. He carefully grasped the fingertips of her glove in his teeth and gently tugged.

Sadie took the hint. She pulled off her glove, knelt down, and took hold of his face again. "I know, big boy," she whispered. "I might be hardheaded sometimes, but I eventually figure things out. I—I'll take good care of your son, Mister MacKeage," she whispered. "I'll see that he's happy and very glad he came to live in this time. We'll give you some grand-babies and tell them all about your visit with us."

Faol whined and lapped her chin, then pulled his head free and turned and looked out at the lake again. He lifted his nose into the air and sent a howl over the valley that carried into the mountains on tremulous waves.

Faol then trotted off into the forest without looking back.

Sadie stepped to where the wolf had been standing and stared at Morgan sitting on the boulder in the middle of the cove, facing her, his large hands braced on the edge of the rock and his feet lazily stirring the water.

He was naked, of course, despite the fact that there was ice lacing the shore of the lake and the air was below freezing. Steam wafted from his wet shoulders, his breath puffed in gentle billows around his head, and the water dripping from his long blond hair made icicles on the rock beside him.

"I'm beautiful, Morgan."

"Aye, Mercedes, you are."

"And I'm your wife."

"I remember our vows."

"I—I'm a modern."

"Nobody promised us a perfect world, lass."

"I'll continue to be strong-minded . . . sometimes."

"Aye. But only sometimes, *gràineag.*"

"I know what that means now. And it's not an endearment."

"But it fits you so well, wife . . . sometimes."

Sadie scowled, thinking this wasn't going well. Not that she'd had a plan when she'd come searching for Morgan, but she had thought the man would be more . . . well, at least more eager to see her. Sadie took a deep breath and continued.

"I broke your sword."

"I noticed that."

"And your waterfall was destroyed."

"I noticed that, too."

"All the magic is gone, Morgan."

"Nay, lass. It's more powerful than ever."

"Dammit, Morgan. I want you to forgive me."

"I did that two days ago, Mercedes."

"Then why didn't you come for me?"

"Because you needed to forgive yourself first."

With trembling hands, Sadie swiped at the tears that had escaped and flowed down her cheeks. This was proving even harder than she'd thought. He was just sitting there like a turtle on a rock waiting for the sun to warm him, his infuriatingly patient and calmly given responses making her insides quake.

Maybe he was a turtle, and she was the sunshine he was waiting for.

"I'm beautiful."

"Aye, Mercedes, you are."

"And you love me."

"I must."

"Dammit, Morgan. This is hard."

"Only because it's important, Mercedes."

"I love you."

"I'm glad. But it's not me you must love, lass."

"I'm beautiful."

"Aye, wife. You are very beautiful."

With hands more shaky than useful, Sadie uncinched the belt at her waist and let her pack slide off her shoulders, catching it and gently setting it on the ground without taking her eyes off her husband.

Morgan lazily watched her as she sat down and unlaced her boots and pulled them off. She tucked her socks inside them and then stood, her trembling hands going to the buttons on her shirt. It took her a long time to get the shirt open, and even longer to work up the nerve to slide it off her shoulders. She let the shirt fall to the ground, reached behind her back, and unhooked her bra, pulling both it and her body sock off, letting them fall to the ground.

And still she watched her husband.

And still he sat there, not saying a word, not moving, not taking his eyes off her.

Sadie unbuckled her belt and unsnapped her pants, pushing them down to her knees and stepping free.

She couldn't quit shaking, and she knew it wasn't the cold making her tremble. Every nerve ending, every taut muscle, every inch of her skin felt as if it were on fire.

She straightened her shoulders and forced her hands to her sides, now facing her husband as naked as he was.

"Do ya see that sunset behind me, lass?"

Sadie could only nod.

"I was sitting here waiting for you to come to me, and I was thinking how the sky is the color of your eyes. It's a very beautiful shade of blue, don't you think?"

She nodded again.

Morgan stood up and held out his hand. "Then come to me now, Mercedes. Bring your beauty into my life."

She took a step forward, and then another. Each step was a bit easier than the previous one, and soon Sadie was running to Morgan.

Until she was up to her knees in the ice-cold water. Sadie screamed at the feel of the icy water on her legs.

"Goddammit, MacKeage! This lake is freezing!" she shouted, scrambling back to the shore.

Morgan dove into the lake and swam until he could stand up. He rose, water cascading down his tall, masculine body, and waded toward her.

Sadie took a step back. Morgan had never looked more like a warrior to her, even though she'd seen him like this before. He was different somehow.

Or maybe she was.

Or maybe it had something to do with the unholy gleam in his eyes, the look of a warrior about to possess the prize of his hard-won battle.

Sadie took another step back.

Morgan had certainly waged a fine war, if not a subtle one. But then, Sadie suddenly thought, stepping toward him instead of away, the prize he was receiving was well worth the effort.

She ran and threw herself into his arms, grabbing his wet hair and kissing his wet face, laughing with the joy of knowing she was about to begin a dream life with this man. He wrapped his powerful arms around her and gently lowered them both to the ground, growling into her ear as he rained kisses through her hair.

With lusty words and whispered promises, Morgan told Sadie as much as he showed her just what he thought of her body. His hands roamed over her skin with feather-light touches, his lips following the trail of his fingers.

Sadie mimicked his actions and his words and made a few lusty promises of her own. She arched her back when his lips grazed her nipples, pushing her breasts into his mouth, yearning to be touched everywhere.

Nothing was off limits any longer. Nothing stood between them, nothing obstructed the pleasure of loving each other. Passion took precedence over shyness, and Sadie was able to give herself freely to the wonder of love.

They played and loved as they had that afternoon in the beautiful, mystical pool filled with the *drùidh's* magic. And Morgan hadn't been lying a moment ago when he'd said the magic was more powerful than ever.

The magic was stronger, their love a brilliant rainbow wrapped around the pure white light of their passion.